Nietzsche
A Critical Life

Ronald Hayman

PENGUIN BOOKS

Penguin Books Ltd, Harmondsworth,
Middlesex, England
Penguin Books, 625 Madison Avenue,
New York, New York 10022, U.S.A.
Penguin Books Australia Ltd, Ringwood,
Victoria, Australia
Penguin Books Canada Limited, 2801 John Street,
Markham, Ontario, Canada L3R 1B4
Penguin Books (N.Z.) Ltd, 182–190 Wairau Road,
Auckland 10, New Zealand

First published in the United States of America by
Oxford University Press 1980
Published in Penguin Books 1982

LIBRARY OF CONGRESS CATALOGING IN PUBLICATION DATA
Hayman, Ronald, 1932–
    Nietzsche, a critical life.
    Reprint. Originally published: New York:
Oxford University Press, 1980.
    Bibliography: p.
    Includes index.
    1. Nietzsche, Friedrich Wilhelm, 1844–1900.
2. Philosophers—Germany—Biography.   I. Title.
[B3316.H44 1982]   193   82-3773
ISBN 0 14 00.6274 2   AACR2

Printed in the United States of America by
R. R. Donnelley & Sons Company, Harrisonburg, Virginia

For Sylvie

However forcefully a man develops and seems to leap from one contradiction to the next, close observation will reveal the *dovetailing*, where the new building grows out of the old. This is the task of the biographer: he must think about the life in question on the principle that nature never jumps.

Friedrich Nietzsche
Menschliches, Allzumenschliches –
Der Wanderer und sein Schatten
(*Human, All Too Human –*
The Wanderer and His Shadow), section 198

I have gradually come to understand what every great philosophy until now has been: the confession of its author and a kind of involuntary, unconscious memoir. At the same time the moral (or immoral) intentions in each philosophy have constituted the real seed from which the entire plant has grown. . . . Nothing at all about the philosopher is impersonal; above all his morality provides decided and decisive evidence about *who he is* – i.e. the relative positioning of the innermost drives in his nature.

Jenseits von Gut und Böse (*Beyond Good and Evil*), section 6

In short, moralities are nothing more than a *sign-language of the emotions*.

Jenseits von Gut und Böse, section 187

Contents

List of illustrations   xi

Acknowledgements   xiii

Chronological Table   xv

Introduction   1

1 Fritz   13

2 Pforta   27

3 University Student   58

4 Soldier and Student Again   89

5 Wagner and *The Birth of Tragedy*   106

6 The Superior Tribunal   148

7 *Volte-Face*   190

8 Mediterranean Sunrise   221

9 Lou Salomé   244

10 Zarathustra   255

11 Revolutionary Revaluations   286

12 Euphoria, Melancholia and Madness   319

13 Self-Denial, Self-Affirmation   351

Notes   362

Bibliography   403

Index   411

Illustrations

(following page 220)

Nietzsche's birthplace

Nietzsche's mother

Nietzsche in 1861

Pencil sketch from Nietzsche's juvenilia (*Nationale Forschungs- und Gedenkstätten der klassischen Deutschen Literatur in Weimar, Goethe- und Schiller-Archiv*)

Friedrich Ritschl

Franconia in 1865

The Philological Society at Leipzig University (1866–7)

Richard Wagner in 1862

Pastor Carl Ludwig Nietzsche

Wagner's house Tribschen

Cosima von Bülow

Nietzsche in 1868

Elisabeth Nietzsche

Carl von Gersdorff

Franz Overbeck

Lou Salomé, Paul Rée and Nietzsche

Nietzsche's house at Sils-Maria

Nietzsche's room at Sils-Maria

Page from the thirteen-year-old Nietzsche's book of poems (*Nationale Forschungs- und Gedenkstätten der klassischen Deutschen Literatur in Weimar, Goethe- und Schiller-Archiv*)

Page of Nietzsche's crayon scrawl, probably 1892 (*Nationale Forschungs- und Gedenkstätten der klassischen Deutschen Literatur in Weimar, Goethe- und Schiller-Archiv*)

Nietzsche during the final year of his illness

Acknowledgements

I am most grateful to the Trustees of the Phoenix Trust for awarding me a grant which I spent on travelling to Weimar, Basel and Sils-Maria. In the Goethe- und Schiller-Archiv at Weimar, Fräulein Eva Beck was extremely helpful, and I am especially grateful for her aid in deciphering Nietzsche's handwriting on the sheets of crayon scrawl written after he went mad. I must thank Dr Berthold Wessendorf for all the help he gave me while I was researching in the archive attached to the public library of Basel University.

Once again I am deeply in Catharine Carver's debt for giving me her valuable reactions to a reading of the first draft, and I should like to thank Margaret Windham of the BBC for the research assistance she gave me while I was working simultaneously on the book and on a radio feature provisionally titled 'When Did the Madness?'

I have to thank Dr R. Catterall, Dr A. Esterson, Dr James Fluker, Dr C. H. Sharma and Dr R. R. Willcox for their interpretations of Nietzsche's symptoms.

I am indebted to a great many previous writers on Nietzsche, and especially to Gilles Deleuze, Michael Haar, Michael Hamburger, Erich Heller, Peter Heller, R.J.Hollingdale, Curt Paul Janz, Karl Jaspers, Walter Kaufmann and J.P.Stern.

Della Couling's editorial help has been a great boon. I should also like to thank Juliet Salaman for not only typing the book, with all my almost indecipherable manuscript emendations, but also making some useful suggestions.

The translations from the German are all my own.

An essay of mine incorporating some of this material has appeared in *Partisan Review*.

Chronological Table

page

14   1844   15 October. Friedrich Wilhelm Nietzsche born, son of Karl Ludwig Nietzsche (b. 1813) and Franziska (*née* Oehler, b. 1826).

17   1846   10 July. Elisabeth Therese Alexandra Nietzsche born.

17   1848   February. Joseph Nietzsche born.

18   1849   30 July. Karl Ludwig Nietzsche dies.

18   1850   January. Joseph dies. Family moves to Naumburg. Fritz goes to local elementary school and then private preparatory school. Beginning of friendship with Wilhelm Pinder and Gustav Krug.

22   1855   Moves to Dom Gymnasium.

25   1856   Erdmuthe Nietzsche (grandmother) dies. Family moves into flat.

27   1858   October. Starts school at Pforta.

30   1859   Easter holiday at Naumburg and Pobles. Poems and abortive play about Prometheus.

31   Summer holiday at Jena and Pobles.

33   August. Joins school choir.

36   1860   Summer holiday with Wilhelm Pinder at Gorenzen.

36   Foundation of Germania.

37   Starts work on an oratorio.

38   1861   February. Sent home to recuperate from an illness.

38   March. Confirmation, and beginning of friendship with Paul Deussen.

39   Essay on Ermanarich.

41   August. Death of Buddensieg.

41   October. Essay on Hölderlin.

44   1862   April. Essay on Fate and History.

46   Visit to Elisabeth in Dresden.

47   Summer. *Euphorion* fragment written during holiday at Gorenzen.

48   August. Sent home again from school to recuperate.

49   October. Essay on Kriemhild in *Die Niebelungen*.

page

53   1864   Easter holidays. Essay on moods.
54   May–July. Essay on Theognis.
57   September. Leaves school. Paul Deussen stays at Naum-
58   burg. They go on a Rhineland holiday.
61   October. Starts studying theology at Bonn and joins
              Franconia.
62   December. Fights a duel.
63   Reads David Strauss's life of Jesus.
63   First Christmas away from home.
64   1865   February. First (unintentional) visit to brothel.
66   Easter at Naumburg. Refuses to take Communion.
67   Summer. Resumes work on Theognis.
67   Correspondence with Carl von Gersdorff crystallizes deci-
              sion to resign from Franconia.
70   October. Arrives in Leipzig. Registers at university to
              study classical philology.
72   Discovery of Schopenhauer.
74   Christmas at home.
75   1866   January. Lecture on Theognis to new philological club.
              Beginning of friendship with Ritschl.
81   June. Lecture on *Suidas* to philological club.
81   July. Ritschl commissions essay on Theognis for *Rhein-
              isches Museum.*
82   August. Reads Lange.
83   Cholera epidemic in Leipzig; to Kösen with mother.
84   November. Starts work on Diogenes Laertius.
84   1867   January. Death of Rosalie Nietzsche (aunt).
87   February. Beginning of friendship with Erwin Rohde.
              c. May–June. Aphorisms on history.
88   Summer with Erwin Rohde.
88   July. Finishes essay on Diogenes Laertius.
88   August. Starts essay on Democritus.
89   September. Medical examination: passed as fit.
              October. Enlisted in artillery regiment stationed in Naum-
              burg.
91   Essay on Diogenes Laertius wins university prize.
91   Resumes work on Democritus when off-duty.
93   1868   March. Damages chest in riding accident.
94   April. Promoted to lance-corporal.
94   Begins essay on teleology since Kant.

page		
95		June. Consultation with Volkmann and treatment in Halle.
95		August. Returns to Naumburg. Works on index for *Rheinisches Museum*.
96		October. Discharged from army. Returns to Leipzig.
98		November. First meeting with Richard Wagner.
102	1869	January. Appointed as professor at Basel University.
105		April. Takes Swiss citizenship and settles in Basel.
107		May. First visit to Wagner at Tribschen.
109		Inaugural lecture.
110		September. First weekend at Tribschen.
118		Christmas at Tribschen.
120	1870	February. Two public lectures on Greek music-drama and on Socrates and tragedy.
125		May. Erwin Rohde in Basel.
127		July. With Elisabeth to Maderaner valley.
128		August. Training course at Erlangen.
129		September. Contracts dysentery and diphthéria. Convalesces in Naumburg.
129		October. Leaves Naumburg to resume teaching.
131		Starts play on Empedocles.
132		Christmas at Tribschen.
137	1871	January. Applies for chair of philosophy.
137		February. Illness, followed by travels with Elisabeth.
141		April. First book, *Die Geburt der Tragödie* (*The Birth of Tragedy*), ready for submission.
142		Whitsun in Tribschen.
143		July. Von Gersdorff in Basel.
144		November. Fritzsch accepts *Geburt der Tragödie* for publication.
145		December. To Mannheim with the Wagners.
149	1872	January. Public lectures on educational institutions.
151	1872	Easter at Tribschen.
153		May. Erwin Rohde's review of book, and Wilamowitz-Möllendorf's hostile pamphlet.
153		Foundation stone laid at Bayreuth.
155		June. Rebuff from Hans von Bülow on his composition.
155		Summer. Essay on Homer and Hesiod.
156		Visit to Splügen.
157		October. Erwin Rohde's pamphlet defending *Geburt der Tragödie*.

page

157		November. With the Wagners in Strasbourg.
157		Christmas. Gives Cosima five prefaces.
159	1873	January. Von Gersdorff in Basel.
160		April. Visit to Bayreuth. Discussion with the Wagners about the essay on philosophy in the tragic age of the Greeks.
161		Essay on David Strauss.
162		May. Eye trouble. Lecturing without notes.
162		July. Dictates essay on truth and falsehood.
165		Summer holiday in Flims.
166		November. Essay on the uses and drawbacks of history.
168		Christmas in Naumburg.
168	1874	January. Visit to Leipzig and meeting with Ritschl.
169		February. Essay on history published.
171		March–September. Writing essay on Schopenhauer as educator.
171		Summer holiday in Bergun.
175		August. Provokes Wagner by leaving a Brahms score on his piano.
176		Christmas in Naumburg rearranging earlier musical compositions.
178	1875	March. Begins to dictate essay on philologists.
179		April. A week's holiday in Berne.
		Summer holiday. At Dr Wiel's clinic in Steinabad.
180		August. Moves into flat in Spalentorweg with Elisabeth.
182		September. Three days' holiday in Burgenstock with Overbeck.
183		Christmas in Naumburg. Collapses on Christmas Day.
183	1876	January. Released from teaching at Pädagogium.
183		7 February. Stops teaching at university.
183		March. Convalesces in Veytaux, first with von Gersdorff, then alone.
183		April. Stays with Hugo von Senger in Geneva. Proposes to Mathilde Trampedach.
184		End of April. Begins working with Heinrich Köselitz (Peter Gast) on the Wagner essay.
184		June. Dictates three final chapters.
187		July. Essay published. Visit to Bayreuth festival.
188		3 or 4 August. Leaves in disgust for Klingenbrunn, where he starts working on a new essay (later to be incorporated into *Menschliches, Allzumenschliches* (*Human, All Too Human*).

page

188   12–27 August. Back in Bayreuth. Leaves with Paul Rée.

191   October. They spend eighteen days together in Bex, going on to stay with Malwida von Meysenbug in Sorrento.

191   November. Final meeting with Wagner in Sorrento.

193   1877   April. Rée leaves Sorrento. Nietzsche stays on with Malwida von Meysenbug.

194   May. Nietzsche goes to Bad Ragaz to take cure.

195   June–August. In Rosenlauibad (Bernese Oberland) he shuffles off his allegiance to Schopenhauer and works on *Menschliches, Allzumenschliches*.

202   September. Returns to Basel. Works with Gast on preparing text for publication.

203   Consultation with Dr Otto Eiser.

203   1878   January. *Menschliches, Allzumenschliches* sent to publisher.

204   March. Hydropathic cure at Baden-Baden. Formally discharged from Pädagogium.

204   April. Copies of *Menschliches, Allzumenchliches* are sent to Nietzsche's friends, who are mostly outraged at the *volte-face*.

205   June. Elisabeth leaves Basel. Nietzsche moves to Bachlettenstrasse.

206   August–September. In Interlaken, trying to convalesce. Wagner attacks him in the *Bayreuther Blätter*.

206   September–October. In Naumburg for three weeks, ill.

       October–December. Back in Basel, still ill, but trying to work on Part II of *Menschliches, Allzumenschliches*.

210   Christmas in Basel.

210   31 December. Complete manuscript of second part sent to publisher.

210   1879   January–February. Bad 'attacks' (headaches and vomiting).

211   March. To Geneva.

212   May. Resigns from university.

213   June. Tries to settle in St Moritz.

214   June–September. Working on Part III of *Menschliches, Allzumenschliches*.

218   October. Lives in a Naumburg tower and attempts gardening work.

219   December. Part III published.

221   1880   February. Travels to Riva, where Gast joins him.

222   13 March. They go to Venice.

page

222   March–June. Nietzsche dictates notes which will be used in *Morgenröte* (*Sunrise*), Part I.

225   29 June. Nietzsche leaves for Marienbad and stays there two months, working on Part II.

225   September. In Naumburg, staying till 8 October.

225   October. In Stresa, where he works on Part III.

225   November. Settles in Genoa for the winter, where he finishes Part IV.

231 1881 February. Manuscripts of *Morgenröte* completed and sent to Gast.

231   May. In Vicenza and then in Recoaro with Gast, who leaves at the end of the month.

231   July. Nietzsche leaves for St Moritz but moves on to Sils-Maria.

233   August. First ideas for *Zarathustra* and conception of notion of eternal recurrence. Material originally intended for *Morgenröte* developed into *Die fröhliche Wissenschaft* (*The Joyful Wisdom*).

235   October. To Genoa.

238   December. Working on *Die fröhliche Wissenschaft*.

241 1882 January. First three books of *Die fröhliche Wissenschaft* completed.

242   February. Completes draft of fourth book. Rée arrives in Genoa. Nietzsche writes verses eventually used in prelude of *Die fröhliche Wissenschaft*.

244   March. Rée leaves on the 13th. Nietzsche goes to Messina on the 29th and starts *Idyllen aus Messina*.

245   May. Meets Lou Salomé in Rome and then Orta and Lucerne.

     24 May. He returns to Naumburg for five weeks.

247   June. Goes to Berlin, hoping to meet Lou. 25 June to Tautenburg, near Jena, to live in a farmhouse.

249   August. Lou comes to Tautenburg. Long walks and talks in the Thuringian woods. *Die fröhliche Wissenschaft* published on the 26th.

251   September. Lou goes to Stibbe to be with Rée. Nietzsche plans for the three of them to live in Paris together.

252   October. The 'trinity' stays in Leipzig for five weeks.

253   5 November. Lou and Rée leave. Breach with Nietzsche follows. He goes to Rapallo.

page

256   1883   January. Writes *Zarathustra*, Book I.

260   February. Makes fair copy for publisher. Learns of Wagner's death. Leaves for Genoa.

262   April. Joins Elisabeth in Rome, where he stays till 12 June. After two days in Aquila, he goes on to Sils-Maria. Works on Book II.

267   September. To Naumburg. Family tension about Elisabeth's impending marriage to Bernhard Förster.

269   5 October–2 December. Two restless months: Frankfurt, Freiburg, Genoa, La Spezia, Villafranca. Finally he settles in Nice for the winter.

273   1884   January. Finishes *Zarathustra*, Book II. Breach with Elisabeth.

273   April. Beginning of friendship with Resa von Schirnhofer. 21 April. Leaves to stay with Gast in Venice for six weeks.

274   15 June. Arrives in Basel to stay for two weeks.

274   July. After a few days in Piora he leaves for Zürich, where he meets Meta von Salis. 18 July. Back to Sils-Maria. Works on *Zarathustra*, Book III.

276   August. Visit from Heinrich von Stein.

276   25 September–31 October. In Zürich. Elisabeth there c. 27 September–14 October. Meets Gottfried Keller.

278   2 November. Arrives in Menton, but decides not to stay. Back to Nice.

278   December. Paul Lanzky arrives. Works on *Zarathustra* Book IV.

283   1885   April. To Venice.

283   22 May. Elisabeth married to Bernhard Förster. Nietzsche spends the day at the Lido.

286   6–7 June. Travels from Venice to Sils-Maria. Starts *Jenseits von Gut und Böse* (*Beyond Good and Evil*).

287   September. Back to Naumburg but leaves for Leipzig after two weeks.

288   October. Returning to Naumburg meets Förster once and leaves for Leipzig. On returning to Naumburg again he avoids Förster.

288   November. To Florence to meet Lanzky, and then on to Nice

289   1886   c. January. Completes *Jenseits*.

296   February. Elisabeth and Bernhard Förster leave for Paraguay.

page

296   March or April. Writes preface for *Menschliches, Allzu-
       menschliches* Part I.

296   30 April. Stays (in Gast's absence) at his Venetian flat.

297   May. Back to Naumburg, via Munich.

298   June. Takes lodgings in Leipzig. Gast comes to keep him
       company for two weeks.

298   August. Publication of *Jenseits*. Writes preface for new
       edition of *Menschliches, Allzumenschliches* Part II and for
       Geburt der Tragödie.

300   25 September. Leaves Sils-Maria for Ruta, near Rapallo.

300   October. Writes fifth book of *Die fröhliche Wissenschaft*.
       20 October. Back to Nice, Pension de Genève.

303 1887 January. Moves to a room in rue des Ponchettes.

304   April. Three weeks in Cannobio, on the Lago Maggiore.

305   28 April–8 May. Ten days in Zürich, before moving on to
       Chur.

305   8 June. Tries to settle in Lenzerheide for the summer, but
       after four days returns to Sils-Maria and settles down to
       work on *Zur Genealogie der Moral* (*On the Genealogy
       of Morals*).

311   30 July. Manuscript sent off to printer.

312   c. 20 September. To Venice, planning to stay for a couple
       of months.

312   21 October. Leaves for Nice.

314   10 November. *Genealogie* published. 26 November Georg
       Brandes enters into correspondence with him.

314 1888 3 February. Claims (in draft of a letter) to have completed
       the first draft of his *Umwertung alle Werte* (*Revaluation
       of All Values*).

315   April. Moves to Turin. Brandes starts a series of lectures
       on him in Copenhagen.

316   May. Working on *Der Fall Wagner* (*The Wagner Case*).

319   5 June. Leaves for Sils-Maria. Starts *Götzendämmerung*
       (*Twilight of the False Gods*) at the end of the month.

324   3 September. Writes a preface for his *Umwertung* and
       starts on *Der Antichrist*. Copies of *Der Fall Wagner* are
       ready by the middle of the month.

327   20 September. Leaves for Turin.

328   15 October. Celebrates his forty-fourth birthday by start-
       ing *Ecce Homo*.

332   November. Enters into correspondence with Strindberg.

page

335   1889   January. Collapses in street. Overbeck comes to Turin and
                escorts him back to Basel, where he is interned in Dr
                Wille's clinic.

337   13 January. His mother arrives in Basel.

338   17–18 January. Overnight train to Jena, where he is
                admitted to Dr Binswanger's clinic.

               June. Bernhard Förster commits suicide.

342   1890   4 March. Nietzsche released from clinic. Lives in a flat at
                Jena with his mother.

342   December. Elisabeth returns to Naumburg.

344   1892   July. Elisabeth goes back to Paraguay after making pre-
                liminary arrangements for a cheap collected edition of
                Nietzsche's works.

346   1893   September. Returns from Paraguay and starts her arrange-
                ments to create a Nietzsche Archive.

347   1894   September. Moves into a separate flat, establishing the
                archive in it.

347   1895   December. Her mother signs a document surrendering all
                her rights to her son's work.

348   1896   August. Elisabeth moves to a flat in Weimar, together with
                the archive.

350   1900   25 August. Nietzsche dies.

Nietzsche

Introduction

'Nothing is definable', wrote Nietzsche, 'unless it has no history.' The case for a biographical approach to his philosophy could scarcely be made more pithily. Any account of what he believed is inadequate unless signposted with dates: his beliefs changed, even more than most writers' do, as he developed. His philosophy cannot meaningfully be separated from his friendships and quarrels, his illnesses and depressions, his teaching and his letter-writing. His withdrawal into solitude was partly the result of physiological and temperamental pressures, partly a criticism of contemporary society, contemporary culture; his writing was partly a critical commentary on his critical life.

Like Heidegger, many writers on Nietzsche have taken the view that it is frivolous to study the tissue of experience from which ideas grow – as if they could be trivialized by their provenance. But Nietzsche himself believed that the best writers – Spinoza, Pascal and Goethe, for instance – were men whose 'thinking constitutes the involuntary biography of a soul'. No one has pointed more insistently than Nietzsche has to the relationship between mood and insight, neurosis and statement, sickness and vision. The sick man, he contended, being more aware of what he lacks than the healthy man of what he possesses, is better qualified to write about health. In Nietzsche's mature philosophy, as in his schoolboy essays, his main weapon was self-observation. Malaise is conducive to introspection, and it was Freud's opinion that Nietzsche achieved a degree of introspection never achieved by anyone else and never likely to be achieved again.[1] Nor has anyone possessed a greater talent for working analogically outwards from self-observation. The historical insights which so impressed Jacob Burckhardt (see page 252) were based less on research than on guesswork. Nietzsche was ingenious at applying self-knowledge to social movements, cantilevering out into the remote past from analysis of his own needs for self-assertion, reassurance, revenge, destruction, hero-worship. Writing about Socrates or Jesus, Schopenhauer or Wagner, he was always writing about himself, but to recognize this is not to depreciate his perceptions. On the contrary, it was his awareness of illogicality in his own consciousness that made him so knowing about the functioning of other consciousnesses. This functioning was determined, he saw, not so much by fact and logic as by mood, accident, prejudice, ambition.

Alertness to human illogicality was rare in the nineteenth century, and it was this, above all, that enabled him to exert such an enormous influence on the twentieth, in which almost every major writer in the German language has been profoundly indebted to him – Rilke, Kafka, Mann, Musil, Benn, Heidegger and Freud, for instance. Freudian psychology is prefigured in his analysis of forgetting; in his recognition that only a small part of the mind's functioning is conscious, and that consciousness is pathological; in his discovery of abreaction and repression, and in his understanding of the sexual and sadistic instincts, and of the retreat into illness.

It has been said that all the major modes of twentieth-century thought were anticipated in Nietzsche's work. Outside Germany the oceanic influence shifted Gide, Valéry, Montherlant, Shaw and D. H. Lawrence. He was the first philosopher to recognize what Camus was later to characterize as absurdity, the disconnection between human nature and an external nature which cannot be explained by reasoning. And, as Camus said, 'In him nihilism became conscious for the first time. . . . He wrote, in his way, the *Discours de la méthode* of his time, without the freedom and precision of the French seventeenth century, which he so admired, but with the mad lucidity characteristic of the twentieth century.'[2]

Even the world of Samuel Beckett, the lonely world in which consciousness can communicate only with itself, is anticipated in Nietzsche's work. In 'A Fragment from the History of Posterity' he imagined the fearful loneliness of the last philosopher, trapped inside his own self-consciousness. 'Nature gapes numbly around him, vultures hover above him. He cries out to Nature: "Grant oblivion. Oblivion." '[3]

Nietzsche saw that we can have no objective knowledge about the facts which determine our condition, that all our perception and cerebration can only be speculative, interpretative. His insistence that there is no fundamental connection between the name and the thing, between signifier and signified, prepared the ground for linguistic philosophy and for Structuralism, while what he called the genealogical method of historical criticism was seminal: the originality of Foucault, who followed Nietzsche in this direction, is still being overrated.

Heidegger called Nietzsche the last metaphysician, and we cannot clear him of the stigma if we agree that to be metaphysical is to use one name for characterizing beings in their totality. But Heidegger was himself working with concepts he had inherited from metaphysics, as Derrida shows, making the Nietzschean point that the entire history of religion and philosophy can be regarded as 'a history of metaphors and metonyms'.[4] A series of different ways has been found for determining the centre of the structure, and in each it is assumed that the centre is not itself structured. As Derrida argues: 'We have no language – no syntax and no lexicon – which is removed from this history; we cannot formulate a single destructive proposition which has not already had to slip into the form, the logic, and the implied hypothesis of exactly what it is trying to refute.'[5] No doubt Derrida will eventually come to be called what he has called Heidegger – the last metaphysician. At least Nietzsche can be called the first of the last metaphysicians.

In launching the first large-scale attack on ethics and ideologies that rested on divine sanction he was also attacking the system that had conditioned all our intellectual habits. Is it possible to reject as much of our moral and linguistic tradition as Nietzsche did without following him down the road to insanity? One of the reasons biography is relevant to the answer is that his drift towards madness cannot be separated from the lifelong history of malaise. Fighting against headaches, pain in and around the eyes, stomach pains, vomiting, debility, he was simultaneously cultivating his potential for madness. His friend Franz Overbeck thought he had been 'living his way towards' the final breakdown. It might seem to us, as it might at first have seemed to him, that, with his inescapable ill health, he could afford to go mad: he would have less to lose than if he had felt comfortable inside his skin. Later it would come to seem more as though he could not afford to remain sane.

There was nothing sudden about his movement into madness. He was only twenty-four when he wrote: 'What frightens me is not the fearful shape behind the chair but its voice; also not the words but the terrifyingly unarticulated, inhuman tone of that shape. Yes, if only it would speak in a human way.' (See page 103.) By 1880 he was able to prescribe methods of going mad. In *Morgenröte* (*Sunrise*) he makes the point that madness – or at least the semblance of it – had been the *sine qua non* of moral evolution. The men driven to reject tradition and propose new norms had had either to feign madness or to induce it by means of fasting, sexual abstinence, solitude, and 'concentrating resolutely on nothing except what provokes ecstasy and derangement'. He appears to have been thinking of himself, St Paul and Plato, who said that 'from madness Greece derived its greatest benefits'.

Writing *Menschliches, Allzumenschliches* (*Human, All Too Human*) in 1877–8, Nietzsche recognized that an interest in degeneracy and ambivalence is an essential prerequisite to self-analysis: where there is no self-division there is nothing to analyse. In 1883, recuperating from the experience with Lou Salomé, he mentioned the possibility that he would have a mental breakdown; when he tried to show that ill health qualified him to make philosophical pronouncements, all his arguments applied equally to incipient madness. Sickliness is normal. Man is the sick animal, insecure, inconstant, indeterminate. Since the healthy cannot be expected to tend the sick, we need sick doctors, sick nurses, sick priests, sick philosophers (see page 310).

It would be hard to think of a philosopher more unlike Nietzsche than Hegel, who comparatively seems so sane, so blinkered, so abstract. The pattern of his life was the obverse of Nietzsche's. He was in his late twenties when the possibility of madness loomed: he wrote later of 'this descent into dark regions where nothing seems firm, distinct or secure, where flashes of splendour abound, but on the verge of great chasms. . . . I have suffered a few years of this hypochondria. . . . Indeed everyone may have a similar turning point in his life.'[6] Four years earlier he had written: 'The first idea, naturally, is the conception *of myself* as a totally free being. Together with the free self-conscious being a whole world emerges from nothing – the sole true and conceivable *creation out of nothing*.'[7] During this Romantic phase, his ideal was 'the complete freedom of all spiritual beings who carry the intellectual world within themselves, and may seek neither God nor immortality outside themselves'.[8] His closest friend at this time was Hölderlin, who shared his anti-social love of rural tranquillity. Like Goethe, they both viewed contemporary discordancies in a critical perspective, based on the assumption that the Greek city-states had been unified and harmonious. For the young Hegel there was no question of coming to terms with the modern world, and even in his 1817 Encyclopaedia the ambivalence about insanity rests on his conception of the ego as wholly free. 'I am, first of all, a totally abstract, indeterminate "I", and therefore open to any arbitrary content. . . . Only Man has the power of apprehending himself in this complete abstraction of the "I". That is why he has, so to speak, the prerogative of folly and madness.'

Since the turn of the century, though, Hegel had been struggling to suppress his anti-social inclinations. To take permanent refuge in an inner world, he maintained, was to miss the chance of coming fully to life; he wanted to be one of those who could 'transcend the negative quality of the existing world to find themselves in it'.[9] In his essay on the German constitution, drawing a contrast between egocentric living and living angled towards the common good, he equates madness with isolation: 'Once a man's social instincts are dislocated, and he is obliged to throw himself into interests peculiarly his own, his nature becomes so deeply perverted that his energy is concentrated on refusing to conform.'

The turning point in Hegel's development coincided roughly with the turn of the century. He still believed that everything was latent in the human mind, that external reality provided no more than a series of impulses towards the development of spirit. As he put it later, 'The authentic truth is the prodigious transference of the inner into the outer, the building of reason into reality – this has been the world's task throughout its history.'[10] The individual's duty to society and the state therefore coincided with his moral duty. As Alfred Adler noticed, the starting point for his system of thinking is the point where repression is involved, the point where thesis turns into antithesis. If biographical factors seem irrelevant to Hegel's philosophy, it is partly because of his success in repressing his anti-social instincts, among others. The man disappears into the philosophy.

What he meant by spirit was not far removed from what Goethe meant by nature: they both believed that a rational principle was working through the whole of creation. Goethe never felt seriously hostile towards his environment, natural, social, or cultural, though he once told Schiller: 'We must step outside our century if we want to work according to our convictions.'[11] Kleist, who would genuinely have liked to opt out of the historical environment, he condemned as 'diese verdammte Unnatur' ('this damned unnaturalness'). Goethe, as Nietzsche put it, lived 'at the very centre of all things . . . in the faith that only the particular is objectionable in its separateness, while everything is sanctified in the wholeness of life'.[12] This quasi-religious cosmic optimism disqualified him, as he realized, from writing tragedy. If his *Iphigenie in Tauris* falls short of tragedy, it is only partly for the reason Schiller gave him: 'You have indeed done everything possible without gods and spirits.'[13] The main reason is that the dramatic texture is imbued neither with a strong enough sense of evil nor a strong enough feeling that human ideas of justice are impotent, irrelevant to the course that events take. Nor can *Faust* be a tragedy when the plot pivots on a wager between the Lord and Mephistopheles about whether the hero can be uprooted from his commitment to life. There is no tragic *hamartia* in the weaknesses Faust reveals: he wants to stop the passing moment; he lusts for knowledge, beauty, youth, superhuman power. Neither God nor the Devil is seriously involved in the extent to which his pleasant vices are instruments to plague him.

Though Nietzsche never wrote a tragedy, his life and his consciousness were oriented to a recognition of the tragic. Like Faust, but with a wilder impatience, he chafed against the confines of the human. And Thomas Mann used Nietzsche as his model for the composer Adrian Leverkühn, the hero of *Doktor Faustus*. As Nietzsche said, 'I want to make things as hard for myself as they have ever been for anybody: only under this pressure do I have a *clear* enough *conscience* to possess something few men have or have ever had – *wings*, so to speak.' (See page 262.) Symbolizing the tragic transcendence of the personal, Dionysus was central to Nietzsche's thinking from the time of writing *Die Geburt der*

Tragödie (*The Birth of Tragedy*) to his final insane identification with the god, whose name he used to sign letters.

Nietzsche was quite unlike Goethe and Schiller in his attitude to the gods, the culture and the civilization of the Greeks. In his 1795–6 essay 'Über naïve und sentimentalische Dichtung', Schiller had praised the Greek poets for being effortlessly at one with nature; against this Rousseauistic Romanticism Nietzsche argued that naive art always represents a triumph of Apollonian order over Dionysian turbulence. Dionysian art makes us look confidently into the horrors of existence, empathizing with primordial being in its rage for life and its terror at impending destruction. Ballasted with Schopenhauerian pessimism and Wagnerian nihilism, Nietzsche crashed past the frontiers of Romantic sentimentalism. After his rejection of Schopenhauer and Wagner, he equated the Dionysian with the superabundance of creative energy that leads to 'desire for *destruction*, change and becoming'. Or, as he made Zarathustra put it, 'Whoever wants to be creative in good and evil, he must first be an annihilator and destroy values.'[14] (Feuerbach said in one of his letters: 'No one without the courage to be absolutely negative has the strength to create something new.'[15] Nietzsche was not echoing him, but the two sentences are post-Hegelian in exactly the same sense.)

In an 1885 notebook Nietzsche identified the Dionysian with 'that acme of joy at which a man can feel apotheosised, can feel that Nature is justifying itself in him'. But 'the slaves of "modern ideas"', the 'children of a fragmented, pluralistic, sick, weird period' had lost that capacity for happiness without which the Greeks could not have participated in Dionysian festivals: the Greek soul had flourished without any need for conditions of morbid exaltation or madness.[16] And in a notebook he kept from March to June 1888, the last year of his sanity, there are some definitions of the Dionysian. It is

a drive towards unity, reaching beyond personality, the quotidian, society, reality, across the chasm of transitoriness: an impassioned and painful overflowing into darker, fuller, more buoyant states; an ecstatic affirmation of the totality of life as what remains constant – not less potent, not less ecstatic – throughout all fluctuation; the great pantheistic sharing of joy and distress which blesses and endorses even the ghastliest, the most questionable elements in life; the eternal will for regeneration, fruitfulness, recurrence; the awareness that creation and destruction are inseparable.[17]

In fact Nietzsche's craving for the Dionysian parallels the need Dostoevsky had – personally and in his fiction – for the epileptic. During his attacks he had muscular convulsions and became unconscious. Epilepsy is an abnormal physical process for instinctual discharge, a safety valve for accumulated pressure that the victim cannot release mentally. Like the Dionysian ritual, the epileptic attack is simultaneously an abdication from the self of everyday life and an intensification of it, bringing energy forcefully into play. In *The Idiot*, Prince Myshkin remembers that just before his paroxysms he always feels as though a flash of light or lightning in his brain is bringing all his vital forces to their highest tension. 'All his uneasiness, his uncertainties, his anxieties were relieved immediately: they were all merged in a lofty calm, full of serene harmonious joy and hope.' But the prince's physical convulsions always ensue immediately on the momentary sense of transfiguration, so it is impossible for him not to associate euphoria with disease. He cannot disentangle 'the highest form of being' from the lowest.

Both Dostoevsky and Nietzsche were deeply religious by temperament; both were terrified of where nihilism could lead. If God is alive, everything is meaningful; if God is dead, everything is permitted, and nothing is comprehensible. 'I made up my mind long ago not to understand,' says Ivan Karamazov in one of the earliest statements about 'absurdity'. 'If I try to understand anything, I shall be false to the fact, and I am determined to stick to the fact.'[18]

Like Dostoevsky, Nietzsche wanted nothing more than to escape into serenity, but he too had to associate it with breakdown. For Nietzsche the risk was madness, though he wanted to believe that 'tragic man' was strong enough to bear even the greatest suffering, firm enough in his conviction that life itself is worthy of reverence. But the image Nietzsche chose to represent the greatest suffering was a symbol of disintegration: 'Dionysus cut to pieces is a promise of life; it will constantly be reborn, constantly return from destruction.'[19] As Plutarch explained in his account of the myth, the god is indestructible. After he has been dismembered, the parts are distributed into winds, water, earth, stars, planets, animals. The story serves as the basis for allegories representing death and destruction followed by restoration to life. But it is dangerous to emulate the god.

This idea of distribution and dispersal was basic to Nietzsche's mental habits. He tried not to think in terms of identities but of forces. The stable identity of the ego disappears, and he was finally unable to differentiate between himself and other people, living or dead: 'At bottom I am all the names in history.'[20] But is insanity the result of rejecting identity and logic? If the old distinctions between truth and falsehood are invalidated, if there is no reality except in appearance, no body behind the panoply of predicates that tradition has forged, there can be no means of rejecting contradictions. Nietzsche was forced into inconsistency. Even if objective knowledge is unattainable, even if we concede that our logic always falsifies, we cannot dispense with it. Without it we cannot gratify either our irresistible curiosity or our compulsion to believe that we are gaining control over what surrounds us. At its most extreme, nihilism is the belief that every belief is false. But that is tantamount to denying the reality of the world, which may be a divine way of thinking – we are nihilist thoughts in the mind of God, Kafka said – but it is not available to humanity. Even if each cave leads only into another cave, even if each mask we pull off the face of reality reveals nothing but another mask, we cannot overcome our resistance to the idea of living with contradictions and uncertainties. Our craving for knowledge, for truth, makes us confuse stability with morality. We are horrified by the flux and destruction that are integral to the continuation of life on the planet.

Nietzsche's conception of the will to power was developed by generalizing from his reactions to observation of his own compulsion towards self-transcendence. It is not merely that he was never satisfied with what he was: his anxiety was that he would dwindle, become less than he was, if he was not becoming more. 'I am the one', says Zarathustra, his *alter ego*, 'who is constantly obliged to conquer himself.' Similarly, the will to power is always battling against itself, and the conflict should propel us towards the Superior Man (*Übermensch*), a concept crystallized out of

Nietzsche's intolerance towards mediocrity and complacency. The Superior Man represents the full realization of human potential. He must take hold of humanity as a sculptor takes his material to give it a new shape. But first he must be liberated from antiquated moral fetters, so that weakness and negativity can be eliminated. (This is itself a negative idea.)

The task Nietzsche was finally proposing for himself was a complete revaluation of all values. In the preface to *Ecce Homo* he warns us that he will shortly be confronting humanity with the greatest demand ever made of it. But the habit of self-conquest was deeply entrenched, and by now he was almost solipsistic enough to identify humanity with the part of himself that he wanted to conquer. *Ecce Home*, with its mad chapter headings ('Why I Am So Clever', 'Why I Write Such Good Books'), was written only three months before the breakdown, and if we could regard him as a victim of syphilitic paresis or *dementia paralytica*, we would have no difficulty in explaining the extravagant self-praise. Delusions of grandeur can begin to take root several years before the breakdown, as brain tissue is gradually destroyed and the self-critical faculties are eroded.

The aetiology of Nietzsche's illness and his madness are especially problematic because contemporary diagnoses are unreliable and the surviving evidence is exiguous. We cannot be certain that his father's epileptic attacks (probably *petit mal*) were syphilitic, or that Nietzsche's childhood illnesses were hereditary. His headaches may have been due to sinusitis, which can cause persistent and extreme discomfort if not effectively treated, while it can hardly have been congenital syphilis that sent Nietzsche mad, or the breakdown would have occurred much earlier. In January 1889, after the onset of madness, he said he had infected himself twice in 1866. If a Leipzig doctor diagnosed venereal disease, he was probably basing his opinion on sores, and it may have been erroneous. We know that Nietzsche went to a brothel in 1865, but he claimed to have come away without touching anything except a piano (see page 64). It is not impossible that, as Thomas Mann conjectures, he went back, but it is unlikely. Unless we can be quite sure that the final madness was syphilitic—and we can't—there is no need to assume that he must, somehow or other, have infected himself with syphilis. We cannot exclude the possibility of cerebral syphilis, which may have caused the stroke he suffered in 1898, but it is improbable that the delusions of grandeur before the breakdown or the madness after it had anything to do with syphilis. For nine years between the breakdown and the stroke, Nietzsche not only remained free from incontinence and from any serious bodily paralysis: he retained at least partial control over his memory. His mother could look after him almost unaided and he could still speak without any slurring. None of this is easy to reconcile with the hypothesis of *dementia paralytica*. Freude, who regarded Nietzsche as paretic, seems to have been wrong, and I can find no evidence to support the rumour, which both Freud and Jung helped to propagate, that he contracted syphilis in a Genoese male brothel. There is no reason to think he was ever a practising homosexual, though Freud was possibly right to explain his obsession with his own ego as homosexual and narcissistic.

One of the reasons his case history is important is that with his headaches, his vomiting and his madness, he was, more directly than any other thinker, living out the consequences of losing faith in a system of belief which is now generally discredited. The relevance of his life is all the greater if the causes of his final breakdown were not organic. It would seem that there is an element of choice in all breakdowns, just as there is a histrionic element in all displays of madness. Without remembering what he had written about situations in which it could be expedient to simulate madness, he gave the impression that he was faking to two of his closest friends (see pages 340–1). Not that he would have gone to these lengths merely to escape the humiliation of failing to keep the promise he had made to revalue all values. Overbeck was right to suggest that he had lived his way towards madness, and Nietzsche had anticipated his own fate in his note about the last philosopher. His way of saying 'Grant oblivion' was to break down.

In any case, his madness invalidates neither his assessment of the demand he was making on us nor the demand itself. We have no option but to follow him into the impasse from which his escape was into insanity. He has left us to find our own way out. If we lose faith in language and truth, how are we to communicate? If we lose faith in the coherence of the self, how can we expect to think coherently? Almost a century has passed since Nietzsche formulated his challenge to our conventions of thinking and expressing ourselves, but we have neither answered it nor found alternative conventions.

1   Fritz

My dear Fritz,

Today, which ought to be a day of real joy for you and your dear ones, is a sad day of mourning, since your dear, good Father, who loved you so much, and was so pleased with you, seeing how well you were doing both physically and spiritually, cannot enjoy the day and cannot pronounce his affectionate blessings.

But the blessed spirit of your Father is nevertheless rejoicing in your birthday, you good child, so prematurely bereaved, and he is looking down on you from the higher world with his best wishes for the welfare of his dear Fritz, which indeed he pronounces before the throne of the Heavenly Father, who so gladly listens to prayers. . . .

The five-year-old child who received this letter from a Lutheran pastor[1] was living in the parsonage of a small village in Prussian Saxony with his twenty-three-year-old mother, three-year-old sister, baby brother, grandmother, two maiden aunts and an elderly maid called Mina. Flanking the church where his father had been pastor, the parsonage was surrounded by trees, fields and farms. It was half an hour's journey from the nearest town. Behind the three-storey house were an orchard and a lawn, which was under water in the spring, when the cellar, too, was flooded. In front of the house were a yard, a barn, a stable and a garden with seats in it. On the far side of a hedge were four fish-ponds surrounded by willow trees. The study was on the first floor, and long before he could read, Fritz liked to look at the pictures in his father's books. Built in 1820, the parsonage had three dormer windows which looked oddly like three eyes staring out of a tiled forehead at the surrounding farms and fields.

Nietzsche's memories of early childhood were happy, though his mother, who had come to Röcken as a seventeen-year-old bride, could not challenge the household matriarchy that had been established when the pastor had invited his mother and his two stepsisters to live with him. Erdmuthe Nietzsche, daughter of a Lutheran archdeacon and widow of a superintendent (the equivalent of a bishop) was sixty-five when her thirty-year-old son married. In poor health and extremely sensitive to noise, she wore a frilly lace-trimmed cap and hardly ever went out. Both Fritz's aunts were sickly too. The highly strung Rosalie, who kept complaining about her nerves, busied herself with church affairs and, unlike most Prussian women, took an interest in politics. She read the *Vossische Zeitung*. Aunt Augusta's affliction was gastric. She was in charge of the housekeeping. 'Do leave me this one consolation,' she would say if anyone tried to interfere. Until Fritz, the first of her three children, was born, Franziska had little to do.

In moving from Pobles to Röcken Franziska had moved from one Lutheran parsonage to another, but the atmosphere at Pobles – another village, an hour's journey away – had been very different. She was the sixth of the eleven children that her mother had borne over a nineteen-year span. Her father, Pastor David Friedrich Oehler, who would have been richer if his father had not lost most of his money during the Napoleonic Wars of 1806–15, could still afford to live like a country squire. He went hunting with a groom to carry his guns, and he enjoyed playing cards. He was fond of music and encouraged visitors to sit down at the piano. Recalling an early visit from her future husband, Franziska later wrote: 'Coffee was drunk amid gay conversation, and then the pastor, already known to us as a pianist, was persuaded to improvise, which he did on this occasion with particular mastery. Afterwards we went into the garden, where he asked me to pick him a bunch of flowers, and a sprig of dill. He loved the smell.'

Karl Ludwig Nietzsche paid almost superstitious attention to anniversaries. He married Franziska on his thirtieth birthday, 10 October 1843, and, just over a year later, he regarded it as significantly auspicious that their first child was born on the king's birthday. Friedrich Wilhelm Nietzsche was named after Friedrich Wilhelm IV of Prussia. At the christening ceremony the pastor said:

Thou blessed month of October, throughout the years all the most important events of my life have occurred in thee; yet what I am experiencing today is the greatest and most glorious of them all! To baptize my dear little child! Oh, blissful moment! Oh exquisite ceremony! Oh inexpressibly holy work! I bless thee in the name of the Lord![2]

There seems to have been little discontinuity between the language in which the pastor prayed and the language in which he thought and spoke. By translating the Bible into German, Luther had given the country a national language, imbued with reverence for authority, divine or human. Nothing encouraged artificiality of diction more than prayer-like piety such as Pastor Gustav Adolf Osswald assumed in his letters, while Elisabeth Förster-Nietzsche's biography of her brother exemplifies the failure to recover from the linguistic conditioning both children received, encouraged by precept and by example to believe that the main function of words was to express reverence.

It was thanks to the king that the pastor was now living at Röcken. The youngest of ten children, he had been sent at the age of fifteen to a seminary in Rossleben, where he stayed for five years. After studying theology at the university of Halle until 1836, he was employed as private tutor in the house of a captain in Altenburg, the city in which the Duke of Saxe-Altenburg had his court. When the young tutor was offered a post there, the three princesses, the duke's daughters, became his pupils, and he must have made a good impression when he was presented to the king, for it was by royal command that he was offered the living in Röcken in 1842. By then his attitudes and manners had been affected by his years at the court, and in the revolution of 1848 his behaviour was more fastidiously monarchist than the king's.

Friedrich Wilhelm IV, who was forty-five when he came to the throne in June 1840, was a lover of the arts and capable of impressive public statements about the pride he took in 'the German nation'. To his father, Friedrich Wilhelm III, the idea of unification had seemed a threat to Prussia, and to the Liberals it had seemed a threat to liberty. The new king gained their confidence by relaxing press censorship just as newspapers could have begun to play an important role in disseminating information. Political thinking in the German states had been largely academic. The Liberal intellectuals had had little contact with the people. Except in Saxony, which was more industrial and commercial, there was no equivalent to the mercantile class which was on the ascendant in England and France. In the other German states about three-quarters of the population was still living on the land.

More of a Romanticist than a Romantic, more concerned with

reviving the glories of the medieval past than with constitutional reform, Friedrich Wilhelm IV surrounded himself with reactionary advisers and armed his soldiers with spiked helmets as if they were Teutonic knights. His nationalism consisted mainly of a dream of reviving the Holy Roman Empire with Prussia as the power behind the Habsburg throne. At the end of 1842 press censorship was again tightened, and early in 1843 the Liberal *Rheinische Zeitung*, which for five months had had Karl Marx as its editor, was suppressed. Marx himself was not unhappy at 'the opportunity to withdraw from the public stage into the study',[3] but the long-term effect on him was to make a reformer into a revolutionary, a Hegelian into a Marxist. But neither the king nor his advisers had any idea of where the real dangers lay. When Bismarck went to Potsdam in 1848, he was disconcerted to find that the king regarded him as a 'red revolutionary'. His response was to shave off his beard.[4] The revolutions of 1848 took the king by surprise. The Paris rising of 24 February, forcing Louis Philippe to abdicate, was the epicentre. The Austrian army was too feeble to crush the insurrection of 13 March in Vienna, where the royal family no longer supported Metternich, who had to resign. But five days later, when fighting broke out in the streets of Berlin, the powerful Prussian army could easily have restored order if the king had not lost his nerve. On 18 March the streets were cleared of rioters, but the next day, unable to assess the new situation or to drop the idea of winning his people's good will, he attempted persuasion. If the barricades were removed from the streets, he promised, he would withdraw his troops. When he ordered an unconditional withdrawal, he was effectively making a rebellion into a revolution. Determined to win back the affection of the masses, he paid homage to the corpses of the Berliners shot by his troops. He drove through the streets wearing a revolutionary cockade, and draped in nationalist colours – red, black and gold. He made speeches to declare himself a devotee of German liberty and German unification. 'Prussia merges (*geht auf*) into Germany,' he said.

Pastor Nietzsche was appalled by the disloyalty of the rebels, and deeply upset by the king's eagerness to condone and appease. When he read in the newspapers that Friedrich Wilhelm had worn the revolutionary colours, the pastor burst into tears and shut him-

self up in his study, afterwards refusing to discuss the incident
with Rosalie or the others. In the autobiographical sketch he wrote
at the age of fourteen, Fritz recalled seeing rebels in wagons,
singing and waving flags.[5]

Though he was soon to become precocious, he did not learn to
speak until he was two-and-a-half. By then he had an extremely
close relationship with his father, who even allowed him in the
study while he was working – the small boy was so quiet and well
behaved. Not that he was always placid: when in a rage he would
throw himself on his back and wave his legs in the air. The best
means of calming him down was music. Even at the age of twelve
months he was responsive to his father's piano-playing. Though
he was not yet five when the pastor died, he afterwards set a high
value on what he owed to him: 'I can enter a world of higher and
more delicate things without specially trying to. I merely have to
wait.'[6]

The pastor often gave the impression of withdrawing into an
inner world. He hated discord in the parish or in the household.
When the women quarrelled, he would sometimes retreat to his
study, shutting himself up for hours, refusing to eat, drink or talk.
If he stayed in the room, he would withdraw from the dispute by
sitting back with closed eyes. He also had attacks of what was
taken to be mild epilepsy. In the middle of a conversation he was
liable to lean back in his chair, staring blankly into space. Afterwards he would have no memory of the attack. Anxious and disconcerted, Franziska spoke repeatedly about her husband's
'condition' to the family doctor, Dr Gutjahr, who was unable to
help.

The second child, a girl, was born on 10 July 1846, eight days
before Fritz's second birthday. Elisabeth Therese Alexandra
Nietzsche was named after the three princesses her father had
tutored at the court of Saxe-Altenburg. The third baby, born in
February 1848, was named after the duke, Joseph. But before the
end of that revolutionary year, the pastor was already in the grip
of the brain disease that would kill him. In the spring he sometimes
felt well enough to take confirmation classes, and he gave a few to
Fritz, who was showing a precocious interest in reading and
writing, but by the beginning of summer the pastor was almost
constantly in great pain. He made a will appointing one of his

relatives, a lawyer, Dächsel, to be guardian of the children, and he asked his mother to take care of Franziska. 'Since last autumn', reported his superior, Superintendent Wilke, in March 1849,

he has been ill with nervous tension and an infection of the brain, needing at first the help of colleagues, and later needing them to deputize fully for him. I would have felt obliged to mention this earlier, were it not that during the first half of the period, from week to week, an improvement in his condition was expected, but, during the second half, mysterious paroxysms supervened, and the illness was now diagnosed as *softening of the brain*.[7] Nevertheless, from week to week, his recovery was still to be expected, according to medical opinion.

He was still in his thirty-sixth year when he died in the early morning of 30 July 1849. The autopsy would later reveal that a quarter of his brain had been affected by the 'softening'.[8]

When I woke up that morning I heard weeping all round me. My dear mother came in tearfully, wailing 'Oh God! My dear Ludwig is dead!' Young and innocent though I still was, I had some idea of what death meant. Transfixed by the idea of being separated for ever from my beloved father, I wept bitterly. The ensuing days were taken up with weeping and with preparations for the funeral. Oh God! I had become an orphan and my mother a widow! – On 2 August my dear father's earthly remains were consigned to the earth. . . . The ceremony began at one o'clock, accompanied by the tolling of the bells. Oh, I shall always have the hollow clangour of those bells in my ears, and I will never forget the gloomy melody of the hymn *Jesu meine Zuversicht*.[9]

Nietzsche's account of a dream he had at the end of January 1850, just before his baby brother died, is evidence of how his father's death was affecting him:

I heard the church organ playing as at a funeral. When I looked to see what was going on, a grave opened suddenly, and my father arose out of it in a shroud. He hurries into the church and soon comes back with a small child in his arms. The mound on the grave reopens, he climbs back in, and the gravestone sinks back over the opening. The swelling noise of the organ stops at once, and I wake up. In the morning I tell the dream to my dear mother. Soon after that little Joseph is suddenly taken ill. He goes into convulsions and dies within a few hours.[10]

Fritz's whole childhood had been lived in the proximity of the graveyard. He had sometimes felt frightened of the huge stone statue in the dimly lit vestry – St George with his menacing weapons – but he had never had reason to feel frightened of the graves, or to think that the body of his father would soon be lying in a vault next to the old wall, overgrown with roses and wild vine, at the edge of the cemetery. Now, suddenly, the tombstones were gateways to an anti-world in which his father lived. His sibling was admitted, but he was excluded. It is hard for a five-year-old to believe that dreams have no effect, and it was impossible for Nietzsche ever fully to exorcise the idea that his dead father was pulling him downwards. This may be one of the reasons he felt safest in high altitudes: mountains will be recurrent in both his life and his imagery.

The family could stay in Röcken only until the beginning of April, when the parsonage would become the home of the new pastor. Meanwhile Fritz was sent to school in the old village schoolhouse, next to the graveyard. Erdmuthe Nietzsche decided she wanted to live in the cathedral city of Naumburg, where she had friends and relations. She found a flat on the ground floor of a house belonging to a railway inspector. Franziska, with her widow's pension of thirty talers (about ninety marks) a year plus eight talers for each child, could not afford to set up house on her own. Except for a small allowance from the Altenburg court, she had nothing else, so it seemed sensible for her to go on living with her mother-in-law. The old lady took the front room in the flat, giving her two daughters the room next to hers, and leaving the two back rooms for the twenty-four-year-old widow and her children, who must have felt very constricted after having so much space at their disposal in the parsonage.

Arriving in a city with a population of fifteen thousand was a frightening experience for two children who had been living in a quiet village. Fritz was shocked and confused by the sight of so many houses, churches, streets, people. The castles and palaces impressed him, and he responded to the beauty of the surrounding countryside with its hills, valleys and rivers. The gates of the city were locked each night at ten o'clock, after a warning bell had been rung from the tower of the town hall. Anyone returning later would have to pay a fine to the watchman who opened up for him.

It was assumed that Fritz, like his father, like both his grand-fathers, and like so many of their forebears, would go into the

Church. Franziska gave him extra reading lessons, and his Aunt Rosalie gave him religious instruction. He was a serious-looking child with shoulder-length blond hair and large but myopic eyes. Early in his life he began to suffer from headaches, though Franziska brought her children up on an exceptionally healthy diet, with plenty of fruit, vegetables and starch but little meat and no beer or wine, though both were normally given to children. Nor did she ever administer medicine. Illnesses were treated with cold compresses, showers, and walks in the fresh air.

Fritz was sent to an elementary school, his grandmother believing that it would improve his understanding of society if he was forced to mix with children from the lower orders, but he was unhappy and isolated. The other boys teased him and called him 'the little minister'. The teasing probably gave him his earliest practice in what he was later to call self-conquest. If he could not get the better of the other boys, he could at least get the better of himself by using his will-power on the weaker side of his own nature, while he might be able to prove his superiority to the others by rising to a higher level of good behaviour. One day the boys coming out of school were caught in a heavy rainstorm. Looking down the Priestergasse, Franziska saw the others running as fast as they could, while Fritz was walking unhurriedly and bareheaded, using his cap and his handkerchief to protect his slate from the rain. She shouted at him, signalling him to hurry. His answer was inaudible, and when he arrived, soaked to the skin, he explained that according to the rules, boys going home from school must not run or jump but proceed in a quiet, orderly fashion.

Erdmuthe Nietzsche's friends in Naumburg were mostly lawyers and their wives. Paul Deussen, who first met Fritz when he was fifteen, says that mixing in the circle of privy councillors in Naumburg left him 'with a certain aristocratic bearing and manner which he never lost'.[11] There was a judge, Herr Pinder, who had two grandsons – cousins – who were the same age as Fritz, and when, after less than a year, he was taken away from the primary school to be sent to the same private school as Wilhelm Pinder and Gustav Krug, the three boys became close friends. Like Fritz, Wilhelm wrote an autobiography when he was only fourteen, and it describes how his friend spoke about his dead father 'always with great reverence'.

His fundamental character trait was a certain melancholy, which was apparent in his whole being. From earliest childhood onwards he liked solitude, and used it to give himself up to his own thoughts. . . . He had a very pious and profound mind, and, as a child, he was already reflecting on many subjects to which most boys of his age pay no attention. . . . As a small boy he occupied himself with many kinds of games, which he had invented himself. . . . So he took the lead in all our games, introducing new methods which made them more entertaining and more varied. . . . He never did anything without consideration, and whatever he did had a definite and well-grounded purpose. . . . Among his other principal characteristics were modesty and gratitude. . . . His modesty often gave rise to a certain shyness, and he felt very ill at ease with strangers.

Life had become much more enjoyable for Fritz, partly because of his friends, partly because of the school, where he stayed until 1854. Starting to learn Latin and Greek, he did not show any flair for them, finding Greek particularly difficult. A great deal of time was devoted to religious instruction, but little to German grammar and composition: he went on making mistakes in his own language. The school curriculum included archery, and Weber, the headmaster, not only took the boys for walks but played such games as 'robbers and policemen' with them.

The two Nietzsche children had a close relationship. By the time Fritz was eight, his six-year-old sister was trying to preserve everything he committed to paper. Whatever he discarded was appropriated and kept in what she called her treasure drawer. Hero-worshipping him, she attached more importance to his things than to her own. His own inclination was often to destroy his productions, and sometimes he would raid the drawer to retrieve a poem and burn it, but his precocity as a writer must have been nourished by her precocity as an archivist.

Fritz was creative in his game-playing. He wrote little plays centring on a china squirrel, one-and-a-half inches in height, called King Squirrel 1. Elisabeth made a crown for him with golden beads, Fritz wrote poems to recite for him, built him a picture gallery with toy bricks, and painted pictures to go in it –

mostly Madonnas and landscapes. Toy soldiers were paraded in front of him, and in 1854, when the Crimean War broke out, the soldiers were used to enact lengthy battles. The boys sided with the Russians. They reinforced their armies with newly bought soldiers, and, after the English and French forces had begun the siege on Sebastopol in October, they would often dig a pool shaped like the harbour, copying from maps in the newspapers, which they read eagerly for news of the latest developments. They reproduced the fortifications and filled the trenches with water. They made pellets with wax and saltpetre, set them alight and threw them on the paper boats. They bought books on military science and they were intending to write a manual of military terms. The siege was protracted, and it was not until the Russians had surrendered that the allied troops entered Sebastopol. When Gustav arrived with the news, the boys were furious with the Russians for not going on with the fight. Too upset to eat his lunch, Fritz wrote a lament in verse. The interpenetration between game-playing and creative art prepared the ground for the interpenetration of both with schoolwork. Once he had overcome his initial difficulties with Greek, Fritz became enthusiastic enough about Homer to collaborate with Wilhelm on a play called *The Gods on Olympus*. The leading roles were written for the authors and Gustav; Elisabeth and Wilhelm's two sisters played goddesses without very much to say. Herr Pinder rehearsed the play with the six children, and in the performance, which was at his house, he had to take over from Gustav, who had gone off in a bad temper. As Jupiter the tall judge was reasonably convincing, but he also had to play a warrior who was defeated by Fritz in single combat. The show went on until the banquet scene, which had not been rehearsed. With blancmange and raspberry syrup to represent ambrosia and nectar, the young actors gave eating priority over declamation.

By this time Fritz was at the Dom Gymnasium. On his first day there he was interviewed by the headmaster, who sent him straight into the second form. This had an immediate effect on his self-esteem, and on his relationship with Elisabeth, who was now told by Fritz that she was a little girl. And he would no longer let Mina collect him from Wilhelm's or Gustav's house at night. If Elisabeth had been invited, Mina would fetch her, but Fritz would walk several paces ahead, pretending to have no connection with them.

Wilhelm's and Gustav's fathers seem to have played as large a role in Fritz's early education as any of his schoolteachers. He sometimes did his homework in the house of Wilhelm, whose father took a lively interest in what both boys were doing. It was Herr Pinder who introduced Fritz to the work of Goethe. When the boys were still very young, the judge would read passages out loud, wanting to accustom their ears to the sound of well-written German. Herr Krug, a privy councillor, played the equivalent role in Fritz's early musical education. He had many musicians, including Mendelssohn, among his friends, and Fritz would often find himself standing motionless in the street outside the house, listening to Beethoven's piano music. Eager to encourage his interest, Franziska bought a piano and took lessons herself so that she could teach Fritz the rudiments of the art. As soon as he had mastered them, she arranged for him to be taught by a woman reputed to be one of the best teachers in Naumburg. She then went on playing duets with him.

Enjoyment of music was, from the beginning, inseparable from the compulsion to create. When Fritz was nine, Handel's 'Hallelujah Chorus' was performed during the Ascension Day church service, and his first impulse was to join in. 'I thought it was like an angelic song of jubilation, and that it was to this sound that Jesus ascended. I immediately resolved to compose something similar.' With most children the resolution would have led only to a daydream; with Fritz it led to an attempt: 'Immediately the service was over I set to work, and I was childishly pleased with each new chord I played.' At the age of fifteen he composed a Christmas motet based on the verse 'Lift up your heads, O ye gates . . . and the King of glory shall come in.' He rehearsed it secretly with Elisabeth in their nursery, and they performed it for the family on Christmas Eve. And, like his father, he had a talent for improvising.

What he enjoyed most of all was writing. His handwriting was extremely neat, and his poems, his lists, and the memos he wrote for himself all show that he took pleasure in forming letters and laying lines of handwriting out attractively on the page. In his notebooks and exercise books there is an extraordinary pride in neatness – hardly ever a blot or any sign of haste or impatience. In the two long poems he gave his mother as a Christmas present when he was thirteen – seventeen seven-line stanzas and eight six-line stanzas – there are only a few slight smudges, and no mistakes or alterations. His handwriting matured early, developing from copper-plate immaculacy into individual stylishness. Sometimes he enjoyed writing in very tiny letters, sometimes he produced elaborate flourishes, especially in the poems he dedicated to Wilhelm. The quantity of the juvenilia is remarkable, and it shows that he was already devoting an abnormal amount of time to what can only be called work. Sometimes he made tiny ink drawings, as in the 1858 notebook titled 'Poésie II', which has sixty pages in it, with a neat list of contents on the first two. The poems are divided into three sections: religious poems, ballads, and descriptions. Sometimes he made little books by folding pages. Some of the books are sewn together, some not.

He stayed at the Dom Gymnasium until 1858, and it was in this period that he became addicted to work. By the time he was in the third form he would usually stay up until eleven or twelve o'clock at night, getting up at five in the morning. He was relentless in his struggle towards self-mastery, callously ignoring the signals of distress his unfortunate body sent out. His headaches were already bad enough to keep him in bed, and from the age of nine onwards he missed a good deal of school through illness. Between Easter 1854 and Easter 1855 he was absent for five weeks and six days. After starting at the Dom Gymnasium in the autumn of 1855, he missed twenty days of schooling in his first year and thirteen in his second. Then when he was twelve he began to have serious trouble with his eyes. He had inherited myopia from his father, and one of his pupils was slightly larger than the other, a feature he had inherited from his mother. This can be a symptom of syphilis, and it could mean that his father had infected his mother with the disease, and that Fritz acquired it congenitally, but even when we take the unequal pupils together with the delayed development in speaking, the headaches, the myopia and the rheumatism he was soon to suffer, the evidence is not conclusive.

His early attempts at writing poetry, unlike his early attempts at composing music, were not based on conscious imitation. During 1854, the year in which he had his tenth birthday, he wrote fifty-five poems. By the age of fourteen, with precocious critical self-consciousness and with a substantial body of work behind him, he was dividing his verse into three periods. He condemned his earliest poems as clumsy and ponderous – bizarre seascapes, descriptions of storms and fires, written with no inkling of how to learn from the work of great poets. But the self-critical fourteen-year-old was probably right to prefer his work as a nine-year-old to that of his second period. Trying to express himself in ornate and striking language, he had written obscurely and affectedly. He dates the third period from 2 February 1858, when he gave his mother another small collection of poems for her birthday. 'From then on I resolved to spend a little more time on practising the writing of poetry, and if possible to write a poem every evening.' At first he tried to express himself simply. 'But I soon gave this up. To be completely achieved a poem must certainly be as simple as possible, but then there must be true poetry in every word.'

That he was an exceptional child was highly evident to the other schoolchildren, and their reactions to him must have encouraged his reclusive tendencies. A boy who was in the third and fourth forms with him later testified that his classmates had almost deified him: 'For there was something extraordinary in his voice and his tone, as there was in his choice of expressions, that made him quite different from other boys of his age.'[12] Another boy, who was a senior when Fritz was a junior, was reminded of the twelve-year-old Jesus in the temple, while at least some of the boys in Fritz's class found his presence inhibiting. According to one boy, 'He looked at you in a way that made the words stick in your throat.'

Home life was changing. Aunt Augusta had died in the summer of 1855, apparently from a lung disease, and in the following April, Fritz lost his seventy-six-year-old grandmother. In her will she left capital sums in trust for both children, the interest meanwhile going to Franziska, enabling her to set up a household of her own. In the summer she moved with the children into a flat in the house of a friend, a pastor's widow. The children enjoyed the garden, and Fritz no longer had to sleep in the same room as Elisabeth. For his new room he was given a stand-up desk. But the flat was too small, and two years later they moved again. During the summer the children would go to stay with their grandfather in Pobles: 'I was never happier than when I was in grandpapa's study, browsing through the old books and magazines.' Once again he was in a pastor's study in a country parsonage, surrounded by books: this was as close as he could come to re-enacting the experience of being with his father at Röcken.

The intensity of the religious feeling in *Aus meinem Leben* is rooted in his need to believe that he would eventually be reunited with his father and in the inevitable identification of God with the absent father:

In everything God has led me safely as a father leads his weak little child. . . . I have firmly resolved to dedicate myself for ever to his service. . . . Like a child I trust in his grace. . . . All he gives I will accept joyfully: happiness and unhappiness, poverty and riches, and boldly confront even death, which will one day unite us all in eternal joy and bliss.[13]

2   Pforta

During the spring of 1857 a school inspector had come to examine the boys in Naumburg. At the Dom Gymnasium, obviously impressed by the answers Nietzsche gave, he made a note of his name. In September 1858 Frau Nietzsche received a letter offering her son a place at Pforta, the most famous classical school in Germany, a boarding-school, where Klopstock, Novalis, Ranke, Fichte and the Schlegel brothers had been educated.

Since the age of ten, when Fritz wrote a poem about the school, it had been his ambition to go to Pforta. But on 5 October 1858, as he caught his first glimpse of it, he thought it looked more like a prison than a school.[1] Built in the twelfth century as a Cistercian abbey, with walls twelve feet high and two-and-a-half feet thick, it was isolated in a valley about four miles from Naumburg. For a Lutheran establishment, the educational system was oddly close to that of the Jesuits. Cloistered behind the thick walls, the boys were cut off from the contemporary world. They saw no newspapers, and the education was calculated to steep their minds in the classical past. They had six hours of Greek every week throughout their six years at the school, eleven hours of Latin weekly during their first three years, and ten during their last three. The object of the teaching was to familiarize them sufficiently with both languages not only to write them but speak them: 'When I have nothing else to do, I transcribe things I may have heard or read into Latin, trying to think in Latin.'[2]

What was peculiarly Prussian about the school was the emphasis on efficiency and the blend of militarism with classicism. Luther himself had been no lover of intellect or culture – in Rome he hated the opulent sensuousness of Renaissance Hellenism – but his legacy to Prussia was spiritual individualism, coupled with the doctrine that freedom is to be found only through obedience to the ruler. Pforta was geared to the same paradoxical combination of asceticism and classicism that had characterized Frederick the Great's court: Voltaire described it as 'Sparta in the morning and Athens in the afternoon'.

Insulated from the distractions of town life by what the Rector called a 'self-contained academic state',[3] the boys were subjected to a discipline which was strenuous and stringent, though not, by Prussian standards, exorbitant. 'They are habituated to the punctual and punctilious fulfilment of duty, to self-control, to serious work, to taking the initiative with originality, inspired by genuine love for their work, to being thorough and methodical in their studies, to systematic organization of the time at their disposal, to self-confident politeness and conscientious reliability in their dealings with their equals.'[4] The day started at four o'clock in the morning when the doors of the dormitories were opened, and the boys had to be out of bed by five during the summer and six during the winter. There were several long periods of invigilated preparation each day, and only short periods of recreation in the garden. Even on Sundays the boys were not free to do as they pleased: there were three periods of preparation and a quasi-military inspection by a prefect before they were marched to church, and they were allowed outside the monastery walls for only two hours, between four and six. Nietzsche would usually walk to the village of Attenburg, half-way between Pforta and Naumburg, to meet his mother and Elisabeth at an inn. They could spend about an hour and a quarter together.

The regimen of the school acted like a hot-house on Nietzsche's inclination to fight for self-mastery. The sadism in authoritarian oppression always tends to generate masochism in the desire to excel through obedience, and, as at the Dom Gymnasium, one of the ways Nietzsche could feel superior to the boys who teased him was by winning the approval of the teachers and earning high marks for good behaviour. The sado-masochism concealed behind his severity with himself came to the surface when he became involved in an argument about Gaius Mucius Scaevola, the Roman soldier who, failing to kill Porsenna, put his hand into a fire to prove his indifference to pain. Taking a handful of matches, Nietzsche set them alight and held them unflinchingly in the palm of his outstretched hand until a prefect knocked them to the ground. He was too late to save the hand from being badly burned.

For a boy who loved solitude and was now almost entirely deprived of it, Nietzsche seems to have settled down remarkably well: 'So far I like Pforta well enough, though not without a mixture of the feeling "just wait – I shall soon be feeling home-sick." ... With friendships [i.e. new ones] nothing happens quickly.'[5] Brave dissimulation cannot be the only reason there are so few signs of homesickness in his early letters home. A mid-November letter is almost apologetic for not missing home life more. 'By the way, I almost believe that homesickness is over-taking me. Now and then I feel signs of it.'[6] To Wilhelm he admitted: 'You cannot imagine how often I wish to be with you in Naumburg. It was all so very pleasant. The happy times are over and I cannot think about them without making myself sad.'[7] But he was precociously appreciative of the educational opportunities on offer. 'Professor Buchbinder's teaching is excellent, though he is strict.'[8] And eight days later, 'I find the timetabling of the day extremely good.'[9]

His desire for self-mastery made him willing to accept a stringent discipline, while his submissiveness was fortified by fanatical piety.

I drove through the gate. My heart was seething with holy sentiments. I was borne upwards to God in silent prayer, and a profound peace came over my spirit. Yea, Lord, bless my arrival and protect me physically and spiritually in this nursery of the Holy Spirit. Send down your angel that he may lead me victoriously through the temptations that I will encounter, and let this place bring me to true blessedness for eternity. Help, Lord! Amen.[10]

If he took precautions, as he claimed later, to protect his private inclinations against the monolithic system of rules, he gave no impression of feeling rebellious, but he must have been grateful that each week there was a day known as *Ausschlafetag*, when the boys were left to their own devices. *Ausschlafen* is to sleep one's fill, but in fact they were allowed only one extra hour in bed. What mattered was that there was no teaching, only preparation. 'These days are particularly suitable for some great private work.'[11]

The curriculum included a fair amount of physical exercise – swimming, games and gymnastics – but, unfortunately for Nietzsche, no one was much concerned about the boys' eyesight. There was not enough light during the day, and in the evening the boys had only feeble oil-lamps on their work-tables. Nietzsche required both reading-glasses and dark glasses to protect his eyes from strong sunlight. In his second letter home he had listed the things he needed: 'Above all a strong pair of spectacles – send them to me as quickly as possible.'[12] In March 1859 he was complaining of headaches, a cold and a cough. 'I still have no appetite, except perhaps for fruit, but I have no money to buy any.' In another letter, three days later, he was still complaining of headaches and of a stomach-ache that was even worse. The malaise seems to have cleared up quickly, but in the autumn he had another period of 'constant headaches'. The only entry for him during 1859 in the school's medical register is 'Rheumatism 15–20.3. Catarrh 2–9.11.'

He spent part of the Easter holiday at Naumburg and part at Pobles. Having had little time for writing during the term, he found himself full of ideas he wanted to explore on paper. This is how he inventoried his Easter output in a letter to Wilhelm:

First an abortive play titled *Prometheus*, stuffed with no end of specious ideas on this subject. Secondly three poems on the same theme, which I do to death in the third. Incidentally this third text is a queer thing. It is not finished yet – only six closely written quarto pages – and titled 'Question-marks and notes including a general exclamation-mark over three poems titled *Prometheus*.' In it a poet is set up against the public, and the whole thing is a mixture of nonsense and rubbish. Among other things there is a sentence that goes on for a whole page. Then there are fearfully stupid distortions, really stupid discussions etc. etc. I do not know what gave me such crazy ideas.[13]

They may have belonged to an adolescent rebellion against the feminine primness which had surrounded him since the death of his father. The unfinished fiction satirizes the dullness and triviality of the constant chatter which he had never previously challenged. Pforta was sharpening his critical faculty: the pleasure of returning to family life was disturbed by intolerance towards its norms. Unable to talk about his ambivalence or the guilt it caused him, he carried the debate into his writing:

Fourthly, a very incomplete study of the question 'All men are good; we ourselves are evil,' which incidentally is quite good to write about, if you bear in mind all the causes and effects. Fifthly, a poem that came out all in one go. It is quite profound, or rather obscure, and all the missing thoughts are indicated by dashes. Incidentally, after a lot of consideration, I gave it the title 'Poetry and faith kept alive'.

Nietzsche's schoolboy humour and his capacity for directing irony against himself were working fitfully. Earlier in the same paragraph his return to school is described in the humourless inflated style of German Romanticism at its worst:

Returning to Pforta at nightfall, I had a very heavy heart. The sky was entirely covered with clouds. Only single spots of brightness were clearly visible, and bright traces of the sunken sun were still prominent. The wind blew hideously through the high trees, which groaningly inclined their branches. My heart was in a similar condition. It too was darkened by clouds of sadness. . . .

His verse matured earlier than his prose. Just over three months after this letter he wrote:

> Flüchtige Rosse tragen
> Mich ohn Furcht und Zagen
> Durch die weite Fern.
> Und wer mich sieht, der kennt mich,
> Und wer mich kennt, der nennt mich:
> Den heimatslosen Herrn.
> Heidideldi!
> Verlass mich nie!
> Mein Glück, du holder stern!

> No fear shakes me
> When wild horses take me
> As far as they can.
> Whoever sees me knows me
> Whoever knows me calls me
> The homeless man.
> Heidideldi!
> Never forsake me!
> My luck, you bright star!

At Pforta, apart from this, he had written only seven poems, but on 20 August 1859, in his diary, he made another resolution to attempt a poem each day.

The first part of his summer holidays was spent with his uncle, Dr Emil Schenk, Oberbürgermeister of Jena, a place 'which I liked almost better than anywhere else', as he said in his letter of thanks.

He went swimming in the Saale, where he was nearly drowned, and his uncle took him along to a meeting of his old student fraternity, Teutonia. They also went for long walks into the hills above the town. In the afternoons he browsed in his uncle's library, where he read Novalis, who had maintained that all experience was magical, using the term *Magische Idealismus* for his conception of a Romantic idealism that would subsume the idealism of Kant.

Nietzsche spent the second part of his summer holiday together with his mother and Elisabeth at Pobles, where on 2 August his grandfather celebrated his seventieth birthday – an occasion for a great family reunion. That night Fritz had a nightmare like the dream about his baby brother. He saw the parsonage lying in ruins and his grandmother sitting alone among the debris. Waking up in tears, he was unable to sleep any more. In the morning he told Elisabeth and his mother, who said neither of them must talk about the dream. Always robust, their grandfather was still in good health. But before the summer was over, he caught a bad chill, which developed into influenza. By the end of the year he was dead.

At Pforta the boys each had a tutor, a teacher who handed out money for expenses – applications had to be made in writing – and gave advice when they wanted to discuss personal problems. Fritz's tutor was Professor Buddensieg, the kindly school chaplain, a forty-two-year-old theology teacher with a sense of humour. The summer holidays ended early in August, and when Fritz succumbed to a bad bout of homesickness, he went to Buddensieg, who prescribed a 'remedy' which Nietzsche noted down in his diary: if we want to learn anything of value, we cannot always stay at home, nor do our parents wish us to. Diligent work is a cure for sadness, and, if work fails, we can pray.

Nietzsche worked and prayed, but the atmosphere at Pforta was affected by the war scare. At the beginning of May 1859, France had declared war on Austria. In June the French won two major victories, at Magenta and at Solferino. Between the two battles Prussia began to mobilize, preparing to intervene, and after the Franco-Austrian armistice of 8 July, the peace seemed unstable:

Professor Steinhardt, the Hebrew teacher, had mentioned the imminent danger of war, which had torn almost everyone from our circle out

of their careers for the appointed period of service. They had, however, only had to report to Naumburg, and forfeited six days of their holidays. When I was in Jena I heard the telegraphic news about the conclusion of peace. But there was no real happiness about it. They were afraid the lion was stepping back only to gather strength for a new assault.[14]

On 20 August he joined the school choir: 'I now sing with it in church, go with it on tour, and enjoy all the advantages and disadvantages of a choirboy.'[15] His life would generally have been pleasanter if he could have held himself less aloof from the other boys, or formed a friendship with one of them, as he had with Wilhelm. 'I longed for Naumburg and for the hours of pleasant conversation with my friends. Here I had no one. The whole school building seemed so bleak, so comfortless, and the duskiness everywhere left me with nothing before my eyes except happy memories from the holidays. Oh Christmas, oh Christmas, how long, how long!'[16]

He also enjoyed the school outings. An expedition into the mountains was an occasion for military-style inspection, marching, singing, dancing, cheering, spirited demonstrations of German and Prussian patriotism being integral to the enjoyment. Nietzsche's diary describes how they marched, with band and singers in front, from the school up into the mountains, flying the school flag. On a plateau where a confectioner had set up his tent for the holiday, the boys all drank and danced. The choir sang 'Hoch, Deutschland, hoch!' At the end, as the boys were lining up in classes ready for the return march, led by the prefect, they gave three cheers for the king, then for the Prince of Prussia, then for the boys taking the final examination, then for the school, the teachers, and the whole assembly.[17]

Demonstrations like this had more to do with high spirits and a sense of national solidarity than with the king, who in 1857 had had a stroke which left him insane. The Prince of Prussia was his more Liberal brother, Wilhelm, who had taken control, though it was not until October 1858 that the reactionary cabinet gave him the title of regent. He was then sixty-two. His son, Friedrich, was married to a daughter of Queen Victoria. The incapacitated Friedrich Wilhelm IV remained king until he died in 1861.

At Pforta generally Nietzsche gave the impression of thinking himself superior to his classmates. One boy ridiculed him by constructing a puppet, made from a photograph of him cut into pieces. Wilhelm continued to be the only boy he was able to treat as an equal, but, having spent half the Easter holiday and the whole of the summer away from Naumburg, Nietzsche had scarcely seen him since the beginning of the year. The friendship continued, but the only vehicle for it was correspondence. '*Semper nostra amicitia manet*', they wrote at the end of their letters to each other. ('May our friendship always remain.') Already Nietzsche was forming the habit of using letters as a substitute for personal contact. Writing frequently and intimately to Wilhelm, and enjoying his equally intimate replies, the fourteen-year-old Nietzsche felt less need for contact with the other schoolboys. At the beginning of the summer term he had even suggested that Wilhelm should collaborate with him in writing about Prometheus: 'I would like it very much if we both wrote down our thoughts about him. So, above all, collect the completest possible account of his life from lexicons and other books. And do the same for the other relevant myth-cycles. . . . You are in a better position to do this because there are not many books at my disposal. Then write down all the ideas that occur to you after more careful consideration of the material, and I will do the same.' He was especially interested in the end of Zeus, which Prometheus anticipated, in relation to the downfall of the German gods, destroyed by the forces of nature. So, while still a believer, he was already attracted to the death of godhead as a theme. 'Meanwhile, instead of succumbing to a simple didactic style, we will write as colourfully, animatedly and strikingly as possible – in short, something brilliant.'

More than at the Dom Gymnasium, his imagination was creatively involved in his work, while he had a phenomenally mature understanding of how important it was not to separate one subject from another. 'Greek and Latin poets should be studied side by side with German classics, and their modes of thinking compared. Similarly, history should be merged with geography, mathematics with physics and music.' In the examination he had to take during the second week in August, he did better in Latin and German than in Greek: he was graded 1 for Latin, 1b for Latin verse, 1b for German, IIa-b for Greek and IIb for mathematics. He was moved into the upper third form with the general grading of 11a in all four subjects. Standards at Pforta were too high for annual promotion to be automatic: some boys were not given their leaving certificate until they were in their twenty-third year.

Sometimes Nietzsche would come top in the class, sometimes third. The boy who came top was called 'Primus' and it was his function to keep the other boys in order when no teacher or prefect or senior was in the room. Nietzsche was 'Primus' when he first spoke to Paul Deussen, later to become a friend. It was during a break, and Deussen was eating his *Näckchen*, his bread roll. 'I can still see Nietzsche wandering between the rows with the uncertain gaze of the extreme myopic, vainly looking for an opportunity to step in. He came over to where I was sitting, bent towards me, and said "Don't talk so loudly to your *Näckchen*." '18

According to the school's medical records, Nietzsche was suffering between 5 and 16 January 1860 from catarrh. He would probably not have been kept in the sanatorium for so long if he had not been coughing so much, or if the doctor had not been waiting for milder weather. 'My cough is almost completely cured,' he wrote to his mother on the day he was discharged, 'but I am still wearing the muffler.' There is no note of any other illness until the 'rheumatism' of 12–26 June, but in the middle of February he does not seem to have been enjoying himself. 'Our life in Pforta consists of no more than constant recollection and constant hope,' he wrote to Wilhelm. 'The former admits sad comparisons with earlier times, while the latter is strengthened and sweetened with the balsam of anticipation, sparing us from all thoughts of the cold, boring present.' Expressing his frustration to Wilhelm made him feel less frustrated, but their correspondence was not a sufficient safety valve. On 6 March he penned a twenty-six line verse letter 'To a friend', the first of several letters to imaginary correspondents:

> So many joys and sorrows have I shared with you,
> And the bond of friendship eased the sharpest pains.
> Well do I know that schooldays must be difficult
> With no evasion of the burdens, worry, work.

Eleven days later, in his letter to Wilhelm on the day before his confirmation, the tone is less discontented and more pious: 'So I hereby wish you the Lord's richest blessings. May he strengthen you with his mightiness to a worthy receptivity towards his divine gifts, and may you always henceforward benefit from the cornucopia of his grace.'[19] If this is reminiscent of Pastor Osswald, it is surprising only because this tone is so rare in Nietzsche's letters, despite the amount of time he must have spent listening to prayers and sermons. Though he was still intending to become a clergyman, the language of the preacher encroached remarkably little on his prose.

The spring holidays lifted him out of his depression, but Pforta seemed very dismal when he had to go back, and his mother, who was usually taken less into his confidence than Wilhelm about his adolescent bouts of melancholia, received a glum letter: 'So once again I have to adapt myself to the inevitable shackles. This subdued, monotonous routine is so totally different from the occupations one chooses in freedom. I really wish I could have the holidays all over again.' But he had to wait till the beginning of July for the summer holiday, when he planned to take Wilhelm with him on a visit to another uncle, Edmund Oehler, pastor at Gorenzen, a village in the Harz mountains.

On one of their walks through the woods Fritz and Wilhelm discussed the idea of regularizing the literary collaboration they had planned for Prometheus. With Gustav Krug and perhaps a few other friends, they would constitute themselves into a club for poetry and science. Their name for the new society – Germania – suggests that the idea may have derived partly from the Teutonia meeting Nietzsche had attended with his Uncle Emil. Returning to Naumburg, they recruited Gustav, whose main enthusiasm was for music, which was therefore included as one of the activities. Everything was done formally. On 25 July, after buying a cheap bottle of red Naumburg wine, the three of them went to Schönburg, an hour's journey from the city, to hold their inaugural meeting in the watch-tower that looked out over the Saale valley. They each made a solemn commitment to contribute a piece of work each month – a poem, an essay, an architectural design or a musical composition – which the others would criticize constructively. Each of them would annually write at least six essays, two of which must be about contemporary issues. According to the constitution, which was drawn up later in the day in Naumburg, the subscription would be five silver *groschen* monthly, the money being spent on music, to be procured by Krug, and on books, to be procured by Pinder. Krug was to act as treasurer and librarian. At quarterly meetings each member was to deliver a lecture. Having pledged themselves to the fraternity, they threw the empty bottle into the valley.

From now on, the teachers at Pforta would not be the only audience for what Nietzsche wrote. But his first contributions to Germania were musical. After his Christmas motet he wanted to compose a Christmas oratorio, and in August he submitted the overture and a chorus. By October he had completed two shepherds' choruses, and by November two choruses of prophets. Among the periodicals bought for Germania was the *Zeitschrift für Musik*, which was the only musical paper to champion Wagner, so Fritz's interest in his work may date from before his sixteenth birthday.

Taking his commitments to Germania more seriously than either Wilhelm or Gustav, and feeling impatient to complete his oratorio, he resented having so little time for anything but schoolwork. In a letter to his two friends he complained that 'holiday thoughts' were distracting him, that there was not enough time for his 'favourite occupations. Indeed it is very much pleasanter to escape from the tyrannous empire of compulsion into the territory of free will.'[20]

While working on the oratorio, he wrote a thoughtful apologia for the form. It was simpler and more elevated than opera, appealing to the ear but to none of the other senses, and it was directly comprehensible to uneducated people. (He may have been thinking of the effect that the 'Hallelujah Chorus' had had on him.) Oratorio should become more popular, as it would if it met three requirements. It should be consistent in character, should go straight to the heart, and should be profoundly religious and exalting.

After sending seven poems to Germania in January 1861, Nietzsche managed to submit a new section of his oratorio in February, despite a long bout of illness, which started in mid-January. Not wanting another spell of confinement in the sanatorium, he did not report it to Dr Zimmermann, the school's medical officer. 'I have constant headaches. They go right through my head, and my neck hurts each time I move, and my larynx when I swallow. For two nights I have not slept at all. I was freezing and sweating alternately. I cannot get my mind clear. Everything around me is like a dream.'[21] He held out until 26 January, but, unable to concentrate on work, he had finally to report to the sanatorium. The doctor gave him medicine, but said that what mattered most was to rest. The pains in his neck and throat eased slightly, only to reassert themselves, while the headaches continued relentlessly. He was quite glad to catch a cold, because it gave him the illusion that when he got rid of it, the other symptoms would disappear. Unable to go home for his mother's birthday, he wrote another of his pious letters. 'May Almighty God be with you throughout the year, and protect you with his blessings. May he bestow good health on you, so that you may live all the year long in perfect well-being.'[22] Nietzsche had been unable to finish a birthday poem for her, but promised to send it as soon as he could.

Within a few days the headaches became sporadic. He was allowed to spend some time out of bed, though neither to read nor write, for fear of bringing them on again, but he was encouraged to go for walks every day. By the middle of February he thought he had recovered, but then the headaches returned: 'The slightest mental effort causes me pain.'[23] Having missed over two weeks of school-work, he was worried about catching up with his class. Dr Zimmermann believed in blood-letting, and now, for the second time, leeches were applied behind Fritz's ears. 'I do not believe it will help. If only I could go for a long walk every day.'[24] He felt sure he would recover more quickly in Naumburg, and permission was given for him to leave Pforta on the 17th. Within ten days the headaches had become less frequent and less painful. He was back at school by the end of the month, only to find that they started again. 'I must gradually accustom myself to them,' he wrote, stoically.[25] By the end of the first week in March, with examinations imminent, he had settled down to work again.

The friendship with Paul Deussen grew out of a shared enthusiasm for Anacreon's poetry: they went for walks together, reciting it.[26] They also took snuff together, secretly, in the dormitory. The son of a pastor, Deussen, too, was intending to go into the Church, and the two boys were confirmed in March 1861 on the Sunday of Mid-Lent, kneeling down together to receive the sacrament. Deussen has written: 'I well remember the holy, other-worldly mood that took possession of us in the weeks before and after the confirmation. We would have been quite prepared to depart this life, to be with Christ, and all our thoughts, feelings and aspirations were irradiated with a celestial cheerfulness.'[27] To some extent, though, he says, the teaching tended to undermine religious faith: Professor Steinhardt interpreted the forty-fifth Psalm as a secular celebration of marriage. But Nietzsche's letters about his confirmation show how seriously he took it. 'May this solemn and holy day constantly remain before my soul throughout the whole of my future life, and remind me of the awe-inspiring oaths I have taken and the professions of faith I have made.'[28]

Not that he had altogether lost the rebellious spirit which had expressed itself in the satirical novel he started during the summer of 1859. In the Easter holidays he had a serious quarrel with his mother, and in April 1861, after returning to school, he deliberately addressed his letter of apology jointly to her and to Elisabeth, so that his sister should witness his contrition. 'Each time I think about it, it causes me great pain that I upset you so much. . . . Do forgive me, dear mamma, but then, I beg you, think no more about this incident. . . . From now on I will try as hard as I can, through my behaviour and through my love for you, to heal the rift.'[29] It may have been a quarrel over religion. In November 1860 she had been shocked when he recommended Elisabeth to read *Das Leben Jesu* by the rationalist Hase.

Perpetually short of money, Nietzsche's mother was renting out his room. Sometimes, when he came home on holiday, he had to sleep in a smaller room. At the end of May, calculating that there were still twenty-five days more of school, and knowing he was to have the larger room for only the first week of the holiday, he was expectantly savouring the sensation of repossessing it. 'It is so pleasingly cool in the room. A table, chair and a bookcase are all the furniture it needs. On the window-sill a few flowers for the sake of their scent. A jug of water for refreshment, my clock, piles of papers and notebooks – that is how I think about the time I will spend there.'

It was probably Koberstein, a literary historian who taught German to the lower second, who acquainted him with the Nordic saga which centred on the Ostrogothic King Ermanarich. Nietzsche became passionately interested, researching avidly and feeling inspired by the subject to write poems and compose music, working 'with the feeling of having so immersed myself in the old saga that it was painful for me to separate myself from it for any length of time'. We have the evidence of Baron von Gersdorff, who was in the lower second with him (but did not become a friend until years later), that when he wrote an essay on the Ermanarich saga, Koberstein was 'full of praise for the scholarship, the insight, the construction and the stylistic accomplishment of his pupil'. Von Gersdorff was living in Koberstein's house. Koberstein, he says, 'was usually fairly silent at meals, but he talked about it to me with pleasure and excitement'. Nietzsche studied the Saxo Grammaticus, the chronicles and the Eddas. 'That twilight of the gods, as the sun goes black, the earth sinks into the sea and whirlpools of fire uproot the all-nourishing cosmic tree, flames licking the heavens – it is the greatest idea human genius ever produced, unsurpassed in the literature of any period, infinitely bold and formidable, but melting into magical harmonies.' It was inevitable that Wagner would have a galvanizing effect on this mind.

Presumably Nietzsche used the essay he had written for Koberstein as a basis for the lecture on Ermanarich he delivered in July 1861 before the 'synod' of Germania. 'Synod' was the name for the disciplinary body at the school, and the three friends continued their extreme formality over Germania, although they had not co-opted any other members. The spectacle of one sixteen-year-old schoolboy lecturing to two others would, to an outsider, have been extremely comic, but Germania, itself a formalization of the friendship with Wilhelm and Gustav, exercised a beneficent influence not only on his prose style but on his working habits. Most schoolboy essays are attempts at communication with teachers. Lecturing to the 'synod', Nietzsche was both identifying with his teachers and communicating with his friends. In June Nietzsche had contributed another chorus for his oratorio and a Moorish song, but the music he submitted in August was not part of the oratorio: it was titled 'Pain is the keynote of nature'. In the Ermanarich saga he had found a subject that would interest him for over two years: during the autumn of 1863, over a period of several weeks, he went on 'grubbing into pigskin-bound volumes and chronicles' until he had produced a sixty-page essay.[30]

Returning to Pforta in August 1861 he found Professor Buddensieg gravely ill. The doctors could not agree on a diagnosis, but thought the disease was rheumatic. In the middle of the month he seemed slightly better, but on the 19th it was clear that he would not survive the night, and he died at two in the morning. He was not yet forty-five. 'Oh you cannot believe how sad my heart is. We all loved him so much. Everybody is deeply disturbed. There is deathly silence everywhere. . . . Oh, it is too painful! Yet what God does is well done.'[31] Having to choose another tutor straight away, he opted for Dr Heinse, who had been at the school less than eighteen months. In May 1860 Fritz had enthused about him in a letter to Wilhelm: 'I very much like his interpretation of Caesar because he often goes into the synonymy.'[32] Asking his mother to visit Buddensieg's widow, Nietzsche described the funeral as 'very beautiful and solemn, but comforting and soothing to the pain that must follow'.[33]

In the September examinations Nietzsche did well, getting 1 in Latin, IIa in Greek, French, history and religious knowledge, and IIb in Hebrew and mathematics. For both conduct and diligence his mark was 1, and he was promoted to the upper second. In October, having to produce an essay on a German writer, he chose Hölderlin, who had died in 1843, but was still almost unknown. It may have been through Wilhelm, who had wanted Germania to buy Hölderlin's poems, that Nietzsche had come to know them. By now he possessed a biography, which was in his bookcase, and he asked his mother to forward it. His own poems owe a good deal to the sonorous musicality of Hölderlin's, and in his essay, which is written in the form of a letter to a friend, Nietzsche boldly calls Hölderlin 'my favourite poet'. Hölderlin's miserable future, the protracted madness that preceded his death, could be heard 'resounding through the melancholy tones of *Empedokles*', his dramatic fragment. His *Hyperion* was remarkable for 'the harmonious movement of its prose. . . . Indeed, this prose is music, soft melting sounds interrupted by painful discords, finally fading into dusky, mysterious funeral songs.'

The influence of Hölderlin's style on the essay is strong, and it is remarkable that so much of what Nietzsche wrote foreshadows the way in which his own later development was to run parallel to the mad poet's. He quotes his imagery friend as complaining:

On me, at least, these turbid, half-mad utterances of a lacerated, ruptured mind have made only a depressing and sometimes repellent impression. Confused discourse, notions from a madhouse, wild outbursts against Germany, divinization of Nature, sometimes animistic, sometimes pantheistic, sometimes polytheistic, all mixed up together – all this has left its mark on his poetry, albeit in accomplished Greek metres.

In defence of Hölderlin, Nietzsche cites *Empedokles* as an example of 'the purest Sophoclean dialogue', an 'inexhaustible plenitude of profound ideas'. Conceding that his imaginary friend's objections may be valid not only for the poems written when Hölderlin was mad but for some earlier ones in which 'cerebration was wrestling with the invading darkness of insanity', Nietzsche praises 'Andenken' ('Remembering') and 'Die Wanderung' ('The Journey') as poems that raise our consciousness to 'the most sublime ideality'. And in *Hyperion*, he says, Hölderlin 'flings sharp and cutting words against German "barbarism". But this revulsion from reality is compatible with the greatest patriotism, which Hölderlin had in the highest degree. What he hated in the Germans was bald specialization, philistinism.'

Discussing *Empedokles*, Nietzsche described the hero's death as due to divine pride, contempt for humanity, world-weariness and pantheism. 'Reading the whole work, I have always found it deeply disturbing. There is a divine majesty in this Empedokles. In Hyperion, on the other hand, though he seems to blaze equally with transfiguring radiance, everything is frustrated and unfulfilled. . . . But the nostalgia for Greece is nowhere revealed in purer tones.' On Hölderlin's 'contradictory' religious views Nietzsche wrote only that he could not refute his friend's animadversions. 'This you must ascribe to my all-too-scanty knowledge of philosophy.'

The teacher (probably Koberstein) who corrected the essay gave it the mark 11/11a, commenting: 'I should like to give the author one piece of friendly advice: to concern himself with a poet who is healthier, more lucid and more German.' Generally Nietzsche seems to have respected his teachers, and especially

Koberstein, Steinhardt and Corssen. But if this comment was typical of their reactions to his work, he must have felt ambivalent over the value of what he was achieving. On one level, as his tone and style indicate, he had complete confidence in his own taste and judgement; on another level he was irremediably insecure, and the death of Buddensieg must have intensified his isolation. As his sister writes, 'He opened his heart and released the flood of ideas from his mind only when his soul was possessed with love and he was convinced of the teacher's good will.'[34] Generally, incomprehension, rigidity, authoritarianism and the monastic duskiness of the building must have inhibited both humour and warmth. Dr Heinse would occasionally invite pupils to dinner, but the supply of good will was not adequate to Nietzsche's needs. Not that any other Prussian school would have been better – none had higher academic standards, and at Pforta boys who could write verse were encouraged. In June 1862, at the speech day, Nietzsche had to read out his poem 'Ermanarichs Tod', which won the mark IIa.

After Hölderlin, the poet he most loved was Byron. In December he wrote an essay on him and lectured to Germania about his dramatic verse, concentrating on *The Two Foscari*. 'The lecturer should have prepared a better script', wrote Gustav Krug in the minutes. Nietzsche's enthusiasm for Byron was in direct line with his earlier passion for Schiller and his play *Die Räuber* (*The Robbers*). 'The characters seem to me almost superhuman (*übermenschlich*),' he had written. 'It is like watching the Titans battling against religion and virtue.'[35] Applying the word *Übermensch* to Byron's Manfred was only one step from calling Schiller's characters *übermenschlich*.

That Shakespeare began to influence Nietzsche at the same time was the accidental result of being given his complete works as a Christmas present. Aunt Rosalie thought Shakespeare was to blame for making him feel so restless and discontented with everything around him. Elisabeth, who concluded that Byron and Shakespeare were equally important as catalysts, points out that later, when he wrote to tell her that every form of strength was in itself refreshing and pleasant to watch, he advised her to read Shakespeare: 'He presents you with so many strong men – rough, hard, powerful, iron-willed. It is in men like these that our age is so poor.'

In January 1862 Nietzsche was working on *Il Principe* in his Italian classes, so when he wrote an essay on 'Napoleon III as President', it had a Shakespearian and Machiavellian perspective. The nephew of Bonaparte had become President in December 1848, after setting himself up as both a champion of his uncle's ideas and a defender of orderly stability. A ruthless opportunist, a mediocre man with a huge, waxed moustache, erratically capable, like Hitler, of brilliant statesmanship, he swore an oath of fidelity to the Second Republic, which he overturned in 1851. After there had been twenty-five thousand arrests and ten thousand deportations, a plebiscite gave him presidential power for ten years, but by the end of 1852, he had successfully proclaimed himself emperor. Regarding Napoleon III as a genius, Nietzsche found it hard to judge his behaviour in moral terms. 'In human affairs nothing can be judged except from the viewpoint of the spirit involved in it.' His assumptions at this stage were pious and Hegelian; while writing about power politics he was often tempted to sidestep into pious generalizations, as he did in a January letter to Aunt Rosalie. These days, he said, it was not enough to pray for the individual: 'Since the welfare of the state affects the welfare of the private person, we must pray for king and country, for peace between the nations.'[36]

Nietzsche did not reject Christianity suddenly, but by the spring of 1862 doubts had begun to set in. He tried to explore them in an essay on 'Fate and History', which he delivered in April as a lecture to the audience of two that comprised the synod of Germania. The prose style now to be sharpened on his Darwinist doubts was still fairly blunt:

The power of habit, the drive towards the higher, the rejection of everything in existence, the dissolution of all social forms, the doubt that humanity may have been led astray for two thousand years by a phantasm, the feeling of one's own foolhardy presumption – all these fight an indecisive battle until finally the pain of the experience, the sadness of the event drives our heart back into the old beliefs of childhood. . . . But we scarcely even know whether humanity itself is only a step, a period in the universal, in evolution – whether it is not an arbitrary manifestation of God. Is humanity perhaps only the development of the stone through the medium of plants and animals? . . . Is humanity only a means, or an end?

Temperament, he argues, is subject to a variety of external pressures, and free will is arbitrary, so fate is a necessity, unless we want to believe that the history of the world has been night-marishly haphazard, that we ourselves are the playthings of our fantasies. If events were determined only by earlier events, men would not be morally answerable for their mistakes. 'Perhaps free will is nothing but the extreme power of fate.'

Not content to leave his first serious excursion into philosophy hanging on an ingenious paradox, he returned to the question of 'Free Will and Fate' in another essay for Germania. Nations that believe in fate sometimes distinguish themselves through strength of will, while Christian submissiveness towards God's will may be no more than a justification for cowardly inaction. For the individual, the principle of free will can mean independence, the separation of self from society, 'but fate puts men back into organic contact with the development of the whole, making it necessary for him – insofar as he wants to master it – to build up powerful opposition. Absolute freedom of the will and inde-pendence of fate would make a man into a god, while the fatalistic principle would make him into an automaton.'

The word 'fate' is used without much precision, but Nietzsche was already taking a comprehensive and dissatisfied view of the human situation. 'All previous philosophy often seemed to me like a Tower of Babel: the object of all the great exertions is to pene-trate into heaven or create heaven on earth.' But his rejection of fate did not lead him to an unequivocal rejection of Christianity. Its principles can permeate our thinking, he said, only when we have stopped trying to blame an external power for misdirecting our lives. We should take God's human incarnation to mean that we must not content ourselves with the prospect of eternity in heaven, but try to make earth more heavenly. In the infancy of the race, aspiration towards 'the other world' had caused confusion. It was only through doubt and conflict that humanity could mature sufficiently to improve this world.

Throughout this crucial period of doubting, he had felt de-pressed and often unwell. According to the school records, he had 'congestion in the head' from 7 to 11 January 1862, headaches from 4 to 13 February, and catarrh from 24 to 29 March. But it did not preclude his involvement in a school production during March. He played the part of Henry de Blançay, a lieutenant, in *Der Oberst von 18 Jahren* (*The Eighteen-year-old Colonel*), a play adapted from the French by L. Schneider. The action was set in 1756 in a fortress at Lille. But this seems to have been Nietzsche's only experience of school theatricals. There was little space in the Pforta curriculum for music, drama or art.

In February 1862 it had been decided that Elisabeth was to complete her education in Dresden, the capital of Saxony. 'I will not like Dresden,' her seventeen-year-old brother decided.

It is not sufficiently first-rate.... However, as a small residential capital and as an artistic centre, Dresden will be quite adequate for E's spiritual education, and in some ways I envy her.... I have plenty of confidence in Elisabeth – if only she would learn to write better. And when she tells a story, you cannot believe how splendid, wonderful and enchanting it would be if she could manage not to keep exclaiming 'oh' and 'Ach'.[37]

In the Easter holidays, he went alone to spend two weeks with her. She was staying with a family called von Mosch. He took her to the art gallery in the Zwinger, and they went for a boat ride on the Elbe. Writing to her from Pforta at the end of April he told her that he had often been dreaming about their time together. 'Above all,' he added, 'try to become really familiar with all Dresden's art treasures. ... You must go through the picture gallery at least once or twice a week, even if you look carefully only at two or three paintings, so that you can send me a detailed description – in writing of course.'[38]

To a seventeen-year-old Prussian familiar with Goethe, Byron must have been fascinating mainly because of the legend surrounding his death on the way to join the Greek rebels. 'Byron is not classical and not romantic,' said Goethe, 'but he is the present age itself. ... He was exactly my man because of his unsatisfied nature and his warlike attitude, which led to his fate at Missolonghi.'[39] In *Faust* Part Two, Euphorion, the child of Faust and Helen, is a Byronic figure who dies like Icarus after defying the warnings of his parents and – in a rebellious gesture that is meant somehow to serve the cause of freedom – hurling himself into space. Nietzsche's Euphorion is anti-romantic and much more modern. The fragment develops the satirical *épater les bourgeois* negativism of the abortive novel written in 1859, and it strikingly prefigures Lautréamont's *Les Chants de Maldoror* (1868):

Opposite me lives a nun, whom I visit from time to time to enjoy her propriety. I know her very well, from head to toe, better than I know myself. She was once a thin, skinny nun – I was the doctor and made sure she soon got fat. Her brother lives with her. They got married just in time. He was too fat and flourishing for me. I've made him lean – as a corpse. He will die shortly – which pleases me – I will dissect him. But first I will write the story of my life. It is not only interesting but instructive, for I am a master in the art of making people age quickly. Who is to read it? My double. There are still plenty of them in this vale of sorrows.

Here Euphorion leaned back slightly and groaned, for he had a consumptive disease in the marrow of his spine.

From Gorenzen, where he had written it, Nietzsche sent this to a recently acquired school-friend, Raimund Granier: 'The plan for my repulsive novel – oh God, you've forgotten it too! Never mind! When I'd written the first chapter I threw it overboard in disgust. I am sending you the monster-manuscript for use as . . . well, as you please. When I'd written it I burst out laughing diabolically – you won't have much appetite for what comes next.'

He had also been composing, he says, and writing poems. Of the two he encloses, one could hardly be more contrasted in tone and attitude to *Euphorion:*

> *Herr ich komme*
> *ich war verloren,*
> *taumeltrunken*
> *versunken*
> *zur Höll und Qual erkoren.*
> *Du standst von ferne:*
> *Dein Blick unsäglich*
> *beweglich*
> *traf mich so oft:*
> *Nun komme ich gerne.*

Lord I come
I was lost
lurching drunken
sunken
to hell and torment tossed.
Distantly, sadly,
your ineffable gaze
sent out its rays
which met me so often.
Now I come gladly.

It is as if Nietzsche, by an act of religious will, was trying to impose harmony on his own impulses. He had been reading Rousseau's *Emile* 'from whom you could pick up a certain amount of naturalness and culture, as well as learning that you must keep your promises'. He had also been busying himself, he said, 'with a refutation of materialism, while you seem to believe in it'.

This prolific summer holiday must have been a period of high tension. Back at school he was suffering from headaches again by the middle of August. After nine days in the sanatorium he was again told that he should go home to recuperate. His mother was away in Merseburg, and, trying not to alarm her, he wrote to say that he would be in Naumburg, leading 'a perfectly quiet life without music or any other excitement. The doctor has given me the necessary diet instructions. . . . So please do not worry, dear mamma. If I avoid all excitement, the headaches will disappear.' The note in the school medical records is: 'Nietzsche was given leave to go home to complete his cure. He is a sturdy, thickset creature with a conspicuously fixed gaze, myopic and often afflicted with recurrent headaches.' It was unfortunate that Dr Zimmermann was not well disposed, but after Nietzsche had been to consult Professor Schillbach of Jena, the doctor had been offended by a letter from him, suggesting that more attention should be paid to the boy's eyes. The situation was exacerbated when Nietzsche, not realizing that the doctor was within earshot, called him 'an old blatherer'.

In September Nietzsche was promoted to the lower first and he was again Primus, but the rebellious mood of his summer writing was soon spilling into his behaviour. As a first-former he had a week of duty as schoolhouse prefect: in military fashion he had to write a report on anything in the dormitories, classrooms or lockers that seemed in need of repair. After four years of rapid mental development against a ground bass of dutiful conformity to the rigid discipline, he felt impelled to a gesture against the humourlessness of the system, and he peppered his report with jokes: 'In classroom number X the lights are burning so dimly that pupils are tempted to have their own lamps lit. . . . The benches in the upper second, which were painted recently, become excessively attached to those who sit on them.' The teachers were not amused. 'My Severe Lords and Masters, astonished to find frivolity introduced into such a serious matter, summoned me to the Synod on Saturday evening and decreed a punishment of no less than three hours' detention and the forfeiture of a few walks.'[40] He was unable to contact his mother in time to save her from walking in vain to Attenburg. Relieved to have his non-appearance explained, she at first reproved him only for lack of tact, but later she remonstrated, suspicious that his new friends were making him cynical and irresponsible. This touched a raw nerve – if only he had friends capable of inspiring him! 'I have a pleasant and varied circle of friends, but there can be no question of influence. First I would have to meet someone I considered to be my superior.'[41] Nor did he involve himself in beer-drinking camaraderie. First-formers were allowed to spend more time in Attenburg, but he preferred chocolate and self-restraint to outings with his class-mates.

No longer intending to go into the Church, Nietzsche was con-sidering a musical career. Like his father, he enjoyed improvising at the piano, and von Gersdorff, who was often in the music room at Pforta with him between seven-thirty and eight, later wrote: 'I do not think Beethoven could have improvised more impressively than Nietzsche, especially when the sky was thundery.' He was also becoming, gradually, more of a Wagnerian. An arrangement of *Tristan und Isolde* had been made for piano duet, and Elisabeth writes that during the autumn of 1862 Fritz and Gustav were playing this arrangement from morning till night, singing lustily to their own accompaniment.

In his school essays he was still trying to analyse what consti-tuted greatness of spirit. In October he wrote 'Towards a Charac-terization of Kriemhild in *Die Nibelungen*': 'The weak, who either laugh at the vital fervour of passionate characters or moralize, are easily intimidated when confronted with the demonic.' In an essay he wrote during January 1863 on Schiller's play *Wallensteins Lager* (*Wallenstein's Camp*), he tried to show how great men can 'become enmeshed with the quotidian and commonplace in a battle from which they seldom emerge as victors, for the weight of the commonplace nearly always submerges even the best of individual powers'. Every schoolboy identifies with the heroes he reads about, but Nietzsche's loneliness and his sense of superiority were combining to give a new slant to the celebration of the heroic. He saw that it is when they act on principle that great men are most isolated, and therefore least capable of noble actions.

He had made no formal break with religion, and could still adopt the old tone of piety, as he did when writing to his aunt Rosalie for her birthday: 'What rejoices your soul and adorns life is inner blessings rather than outward benefits, which are futile and transient.'[42] Not that he was being insincere. He still felt a strong pull towards the values he was brought up to honour, and when Dr Heinse, who had been offered a professorial position at Oldenburg, left Pforta, it was once again the chaplain whom Nietzsche selected as his tutor. And at the beginning of March 1863, when Pastor Kletschke chose him to act as his assistant, he was delighted. But the spirit of his *Euphorion* fragment was still alive in his verse. In one poem a drunkard throws a bottle of *schnaps* at the figure of the crucified Christ.[43]

Nietzsche himself did nothing comparable, and his one lapse into drunkenness was followed by intense embarrassment and contrition:

Dear Mother,

If I write to you today, it is about one of the most unpleasant and painful incidents I have ever been responsible for. In fact I have misbehaved very badly, and I do not know whether you can or will forgive me. I pick up my pen most reluctantly and with a heavy heart, especially when I think back to our pleasant life together during the Easter holidays, which was never spoiled by any discord. Last Sunday I got drunk, and I have no excuse, except that I did not know how much I could take, and I was rather excited in the afternoon.[44]

But his teachers did not view his inexperience in drinking as an extenuation. Called in front of the synod again, he was degraded in rank to third, and he forfeited an hour of his Sunday walk. He felt wretched at letting down Kletschke, who had shown such confidence in him. 'Once again I had acquired too much self-assurance, and now, in the most frightening way, I have lost it.'[45]

In this letter he complained of hoarseness and pains in the chest, asking for his muffler to be sent. Exacerbated by guilt and depression, his condition deteriorated. According to school medical records, he had catarrh from 24 April to 5 May and a mastoid condition from 7 to 20 May. He was miserable to be in the sanatorium again. On Sunday 26 April a pair of leeches was applied to his neck. 'They sucked well,' he wrote the day after. 'It is also a little better. I must diet carefully and keep warm and not talk much.'[46] On 2 May the hoarseness was no better, and the sunny weather made confinement in the sanatorium almost unendurable. Though trying to work, he was accomplishing little, 'because this or that book, which I need, is always missing'. Nine days later he was still there. 'You have no idea how completely cut off one feels, living in the sanatorium. How seldom people come over, and scarcely at all in good weather. And there's nothing to write with. Till Thursday I was lying in bed with one ear suppurating, and it's suppurating still.'[47] On the 16th he had an attack of coughing that lasted for two hours, with his nose blocked and his eyes streaming. He had become increasingly distressed at getting no better and at missing so much work, but his fundamental anxiety, all this time, was about the future. 'The decision about which subject to study', he wrote on 2 May, 'will not come of its own accord.' In choosing, he said, he must not let himself be distracted by momentary predilections or feelings of obligation towards family tradition. 'Now I am in the particularly unfortunate position of being interested in a number of the most varied subjects. . . . It is clear that I shall have to cast some of them aside. . . . But which will be the unlucky ones that get thrown overboard? Perhaps my very favourite children!'

Discharged from the sanatorium on 20 May he began to work hard, but little more than a month was left before the holidays. He asked his mother to prepare the room 'so that it doesn't smell so, and is quite fresh',[48] and he told her what his daily routine would be. He would get up between four and five to start working, drink coffee with her at six, work till nine, play duets with Gustav either at their house or the Krugs', go swimming, come home for lunch, 'and in the afternoons I will be entirely at your disposal, so long as you don't want to drag me into being sociable every day.'[49]

His first infatuation occurred in September 1863, when Anna Redtel, the sister of a school-friend, came to visit her grandparents in Kosen. She could play the piano, and Nietzsche soon found himself sitting down to duets with her. Either forgetting that his possessive seventeen-year-old sister was likely to be upset, or perhaps wanting to provoke her, he wrote asking her to forward four scores from Naumburg, including Schumann's *Fantasien* and *Kinderszenen*. He had promised them to Anna. Elisabeth did not send them, and Anna had to be content with the poems and the rhapsody he dedicated to her. As for Elisabeth, it is likely that fixation on her brother was one of the reasons she turned down several early proposals, not finally marrying until 1885. Later, after reading in Schopenhauer that human life moved in a causal chain, she asked her brother not to think badly of her if the chain ended with her as a spinster.

Writing to his mother and sister at the beginning of December, Fritz was looking forward glumly to what seemed likely to be their last Christmas together for a long time. 'Next time I shall be alone in a rather distant university city or fighting a winter campaign for Schleswig-Holstein.'[50]

In September 1862 Bismarck had become Prussian Premier and Minister for Foreign Affairs. The new king, Wilhelm I, had appointed him at the suggestion of Roon, the Minister of War. The one reactionary in a Liberal cabinet, Bismarck provoked a constitutional crisis with his plans for improving the army and reducing its dependence on conscripted reservists. The *Landtag* would have been prepared to spend more money on the army, but not on Roon's reorganization of it. Wilhelm, who had been brought up as a soldier, was ready to abdicate over the issue. Bismarck taught him that increased taxes could be collected and the army strengthened without parliamentary support. Convinced that Germany could be united under Prussian leadership only after Austria had been defeated, Bismarck was confident of Wilhelm's support in his struggle against the Liberals.

In November 1863, formulating a new constitution which incorporated the duchy of Schleswig into the state, Denmark violated a Protocol signed ten years before. Bismarck was now in favour of seizing both Schleswig and Holstein. War seemed inevitable, and for the nineteen-year-old Nietzsche, the prospect was that school would be followed by compulsory military service.

In December, Saxon and Hanoverian troops entered Holstein. On 16 January 1864 Prussia and Austria delivered an ultimatum to Denmark, demanding the repeal of the new constitution, and on 1 February Austro-Prussian troops entered Schleswig. Nietzsche was given a medical examination, and in March he heard that he would be called up not later than 1 October 1867. The army doctors had found him quite fit, apart from his myopia.

'My eyes are obviously becoming worse. Working by lamplight is a great effort and a great strain.'[51] He was looking forward to summer daylight and to university life, resolving to be more careful with his eyesight than he could be at Pforta. He had also been suffering from catarrh again, and had been expecting to succumb to the epidemic of mumps that had filled the sanatorium. He escaped, but had to put up with a long bout of hoarseness.

In 'Über Stimmungen' ('On Moods'), which he wrote at Naumburg during the Easter holidays, he dramatizes his own actions as a writer and his own daily routine:

It can be visualized that on the evening of the first day of Easter I am sitting at home, wrapped in a dressing-gown; outside it is drizzling; no one else is in the room. Pen in hand, I stare for a long time at the white paper in front of me, troubled by the confused crowd of themes, experiences and thoughts all demanding expression in writing.

Some, he said, were young and importunate, others mature and familiar. 'Our state of mind is determined by the conflict between the old and the young worlds, and mood is what we call the current state of the battle.'

He had been playing Liszt's 'Consolations', and, having had a painful experience, he noticed how sounds and feelings became mixed:

What the soul cannot reflect makes no impact on it; but since the willpower can control whether the soul reflects something or not, the soul meets only what it wants to meet. . . . But one of the soul's strongest impulses is greed for the new, an inclination towards the unfamiliar, and this explains why we so often let ourselves be put into bad moods. . . . The soul is made from the same material as experiences, or from something similar, which is why an experience which finds no counterpart in the soul presses heavily on it, gradually producing such imbalance that it compresses and constricts the soul's other contents.

So moods are formed either from inner conflicts or outer pressures on the inner world: a civil war between two armies or oppression of the people by one class, a small minority.

When I eavesdrop quietly on my own thoughts and feelings, it is often as if I had heard the noisy battle of wild parties. . . .

Conflict is the soul's staple diet, and it knows how to extract enough sweetness and nourishment from it. By annihilating, it gives birth to new things. By fighting fiercely it gently makes its opponent into an intimate ally. Most wonderful of all, it disregards the external: names, persons, places, fine words, flourishes, all these are of secondary importance. What counts is what is inside the shell.

He may have been reading Kant's essay on the philosophy of history, which suggests that man wants harmony while nature arranges conflict.[52] But the mixture of the metaphysical with the psychological is as characteristic of Nietzsche's early work as the identification of microcosm with macrocosm. Knowing no consciousness but his own, and knowing nothing of the outside world except what was in his consciousness, he had unlimited curiosity about the relationship between the two, and a strong compulsion to trap as much as he could of consciousness into images on paper. He had a formidable talent for using his ability to eavesdrop on his mood changes as a means of drawing inferences about the nature of reality. But he had no vocabulary to articulate his feelings, and no categories in which to analyse them. Writing in terms of willpower he could not yet arrive at any precision.

After returning to Pforta at the end of the 1864 Easter holidays, he would have to select a university. He did not want to go to Halle, where his father had studied theology, but otherwise he was undecided. He soon became involved in writing a dissertation in Latin on the sixth-century Greek poet Theognis of Megara. Less than 1,400 lines of his work survive, and their authenticity is disputed. It was probably a young teacher, Dr Volkmann, who proposed the subject, and the nineteen-year-old Nietzsche was quick to see its potential: 'I have involved myself in a great deal of surmise and guesswork, but I plan to complete the work with proper philological thoroughness, and as scientifically as I can. I have already worked out a new approach to this man, and on most points my judgements are at variance with the usual ones.'[53] As he pointed out in the essay, Theognis was a passionate partisan of the aristocracy against the populace, but, far from identifying with his attitudes, Nietzsche characterized him by comparison with the *Junkers*, the landowning class that dominated the Prussian civil service and the commissioned ranks in the army. Bismarck was only half *Junker* by birth, but he called himself a *Junker*, dressed accordingly, and spoke with affected *Junker* brutality. But for his support against Liberalism and industrialism, Junkerdom would not have been such a powerful force in nineteenth-century German history. The enlarged army he needed was unacceptable to the Liberals, who were nervous that it might be used as an instrument of internal repression.

Wilhelm Pinder was now at the University of Heidelberg, and Nietzsche settled on Bonn. The two universities were often bracketed together,

but they are far enough apart to go on separating us as we are separated now. We shall see each other, heaven willing, once or twice a year. Otherwise there will be a space between us, often bridged by thoughts but seldom by paper or postage. Otherwise, believe me, whatever you want from me is yours, even if it is a million, paid, of course, Falstaffian fashion, in love.[54]

At five o'clock in the afternoon of Friday 8 July 1864 he finished the dissertation on Theognis and picked up what he had written to feel the weight of it in his hand. It consisted of forty-two closely written pages, which would spread to at least sixty when he made the fair copy. 'Am I satisfied with it?' he asked in the letter he immediately began to Paul Deussen. 'No, no. But I could scarcely have said anything better, even if I had made still more effort. Some passages are boring, others stylistically awkward.'[55] Then he indulged in a description of his daily routine. An early start to the day. A cup of coffee. Wearing his dressing-gown, he would then go to his room, where the large table was covered with books, mostly open. Work till about one. Lunch with mother and sister, followed by a glass of hot water, a session at the piano, and another cup of coffee. Work till about six, when tea and supper would be brought to his room.

I drink and eat and write. It gets dark. I pull myself together, look at the time: half past eight. I dress quickly, leave the house, and in the gathering darkness of the night, hurry into the Saale, which is cool, cold, therefore refreshing. The river makes its noises; everything else is silent. The mist and I rest on the water. The wind blows as I go home.[56]

Having completed his forty-two pages in Latin, he felt entitled to some self-dramatization. It is the literary chatter of a man with no one to listen to him.

He was keeping himself busy, though: in the same letter he complained of having no time to write down the melodies that came into his head. But he was capable of thinking out music in some detail without writing down a note. In the list he made of the work done in 1863, he noted that he had worked out – but forgotten – the Allegro of a sonata for piano duet. He also worked out the Adagio, and did not forget it.

It was self-sacrificial for Nietzsche to abandon all idea of an artistic career, opting for philology. He wanted, he wrote, 'a science that could be pursued with cool reflectiveness, logical coldness, equable effort, and would not yield results that seize hold of the heart.' The headaches must have been making him wary of over-stimulation. His Lutheran upbringing and his Prussian education had conditioned him to value self-discipline, while one advantage of philology was that it would be easier for him to regulate his own activities than it would have been had he become an artist. In the autobiographical sketch he was required to submit before leaving the school, he wrote: 'I propose one categorical law for my future acquisition of knowledge: to resist my tendency to wide-ranging sciolism, and to foster my interest in pursuing a subject to its deepest, remotest roots.' At Pforta languages were regarded as sciences, and, as a philologist, Nietzsche would be able to submit himself to scientific discipline. He was also casting himself in the same role as the father-figures he admired, Steinhardt, Corssen and other teachers he regarded as philologists. At the same time he would be giving himself opportunities to immerse himself in the classics. His first book, *Die Geburt der Tragödie aus dem*

Geist der Musik (*The Birth of Tragedy from the Spirit of Music*), had roots in the work he did during his last year at Pforta. His commentary on the first chorus in Sophocles' *Oedipus Tyrannus* contrasts German drama, which developed out of the epic, with Greek drama, 'which had its origins in the lyric, combined with musical elements'. The great advantage of the tragedians was that they were not only poets but also composers.

Formidable though it was, the combination of school discipline and self-discipline was patchy in its effects. He had not developed much interest in mathematics, and in the final certificate he received from the school, he was accused of being 'deficient in application and regular industry'. The mathematics teacher, Buchbinder, had wanted him to be refused a leaving certificate, but had to give in when Corssen called Nietzsche the best pupil he could remember at Pforta. He was awarded the highest grading in religion, German language, and Latin. In Greek he was considered to be 'good', and in French, history and geography, and natural sciences, 'satisfactory'. His worst subjects were Hebrew, mathematics and drawing. So in spite of all the pressure on him, the pattern had changed very little since the examination he had taken in 1859.

On 7 September 1864, together with eight other boys who were leaving, Nietzsche had to make a speech, thanking God, the king, the school and the masters. A garlanded carriage with postilions in bright costumes was waiting to take them away from the school for the last time. He was nearly twenty, but he could not leave without regret. His ambivalence is expressed in the poem 'Dem unbekannten Gott' ('To the Unknown God'):

> Once again, before I depart,
> Before I look at the road so lonely,
> I raise my hands to you, the only
> Refuge for my high-flying heart.
> Deep inside me is your altar,
> So however much I falter,
> And whatever may befall me,
> Your voice will always call me.

3 University Student

Believing that one of the soul's strongest impulses is greed for the new, Nietzsche was aware of how tightly the discipline of Pforta had, for six years, shackled him to the familiar. The sense of liberation must have been exhilarating but frightening: he had good reasons – quite apart from his headaches – for feeling afraid of the future, and it may have seemed to him that the greatest danger was isolation. During his year of studying theology at Bonn he would make a vigorous effort to escape into the comforts of gregariousness. He was still self-ignorant enough to believe that he could transform himself. According to his theory of moods, it is willpower that determines which external elements the soul goes out to meet. Applying his formidable willpower to the task of making himself more extrovert, he behaved as if there was nothing he regretted more than not having gone out with his classmates at Pforta to drink beer in Attenburg.

According to Elisabeth, he considered himself 'something of a stranger to the practical world', and resolved, accordingly, 'to keep his eyes open and note down everything of importance, even in matters of eating and drinking' while he was on holiday with Paul Deussen, who was also going to study theology at Bonn.[1] In September 1864, after Deussen had been the Nietzsches' guest for a few weeks at Naumburg, the two boys left together for the Rhineland. Their first stop was at Elberfeld. 'The town is extremely commercial, the houses mostly slate-clad. Among the women who are to be seen, I noticed a strong predilection for letting the head hang piously.'[2] Here, as elsewhere, he was gratified by the reactions he got to his improvisations at the piano. 'Wherever I am I have to play, and there are shouts of "Bravo!" It is quite ridiculous.'[3] There was a great deal to enjoy, including the food and drink. 'They eat well here and drink still better, but the food is different from ours. Swiss cheese and *pumpernickel* three times a day.'[4]

They had dinner one evening at the house of Ernst Schnabel, a distant cousin of Deussen's, and the three boys made an excursion, which Deussen has described, to Königswinter:

Intoxicated with wine and camaraderie, we allowed ourselves, in spite of having so little money, to be talked into hiring horses to ride up the Drachenfels. It is the only time I have ever seen Nietzsche on horseback. He was in a mood to interest himself less in the beauty of the scenery than in the ears of his horse. He kept on trying to measure them, and to make up his mind about whether he was riding a donkey or a horse. In the evening we acted still more insanely. The three of us were wandering through the streets of the little town making overtures to the girls we assumed to be behind the windows. Nietzsche whistled and cooed 'Pretty darling, pretty darling'. Schnabel was talking all kinds of nonsense, making out that he was a poor Rhenish boy, begging for a night's shelter.[5]

In the end a man came out from one of the houses and 'drove us away with curses and threats'.[6]

Nietzsche went on to stay with Deussen and his parents at Oberdreis, near Koblenz. The pastor's wife impressed him as 'a woman of such culture, such delicacy of feeling and expression, and such capacity for hard work as to be almost unique'.[7] She overshadowed her husband, 'a good man but not always consistent', while their daughter made a more favourable impression on their young guest. 'Marie Deussen is, despite her youth, a quite splendid, very spiritual girl, who really, dear Lisbeth, occasionally reminds me of you, so I cannot withhold my especial goodwill.'[8] He expressed it by dedicating some music to her, as he had to Anna Redtel.

Since Frau Deussen's birthday coincided with Nietzsche's, his twentieth, there was a joint celebration on 15 October. Afterwards, 'we crossed over the hills of the Westerwald into the valley of the Rhine to Neuwied, where a steamer took us to Bonn in a few hours.'[9]

The room Nietzsche found for himself was opposite a church tower, and he would often wish that he could move into the tower, so as to be further away from the noises of the street. Deussen arranged to have his lunch in Nietzsche's lodgings every day. They had been intending to find lodgings they could share, but, surprisingly, the double rooms cost at least twice as much as the

singles, so there was no economy in it, and it was soon obvious that
university life would be more expensive than they had calculated.
Deussen had budgeted for outgoings of twenty *talers* a month,
Nietzsche for twenty-five, but he would have to spend five on rent,
ten on meals, three on hiring a piano, about two on laundry, and
twenty silver *groschen* on the boy who cleaned the boots.[10] He
would also have to buy books, exercise-books, an oil-lamp, oil
and so on.

In spite of his commitment to philology, he had found himself
incapable of breaking completely with the family's past, and he
had registered as a theology student, intending to compromise by
concentrating on 'the philological side of Gospel criticism and the
investigation of the New Testament's sources'. He may have had
some idea of resolving his religious doubts by confronting the
theological problems, but his motives were also confused not only
by his continuing veneration of his father, whose photograph was
placed over the piano, underneath a painting of the deposition from
the cross, but also by procrastination over telling his mother that
he was not going to become a clergyman. In any case he would not
be restricted to attending theology lectures, and, according to
Deussen, he and Nietzsche had both been attracted to Bonn by the
presence of two philologists, Albrecht Ritschl and Otto Jahn.
Jahn was a pioneer in the study of Greek art; Ritschl was known for
his work on Plautus and early Latin.

Despite the letter of introduction they had from the teacher of
religion at Pforta, both lecturers were unwelcoming when they
presented themselves. Jahn merely said: 'If I can be useful to you
in any way you have only to come to me.' They went on to
Ritschl's house, where students were coming and going. He read
the letter hurriedly. 'Oh, my old friend Niese. So what is he doing?
Is he well? So your name is Deussen. Right, come to see me again
soon.' Embarrassed, Nietzsche had to point out that he too was
mentioned in the letter. 'Oh yes, there are two names – Deussen
and Nietzsche. Delighted, delighted. Right, gentlemen, come to
see me again soon.'

The only cordial reception they received was from Schaarschmidt, a friendlier man, who had been at Pforta himself.
Gradually they both settled into a routine of attending his lectures
on the history of philosophy and on Plato, as well as Jahn's on the

Symposium, and Ritschl's. Nietzsche also went to Professor Sybel's lectures on history, and some lectures on the history of art by Professor Springer.

But after six years of working intensively and single-mindedly, giving himself very little time for relaxation, Nietzsche had strong reasons, partly conscious, partly unconscious, for not wanting to continue the same pattern of living. The commitment to gregariousness was conscious. Regretting the disdain he had shown towards the beer-drinking camaraderie of the first-formers at Pforta, and remembering his evening in Jena as his uncle's guest at a meeting of Teutonia, he joined Franconia, another of the student fraternities. A characteristically German phenomenon, these *Burschenschaften* had been started in the universities during 1815 as part of a movement aiming at a liberal and united Germany. Duelling was *de rigueur*. Members sang patriotic songs and paraded through the streets in uniform, marching behind a military band. During the 1930s the Hitler Youth would be built up over the tradition of the *Burschenschaften*, taking advantage of the fact that, as in the nineteenth century, boys would join not for political or ideological but for social reasons. The main attractions were the feeling of solidarity with other boys of the same age, and the fun they had together at organized events. Of the twenty-nine students in Franconia, twenty-seven had been at Pforta. The advantages of belonging to a group were unfamiliar to Nietzsche, and he found a new pleasure in using the first person plural: 'We are nearly all philologists, as well as being lovers of music.'[11]

Arguing in his letters home that the fraternity did not distract him too much from his work, he was also arguing with himself: 'It is really helpful that for the most part it is philologists who are coming together.'[12] He kept emphasizing the serious 'tone' of the meetings: 'In general a very interesting tone prevails in Franconia.'[13] 'A Parliamentary tone is vigorously sustained. . . . I wish you could hear the lively debates at our assemblies.'[14] Obliged to participate in evenings of heavy drinking, he made valiant efforts to convince himself he was enjoying them, though he much preferred coffee and cakes to beer and wine. Writing to Elisabeth about a hangover, he took his usual pleasure in dramatizing the moment of writing, but found it unusually hard to present himself in a favourable light:

Having just wrenched myself out of bed, I am writing this morning in direct refutation of the opinion that I had a hangover. [The German word for it, 'Kater', also means tom-cat.] You will not know this hairy-tailed animal. Yesterday evening we had a great assembly, ceremonially singing 'Father of the People' and endlessly drinking punch. . . . Yesterday's *Gemütlichkeit* was splendid, edifying. You know, at assemblies like this there is a general buoyancy of the soul. It is not just beery *Gemütlichkeit*.[15]

But the commitment to theology was making him less interested in working, and he got into the habit of rising at eight instead of six.

Duelling scars were almost like membership badges, and Nietzsche did not baulk at the necessity of obtaining one. Walking one day in the marketplace, he struck up an acquaintance with a pleasant-seeming boy from another fraternity. As Nietzsche told Deussen, 'We had a very animated conversation about all kinds of things, artistic and literary, and when we were saying goodbye, I asked him in the politest way to duel with me. He agreed, and the next thing is we're going to have a go at each other.'[16] Deussen felt quite worried for his myopic, corpulent friend, but there was nothing he could do to stop the duel.

They locked swords, and the glinting blades danced around their unprotected heads. It scarcely lasted three minutes, and Nietzsche's opponent managed to cut in low *carte* at the bridge of his nose, hitting the exact spot where his spectacles, pressing down too heavily, had left a red mark. Blood trickled to the ground, and the experts agreed that past events had been satisfactorily expiated. I packed my well-bandaged friend into a carriage, took him home to bed, assiduously comforted him, forbade visits and alcohol. Within two or three days our hero had fully recovered, except for a small slanting scar across the bridge of his nose, which remained there throughout his life and did not look at all bad on him.[17]

Later, looking back on his year in Bonn, Nietzsche described himself as having been in a state of dreamlike indifference towards the future.[18] He went on studying theology until Easter 1865, though he was thinking more critically about the scriptures. David Strauss's analysis of the gospels had caused a fury of controversy in 1835–6 when it was published in two volumes under the title *Das Leben Jesu kritisch bearbeitet*. (George Eliot's translation of the fourth German edition was published as *The Life of Jesus Critically*

Examined.) In 1864 Strauss brought out a new version, *Das Leben Jesu für das Deutsche Volk bearbeitet*, and when Nietzsche bought a copy, Deussen, following his example, found Strauss's arguments irresistible. Nietzsche, who was eventually to be so thoroughgoing in his rejection of Christianity, was initially more cautious: 'There is a serious consequence – if you give up Christ, you will have to give up God too.'[19]

The twenty-first Christmas of his life was the first he would have to spend away from home. Under the influence of Schumann he composed eight songs as a present for Elisabeth, and he bound the manuscript for her in lilac-coloured morocco with a silhouette of himself stuck to the front. He posted it to her with careful instructions about how to perform the songs. Two of them were to be sung 'as tenderly, as simply, as ingenuously as possible'; one 'seriously, mournfully, and with determination until the middle verse, which forms a contrast with what comes before and after'. One 'must be performed with drive, pertness and grace', another 'with unrestrained passion'. Later they would laugh at the way her 'delicate, fair, rosy and smiling appearance' (as she describes it) belied the seriousness, mournfulness and determination she tried to muster.

On Christmas Eve he lay down on the sofa in his room without lighting the lamps, picturing the scene at Naumburg as his mother, sister and aunt gave each other presents. After eating his evening meal he went to find his fellow Franconians in the clubhouse. 'Then we gave each other silly little presents. For example one man who has run up a lot of bills was given a savings box.'[20] In the morning a package of Christmas presents arrived from Naumburg, with a poem Elisabeth had written for him. He wanted to write some New Year verses for his mother, but found he was unable to: 'It may be that I now demand much more of a poem. It may be that I am slightly more sober and practical, which would not be a bad thing. It may be that the diabolical toothache which torments me is driving out any possibility of rousing enthusiasm.'[21] He liked New Year's Eve and birthdays, 'because they give us hours ... when the soul stands still. ... For a few hours we are elevated above time, and almost step outside our own growth.'[22] His fragment 'A New Year's Eve Dream' may have been based on an actual dream or, more likely, on a fantasy:

It is the last few hours before midnight. I have been rummaging among my manuscripts and letters, drinking punch and then playing the Requiem from Schumann's *Manfred*. Now I want to shut out every-thing alien and think only of myself. . . . The spirit flies swiftly through the towns it loves, lingering in Naumburg, then in Pforta and Plauen, returning finally to my room. My room? What do I see in my bed? Someone lying there – moaning faintly, a death-rattle in his throat – a dying man.

It is both the old self and the dying year. Around it are shades, some cursing it for failing to fulfil its promises, some blessing it for being so gentle. Suddenly everything brightens. The walls of the room vanish, the bed is now empty, but a voice is heard saying 'The fruit will fall when it is ripe, not before.'

In February 1865, while he was visiting Cologne to see the sights, Nietzsche told a street porter to take him to a restaurant. Instead the man led him to a brothel. As he afterwards told Deussen, 'I found myself suddenly surrounded by half a dozen apparitions in tinsel and gauze, looking at me expectantly. For a short space of time I was speechless. Then I made instinctively for the piano as being the only soulful thing present. I struck a few chords, which freed me from my paralysis, and I escaped.'[23] At Pforta he had told Deussen he was going to need at least three women, but his friend was left with the impression that Nietzsche remained a virgin throughout his life. Thomas Mann uses this brothel incident in *Doktor Faustus* (Chapter 16), making his hero go on thinking so much about a snub-nosed gipsy girl who has brushed his cheek with her arm that he returns. In an essay on Nietzsche, Mann has suggested that he, too, went back to the brothel.[24] In 1889, answering questions in the asylum, Nietzsche said that he had infected himself twice in 1866, but it is also possible that he misunderstood what he was being asked.

In any case his sexual drive must have been abnormally low, and since his madness probably had nothing to do with syphilis, he may never have been infected. When he was twenty-six he included sex in a list headed 'Delusions of the Individual'. We have the testimony of a fellow Franconian – later Professor Hersing – that Nietzsche was 'not a student who liked having fun. There was no sign of any need to sow wild oats.'[25]

He may have felt that while a duelling scar was proof of virility to the outside world, he also had to prove his manliness by losing his virginity or he may have baulked at this form of self-conquest. In any case he was determined to make himself into an extrovert, but his capacity for gregariousness was impaired by a tendency towards sadistic didacticism. He would goad his companions, as he goaded himself, compulsively demanding more than was compatible with comfort. He hated self-satisfaction: no one should be allowed to settle for anything less than the fullest realization of his potential. Writing home about his reputation among the students, he said he was regarded as 'something of a freak (*Kauz*)', though respected as an authority on music. 'I am by no means disliked, though I am considered to be something of a scoffer, and ironical. ... I can add that I do not consider myself a scoffer, that I am often unhappy and too moody and like being a thorn in the flesh (*Quälgeist*) not only to myself but to others.'[26] This was confirmed by Deussen, who was disappointed but relieved when his friend left at the end of the year. Both at Pforta and Bonn, he wrote, Nietzsche's personality had exerted an influence on him by putting him under severe pressure. He always showed 'a tendency to play the pedagogue, constantly correcting me, and sometimes really to torture me'.[27] Dissatisfied with himself for not working harder, Nietzsche was venting some of his frustration on his friends.

His nervous energy was finding no outlet either in composing or in writing verse. The reason he gave was that he wanted to concentrate on developing his critical faculty. The abstention from song-writing may have been connected with embarrassment over money. He had shown the last eight songs, written for Elisabeth, to the director of the musical faculty, Brambach, who suggested that he ought to take tuition in counterpoint. 'I lack the means,' he explained in his letter home.[28] He was getting into debt. 'It is unpleasant to have the Philistines banging on the door each morning when one has nothing to give them.'[29] It was clear by now that he could not afford to stay for more than a year at Bonn, where life, he said, was more expensive than at other universities, and he was thinking of enlisting for army service in Berlin.[30] He had been spending money on concerts, opera and theatre, but it would have been foolish to miss the opportunity of hearing such singers as Patti and Burde-Ney, and seeing such actresses as Marie Seebach and Friederike Grossmann. 'We

Franconians were naturally in love with her to a man. We shouted her songs across the beer-table and drank toasts to her.' Though he claimed to be spending less on food and drink than other students were, 'the fraternity is undeniably costing a lot of money. But I am daily growing more partial to it. It is now in the hands of men from Pforta, and our spirit is the prevailing one.'[31]

Generally, he said, he was trying to live in the same style as before coming to Bonn – 'that is to say without being extravagant, but without setting narrow limits or being parsimonious. It would have been wrong to give the impression of being a poor man.'[32] At the end of May he effectively forced his mother to take the decision about whether he should resign from Franconia. It would be 'madness', he said, to miss the assemblies and celebrations that were planned for the immediate future, but she must let him know exactly how much money she could send before the end of term.[33]

When he came home for the Easter holidays, Elisabeth noticed a big difference in him after the six months of separation. He was more self-assured and was no longer willing to attend church services. In spite of everything his mother said, he refused to take Easter Communion. She began to weep and the quarrel would have become fiercer but for aunt Rosalie's intervention. Tactfully she explained to her sister-in-law that every great theologian had to go through periods of doubt. At such times it was best to avoid discussion. This obviated much unpleasantness, but the nineteen-year-old Elisabeth was drawn painfully into a crisis of uncertainty. Since early childhood her faith in her brother's judgement had been almost religious, and their mother, alert to the danger, forbade them to discuss what they believed or to exchange letters on the subject. Tormented by doubt, Elisabeth decided she must have talks with the two uncles who were pastors. Neither of them could produce any arguments that made as much impression on her as the letter from her brother:

If we had believed from youth onwards that the soul's salvation depended on someone other than Jesus – on Mahomet, say – we would no doubt have felt equally blessed. Surely it is faith alone that imparts blessedness, not the objective behind the faith. . . . Genuine faith never fails. It fulfils whatever the believer expects from it, but it does not offer the slenderest support for a demonstration of objective truth.

Here the ways of men divide. Do you want to strive for peace of mind and happiness? Then believe. Do you want to be a devotee of truth? Then seek.[34]

The letter, of course, was written partly to himself, confirming his resolution to be a seeker.

By the end of April he had given up the idea of enlisting, but he still wanted to leave Bonn at the end of the academic year, though he was glad to have been there. 'For a philologist the essential thing is to learn method, and there is nowhere better for doing that.'[35] At Pforta he had already discovered that language, literature, psychology and politics were areas of study that should not be kept separate. He had been made to write critical commentaries on passages of Sophocles and Aeschylus, for instance, and in his study of Theognis he had combined psychological analysis of the man with political analysis of his background. At Bonn he learned a good deal about how to organize his material while improving his technique of self-expression. In his final term at the university he returned to his work on Theognis. 'With a pair of critical scissors, attached to a methodical cord, I daily snip a few bits of fraying tinsel from him.'[36]

Though he benefited little from the presence of Ritschl, he did come to appreciate how much the professor had to offer. The news that he was leaving for Leipzig University crystallized Nietzsche's decision to go there. At the beginning of May he had been hesitating about whether to opt for a foreign university or one in the south of Germany.[37] Though Steinhardt had been critical of the philological faculty at Leipzig, Nietzsche had been considering it before he heard of Ritschl's decision, which clinched the question: 'This makes Leipzig's philological faculty the most important in Germany.'[38] At Bonn, where he had been involved in an acrimonious feud with Jahn, Ritschl had also been burdened with a variety of administrative responsibilities; at Leipzig he would be free to concentrate on teaching. 'There will be a small colony emigrating from Bonn with him.'[39]

Nietzsche was planning to study music at Leipzig, as well as philology. He was still writing no verse, but he had started composing again. And he was pleased at the prospect of being reunited with Baron von Gersdorff, who was going to study literature there. The letters they now began to exchange helped to clarify Nietzsche's feelings about student fraternities. As his ambivalence surfaced, he recognized that it was partly an ambivalence towards the German people: the *Burschenschaften* represented the rising generation. Surely he could insulate himself from it without becoming totally isolated. All he needed was one or two friends, like von Gersdorff, who shared his views: they would give him courage to remain a nonconformist. He had become overtolerant not only towards drunkenness but towards intolerance:

> We must be careful not to let ourselves be influenced too much. Habit is monstrously powerful. We are losing a great deal if we do not keep our capacity for moral indignation over the bad things that happen daily in our circle. This is relevant . . . to the contempt and denigration of other people, other opinions.[40]

Like Nietzsche, von Gersdorff had been joining in all the activities of the fraternity, but now, confiding in each other, they opened the floodgates to the misgivings they had both inhibited. Nietzsche admitted 'that I often found the expressions of good fellowship in the clubhouse extremely distasteful, that I could hardly bear certain individuals, because of their beery materialism'.[41] It was like another loss of faith. A new tone of embittered scepticism emerges in his account of a joint assembly with two other fraternities: 'Hurrah! What beatitude! Hurrah! The things the fraternity has done! Hurrah! Are we not the future of Germany, the nursery of the German Parliament?'[42] By the end of August 1865 he was admitting that it had been a mistake to continue as a member of Franconia: he should have left at the beginning of the summer term. 'I went against my principle of not surrendering myself to people or things for longer than it takes to understand them. . . . In my view they have little political judgement. They depend on the leaders of opinion. I find their outward behaviour plebeian and repulsive.'[43]

Again, as at Pforta, letter-writing had become very important for him as a means of finding out his true feelings and sharing them with a circle of close friends. As a boy he had derived so much satisfaction from Germania that throughout the rest of his life he needed a substitute for it, and the closest approximation he could find was in the exchange of letters. Correspondence made him the member of an exclusive club which did not need to be formally constituted. Literary intimacy did not yet become a replaecment (as it did later) for personal contact, but it was more than a by-product of it. Correspondence helped to give both his relationships and his ideas the quality they had. While his critical acumen was combining with his shyness and his malaise to swing him away from the comforts of camaraderie, he needed the consolation of exchanging ideas with friends, of feeling that their critical standards were the same as his. This unreliable line of defence against isolation was the only one he had.

He became less patriotic. In June 1865, to celebrate the fiftieth anniversary of the incorporation of the Rhineland into Prussia, King Wilhelm made an appearance in Cologne with the general staff and 'sundry ministers', as Nietzsche put it.[44] According to the newspapers, the populace was jubilant; 'I have been in Cologne myself and can judge this jubilation. I was almost astonished that the crowds were so frigid, though I really cannot imagine how anyone could muster enthusiasm for the king and the minister.'[45]

Progressive students and German Liberals would mostly have shared this view. Bismarck's cavalier disregard for constitution-alism and his loyalty to the *Junkers* made the liberal Austrian régime seem more attractive, and in August 1863, when the Austrian emperor, Francis Joseph, had made a grand gesture towards the unification of Germany, inviting all the princes to a meeting in Frankfurt, Bismarck shrewdly stopped Wilhelm from attending. There was nothing the canny Premier wanted less than the destruction of *Junker* Prussia in a new pan-German state, and he knew that with only one of the two great German powers represented at the conference, no progress would be made. During the first half of 1865 war could easily have broken out over Schleswig-Holstein, and it could have drawn Nietzsche into the army. Bismarck had been pretending to want an alliance with Austria, while secretly doing all he could to ready his country for war. Austria had not been admitted to the *Zollverein*, the German customs union, and it was obvious that Austria and Prussia could not continue indefinitely as joint custodians of the duchies.

During his last weeks in Bonn, Nietzsche's health deteriorated again. In a June letter he had complained that since the Easter holidays his left arm had been rheumatic,[46] but generally he had felt much better than when he was at Pforta. At the end of July, though, and the beginning of August, he took once again to his bed. The rheumatic pains had spread from his arm to his neck, his jaws and his teeth, joining forces with the headaches, which renewed their attack. For much of the time, consequently, he felt apathetic about work, though there was much to be done. He had become secretary of the Gustavus Adolphus Society, a student union, and, having resumed his habit of rising at six, he was attending a daily philosophical seminar at seven. Though eagerly looking forward to the summer holiday, he warned his mother and Elisabeth that he was liable to be irritable and sarcastic.[47] Back in Naumburg, he reported that 'I am not being sociable. My nervous irritability has not yet been assuaged.'[48]

What peeved him most was that he had wasted his opportunities of settling down to serious work. After achieving so much at Pforta, he could not feel proud of what he had done at Bonn – except for a lecture to Franconia about Germany's political poets, a lecture to the Gustavus Adolphus Society about the ecclesiastical conditions of the Germans in North America, and the additions he had made to his study of Theognis. Hard though he had tried to convince himself that Franconia had at least taught him about himself and about the rising generation, he knew he had mismanaged his first year of university. Even when he went to spend a fortnight in Berlin at the invitation of his friend Hermann Mushacke, he was too depressed to behave properly towards students wearing *Burschenschaft* colours. He met some at a concert: 'And I was boorish enough, after the necessary greetings, to spend a whole evening sitting beside them without saying anything. When one of them thought it was his duty, nevertheless, to invite me to their clubhouse, I went there out of civility to my friend Mushacke, but remained just as silent and unapproachable as at the first meeting.'[49]

On 17 October 1865, together with Mushacke, Nietzsche arrived in Leipzig. He formed a favourable first impression of 'the high-gabled houses, the streets so full of life, the bustling activity',[50] but his elation evaporated as they began to view the lodgings advertised in the newspapers. Most were smelly, dirty and uncomfortable. But a second-hand bookseller who had rooms to let, Herr Rohn, led them into a narrow side-street called Blumengasse. He took them through a house, into a garden and then into another building, where he showed them a small room with an adjoining bedroom. Nietzsche agreed at once to rent the rooms, and Mushacke found rooms in the house next door. Unfortunately for Nietzsche, the bookseller had young children, 'who scream rather a lot'.[51]

The rain drips quietly onto the zinc-covered roof under my two windows. A lot of people live all round me, and I can see into their rooms. Thoroughly disagreeable faces! And in the gardens that spread out on both sides, everything is yellow, as if mummified, desolate. This is now my world.[52]

The next day, going to register at the university, he found himself in the midst of a celebration. It was the centenary of the day Goethe had registered. This Nietzsche took to be a good omen, though the rector, shaking all the newcomers by the hand, warned them against modelling their university career on Goethe's. Genius had wayward and devious ways of reaching its objectives, he said.

The row at Bonn about Ritschl's departure had been given such wide coverage in the newspapers that when he arrived at Leipzig to give his inaugural lecture the great hall was thronged, not only with students and lecturers but with curious citizens unconnected with the university. He made his entrance in immaculate evening dress, white tie, and felt slippers. Elated at seeing so many familiar faces, he wandered from group to group at the back of the hall, shaking hands and chatting. 'Hey', he called out suddenly. 'So Herr Nietzsche is here too!' And he waved. When the senior dignitaries of the university made their appearance, he mounted the platform. He delivered his Latin oration, which was about the value and use of philology, very animatedly.

At the age of fifteen, solemnly lecturing to the synod that consisted of his two friends, Wilhelm and Gustav, Nietzsche had already found himself playing the pedagogue, emulating teachers; now, a twenty-one-year-old student, he discovered that while listening to Ritschl and the other professors he was concentrating more on their method of teaching than on what they said. Confident that he would not end up with too little knowledge, he focused his energy on learning how to teach: 'My goal is to become a truly practical teacher, and above all to be able to stimulate the necessary thoughtfulness and self-examination in young people, so that the Why? the What? and the How? of their science can be kept constantly in the forefront of their minds.'[53]

One day, probably late in October 1865, Nietzsche was browsing among the books in his landlord's shop when he picked up a copy of Schopenhauer's *Die Welt als Wille und Vorstellung* (*The World as Will and Representation*), which had been published in 1819 but made little impact until the fifties, partly because it ran counter to Hegelian ideas, which were irresistibly in the ascendant.

I took it in my hand as something totally unfamiliar and turned the pages. I do not know which demon was whispering to me: 'Take this book home.' In any case, it happened, contrary to my principle of never buying a book too hastily. Back at the house I threw myself into the corner of the sofa with my new treasure, and began to let that dynamic, dismal genius work on my mind. Each line cried out with renunciation, negation, resignation. I was looking into a mirror that reflected the world, life and my own mind with hideous magnificence.[54]

The book starts arrestingly with the assertion that the world 'is my representation': the world as perceived is the creation of the perceiving mind. In his analysis of the self that forms the idea, Schopenhauer reinterprets Kant's division of the mind into the part that perceives and the part that thinks. Thinking is establishing relationships between ideas. The only knowledge we can have directly is knowledge of the self. We know our body as an object, extended in space and time, while we are directly familiar with our inner world of sensations and desires. 'Will' was the word Schopenhauer used for this inner world, and the single insight that, according to him, constitutes the whole of his philosophy is 'My body and my will are one.' For Kant there had been two worlds: one was the world of appearances or phenomena; the other was the real or noumenal world, the world of the *Ding an sich*, the thing in itself. For Schopenhauer the body is the phenomenal form of the will, the will the noumenal form of the body. Thought therefore came to seem more physical than was previously believed.

Hegel and Kant had both written from a Christian standpoint; Schopenhauer was unorthodox among German philosophers not only in recognizing that the universe was not constructed according to the rational architecture of a benevolent deity, but in providing an explanation of human behaviour that did not make all motivation stem from the calculating intellect. Anticipating Freud's account of the unconscious, he represented the will as a blind man carrying everything, including the lame man, intellect, on its back.

The schoolboy essay 'On Moods' had argued that conflict was the soul's staple nourishment; though Schopenhauer did not regard conflict as nourishing, his emphasis on it must have appealed to Nietzsche. Will is fundamentally appetite for life, which puts us in conflict with people whose drives run counter to ours. The suffering caused by this conflict is not only the norm but the purpose of human existence. Happiness is only a diminution of suffering, so it is negative, while pain is positive. I am aware of discomfort where the shoe pinches, not of the comfort that the rest of my foot is enjoying. The only escape from suffering is in the use of the intellect, first to understand the will and then to suspend it. Schopenhauer's pessimistic temperament had responded strongly to the Buddhist idea of using contemplation as a means of negation. After studying Plato and Kant, he had discovered the *Upanishads* in a Latin translation of the Persian version. Unable to enjoy his life, he was predisposed to believe that the will was evil, and that contemplation or philosophizing was a means of countering it.

The immediate effect of Schopenhauer on Nietzsche was to make him so self-contemptuous that he wanted to impose penances on himself. For two successive weeks, applying his formidable willpower, he allowed himself no more than four hours of sleep each night. The impact is also visible in his third letter home from Leipzig:

Do you really take it so lightly, this existence in which so much is contradictory and nothing is clear except that it is not clear? It seems to me that you always evade the point by joking. . . . There are two ways, my dears: either we make efforts to live as narrowly as possible, accustoming ourselves to that, screwing down the flame of spirit as low as it will go and seeking riches to live with the pleasures of the world. Alternatively, we know that life consists of suffering, that the harder we try to enjoy it, the more enslaved we are by it, and so we discard the goods of life and practise abstinence, being mean towards ourselves and compassionate towards everyone else, since we pity our comrades in misery.[55]

Nonplussed by the letter, his mother replied that she did 'not like that kind of display or that kind of opinion so much as a proper letter, full of news'. It only made her worry about him. He should entrust his heart only to God, not to the worldly wisdom he found in books. It was his task in life to support his mother, and later his sister. That was what he should be thinking about.

Schopenhauer's influence on Nietzsche was to be enormous, but it did not prevent him from responding with cheerful obedience (and delicate irony) to his mother's injunctions. His next letter home was quite different. Announcing the intention of 'entertaining' her with a 'ragout' of his experiences, he described his daily routine. He rose at six-thirty, worked till eleven, went into college, ate lunch in a restaurant, and went home before spending another two hours in college between three and five, working afterwards until bedtime. 'My stove heats well. The children next door make a frightful noise. I have double glazing. How do you get rid of bugs? (Pious ejaculation!) The weather is bad, rainy, the streets dirty. So I never go out without galoshes.'[56]

It had been Nietzsche's intention to make up for the time he had wasted at Bonn by settling down to an intensive routine of work. If he failed, it was less because of the noisy children than because Schopenhauer's philosophy suddenly made philological niceties seem trivial. Apart from the reading and thinking that ensued on his visit to Rohn's second-hand bookshop, the most decisive event of the term occurred when Ritschl invited several of his students to dinner at his house. When the ladies had left the table, he suggested that a student philological club ought to be founded. He knew from experience how useful and influential clubs could be. With his memories of Germania, Nietzsche could hardly fail to respond enthusiastically, and so did three other students, including Wilhelm Roscher, whose father was Professor of Economics. The four of them invited potential members to a meeting in the *Deutsche Bierstube*, and this led to a second meeting a week later.

Leipzig was so close to Naumburg that it was easy, this time, for Nietzsche to spend Christmas at home, where he found

Elisabeth in a gloomy state, throwing out uncharacteristic remarks about suffering and the contradictoriness of existence. Under the influence of his Schopenhauerian letter, she was doing her best not to take life too lightly, but it was easy for him to restore her high spirits as they began to share jokes.

The philological club, which consisted of ten members, held the first of its regular weekly meetings on Thursday 11 January 1866 in a pleasant, vaulted room in a restaurant in Nikolaistrasse. Proceedings were conducted formally but no president was appointed. At the beginning of each meeting a chairman was elected for the evening. At the second meeting Nietzsche gave his first talk. Though he had chosen a subject he knew well – the original edition of Theognis' poems – he was nervous at first, but gained confidence while speaking. Encouraged by the reactions of his friends, he showed his manuscript to Ritschl, who sent for him a few days later. 'For what purpose did you do this work?' As the basis of a lecture, Nietzsche answered, so it had already fulfilled its purpose.

Ritschl then began to ask Nietzsche questions he had never previously put. How old was he? How long had he been a university student? Finally the professor pronounced it to be the most rigorously methodical and the most securely structured piece of work he had ever read by such a junior student. 'This was the moment of my birth as a philologist. I was pricked on by inklings of the acclaim I could win in this *métier*.'[57] And this was the moment that made it possible for Nietzsche to start working as hard as he had at Pforta, or even harder, with encouragement from an excellent teacher whose interest grew into friendship. About twice a week Nietzsche went to see him at lunchtime; he was usually to be found in his armchair with a glass of red wine and newspapers from Bonn and Cologne, to which he was still addicted. Like Goethe he preferred to be uncomfortable while he was working. He sat on a backless wooden seat he had upholstered by cutting the embroidery off a cushion. He was undiplomatically critical about the university and about his colleagues, while his wife was undiplomatically critical of his eccentricities. Until recently he had been in the habit of concealing banknotes in books so that he would be pleasantly surprised when he found them.

Impecunious students to whom he lent the books would assume that he had found a tactful way of helping them.

At the end of January, when King Wilhelm came to Leipzig, Nietzsche's reaction to him was quite different from what it had been in June. Together with a minister and a general, the king spent several days at the university from early morning to evening, sitting in on lectures, including Ritschl's. 'I feel extraordinarily fond of him,' Nietzsche wrote. 'It is a fine, scholarly head, and there is something sincere and mild in him. Unlike other kings, he has nothing of the non-commissioned officer about him.'[58] At the same time Nietzsche's attitude to Bismarck was changing, although the chancellor was still patiently manoeuvring to upset the peaceful balance established at the end of the Napoleonic Wars. Napoleon III also wanted to disturb it, so Bismarck easily secured the neutrality of France in the war he was determined to foment with Austria, and in April he made an alliance with Italy. Later in the month Nietzsche was as patriotic as he had been at Bonn. He signed a letter home with the phrase 'One who is ready for war',[59] and he was calling himself 'proud to be a Prussian'.[60] He made two attempts to enlist in the army, but was rejected as too myopic.

He was spending one evening a week reading Greek with von Gersdorff, and one a fortnight 'Schopenhauering' with him and Mushacke. Towards the end of February 1866 he gave notice of wanting to leave his lodgings. The mother had scalded one of her children with boiling water, so the screaming was worse than ever. He was also suffering from a cough he could not throw off. By the end of March the fits of coughing were rarer, but felt almost asphyxiating.[61] He was spending more time at his lodgings, attending lectures less regularly and thinking of going home early for the Easter holidays. Encouraged by Ritschl, he had undertaken to prepare a new edition of Theognis' work with a long introduction, and he had only six weeks to get the book ready for the printer. He wrote excitedly to his mother and sister about the project, telling them to prepare his room for him and to keep the news secret.[62]

But there was a strong counter-current to his elation. He had begun to feel that philology and philosophy were pulling him in different directions. It would not have been so easy for him as it is for us to see that his passion for philosophy derived some of its impetus from his interest in the relationship between the ideas expressed in classical literature and their background, political, social, religious and cultural. Even if he was aware of this, it would still have been frustrating in many ways to be in the hands of a teacher like Ritschl, whose interest in philology was too narrow: 'He was possessed by an overvaluation of his subject, and disapproves proportionately when philologists become involved in philosophy.'[63] Nietzsche was now resenting the time he had to spend on Theognis, and, taking pleasure in almost nothing but Schopenhauer, Schumann and solitary walks.[64] Like the Romantics, he was finding solace in the savagery of natural forces. One day when a storm was threatening he walked up a nearby hill, and, at the top, just before the storm broke, found a man slaughtering two kids. Standing on the hilltop, amid hail and thunder, Nietzsche could feel that personal anxieties were trivial and ethical imperatives absurd. 'How different lightning, storms and hail are – free forces, amoral. How happy and how powerful they are: pure will, with no intellect to oppress them.'[65] Like Schopenhauer, he was identifying 'will' with 'force'.

His admiration for the blind forces of nature may have been intensified by his recoil from an intolerant sermon about Christianity, 'the faith that has conquered the world'. The preacher, Friedrich August Wenkel, chief Protestant minister in Naumburg, had spoken scathingly about pagan cultures, arguing, confusingly, as if the word 'Christianity' were synonymous with 'sense of sinfulness'. Nietzsche was provoked to write: 'If Christianity means belief in a historical event or a historical person, then I want nothing to do with it. But if it means no more than a feeling of need for redemption, then I can set a very high value on it, without taking it amiss that it tries to discipline philosophers.'[66] This sermon may have prompted the 'Gedanken über das Christentum' ('Thoughts about Christianity'), which fulminate against 'the monstrous fallacy of taking theism and morality to be identical'.[67]

By the end of the Easter holidays he had organized all the material he needed for his Theognis essay, but not started on the actual writing. He decided that he could not have the book ready for publication until the summer holidays and, when term began, he would have no qualms about giving it priority over lectures and seminars. He had taught himself more in the five weeks of working on his own, he felt, than in his whole time at the university.

Before leaving Naumburg he had written to place an advertisement in the *Leipziger Tageblatt* for a ground-floor room, 'cool and quiet in a non-commercial area'. He wanted to get away from the Jews, he said. In Elisenstrasse he found a newly decorated room which had not yet been furnished, and the landlord, who owned a machine-tool factory, allowed him to choose what he wanted. The room was 'very high, cool and quiet – so far as I can tell – beautiful carpet, large looking-glass, large gold-framed oil-painting of an old man ... bureau, washstand, stove, bed, book-shelf and two chairs.'[68] In another letter he called it 'three times more decent than my last room'.[69]

But the mindless bonhomie of the *Burschenschaft* had broken his lifelong habit of working remorselessly, and in the new room he lapsed into depressive lethargy. He got up late. Breakfast consisted of two glasses of milk, drunk while reading either Schopenhauer or a book on prosody. 'Then I saunter along to the university, usually arriving two hours too early, because I have no watch, and in my isolation I hear nothing. At Curtius's lectures I almost fall asleep, then eat at Mahn's then go to the Café Kintschy, where I rest.'[70] Mahn's was a restaurant near the old theatre. Between three and seven he would attend three or four lectures, including one by Ritschl, who was offended that Nietzsche did not come to his seminar. 'Such people overvalue themselves prodigiously.'[71] Though he was enjoying Friedrich Zarncke's lectures on literature, Nietzsche was finding the university generally tedious and was hoping that within two weeks or so he would feel strong enough to go back to his work on Theognis.[72]

The possibility of being enlisted made it harder for him to concentrate. Staying in Leipzig over Whitsun he made some headway with his work, but read the newspapers anxiously. Bismarck had made an uncharacteristically radical proposal for a German national Parliament, with Austria excluded and with every adult male given a vote. At the same time, he had accepted Napoleon III's proposal for a European congress. 'All our hopes are pinned on a German Parliament', Nietzsche wrote, 'but I hope the Paris congress enjoys defecating.'[73]

On 1 June, Austria appealed to the federal Diet at Frankfurt to decide the fate of Schleswig-Holstein. Bismarck's answer was that Austria had violated the agreement of August 1865 that joint rule should end, that Prussia should control Schleswig, and Austria Holstein. Joint rule, he said, should automatically come back into force, and on 8 June he marched his troops into Holstein. Austria again appealed to the Diet, and on 14 June, when some of the German states voted for mobilization against the aggression, the Prussian delegates declared that the German Confederation no longer existed. Under cover of darkness on the night of the 15th the Prussian army invaded Saxony, Hanover and Hesse. By the end of the month it was in control of Hanover, but Nietzsche did not see how Bismarck could go on to impose unity on Germany by force. 'He has got courage and ruthless consistency, but he underestimates the moral strength of the people. All the same, his latest moves are masterly. Above all he knows how to throw a large – if not the largest – part of the blame onto Austria.'[74]

On the day Nietzsche wrote this letter, a state of war was declared for the whole of Saxony. 'It is gradually becoming more like living on an island, because telegraph despatches, postal connections and railways are constantly disrupted.'[75] Lectures were going on as usual, but he was more impatient than ever to be called up. His country was in serious danger, he thought. 'It has become dishonourable to stay sitting at home while the fatherland is at the beginning of a life-or-death struggle.'[76] He was not to know how quickly the war would be over. The Prussian army was well organized and well equipped: the new needle-gun was a powerful weapon, and the campaign was skilfully fought. On 3 July the Austrian army was routed at Sadowa. 'The news was announced in the evening of the day before yesterday through our city commander, who immediately had an immense black and white flag flying from his hotel. The feelings of the people are very mixed.'[77] So were Nietzsche's. Writing to Wilhelm Pinder, he condemned Bismarck: 'The highest good cannot be attained by evil means.'[78] The French newspapers were right to call him a revolutionary. Much could be learned from times like these, when the ground shook under their feet, and the masks fell away from ugly, self-seeking faces.

But he was disconcerted to see how irrelevant intellectual

activity was to power politics. 'What is most noticeable of all is how slight the power of thought is.'[79] The preoccupations of academics had no bearing on the events that determined the fate of the German people. Combined with the influence of Schopenhauer, the six weeks of war made Nietzsche feel that he had been living under comfortable illusions. 'Since Schopenhauer took the blindfold of optimism from our eyes, we see more clearly. Life is more interesting but uglier.'[80] A day later, writing to von Gersdorff, who was now in the army, Nietzsche was ready to concede: 'In the last fifty years we have never been so close to the fulfilment of our German hopes. I am beginning gradually to understand that there was probably no softer alternative to a horrific war of annihilation.'[81] By the middle of August he was 'thinking very optimistically about Prussia'[82] and Germany's immediate future, and by the end of the month, after the Peace of Prague had consolidated Prussia's annexation of Hanover, Hesse, Nassau and Frankfurt, and led to the formation of a new North German Confederation under Prussian leadership, Nietzsche felt unreservedly in favour of Bismarck's achievement. 'For me it is also – quite frankly – a rare and totally new pleasure to feel totally in accord with the existing government. . . . This time, success is there: the achievement is a great one.'[83]

Bismarck had managed to shut Austria out of German affairs, gaining both Schleswig and Holstein. There was a proviso that Northern Schleswig should be returned to Denmark if this was the decision of a plebiscite, but no plebiscite was held. Within a year, the new North German Confederation had its constitution, with the king as head of it and Bismarck, as chancellor, effectively superior to all other ministers and officials. The North German states which were not annexed – including Brunswick, Anhalt, and Oldenburg – were incorporated in a loose federal structure designed to make it easy for Bismarck to extend his dominion to the southern states. In the *Bundesrat* (the federal council), Prussia had seventeen votes while no other state had more than four. In practice Bismarck was already in control of all German territory north of the river Main, and after signing treaties with Bavaria and other southern states, he was in a strong position to exert influence on them. Liberalism was on the wane, but nationalism was gathering force, with him as its hero.

The work on Theognis had led Nietzsche to *Suidas*, a lexicon which had been completed about the end of the tenth century AD. Though some of the text is corrupt and much of it based not on original sources but abridgements and selections, it contains evidence of work done by the earliest classical scholars, and in trying to track down its sources Nietzsche could apply the same critical methods he had used on Theognis. The valuation he set on *Suidas* was extremely high. His second lecture to the philological club, delivered on 1 June, had the title '*Suidas* is incontestibly the most important source for the classical period of Greek literature, though it came one-and-a-half thousand years later.'

Two days after the Battle of Sadowa, Nietzsche was in no hurry to round off his work on Theognis: it would be impossible to publish it before the war was over.[84] But within a week he was planning to complete it by the end of the month, though not for publication as a book. On 10 July he discovered that two scholars already had a new critical edition of Theognis in hand, and Ritschl advised him to bring the work rapidly to a conclusion for publication in a periodical he edited, *Das Rheinische Museum für Philologie*. This was the first time he had ever invited one of his students to contribute. By the middle of August two-thirds of the text were in Ritschl's hands, and the whole of it by the end of the month. 'I have never worked on anything with so little enthusiasm. At the end I was churning the stuff out in the most monotonous way. But Ritschl was very satisfied with the part he has read. It will probably be out in October.'[85]

Ritschl liked helping his pupils to obtain paid work as early as possible, and while breaking the news to Nietzsche about the scholarly critical edition of Theognis, he was able to tell him that a colleague, Wilhelm Dindorf, might be interested in employing him to work on an Aeschylus lexicon. The proposal was attractive for several reasons. The work would familiarize him with Aeschylus, while he would be given access to Dindorf's collation of the *Codex Medicens*. He would be able, incidentally, to prepare for future use a lecture on one of Aeschylus' plays, and the remuneration was likely to be quite high. Ritschl would negotiate it with Dindorf for him once he had proved himself by submitting a sample passage. He had been thinking of leaving Leipzig before the end of the year; this made him want to stay on.

But all this did not stop him from feeling more attracted to philosophy than philology. In 1866 F. A. Lange, 'a most enlightened Kantian and natural scientist',[86] published his *Geschichte des Materialismus und Kritik seiner Bedeutung für die Gegenwart* (*History of Materialism and Critique of its Significance for the Present*). Nietzsche's first reaction was that it was undoubtedly the most significant philosophical work to have appeared during the last hundred years.[87] According to Lange, the age of idealism had ended in 1830 with the July Revolution that overthrew the monarchy of Charles x to restore constitutionalism under Louis-Philippe. Since then the pressure of material interests on spiritual life had been engendering a new realism. The rapid growth of industrialism, the development of the railway system, and the popularity of David Strauss's *Das Leben Jesu* had all contributed to a revival of interest in philosophy as an alternative to religious idealism, but though a revolutionary impulse was visible among philosophers, they had not caught up with the implications of the new materialism.

By asserting the unity of the body and the will, Schopenhauer had gone some way towards refuting Kant's Platonically based assumption that the world of phenomena is distinct from the world of the *Ding an sich*. Lange argued that no such distinction could meaningfully be made. If there is a borderline between appearance and reality, we cannot hope to locate it, so it is pointless to speculate about it. For Schopenhauer the ultimate reality was the will, and the account he gave of it was central to his philosophy. For Lange the ultimate reality was totally unknowable. Any conception we form of it belongs to the world of phenomena, as does everything that enters our minds, which means that we can have no apprehension of how the *Ding an sich* differs from the phenomenon. Nor can we have any accurate knowledge of our own body, which, like other parts of the visible world, is only a manifestation of an unknowable reality. Everything in our awareness is produced by interaction between the perceiving mind and the world of phenomena, but we can be aware of neither independently.

Nietzsche wrote about the book to von Gersdorff, who was still serving in the army. Nietzsche's letters to him are full of pleas that he should try to get himself transferred to Leipzig. 'Who is there in the whole world I can really confide in? With the bulk of my acquaintances it is truly impossible, though there are likeable, decent people among them. ... But the days are over when one could quickly make a friendship – which really means more than friendship.'[88] Mushacke had gone to Berlin. Deussen was studying theology in Tübingen in spite of Nietzsche's insistent letters arguing that he lacked the requisite faith, and that he was wasting his talents as a philologist. Ritschl was now a friend, but not one with whom Nietzsche could have philosophical conversations.

He was still in Leipzig when an epidemic of cholera hit the city. He referred to it casually enough in a letter written on 18 August: 'I am not yet ill with cholera. Besides, it has made only a mild appearance in Leipzig.'[89] But it became more severe before he returned to Naumburg. According to his sister, he had to spend a night in a house with a cholera corpse, and claimed that he had twice cured himself of infection by drinking large quantities of hot water to induce sweating,[90] but there is nothing in his own writing to substantiate either of these stories. The epidemic spread over Saxony and Thuringia, reaching Naumburg. In the middle of September Nietzsche and his mother retreated to Kösen, a spa which remained unaffected, while Elisabeth went to stay with relations in the Voigtland. Waiting for the epidemic in Leipzig to subside, the university authorities postponed the beginning of the new academic year, so Nietzsche stayed on with his mother in Kösen through most of October. They were living in an unheated room. 'The last few days have been extremely cold. I am writing to you in my overcoat with a blanket around my feet.'[91] But they had done well to move away from Naumburg: the comb-maker who lived on the ground floor of their house died of cholera.

Returning to Leipzig, Nietzsche attended Ritschl's course on Latin grammar, which he had already heard once, and he joined Ritschl's philological society, as did most of the other society's more active members, so the two clubs continued 'almost hand in hand' with each other.[92] For his third lecture to the student society Nietzsche was planning to broach another question of textual corruption: how much dialogue in the classical tragedies had been interpolated by the actors or other people? But he decided to make this the subject of an essay, and to lecture instead on the sources of Diogenes Laertius. About the end of the third century AD

Laertius had edited a compendium of excerpts from the work of ancient philosophers interpolating biographical material, some of which he had written himself, however eclectically. Unconscientious though he was, the compendium is an important source of information, and, as in his work on *Suidas*, Nietzsche had a chance to use his flair for investigating sources.

Taking the risk that he would be accused of favouritism and injustice, Ritschl asked Nietzsche whether he would be interested in continuing his research on Laertius if he were given an incentive. Though his answer was yes, he was not told what the incentive was to be. After a period of puzzling, he guessed that the theme might be set for one of the prize essays, and later he read in the newspaper *Leipziger Nachrichten* that it had been. The competition did not close until the beginning of August 1867, but he started eagerly on the work, quite confident that he could win.

His relation with Dindorf had started well, but it failed to develop fruitfully. Not feeling that Nietzsche could yet be entrusted with a critical lexicon, Dindorf had given him only the job of preparing an index. With less incentive to stay in Leipzig, Nietzsche had been thinking of taking his doctorate in the winter and moving on to Berlin, so Ritschl's sleight-of-hand may have been a stratagem to keep his most brilliant pupil for the rest of the academic year.

Usually Nietzsche looked forward eagerly to going home for Christmas, and he had kept up the childhood practice of listing the presents he wanted from his mother and sister. But now his aunt Rosalie was dying. Writing home a week before Christmas, he offered to pay for anything that could be done to help her.[93] She survived into the New Year but died on 3 January:

> With her I have lost a large piece of my past, especially my childhood. ... A few hours before dying she broke a blood-vessel. It was in the twilight. Outside snow-flakes were drifting. She sat quite upright in bed, and gradually death came with all its sad symptoms. To have once watched this, fully conscious, is an extraordinary experience, which does not disappear quickly from the mind.[94]

Nietzsche needed the relief he got from the act of writing. As he explained at the beginning of this letter to Mushacke, there was an unposted letter to him in Leipzig, containing nearly all the same news. 'But today I feel such a need to converse with one of my friends and cheer myself up by writing that I prefer to start a new letter.'[95] When he took time for letters Nietzsche had the feeling that he was keeping *Suidas* and Laertius waiting. 'I daily set more and more value on steady, concentrated work.'[96] He found writing both pleasant and painful: it was difficult for him to write well.

It will amuse you if I confess what has given me most trouble and anxiety: my German style. The scales are falling from my eyes: I have lived all too long in stylistic innocence. I have woken up to the categorical imperative: 'Thou shalt and must write'. In fact I tried what I had never tried except in school: to write well. And suddenly the pen was paralysed in my hand. I could not do it, and I was angry.[97]

He comforted himself by remembering that Lessing, Lichtenberg and Schopenhauer all believed that a good prose style could be attained only by hard work. 'I honestly want never to write again so woodenly and drily as I did, wearing logical corsets, in my Theognis essay, for example.'[98] While English and French are both conducive to good prose, the exigencies of clarity being the exigencies of elegance, German is resistant to good prose style. Clarity is compatible with uncouth syntactical cluttering, and the would-be stylist must strike out on his own. Nietzsche started to think that he might be able to use improvisation as a model. 'Above all, some gay spirits in my style must be given back their liberty. I must learn to play on them as on a keyboard, not like pieces I have learned, but impromptus, as free as possible, though always logical and beautiful.'[99]

Sometimes he felt repelled by his image of himself sitting at a desk spread with layers of open books. 'Our whole way of working is quite ghastly. The hundred books in front of me on the table are like fire-tongs for overheating the nerve of independent thinking.'[100] As an occupation, soldiering seemed comparatively honourable. Von Gersdorff, who was now an officer, had 'the best lot of all. That is an effective contrast, a reversal of attitude, an opposite viewpoint towards life, humanity, work, duty.'[101] Without being pro-military, Nietzsche admired the way his friend had turned his back on his former life. It seemed like a negation. Later Nietzsche was to write: 'The belief in truth starts with doubt of all the truths in which one has previously believed.'[102] He also appears to have been influenced by Schopenhauer's contempt for academic institutions. 'Truth seldom lives where temples have been built for it and priests ordained. It is we who have to suffer the consequences of our good or stupid actions, not those who have given us good or stupid advice.' The more independent we can be, the better. 'Our egoism is not sufficiently clever, our intellect not sufficiently egoistic.'[103]

Of the three writers Nietzsche mentioned in the letter, both Lichtenberg and Schopenhauer had written aphorisms, and in an attempt to bring his prose stylistically closer to his piano impro-vizations, Nietzsche wrote his 'Aphorismen über Geschichte und historische Wissenschaft' ('Aphorisms on History and Historical Knowledge').[104] The prose is all too obviously striving for paradox; from these aphorisms it would have been impossible to predict that he would cultivate style so successfully. What is impressive is the width of vision and the ability to produce a thoughtful anti-Hegelian argument by co-ordinating insights gained from Schopenhauer and Lange with knowledge gained from philological research and personal impressions formed during the 1866 war. Lange had alerted him to the way political leaders take advantage of their followers' social conscience. To be a leader, Nietzsche now argued, was to bring forces into action that would carry through an idea. The leaders manipulate the needs of the masses, and history, as we know it, is the history of the masses, involving the individual only insofar as he has made himself publicly felt. The historian's task is to recognize the needs that have motivated the group, but he cannot demonstrate the movement of historical necessity. 'The historian is looking through a medium con-stituted by his preconceptions, those of his period and those of his sources. There is no hope of penetrating to the *Ding an sich*.' Having been appalled by the gulf between intellection and political events, Nietzsche was now trying to bridge it by analysing them.

Ambivalent though he felt about the academic priesthood, the personal link with Ritschl was becoming closer. 'He is the only man from whom I am glad to hear adverse comments, because his judgement is always so sound and healthy, with such delicate feeling for the truth that he is a kind of intellectual conscience for me.'[105] Nietzsche was worrying about how long his teacher could live. He had erysipelas, a local febrile disease, on his foot, and he was seriously ill several times. Some of his lectures had to be cancelled and, when they resumed at the end of May, he had to be carried in a chair to the entrance of the lecture hall. To be with him, Nietzsche decided to stay in Leipzig over the summer. He was thinking about attempting a critical history of Greek literature, and meanwhile, to qualify for a doctorate in the autumn, he started to prepare a thesis on the mythical hexameter competition between Homer and Hesiod, also discussing Orpheus and Musaeus as representatives of a new Greek pessimism. He may have been responding belatedly to a suggestion made early in 1866 by von Gersdorff, who wanted him to write about classical pessimism, but his involvement in the question was Schopenhauerian.[106] Gratifying his interest in conflict, the project led to his choice of topic for his July lecture to the student philological society – the song contest in Euboea. He took the view that between Homer and Hesiod there was no antinomy between rival views of art; it was just that the notion of competition (*agon*) was fundamental in Greek culture.

Of all Nietzsche's friendships the slowest to ripen was the one with Erwin Rohde, who was a year his junior. The son of a Hamburg doctor, he had been at Bonn, leaving at the same time to follow Ritschl. In June, after seeing a play, Nietzsche had a meal with him at Mahn's, and they then began to meet more often, though at the end of August Nietzsche described him as having 'a very acute but perverse and obstinate brain'.[107] By February 1867 they were meeting every day at Kintschy's, together with another student, Otto Kohl, and in the summer Nietzsche and Rohde took riding lessons together and practised together with pistols at a shooting-range. Rohde had long been passionately enthusiastic about music, and by the time he started to live on a different floor of the same house as Nietzsche he was also an avid Schopenhauerian. Rohde described their summer together in a November letter to a friend: 'The whole summer our life was very strange, as if we were inside a moving magic circle, not coldly closed to other people though we were nearly always alone together. We would use up half the day, almost the whole day in happy idleness and I, at least, profited very richly from this duet in supinity – more richly than I could have from philological drudgery.'[108] Not that they were usually in agreement on anything except the affectations and vanities of philologists. Rohde's gift for mimicry gave them plenty of amusement, but it seemed strange that such a feeling of harmony could emerge from incessant differences of opinion. So far, wrote Nietzsche, 'I have had only this one experience of a friendship that formed itself against a philosophical and ethical background.'[109]

By the end of June he had decided to leave at the end of August for Berlin.[110] Either he would attend the university there, or, if he had to enlist for military service, that was where he would least dislike having to do it. He asked Mushacke to find lodgings for him, suggesting they might found a philological society together in Berlin, where they would not have to reckon, as in Leipzig, with 'Saxon slowness and sleepiness'.[111]

Nietzsche finished his essay on Laertius two hours before midnight on the last day in July. Rohde had a glass of wine waiting to revive him after the final burst of energy. Then in August they went on holiday together into the Bohemian woods. They ended up in Meiningen, where Franz Liszt was directing a musical festival with performances of music by Schumann, Berlioz, Cornelius, Volkmann and Liszt himself – *Zukunftsmusik* (music of the future), as Nietzsche said, adopting the derisive term that journalists had portmanteaued out of Wagner's phrase *Kunstwerk der Zukunft* (artwork of the future).

Nietzsche spent the last two weeks of the summer holiday at home in Naumburg, where he immediately started work on an essay about Democritus, who had been praised by Aristotle for identifying mind with soul and thought with sense. Nietzsche had been infected with Lange's enthusiasm for him. Had the essay been finished, it would have been one of a series presented to Ritschl as a tribute from his pupils, but Nietzsche's hopes of exemption from military service were disappointed. A new regulation had been introduced about myopia: men wearing spectacles no stronger than Grade 8 were to be admitted to the army. When Nietzsche presented himself for a medical examination at Naumburg on 26 September, he was wearing pince-nez of that grade. According to his sister, they were too weak for him,[112] but it was not his eyes that were examined, it was the pince-nez.

4   Soldier and Student Again

On 30 September 1867, four days after his medical examination, still believing he would be exempt from military service, Nietzsche left Naumburg to attend a three-day philological congress at Halle. On the platform of the railway station he met the commanding officer of the artillery division stationed in Naumburg, Colonel von Jagemann, who told him about the new regulation, which meant that he would be required to join the army on 9 October. When Nietzsche said that he would prefer to serve in Berlin, the colonel promised to give him a certificate he could present to a guards regiment there. Meanwhile he was free to attend the congress.

There were about five hundred delegates. Ritschl, who had promised to be there, was not well enough to brave the cold weather, but several other philologists had come from Leipzig.

Troupes of teachers like these make a better showing than I would have expected. It may be that all the elderly spiders were staying in their webs. In short the clothes were decent and fashionable, while moustaches are very popular. True, old Bernhardy was the worst possible chairman, and Bergk's three-hour lecture was boring and incomprehensible. But most things went well – especially the dinner, at which old Steinhardt's gold watch was stolen. So you can imagine the general mood.[1]

Arriving in Berlin on 5 October, he was chagrined to find that the guards regiments were no longer accepting one-year 'volunteers'. Back at Naumburg, he had 'to embrace the local cannons – with more fury than tenderness'.[2] He had wanted to avoid the artillery, which was reckoned to be the worst section of the army to serve in. Recruits had to train on the parade-ground, in the saddle, and on the rifle-range, as well as learning how to handle the horse-drawn cannons, pulling shells out of the limber, and cleaning the oily bore with a cloth. He was on duty from seven in the morning till six in the evening, with only a thirty-minute break for lunch. The one compensation was that he could live at home. He would wake at four-fifteen, in time to be at work in the stables by five-thirty, cleaning away dung by lamplight and grooming his horse, Balduin, with a brush and a comb. Everything he had learned at the riding-school in Leipzig he now had to put out of his mind. With a blanket over the horse, he rode with spurs but no riding crop, trying to preserve a military posture. 'Philosophy can now be of practical value to me. I have not yet been depressed for a moment, but very often smiled, as if I were reading a fairy-tale. From time to time, concealed underneath the horse's belly, I mutter: "Schopenhauer, help!" And if I come home exhausted, with sweat all over me, I get comfort from a glance at the picture on my desk.'[3] Rohde had given him a photograph of Schopenhauer.

In the evening he would try to concentrate on philological work and preparation for the officers' examination. When he had time to think about philosophy, he was irked by the unlimited capacity of contemporary thinkers for self-delusion. 'So be it. If a slave in prison dreams about release and freedom, who will have the heart to wake him and tell him it was a dream?'[4]

Knowing that he would have more time to himself after the first few weeks of training, Nietzsche wrote to tell Ritschl that he would still be able to fulfil his commitment to make an index for the first twenty-four volumes of the new series of *Rheinisches Museum*.[5] From the sixth week, when he had a boy to do the stable work for him, the daily routine became less arduous. He would usually be on duty from seven until ten-thirty and from eleven-thirty until six, drilling on the parade-ground for most of this time. Among the thirty recruits in the division there was only one other one-year 'volunteer', and four times a week the two of them would be given a 'lecture' from a lieutenant to prepare them for the officers' examination. 'The riding lessons give me the most pleasure. I have a very pretty horse, and am supposed to have a talent for riding. When I hurtle out into the big exercise yard on my Balduin, I feel very satisfied with my lot.'[6] Having written eight months earlier to congratulate von Gersdorff on negating his previous life by becoming a soldier, Nietzsche was finding himself plunged into an existence that could hardly have been more different from studying at university. He was not unhappy, though he did feel isolated. 'I am fairly lonely in Naumburg. I have neither a philologist nor a Schopenhauer enthusiast among my acquaintances, and in any case I see little of them, because duty claims so much of my time.'[7] More than ever, he depended on letters to give him the illusion of intimate contact with friends. He paid epistolary tribute to Rohde as 'a friend who is not only a comrade in studies or linked to me by common experiences, but who is really as serious about life as I am, and who follows approximately the same rules as I do in his appreciation of things and people, and whose whole being, finally, has a strengthening, bracing effect on me'.[8]

Combining the hardships of camp with the comforts of living at home, Nietzsche's life also combined soldiering with classical scholarship. After submitting to regimentation, obeying raucous orders on the parade-ground, he could withdraw luxuriously into his quiet room, where work had to be done in a leisurely way if it was to be done well. The end of October brought the news that his essay on Diogenes Laertius had won the prize. He could not attend the ceremony, at which Ritschl, speaking in Latin, eulogized his work, but he was sent a transcript, which spurred him 'to go further along a path which scepticism sometimes tempts me to abandon'.[9] The best teachers can exert influence *in absentia*: Nietzsche could now muster the energy to resume work on Democritus, while emancipation from the academic routine was conducive to the germination of his own philosophical ideas. He was influenced by Democritus' doctrine that the ultimate principles are atoms and void – innumerable tiny particles, homogeneous in substance, but varied in form, and infinite empty space, unreal but existent. Plato and Christian theologians had been equally nervous of Democritus, believing his teachings to be dangerous. This made him all the more attractive to Nietzsche, who admired him as a revolutionary wanting to liberate humanity from superstitious fear of the gods, and as the first philosopher to understand that the scientific method had ethical implications. He was therefore, as Nietzsche saw, a precursor of positivism, comparable with Auguste Comte, who adapted the word 'positive' to signify six qualities: being real, useful, certain, precise, organic, and relative. Like Democritus, Comte adopted a critical attitude to logical argument: he maintained that human thought had evolved from a theological phase (postulating gods) through a metaphysical (postulating essences) to a scientific (limiting itself to the observable). Democritus, wrote Nietzsche, 'devoted his life wholly to an attempt at penetrating into all kinds of things with his method. So he was the first to work his way systematically through *everything knowable*.'[10]

Lecturing to the student philological society, Nietzsche must, to some extent, have been emulating university lecturers, having already found himself concentrating more on their teaching methods than on what they were saying. Working on Democritus, and emulating his scepticism, he found that he was rebelling against the work earlier philologists had done. His research on Theognis and *Suidas* had encouraged him to be suspicious of accepted ideas, but at the same time he had been pulled in the opposite direction by the reverential authoritarianism that permeated the educational system. But now, with army drill to provoke revulsion against discipline, he was more than ever disposed not only to be disrespectful towards *ex cathedra* pronouncements by pundits, but to be suspicious of all evidence and all witnesses. 'Progress has been made with research into literary history only because one is no longer satisfied with one answer, but goes on asking questions. ... Doubt is now *de rigueur*, just as belief used to be.'[11] Knowledge now had to be conceived not as static but as a *perpetuum mobile*.

This phase in Nietzsche's development involved him in a new relationship with negativity. The convergence of his philosophical and philological interests in the work on Democritus made it all the harder for him to write the essay in a form that satisfied him. The preliminary work was partly destructive: he had to fight his way through current misconceptions. The impression he evolved of Democritus' personality was not totally at odds with the traditional view. At first he had had the impression of wholesale literary counterfeiting, 'But finally, taking all the inferences sceptically into consideration, I found the image in my hands was inverting itself. I achieved a new overall impression of his remarkable personality, and from this high watch-tower of observation I saw tradition reasserting itself.'[12] Or, as he put it in the essay, 'With scepticism we dig a grave for tradition; with the consequences of scepticism we ferret the concealed truth out of its burrow, and find, perhaps, that tradition is right, though it stands on clay feet. So a Hegelian might say we were trying to convey truth through the negation of negation.'[13] His object in the essay was to reproduce the process by which he had arrived at his insights. 'I try to stimulate in the reader the same sequence of thoughts that suggested themselves to me so spontaneously and so forcefully.'[14]

This view of negation was partly conditioned by the experience of military service, just as his attitude to military service had been conditioned by his idea of negation ever since his letter to von Gersdorff about rejecting his student past. Considered as an *entremets*, Nietzsche's experience of soldiering was not merely acceptable but useful. 'It is continuously an appeal to a man's energy and it is specially effective as an antidote to the paralysing scepticism whose effects we have frequently observed in each other.'[15]

He was pleasantly surprised to find he was the best horse-rider among the thirty recruits.[16] The officers praised his posture in the saddle,[17] and predicted he would reach the rank of captain. He had not expected either that he would have the potential for doing well in this métier, or that he would want to.[18] But his progress towards a commission was humiliatingly interrupted. Myopia had made him a bad judge of distances, even at short range, and in the middle of March, jumping into the saddle, he threw himself so hard against the pommel that he tore two muscles in his chest. He felt a sharp, twitching pain in his left side, but rode on with Spartan determination. In the evening the pain became so intense that he fainted twice. For ten days he lay in bed, immobilized; he was in constant pain, with a high temperature. Ice-packs gave him little relief, and he would not have slept but for doses of morphine. A chill in his stomach added to his discomfort. At the end of ten days the military doctor made incisions in his chest. 'Since then I have had the Philoctetesian pleasure of chronic suppuration. . . . I am understating it if I say that already four to five cupfuls of pus have come out of each wound.'[19] He could not lever himself up into a sitting position without help, and when he tried to walk he could hardly put one leg in front of the other. Exhaustion rapidly ensued from any effort, mental or physical. A letter he started at the end of March remained unfinished for several days.

On 1 April his morale was boosted by the news that he had been made a lance-corporal and he began to feel better, but the wound would not heal. By the end of May the suppuration had begun to infiltrate the bone: 'Recently, to my astonishment, a piece of my frame, a small bone, came into view. Now I assiduously bathe the inner pus-cavities with camomile tea and nitrate of silver solution, and three times a week I take a hot bath.'[20]

Physically at a lower ebb than he had been since the worst of his confinements to the sanatorium at Pforta, he was intellectually at his best. After reading Kuno Fischer's book on Kant and re-reading Lange, he started work on his first important philosophical essay, 'Die Teleologie seit Kant' ('Teleology since Kant'). Initially he thought of it as a dissertation for his doctorate, only to realize that it was unsuitable, even if he was writing better than ever before. The aphorisms he had attempted less than a year ago had been broken-backed and laborious; now, at the age of twenty-three, he was writing philosophical aphorisms with an economy, lucidity, precision and incisiveness that look forward to Wittgenstein. The influence of Democritus was converging interestingly with the influences of Kant, Schopenhauer, Lichtenberg and Lange. Liberated from the compulsion to assume that the world must be intelligible, and alert to the connection between optimism and teleology – they always go hand in hand, he argued – he could formulate trenchant criticisms of the cosmological argument for God's existence: that since everything requires a cause, God must exist as the first cause. Kant had conceded that even if the appearance of order in the universe is evidence of design or purpose, the existence of a creator cannot be deduced from the existence of an architect. Nietzsche went much further, producing strongly anti-metaphysical arguments. He saw that it was no longer necessary to assume that there was any premeditation behind natural phenomena, even if the complex patterns in organic growth make it hard for us to conceive of them as resulting from accident.

Most philosophers have left the body out of account; Nietzsche lays great stress on it, building up this essay on a basis of quotations from Kant and Goethe: 'An organism is that in which everything is an end and, contrariwise, also a means.'[21] – 'Each living thing is not singular but plural: even in so far as it appears to us as individual, it remains a collection of living, independent beings.'[22] Each of us is plural. Like the concept of wholeness, the idea of purpose derives less from observation of things than from the observer. The origins of organic life are beyond human comprehension, so we let the appearance of purposefulness in nature lead us to the idea of nature as an entity, coherent in itself and consistent in the means it employs. But the life of the organism contains no evidence of a higher intelligence. In nature, aims and forms are identical. Why should we assume that the existence of the dog was preceded by a notion of what a dog should look like? To trace the existence of the universe to a single cause is to assume that the idea of the whole was present, causally, in its inception. This is to predicate a phenomenon as noumenal and pre-existent, to assume that the *Ding an sich* must manifest its unity in the harmony of all appearances.

He wrote the essay in the spring, while the purulence persisted. By the end of May it was clear that he had damaged his breastbone. This was why the wound would not heal, and now the bone itself was going soft. It is possible that his sternum had syphilitic *gummata* on it, but these would have taken between three and seven years to develop if they resulted from a syphilitic infection. If he was the victim of congenital syphilis, the softening may have been due to it, but it is more likely to have been due to osteomiolitis of the bone. Without penicillin, suppuration could be treated only by irrigation, which did not kill the germs. On 6 June the army doctor said that an operation would be unavoidable. The soft part of the bone would have to be cut off and the breastbone 'reduced'. He felt very frightened: 'No sooner are you under the knife and the saws of the surgeon than you realize what a frail thread the thing called life is hanging on.'[23] But the case was sufficiently unusual for the doctor to want the opinion of a specialist. On 25 June, Nietzsche was sent to Halle for a consultation with Richard von Volkmann, who held out little hope of avoiding surgery. He recommended Nietzsche to take the cure at the salt-water baths in Wittekind, but was himself surprised at the speed of the results. The inflammation was soon reduced, the suppuration stopped. After a painful series of visits to Volkmann's clinic for the wound to be painted with iodine, Nietzsche was discharged. On 2 August, after five months of illness, he returned to Naumburg. Sitting on the veranda of his mother's house, he worked with Elisabeth's help at the index for Ritschl, and soon nothing was left of the wound except a deep scar across his chest, 'to remind me how serious – indeed how dangerous – my condition was.'[24]

It was taken for granted that he should not continue with his military career. He was declared 'temporarily unfit for service', and on 15 October, his twenty-fourth birthday, he was a civilian again. But since there was no prospect of continuing peace or of permanent freedom from having to wear uniform, he wanted a commission, so he arranged to do another month's service in the spring to qualify himself with the necessary knowledge about gun-hauling exercises.

Though he went back to Leipzig University, he could no longer think of himself as a student. 'It is already over a year since I threw off that intolerable condition. Here I am rather the future Leipzig lecturer, and I organize my life according to this intention.'[25] Confidence in his academic future was boosted by reactions to a lecture he gave on Varro and Menippus to the philological society. Instead of reading a paper, as most lecturers did, he spoke to the audience of forty with only a few notes in his hand. He had briefed his friend Heinrich Romundt to be his critic, concentrating on 'the theatrical side' – delivery, voice, style and organization of material. But it was obvious that everything was going well.[26]

He had arranged to live as a paying guest in the house of Professor Biedermann, a former member of the *Landtag* and now editor of a newspaper, the *Deutsche Allgemeine*. Nietzsche, who ate with the family, had a large, rather bare room with a good view, and a spacious bedroom. He was pleased with the acquaintances he was able to make through the professor, 'witty ladies, pretty actresses, important writers and politicians, etc.'[27] He was able to attend concerts and lectures as a reviewer for the *Deutsche Allgemeine*, and he was invited to become its opera critic. He was also taken on by Friedrich Zarncke, editor of the periodical *Literarisches Zentralblatt*, as a book reviewer, covering the whole field of Greek philosophy except Aristotle.

'I have come back to Leipzig with utterly different demands on life.'[28] There was a new balance in his division of loyalty between philosophy and philology, even if it was mainly to provoke Paul Deussen that he wrote: 'I regard Philology as the misbegotten child of the goddess Philosophy, spawned by a cretin or an idiot.'[29]

On the evening of 27 October, when he heard an orchestral performance of the Overture to *Die Meistersinger* and the Prelude to *Tristan*, which he had known only from a piano version, his attitude to Wagner changed. 'I cannot bring myself to take a critically cool view of this music. It sends a thrill through every fibre, every nerve, and for a long time I have not had such a sustained feeling of being carried away (*Entrücktheit*) as the Overture gave me.'[30] Analysing his reactions to different pieces of music in about the spring of 1867, he had used the phrase 'krystallne Entrücktheit' à propos the song of the Blessed Boys in Schumann's *Faust*.[31] Less than two weeks later, returning to his rooms after a meeting with Ritschl, he found a note from his friend Ernst Windisch, a fellow-student who had often been to the café with him: 'If you want to meet Richard Wagner, come to the Theatre Café at 3.45 p.m.'

When Nietzsche arrived there, Windisch explained what had happened. Wagner was paying a secret visit to Leipzig, his native city, where his sister Ottilie still lived, and he was staying with her and her husband, Professor Hermann Brockhaus. They had warned their servants and friends that the newspapers must not learn of Wagner's presence in Leipzig. Frau Brockhaus was a friend of Frau Ritschl, who was invited to meet the composer. When he played her the Prize Song from *Die Meistersinger*, she told him that thanks to a student of her husband's she already knew it well. Feeling that he needed more contact with the younger generation, and loving nothing more than admiration, Wagner asked to meet the young man. Windisch took Nietzsche straight to the Brockhauses' home, only to find that Wagner had just gone out. Nietzsche was invited back the next evening, a Sunday.

Assuming it would be a formal party, he decided to wear the evening dress which was to be delivered that day by his tailor. He stayed in his room most of the day, unable to concentrate. After lunch Wilhelm Roscher arrived to discuss the thesis he was writing. It was getting dark when he left, but the tailor had not come. Nietzsche went impatiently to the shop, where several apprentices were working on the suit. It would be delivered in three-quarters of an hour. Reassured, he went to Kintschy's, where he read in *Kladderadatsch*, a humorous illustrated paper, that Wagner was in Switzerland.

At about six-thirty a little old man arrived at the Biedermanns' house with a package and a bill.

I take it politely: he wants payment on receipt of the goods. Flabbergasted, I explain that I want no dealings with him, my tailor's employee, but only with the tailor himself, from whom I ordered the suit. The man puts more pressure on me; the time puts more pressure on me. I seize the things and begin to put them on; the man seizes the things and prevents me from putting them on. Force on my side; force on his. Scene: I am fighting in my shirt because I want to step into the new trousers.[32]

The little old man must have been stronger than he looked. He went off with the suit, leaving Nietzsche sitting on the sofa in his shirt, swearing revenge against the tailor, and asking himself whether a black jacket was good enough for an evening with Richard Wagner.

Nietzsche was late for the meeting he had arranged with Windisch at half-past-seven in the Theatre Café. They hurried to the house, to find that Wagner was the only other guest. He bore a striking resemblance to Pastor Nietzsche, who had been his junior by five months. We have no means of knowing whether the impact he made on Nietzsche had anything to do with this resemblance; what we do know is that from now on Nietzsche hardly ever referred to his father. Normally he did not enter quickly into feelings of intimacy, but two days later, writing to Erwin Rohde, he referred to Wagner as Richard.

Wagner wanted to know in detail how Nietzsche had come to be familiar with his music, and he spoke scathingly of all except the Munich productions of his operas, mimicking the conductors who equably asked for 'more passion' from their orchestra. 'He really is a fabulously vivacious, fiery man, who talks very quickly and wittily, brightening up a party of this very private kind.'[33] He sat at the piano, playing from Die Meistersinger and exuberantly singing all the roles himself. He also read an excerpt from the autobiography he was writing – 'a hilarious scene from his days as a student at Leipzig. I still cannot think about it without laughing'.[34] In between, he told Nietzsche about his admiration for Schopenhauer, the only philosopher to have understood the essence of music, he said. He had become an enthusiast as soon as he had discovered Schopenhauer's work, fourteen years earlier.

In 1848, while he was second conductor at the Dresden opera house, Wagner had been a friend of Bakunin and a disciple of Feuerbach, who held that 'The need for preservation is something artificial. . . . No one without the courage to be absolutely negative has the strength to create anything new.'[35] In June 1848 Wagner made a speech to the *Vaterlandsverein*, demanding the abolition of nobility and privilege and the creation of a republic headed by the Saxon king. Only a prince would be capable of representing the people, united in a classless society. Together with Bakunin he helped to organize the revolt in Dresden at the beginning of May 1849. Having to live in exile after this, he settled in Zürich for ten years. In December 1851 the success of Louis Napoleon's *coup d'état* made him repudiate not only politics but aspiration to realism: 'I turned away from the investigation of this enigmatic world as one turns one's back on a mystery that no longer seems worth trying to fathom.'[36] After finishing *Lohengrin* in 1847, he wrote no music until he began composing *Der Ring des Nibelungen* in 1853, but he drafted the libretto of the *Ring* between 1848 and 1853 – though when he read Schopenhauer he arrived at a new interpretation of what he had written: 'I had built up an optimistic world, on Hellenic principles, believing that for man to bring such a world into realization, it was necessary only for him to wish it.'[37] Siegfried had been intended to represent the possibility of a future existence devoid of pain, while instinctively Wagner had 'grasped the essence and the meaning of the world in all its possible phases, and I had realized its nothingness'.[38] Schopenhauer made him intellectually aware of what he had understood only intuitively, and Siegfried was displaced from his central position by Wotan, the god who longs for his own annihilation:

I am eternally sickened to find nothing but myself in everything that I bring about. . . . Whatever I love I have to abandon, those whom I woo I murder, deceitfully betray whoever trusts me . . . destroy what I have built. . . . My work I abandon. I want only one thing – the end, the end. . . . What profoundly disgusts me I give to you as your inheritance – the futile splendour of the divine.[39]

When Wagner had sent Schopenhauer a text of *Der Ring*, printed on impressively thick paper and finely bound, the old man, who loved Mozart and Rossini, had ironically replied that Wagner should perhaps cultivate his poetic talent. Overlooking the irony, and unaware of the hostile annotations that the philosopher had made in the margins, Wagner now told Nietzsche that Schopenhauer had liked his writing. Nietzsche, who had never encountered such a strong personality, felt very honoured at the end of the evening when the composer shook him warmly by the hand 'and very cordially invited me to visit him for music-making and philosophical conversation. He also entrusted me with the task of familiarizing his sister and her family with his music, which I have solemnly undertaken to do.'[40] Within two weeks Wagner was a hero to be worshipped next to Schopenhauer. When Ritschl rejected an essay of Rohde's that Nietzsche had submitted to *Rheinisches Museum*, he wrote to console his friend: 'Think of Schopenhauer and Richard Wagner, of their inexhaustible energy which kept their faith in themselves intact despite the jeering of the whole "cultured" world.'[41]

In Wagner's absence, Frau Brockhaus was glad to have such a good audience for reminiscences about her brother, and, listening to her, Nietzsche had the impression of coming to know Wagner better. Reading his verse, Nietzsche thought highly of it, though not so highly as his friend Romundt, who judged Wagner to be by far the best poet of his generation. Intoxicated in his new allegiance, Nietzsche wished Rohde could have been there to share the manifold pleasure he was taking in Wagner. 'Together we could march to the bold, indeed giddying rhythm of his revolutionary and constructive aesthetic. We could finally let ourselves be torn away from the passionate surge of his music, from this Schopenhauerian sea of sound. I feel so involved in the beating of its most secret waves that, for me, listening to Wagner's music is a jubilant intuition, indeed an astonishing self-discovery.'[42] Even Nietzsche's prose style had become more Wagnerian.

He was writing home less frequently and more tersely than ever before. He was going to concerts and to the theatre – sometimes escorting Frau Ritschl – while his social life was fuller than it had been since Bonn, and more enjoyable than ever. He was invited often by the Ritschls and the Brockhauses, sometimes by other friends and acquaintances. He would occasionally give a party, mainly to repay hospitality, and he had taken up riding again.

Though he had not quarrelled with his mother and sister, even the approach of Christmas failed to bring any renewal of the old closeness. His intention was to spend only three-and-a-half days at home with them, while he excused himself from writing the songs they had requested. 'For some of them I have no music and for none have I any words.'[43] Wagner was already so important as a father-figure that the need for mother and sister was dwindling, while Nietzsche was conscious that the bonds of family life had come to mean less to him than the bonds of friendship:

> The man who is lonely owing to a quirk of nature or a strange brew of whims, talents and aspirations – he knows what 'an inestimably great marvel' a *friend* is; and if he is an idol-worshipper, he must first of all erect an altar to 'the unknown god who created the friend'. . . . The cosiness of wearing a dressing-gown, the most quotidian, most trivial things glimmering out of this snugly expansive feeling – that is happiness in family life, and it is far too common to be of much value.[44]

Fantasies about family life, unlike fantasies about friendship, could never be heroic.

Half-way through this letter of 10 January 1869 to Rohde the letters 'NB' indicate the point at which Nietzsche was interrupted by a message to call on Ritschl. 'Now that I have come back I am trembling in every limb, and cannot release myself from the tension by pouring out my heart to you.'[45] But he wrote again, six days later, to let Rohde into the secret a day before he confided it to his mother and sister. The Chair of Classical Philology at Basel University had fallen vacant, and it was virtually certain that the twenty-four-year-old Nietzsche, who did not yet have his doctorate, was about to become a professor. A former pupil of Ritschl, Adolf Kiessling, who had been only twenty-five when he was appointed to the Chair seven years earlier, was giving it up to accept a position in Hamburg. After reading Nietzsche's contributions to the *Rheinisches Museum*, he had written to Ritschl for information about him. Ritschl's answer was that he had never known a young man 'who became *so* mature so early. . . . If God grants him long life, I prophesy that he will one day stand in the front rank of German philology.' Kiessling passed on Ritschl's recommendation to Professor Wilhelm Vischer-Bilfinger, Ordinarius for Classical Philology and President of the Education

Institute, while Ritschl wrote to tell him that although Nietzsche's studies had centred on Greek literary history and especially the history of Greek philosophy, his great talent would enable him to work his way into other academic areas. 'Whatever he wants to do he will be able to do.'[46]

The position would carry the title of Professor Extraordinarius and a salary of 3,000 francs – about 800 *taler* or 2,540 marks – a very large income compared to what he had been living on. Nietzsche even thought of employing a manservant and asked his mother and sister to find a man, preferably an ex-soldier, whom he could take to Basel. He would also have to teach for six hours each week at the Pädagogium, a public school which had originally been part of the university. One of the attractions of the offer was that Basel was only about fifty miles from where Wagner was living, outside Lucerne. After hearing the news Nietzsche spent that whole afternoon walking and singing melodies from *Tannhäuser*. Coincidentally, he received his first letter from Wagner, and he decided that he would go to *Die Meistersinger* in Dresden at the end of January. His only regret was that he would not be able to have a year in Paris with Rohde.

But amid the flurry of telegrams and letters of congratulation, the flattery and the invitations, the admiration and adulation, Nietzsche's euphoria quickly evaporated: 'What does this wonderful luck, this enchanting novelty consist of? Sweat and effort. . . . But you have only skimmed off the cream, which may well have tasted good. What remains for me is the stale milk of the job's daily monotony, the friendless isolation, etc.'[47] He would also have to work extremely hard to be ready to take over his new responsibilities immediately after Easter. In February it looked as though, besides preparing lectures for Basel, he would have to finish a thesis to gain his doctorate before leaving Leipzig. He could not have anticipated that it would be awarded to him gratuitously, as it was on 23 March, in recognition of the essays he had published in *Rheinisches Museum*. Meanwhile the sense of pressure undercut the pleasure he took in being, suddenly, so much in demand socially. Writing to Rohde on 22 February, Schopenhauer's birthday, he may have been self-consciously assuming a melancholy tone, but the underlying depression seems genuine:

In fact I live here in the ash-grey cloud of loneliness, which is all the worse for having so many sociable arms held open to me on many sides, and almost every evening the dismal flow of invitations keeps up its pressure. In these gatherings I hear so many voices. I never come to myself at all. . . . At the moment, dissipated and pleasure-seeking, I am living through a desperate carnival before the great Ash Wednesday of the profession, philistinism. It grieves me to the heart, but none of my present acquaintances notices anything of this. Dazzled by the title 'professor', they think me the luckiest man on earth.[48]

Not that there was any danger of his failing to take his new responsibilities seriously. He was too deeply steeped in Schopenhauerian *gravitas* not to be interested in the opportunity of exerting influence. He had no intention of being a 'drill sergeant for competent philologists';[49] he wanted to transmit seriousness to his students. 'If we have to let our life run its course, let us try to use it in such a way that other people will bless it and esteem it when we are fortunate enough to have been released from it.'[50] This is to take it for granted that the pains of being alive exceed the pleasures: either the new appointment or the superficiality of the philistines' reaction to it had provoked a recrudescence of Schopenhauerian pessimism.

'What I am afraid of', he wrote in a note, 'is not the frightful shape behind my chair, but its voice; also not the words, but the terrifyingly unarticulated and inhuman tone of that shape. Yes, if only it would speak as human beings do.'[51] Hallucination? Madness? Prescience? Unless other pieces of similar writing have been suppressed by his sister, this paragraph is unique in Nietzsche's early work – an isolated outcrop of delusionary language. His life had been a chain of events and efforts, but had the chain been formed by 'the coincidences of external fate and baroque moodiness' or had 'the groping hand of instinct' felt its unerring way to the point he had reached? Had he created his own fate? In 1868 he had written nine aphorisms under the title 'Selbstbeobachtung' ('Self-Observation'). The first is 'It misleads'; the sixth is 'Instinct is best'; the last is 'Our deeds must happen unconsciously.' A precursor of Freud in his recognition that the self is multiple and that its components are in conflict, Nietzsche was also aware of the dangers of self-analysis. The second aphorism is 'Acknowledge yourself'; the third 'Through action, not observation'. But in 1869 he was forced to recognize the consequences of his unconscious actions.

The habit he had learned at Pforta of organizing his time tended to reduce each activity to equal importance. His inclination towards art had been partly a reaction against systemization. Nearly all his best writing had been done when he had broken away from the academic system to work on his own. But he needed the discipline to protect him from randomness and over-excitement in his passion for what he called 'universal knowledge'. By 1869 he was aware that his philosophical seriousness and his compulsion to hunt down 'the naked truth' made him not only willing but eager to confront unpleasant realities. It seemed possible that a negative force had been operating on him, inducing him to opt for narrower fields of activity. He had moved from art to philosophy and philology. If only there had been better musical opportunities at Pforta he might have become a professional musician; as a fully-fledged artist Wagner was an attractive realization of the potentiality Nietzsche had failed to develop. But the compulsion to hunt down the naked truth committed him to precision, objectivity, penetration, and the field of activity had to be chosen accordingly, even if this meant that the means was determining the end.

I should think that a man of twenty-four already has behind him the most important things in his life, even if it is not until later that he produces what makes his life worthwhile. Until about this age the young soul still extricates what is typical from all its experiences of living and thinking, and it will never be prised away from the world of these types. Later on, when this idealizing gaze is extinguished, we remain under the sway of that world we receive as a legacy from our youth.[52]

But the autobiographical habit had been only of limited usefulness to him. He could make his own life into history, understanding both how his past had led to his present and how it was likely to impinge on his future, but this historical self-awareness could not protect him from the catastrophes that would come to seem inevitable.

If war broke out, university professors would not be exempt from military service, and Nietzsche was asked by his new employers whether he would take Swiss nationality. Applying for a change of national identity must have heightened the feeling that one phase of his life was drawing to a close. His twenty-four-and-a-half years as a Prussian ended in April 1869, and on the 13th, wearing clothes chosen to make him look older, he was taken to the station at Naumburg in an old-fashioned fly-coach, driven by the coachman who in 1843 had taken his parents to their wedding. Dividing the journey into leisurely stages, partly in order to prepare his inaugural lecture en route, he spent a day in Cologne and one in Bonn. The next day was spent on the Rhine in a steamer. He had planned to arrive in Basel on the seventh day of the journey, but on a train just before it stopped at Karlsruhe he overheard a passenger's remark about a performance of *Die Meistersinger* there that evening, and he decided to break his journey to hear his 'favourite opera. This is how I took leave of German soil.'[53] The next day he crossed the border.

5 Wagner and *The Birth of Tragedy*

Nietzsche had never been outside Germany. This had possibly been one of his reasons for thinking of going on from Bonn to a foreign university, and, more recently, for wanting a year in Paris with Rohde. To an Englishman or a Frenchman, the atmosphere of Basel would have seemed very German, as it still does, but to Nietzsche it seemed un-German, partly because there was no evidence of a self-assertive state. Monarchy and militarism had made their marks neither on the urban landscape nor on what was visible of communal life, which revolved, more democratically, around church and university. There were no princely palaces, no flag-waving processions led by military bands. But his first impressions of an alternative political system were unfavourable: 'Here one can be cured of republicanism.'[1] Though the local authorities were demolishing the city wall and laying out new parks, there was a great deal that struck him as medieval: the old houses with their quaint facades, the ancient customs and usages, the low-German dialect, the church-going in family groups.[2]

Until his lodgings were ready at the end of his second month in the city, he lived in the cramped quarters he had originally intended for his manservant. From the outset his routine was strenuous. He had to pay about sixty courtesy visits to university colleagues. He lectured six days a week at seven o'clock in the morning, speaking about the history of Greek verse on Monday, Tuesday, and Wednesday; on Aeschylus's *Choephori* on Thursday, Friday and Saturday. His audience consisted of only eight, including a theology student. Wanting to introduce seminars like Ritschl's, he held one on Mondays, the only weekday he did not have to teach at the Pädagogium, where he had two periods on Tuesday and Friday, one on Wednesday and Thursday, but he found these quite enjoyable. 'Translating the *Phaedo* gives me the opportunity to infect my pupils with philosophy. By giving them exercises to do in class, which is quite unprecedented here, I rouse them very roughly out of their grammatical slumber.'³ The constant obligation to make the acquaintance of new people he found burdensome,⁴ but he loved the mountain scenery, and he made excursions into the Jura valley, the Vosges, and the Black Forest.

He had been in Basel for less than a month when he decided to visit Wagner at Tribschen, the isolated villa beautifully positioned between Lake Lucerne and Mount Pilatus. He was living with the thirty-one-year-old Cosima von Bülow, second of the three illegitimate daughters born to Franz Liszt by the Comtesse Marie d'Agoult. Cosima had been Wagner's mistress since 1863. His first wife, Minna, had died in 1866, and Cosima, who had already borne him two daughters, was now pregnant by him for the third time, though not yet divorced from the conductor Hans von Bülow.

On Saturday 15 May, Wagner was working on the third act of *Siegfried*. 'I stood still for a long time in front of the house, and heard a painful chord repeated constantly.' The manservant who came to the door said that his master could not be disturbed before two o'clock. After leaving his card, Nietzsche was walking away from the house when the servant came hurrying after him. Was he the Herr Nietzsche the master had met at Leipzig? When he said yes, he was asked to wait. On his third appearance the servant invited Nietzsche to come back for lunch. Committed to rejoining some acquaintances, he could not accept and, after disappearing inside the house once more, the servant invited him to come back on Monday.

The villa was like a museum in which the main exhibit was still alive. Rebuilt at the beginning of the century on medieval foundations, the large, square, three-storied house had been redecorated for Wagner in a rococo style, with a great deal of pink satin and many small cupids. In the drawing-room were large busts of Wagner and Ludwig II, an oil painting of Wagner, a *Tannhäuser* picture, and Genelli's *Dionysus among the Muses*. Gifts from the king were prominently displayed, including silver bowls and statues of Tannhäuser and Lohengrin. In what Wagner called his 'gallery' were engravings and photographs of sequences from productions of his operas, and a Buddha given to him by the

Comtesse d'Agoult. The household was large, with four children (Daniela and Blandine von Bülow, and Isolde and Eva Wagner), a governess, a nurse and five servants. They had two dogs, several cats, two peacocks, two horses, sheep and chickens. Wagner habitually dressed in the style of a seventeenth-century Flemish painter, wearing a black velvet coat, black satin breeches, black silk stockings, a tam o'shanter, and a satin cravat tied in a large bow on his lace and linen shirt. But Nietzsche, who was beginning to love this man more than he had ever loved anyone since his father, was in no state to be critical. At the end of the afternoon Wagner presented him with a photograph of himself and invited him to pay another visit. 'He is really everything we hoped he would be, a lavish, rich and great spirit, an energetic character, and an enchantingly likeable man, with a strong craving for knowledge. I must stop or I shall be singing a paean.'[5] Four days after his visit to Tribschen he received a note from Cosima inviting him to return on Saturday to celebrate the Master's birthday with them and to stay the night. Not being free to accept, he wrote an adulatory letter hailing Wagner as Schopenhauer's spiritual brother. This must have pleased Wagner enormously. *Die Welt als Wille und Vorstellung* had become so important to him that he nicknamed himself 'Will' and Cosima 'Vorstell'. Nietzsche's letter was probably the most sycophantic that he ever penned, praising Wagner for his awareness of a spiritual world, an awareness 'we poor Germans have lost in the night through every possible kind of political wretchedness, through philosophical nonsense and through Jewish greediness'.[6] (Some of Nietzsche's letters from Leipzig had contained disparaging remarks about Jewish citizens, and conversation with Wagner and Cosima had already revealed how anti-Semitic they were.)

Of the other lecturers at Basel the most interesting was Jacob Burckhardt, who was Nietzsche's senior by twenty-six years. A native of Basel, he was now in the tenth of his thirty-five years as a professor there. Though best known for *Die Kultur der Renaissance in Italien*, which had been published in 1860, he was also a student of Greek civilization; his influential four-volume history of Greek culture was to be published posthumously. Nietzsche, who attended some of his lectures, had several conversations with him. To Elisabeth he described Burckhardt as 'the person I see a great deal of',[7] and to Sophie Ritschl as 'closer to me' than other colleagues. But, rich though he was, he chose to live in 'the most tasteless parsimony', fraternizing regularly with 'the philistines of Basel' in the pubs.[8] The word 'philistine', picked up from Hölderlin, was to bulk large in Nietzsche's criticism of his contemporaries, as it did in Matthew Arnold's.

The lecture notes Burckhardt prepared in 1868–71 were published posthumously as *Weltgeschichtliche Betrachtungen* (*Reflections on World History*), and it is easy to see why Nietzsche warmed to his Schopenhauerian mockery of the Hegelian idea that a world spirit had been marching rationally through history, that humanity had made progress towards freedom as the mind had become more aware of its own significance. Like Plato, Schopenhauer believed that reality was essentially the same at all times. Burckhardt was echoing him when he said: 'An authentic philosophy of history should concern itself with what constantly *is* and never *develops*.' For him, as for Schopenhauer, history must be pathological, dealing as it did with man and human nature. Disappointing though it was to find that his colleague felt nothing but contempt towards Wagner and his music, Nietzsche would have liked to become his friend; it was the older man who held back. But he was indebted to Nietzsche's insight about contests and competitions in Greek life: their importance is emphasized in his posthumous history of Greek culture.[9]

Burckhardt attended the inaugural lecture Nietzsche delivered on 28 May, speaking to a large audience in the main hall of the museum on 'Homer und die klassische Philologie'. Philology, he said, was not a pure science, but overlapped inextricably with art. 'Life is worth living, says art, the loveliest seductress; life is worth seeing for what it is, says science.' Classical philology must straddle the contradiction, and the philologist's procedure should be neither rigidly scientific nor chaotically unsystematic. The idealization of antiquity probably derived from the German nostalgia for the south, but the classicist should bridge the gap between the ideal and the real.

Six-and-a-half years previously, in the essays he wrote at Pforta on *Wallensteins Lager* and on Kriemhild in *Die Nibelungen*, Nietzsche had explored the relationship between the individual poet and the folk consciousness. His basic feeling had not changed.

It was dangerous, he told his audience, to believe in a polarity between folk poetry and individual poetry. Nothing truly great or far-reaching could be incarnated in anything as weak or short-lived as the individual. 'We have finally become aware of the great mass instincts and the unconscious popular pressures as the real supports and levers of the so-called history of the world.' But it was absurd to credit the masses with poetic genius: poetry always needed the mediation of an individual. 'As the poet of the *Iliad* and the *Odyssey*, Homer is not a historical tradition but an aesthetic judgement.' Individuals had been at the source of both of the Homeric epics. Then came bloating and distortion through oral transmission, and, finally, the systematic completion of both works. 'We believe in the great poet who wrote the *Iliad* and the *Odyssey, but not in Homer as this poet.*' Like Orpheus and Daedalus, Homer was the mythical pioneer of a new art-form.

The credo at the end of Nietzsche's lecture must have surprised his audience: 'All philological activity should be embedded and enclosed in a philosophical *Weltanschauung* so that all individual or isolated details evaporate as things that can be cast away, leaving only the whole, the coherent.' This was unconventional and provocative, but the lecturer was undeniably impressive. 'This inaugural lecture convinced the people here of various things, and it is obvious to me that it has made my appointment secure.'[10]

A few days later Nietzsche received a letter from Wagner, thanking him for the 'beautiful and significant' birthday tribute, and pressing him to spend a weekend at Tribschen. 'Do come—you have only to send me a line in advance. . . . So far my experiences with my fellow-countrymen have not been altogether pleasant. So come and restore my faith in what I, together with Goethe and a few others, call German liberty.'[11] He had not expected Nietzsche to respond so promptly, but, not knowing that Cosima was about to give birth to her baby, he wrote back by return to say that he would come on Saturday. Wagner wanted to put him off, but she felt it was better that he should come.[12] From half-way through Saturday, 5 June the entries in her diary are in Wagner's handwriting: 'A tolerable evening spent with Nietzsche. Said good night about eleven. The labour pains begin.' At one o'clock in the morning she got out of bed to tell the Master, and to insist 'that there should be no change to arrangements for the day, that Nietzsche should stay for lunch with the children'. The midwife arrived at three in the morning, and at four Cosima bore her fifty-six-year-old lover his first son. 'R. felt an urge to demonstrate his joy throughout the house. He had handsome presents given to all the servants.'[13] He stayed with her all morning, leaving at noon to have lunch with Nietzsche and the children. He afterwards considered it a good omen that Siegfried's birth had coincided with his young friend's first overnight visit, while Nietzsche could not have been more impressed with his host: 'He fulfils every wish we could possibly have. The world knows nothing of the human greatness and singularity of his nature. I learn a great deal in his presence: this is my practical course in Schopenhauer's philosophy. The presence of Wagner is my consolation.'[14]

Nietzsche immediately considered himself a member of the Wagner household: 'We live there together, having the most stimulating fun in the most affectionate family circle and without any of the usual social trivialities. For me it is truly a great stroke of luck.'[15] Love is the only word for what Nietzsche felt towards Wagner and towards Rohde, however little he saw of either. Rohde was told: 'Something else we have in common is that we can both bear solitude. Indeed we love it. And when we are together, it is really no duality but a true and authentic monad. It is only then that we are really lonely and cut off from the whole importunate world.'[16] Having no relationship with a woman and only an attenuated relationship with his family, Nietzsche wanted to involve his best friend in his surrogate family: 'It will give him (and me) pleasure if you write to him soon, and at length.'[17]

By the time Nietzsche moved into his lodgings at the end of June or beginning of July, he had grown accustomed to his job. 'The whole thing could not suit me better. It fits like a glove. Yes, I am quite obviously in my natural element. . . . Though it will take a while for my nature to accustom itself fully to this activity. At present I still frequently feel under a great strain.'[18]

His extrovert predecessor, Kiessling, had gone for long walks with six or seven colleagues. Nietzsche seems to have made good use of the *Baedeker* he possessed, but he preferred walking solitarily. 'With my "colleagues" I make a strange discovery: amongst them I feel as I used to amongst students. On the whole I feel no need to concern myself more closely with them, but I feel no envy. To be precise, I am aware of a small grain of contempt for them.'[19]

The summer holidays would bring leisure for expeditions into the mountains, but to his mother he made out that he felt badly in need of a rest: 'the schoolmastering and the daily reading are formidably strenuous, and I am really in dire need of a holiday. But then I must settle down to serious work, since there is much to be done for which I cannot find time in the daily course of the academic routine.'[20] It would be better if she did not come to see him until October, when he would have another fortnight's holiday. But when the term ended he did not greatly relish the prospect of four weeks' freedom. 'The icy mountains are not so very enticing, though it would be a delight to explore the lovely hills of Bavaria and Bohemia once again if I could do so in your company,'[21] he told Rohde.

Though welcome at Tribschen, he did not want to spend as much time with Wagner and Cosima as they would have liked. He was there for the weekend of 31 July to 2 August. 'Visit from Professor Nietzsche,' she wrote in her diary. 'A cultured and pleasant man.'[22] They talked about her father's oratorio *Sainte Elisabeth*, which Wagner did not like, and Nietzsche said: 'It smells more of incense than roses.' (One of the legends of the saint concerns roses.) But on 5 August, when he was climbing Mount Pilatus, she wrote humorously to rebuke him for deserting them in favour of the mountains. If bad weather had confined him to his mountain hotel for three days, it had been 'to punish you for having so little time for Tribschen, and for refusing or being unable to postpone your Pilatus trip even for a single day'.[23] She invited him for the following weekend, but he did not go again until the weekend of 21 to 23 August, though he then returned for the following weekend, when the Brockhauses were staying there. Von Bülow was now divorcing Cosima, who 'sobbed uncontrollably the whole morning' on the Saturday. 'At lunch, the Brockhaus family and Professor Nietzsche, all very kind.'[24]

Wagner, who was starting work on *Götterdämmerung*, was still rising in Nietzsche's estimation: 'With him I feel in the presence of the divine.'[25] Wagner was 'ill with grief'[26] about *Das Rheingold*, which had been completed in 1854. He did not want it to be performed, but he had accepted an income from King Ludwig II when, at the age of eighteen, he had come to the Bavarian throne. Now he was too impatient to wait, and Wagner could not prevent him from mounting the opera in Munich, though he refused to supervise the production. On Saturday, telegrams and letters began to arrive from Munich, reporting that the dress rehearsal had been disastrous. Wagner sent a telegram to the king demanding a postponement of the opening, and on Sunday a telegram arrived from him, thanking Wagner for his birthday present but ignoring the demand. Another telegram arrived from the conductor, Hans Richter, saying that he had resigned, and another telegram from the Weimar theatre director, Loën, who was in Munich, asking whether his conductor, Lassen, could take over. In the evening the news arrived that Richter had not resigned but had been suspended by the management because of his refusal to conduct unless the scenery was improved. Wagner and Cosima can have been in no state to concentrate on the needs of their house-guests.

Writing to Gustav Krug, the first Wagnerian he had known, Nietzsche called his days at Tribschen 'certainly the most valuable result of my professorship at Basel'.[27] Wagner had recommended such neglected German classicists as Otfried Müller, Friedrich Creutzer and Friedrich Welcker; Nietzsche was then able to borrow their books from the library in Basel and make extracts in his notebooks. More important, Wagner had shown him some of his early aesthetic and philosophical essays, which would exert a strong influence on *Die Geburt der Tragödie*. At school in Dresden, Wagner had been so excited by Greek mythology that his teacher, Sillig, wanted him to become a classicist. Like the schoolboy Nietzsche, he had come to love the Icelandic sagas and Teutonic legends, which were eventually to be his sources for *Der Ring*, and had seen them in a perspective formed by the Greek cult of the heroic. Even the nationalist element in Wagner's work may derive partly from his early study of Greek civilization and his early identification with Greek heroes. He believed in art as an expression of national consciousness: poetry was distilled out of a collective experience of crisis.

Before beginning on the music of *Das Rheingold* in 1854, Wagner had evolved his theory of opera as a *Gesamtkunstwerk*, a union of all the arts. In 'Die Kunst und die Revolution' (1849) he argued that Greek theatre was a focus of communal life and that all the individual arts had been components of tragedy, which, at its best, was the highest form of art. The achievement of the Greek tragedians had never been surpassed or equalled, because subsequently the arts had separated. In the classical drama 'every artistic impulse stood still before philosophy', but the two thousand years which had followed 'belong to philosophy and not to art'. Wagner's aim, therefore, would be to reunite theatre with music and the other arts.

In 'Das Kunstwerk der Zukunft' ('The Art-Work of the Future'), published in 1850, Wagner put forward the argument that Nietzsche had been attacking in his inaugural lecture without knowing that Wagner was one of its champions: that the individual artist is only the mouthpiece for the genius that resides in the masses, who must be alerted to their redemptive mission. They must restore to art the instinctive laws of Nature. In the art of the future, cooperation between musician, poet, painter, actor and architect must give expression to the underlying genius of the people. Discussing Homer, Wagner presented speculations as if they were facts: before these 'epic songs' were written down, they had 'flourished among the people as a physically enacted art-work, reinforced with voice and gesture'. Nevertheless, when Nietzsche gave him a printed copy of his inaugural lecture, Wagner made Cosima reply: 'Herr Wagner gratefully wishes to say that he can only concur with all your views on aesthetic questions, and in regard to the subject of the lecture he congratulates you on having correctly posed the problem, which is indeed the beginning and perhaps the end of all wisdom, though it is usually ignored.'[28]

Wagner's 'Oper und Drama' (1851) contended that the fallacy of opera had been to make a means of expression (music) into an end, and the end of expression (drama) into a means. He was discussing Meyerbeer, but thinking, no doubt, about his own forthcoming cycle of operas when he wrote: 'Thus the operatic composer became, in the full sense, the redeemer of the world, while the profoundly inspired composer, irresistibly exalted by self-lacerating visionary zeal, must be acknowledged as the modern Messiah.'

Nietzsche had already been quoting from 'Oper und Drama' during his first term's lectures,[29] and by the end of September 1869, when he began making notes for two public lectures he was to deliver early in the new year, Wagner's ideas were altering his view of Greek tragedy:

Today, speaking or hearing about Aeschylus, Sophocles, Euripides, everyone automatically thinks of them as poets of literature, because he has come to know them through *books*, in the original or in translation. But this is more or less like mentioning *Tannhäuser* and meaning only the libretto. These men should be discussed not as librettists but as opera composers.

The notes go on to dismiss French tragedy as artificial, but to credit German tragedy with Dionysiac roots. Drama had its origins in the ecstasy of carnivals. Nietzsche quotes from Wagner's architect friend Gottfried Semper: 'The dimness of carnival candle-light is the true atmosphere of art.'[30] He follows Wagner in insisting on the pagan quality of art. Admiration for beauty, Wagner had argued in 'Kunst und Revolution', was essentially non-Christian. Aphoristically, Nietzsche writes: 'The development of operatic melody is heathenness in music.' The next aphorism is 'Absolute music and everyday drama: two splintered pieces of music-drama'. The whole tenor of the notes is Wagnerian, and it is on this matrix that Nietzsche conceived the idea for his first book: that tragedy is born from the soul of music. The seminal entry in his notebook was: 'Music as mother of tragedy.'

He had been paid at the beginning of July for his first three months' work, but his salary for the second half of the year was not due until 1 January, so by the end of August he was short of money. He wrote asking Elisabeth to cash a state security bond for him, but she was away from Naumburg, and the letter was read by their mother, who could not stop herself from writing him an admonitory letter about the importance of saving money from his salary. He replied tersely: 'N.B. I must ask you to reconsider whether the expressions and observations in this letter were *appropriate*. F.N.'[31]

His conversion to vegetarianism was very abrupt. Carl von Gersdorff had eaten no meat for three months when, on 8 September 1869, he wrote to Nietzsche from Berlin, enclosing two pamphlets. His letter told the story of a doctor who had been suffering acutely from piles until, one-and-a-half years ago, he had given up meat. 'Now, as he says himself, he feels as well as a god.'[32] Nietzsche, who had been having digestive troubles,[33] found that he felt better on a diet of bread, milk, soup, grapes and other fruit; but when he spent the weekend of 18–19 September in Tribschen, his sapling vegetarianism, which had scarcely taken root, had to weather a hurricane of Wagnerian argument. Wagner had not only experimented with a meatless diet, he had seen a friend die of it, and he was convinced that he would not be alive himself if he had persisted. Nietzsche told Wagner that he had taken a vegetarian oath, but by the end of the month he was eating meat again. 'The rule yielded by experience in this area is that intellectually productive and emotionally intense natures *must* have meat. The other way of life is for pastry-cooks and peasants, who are nothing but digesting machines.'[34]

Bracketing vegetarianism with socialism and cremation, he saw it as optimistically inconsistent with Schopenhauerian principles, 'as if happiness and harmony could be achieved merely by extirpating a sinful and unnatural phenomenon. Whereas our sublime philosophy teaches that whatever we grasp at, we come in contact with sheer perdition, the pure Will to Life, and here all palliatives are pointless.' While conceding that respect for animals was a noble trait, he depicted Nature as a cruel and immoral goddess who had implanted carnivorous instincts in those who live in colder climates. In hot countries men could follow the vegetarian regimen of the monkeys.

Though the university term ended on 25 September, Nietzsche had to go on teaching at the Pädagogium until 3 October, when he was expecting his mother and sister to visit him in Basel. But at the end of September he was disconcerted to receive a telegram saying they were not coming. His mother had become nervous about the weather in the Swiss mountains. What was it, Nietzsche demanded – clairvoyance or pessimism?[35] But since he would not be going home for Christmas, when he would have only six days of holiday, he decided to spend ten or twelve days there now. They should remember, though, that apart from working on the index he had to prepare his lectures for next term.

As a teacher he was conscientious and concerned. His students often came to him for advice,[36] and he was gratified when the best three of them went on to Leipzig. But learning was integral to teaching, and by the middle of July he had made up his mind to lecture on subjects he wanted to study.[37] For his public lectures he could work out part of an aesthetic system.[38] Using Wagner as a model, it should be possible to overturn the aesthetic theories of Lessing, whose presuppositions were inimical to the notion of the *Gesamtkunstwerk*. Nietzsche was now convinced that, just as Schopenhauer was the greatest philosopher since Plato, Wagner represented the highest point in the evolution of modern music. If the function of music was to arouse emotion and to express what would otherwise remain unconscious and ineffable, German Romanticism had advanced beyond the achievements of Bach and Beethoven. Music had become less abstract, more poetic, but, because of the separation of the arts, the whole development of modern music was artificial.[39] Wagner was not only the greatest Romantic composer: as a poet and dramatist, he was the artist who could reunite music with drama – a momentous cultural achievement which would have the effect of bringing art and philosophy together again after two thousand years of divorce. If this was true, no praise could possibly be too high. 'The *greatest genius* and *greatest man* of this age, totally incommensurable.'[40] 'Schopenhauer and Goethe, Aeschylus and Pindar are still alive – believe me.'[41]

Nietzsche's misgivings about contemporary culture had to be reinterpreted in the light of his conversion to Wagner's theory. 'Unfortunately we have become accustomed to enjoying the arts individually: madness of art galleries and concert halls. The *absolute arts* are a pathetic modern non-art.'[42] The best contemporary analogy for the ancient music-drama was the Catholic Mass, which was enacted symbolically – not in narrative terms. 'This alone can give us an impression of the pleasures of theatre-going in the time of Aeschylus, though everything was then much brighter, sunnier, more trusting, clearer; indeed also less inward, intense, mystically infinite.'[43]

Nietzsche attempted a definition of art in Schopenhauerian terms: 'Reproducing the world of will without investing the product with willpower. So it is a matter of *instinctively* using the will to manufacture the will-less. ... Music is fundamentally symbolic of impulses which are understandable to everyone as such in their simplest forms (tempo, rhythm). It is also always more generalized than any single plot. Therefore it is more comprehensible to us than any single plot. Music is the key to drama.'[44]

Though Nietzsche spent little time at Tribschen during the autumn, Cosima kept him informed by letter of the events surrounding the première of *Das Rheingold*, while he kept her in touch with what was appearing in the newspapers about the quarrel between Wagner and Ludwig II. Wagner had made a secret journey to Munich, where the king refused to receive him, but agreed, through his secretary, to a postponement of the opening. Franz Wullner took over as conductor, and Wagner's disaffection was expressed in the pamphlet 'Über das Dirigieren' ('On Conducting'). The opera was premièred on 22 September.

Feeling that the whole world was hostile to 'the Master', Cosima was reluctant to leave Tribschen. For three months before the Christmas he shared with them, Nietzsche was asked to do her a series of favours. The first was to locate a portrait of Adolph Wagner, Richard's uncle, who had probably given it to his maid-servant in Leipzig. Nietzsche enlisted the help of his sister, who was now studying at Leipzig University, and she tracked down the picture, which Cosima wanted to buy as a Christmas present for Wagner. Nietzsche also had to go shopping for her in Basel whenever she could not buy what she needed in Lucerne. He had to find a Dürer engraving, some antiques, and a selection of Greek and Latin texts. He was to have the Greek books bound in reddish-brown, and the Latin classics in yellowish-brown, both with leather backs and marbled endpapers. He was to find toys, dolls and a toy theatre. He took his tasks seriously. The king provided with the toy theatre did not strike him as sufficiently regal or the devil as sufficiently black. Dissatisfied with the robes of all the Christmas angels on sale in Basel, he ordered one from Paris.[45]

On Christmas Eve he helped Cosima to set up the puppet theatre, and in the morning she read to him from Wagner's draft of *Parsifal*, afterwards noting in her diary: 'Renewed feelings of awe.' This must refer to her own impression, since Nietzsche's was not being renewed. Afterwards the Master philosophized 'sublimely' about the history of music: she hoped he would write down what he said. Nietzsche may have been surprised by the religious tone of the libretto, but his general feeling towards his surrogate family remained extremely positive. 'My true refuge here, which I cannot sufficiently praise, is still Tribschen, near Lucerne. . . . I spent the Christmas holiday there – most beautiful and elevating memory.'[46]

He was slow in writing to thank them for their hospitality, and Wagner was not slow to rebuke him. 'My dear Friend! Your silence strikes me as strange: it is to be hoped that you will soon dispel this feeling.'[47] He went on to ask a favour. Some family letters sent to him for a Christmas present had revealed a chronological mistake in his autobiography, which was already in proof. Would Nietzsche go through the proofs for him, correcting all chronological and typographical errors?

The tone of Nietzsche's correspondence with Rohde, who was in Rome, had become more loving than ever. In November Rohde had written: 'Every day, dear friend, I yearn for your presence, morning, noon and evening. What an existence we would want to have together. It would be like writing poetry, as Jean Paul puts it, not with a pen but with our whole being and life, our whole essence resounding like passionate music.'[48] Nietzsche was hardly less rapturous:

> Now I will say one really urgent thing to you. Think about living with *me* for a time on your way back; you know, it could be the last chance for a long time. I miss you so much it is incredible: give me the comfort of your presence and take care that it is not too brief. It is really a new sensation for me to have *no one at all* on the spot to whom the best and the most difficult things in life can be told. . . . In such a hermit-like situation in such young and difficult years, my friendship is really becoming pathological. As a sick man entreats, I entreat you: 'Come to Basel!'[49]

It was not, of course, a new sensation for him: similar complaints are to be found in earlier letters from Pforta, Bonn, Leipzig and the army. The hermit simile recurs in a February 1870 letter to Paul Deussen: 'It is our lot to be intellectual hermits and occasionally to have a conversation with someone like-minded.'[50] But there is an unmistakable admixture of love for solitude in his hatred of it. Letters were more and more becoming a satisfying substitute for conversation, and the pressure that made him pick up his pen was relieved before he put it down. A letter could then remain unposted, as the one to Rohde did for over two weeks. The mid-February postscript began, 'I am now very anxious about whether your letters are reaching me, and mine you: I have heard nothing since November.'

He went on to report that the public lecture on 'Sokrates und die Tragödie' had 'aroused fear and incomprehension'. Taken together, the two public lectures can be regarded as a rough draft for *Die Geburt der Tragödie*. In 'Das griechische Musik-drama' Nietzsche suggested that the chorus of men dressed as satyrs had been a pointer to the sufferings of Dionysus. Later the god was introduced, so that he could tell the story of his adventures while exciting the chorus of followers to passionate involvement. During the choruses the actor would represent the living statue of the god. 'Indeed, the antique actor has something of Mozart's stone guest about him.'[51] The emphasis of the drama had been on suffering, not action, and we should imagine the dialogue sung in semi-recitative. The function of the music was to arouse sympathy in the public for the sufferings of the gods and the heroes.

In the second lecture, 'Sokrates und die Tragödie', Nietzsche blamed Socrates and Euripides for the decline of Greek tragedy. The characters of Aeschylus and Sophocles had been profounder than the words they spoke. The playwrights had not been afraid of mystery, but Euripides was the poet of Socratic rationalism. The playwright's principle – 'to be beautiful, everything must be known' – was parallel to the philosopher's principle: 'to be good, everything must be known'. Socratism looked down on instinct, and therefore on art. In all fertile minds, the unconscious was creative and affirmative, the conscious mind critical and restrictive; in Socrates instinct was critical, consciousness the creator. The next step was for Plato, his disciple, to deride the poet's creativity, to deny him the power of seeing into the true essence of things. It was significant that Socrates was the first great Greek to be ugly. Everything about him was symbolic. He was the father of logic, the exterminator of Greek music-drama.

Everything that Nietzsche took from Wagner could be fitted comfortably within a Schopenhauerian framework. Tragedy was essentially pessimistic, representing existence as frightful and humanity as absurd; dialectic was essentially optimistic, postulating connections between cause and consequence, guilt and punishment, virtue and happiness. Socrates optimistically equated know-

ledge with virtue, and in this atmosphere the tragic hero, stumbling in ignorance, is liable to forfeit our sympathy. Unlike Antigone, Oedipus, and Elektra, the Euripidean hero can amount to no more than what he says. Abruptly, at the end of the lecture, Nietzsche asked whether music-drama was really dead. This was the 'most serious artistic question' of the time.

No longer needing to prove himself, as he had in his inaugural lecture fourteen months earlier, Nietzsche was giving two assured public performances in a role he had been rehearsing ever since his schoolboy lectures to the synod of Germania. But he no longer saw himself merely as a lecturer: he was simultaneously casting himself in a more heroic role as the champion of Wagnerian opera, and he dropped carefully worded hints of the possibility that tragic music-drama could be revived in Germany. The audience-provocation in the lectures was carefully calculated: with encouragement from Wagner and Cosima, Nietzsche began to think of writing a book on the same subject as the second lecture. It would not achieve its purpose unless it unsettled its public, so he was cultivating his aphoristic style, and he was not displeased to report that the lecture 'has been taken for a chain of paradoxes'.[52]

What this meant was that the style of his notes had survived in the end-product. He had been making copious jottings which correspond in manner to the decision he had made in April 1867 to write more as if he were improvising at the piano. The book *Die Geburt der Tragödie*, which was first submitted to a publisher in April 1871, consists of about 38,000 words, based on roughly 100,000 words of unpublished notes written between the autumn of 1869 and the spring of 1871.

Nietzsche's method of composition was Schopenhauerian. *Die Welt als Wille und Vorstellung* was written between 1814 and 1818, but the preliminary notes were begun earlier. 'Under my hands,' Schopenhauer wrote in 1813, 'and still more in my mind, a work is growing, a philosophy that will combine ethics with metaphysics, which have previously been dichotomized as fallaciously as man has into body and soul.' He went on jotting down ideas as they occurred to him, confident that they were all rising from 'a single foundation', and would therefore cohere. He said that his system was developing like a child growing inside its mother's womb.

Nietzsche similarly noted down ideas as they occurred. Like Schopenhauer he could write better prose than any earlier philosopher in the German language. They both despised Hegel's prose and, consciously or unconsciously, they both depended partly on style to unite heterogeneous material.

Writing the notes, Nietzsche did not need to worry about structure, but it was already his ambition to break down the barriers between creative and critical writing. Polarized by Wagner and the idea of the *Gesamtkunstwerk*, he would go on – long after his rejection of Wagner – trying to combine philosophy with poetry, fact with creative fiction. His best books are uncategorizable. An early note attacking 'the conventional distinction between creative and critical natures'[53] shows how irked he was by the assumption that great artists belonged to a different species of men from great thinkers. In both, he insisted, 'the quite infallible wisdom of their instincts' enabled them 'to discover authenticity and truth under unattractive coverings'. Behind the argument was a strong personal pressure. Though, consciously, he was content to recognize Wagner as a paragon of artistic genius, superior to all his contemporaries, Oedipal forces were at play. Cosima, whom Nietzsche liked and admired more than any other woman, was his senior by only six years, and she had borne three children to a man as old as his father would have been and only two years younger than her own father. But it was not until nineteen years later, when Wagner was dead and Nietzsche was mad, that he addressed a love-letter to her. Towards Wagner, Nietzsche was not conscious of feeling envy, only loving admiration, but he had sacrificed his artistic ambitions on the altar of philology and had become impotent as a composer, while Wagner was still at the height of his powers, translating libidinal impulses into massive surges of throbbingly sensual operatic sound, with a king to act as his producer. There was no possibility for Nietzsche to set himself up as a rival to his surrogate father. At most he could aspire to a mastery over words comparable to Wagner's mastery over music, but he was masochistically disparaging words as inferior. 'Language signifies only through concepts, so sympathy arises through the medium of thought. This sets a limitation on it.'[54] Written language, in which music played no part, was more limited than spoken language, in which pauses, rhythm, tempo,

volume and emphasis 'are all symbolical of the emotional content to be communicated. The great preponderance of emotions cannot be expressed through words. Words can do no more than indicate. They are the rippling surface of the lake, while turbulence rages in its depths.' (Schopenhauer had written: 'Consciousness is the mere surface of the mind, of which, as of the earth, we do not know the inside but only the crust.')

Nietzsche's devaluation of the word may strike us as modern, but he was only developing the views of Schopenhauer, for whom music represented the fullest development of the aesthetic. Nietzsche even made the Schopenhauerian point that self-oblivion was the starting-point for both dramatic and epic art.[55] The individual will was extinguished in the process of empathizing with the characters. 'Dramatic art arises out of a strong drive – belief in the impossible, the wonderful: a higher grade of emotion than in epic, whose whole inheritance it takes over.' His reaction to the St Matthew Passion was similarly Schopenhauerian. During the last week in April he heard three performances of it, 'each time with the same feeling of boundless wonder. Whoever is fully cured of Christianity can really listen to it as to an Evangelist. This is music of the negation of the will, without any reminder of asceticism.'

The provocative aphorisms in the notebooks could excite only Nietzsche himself. He was outraging the part of his mind that demanded a scholarly accuracy worthy of Ritschl. In his cult of the paradoxical he was generalizing and simplifying, but he was also rehearsing for the book, which would make more impact if it broke with convention not only in its substance but in its form. The other advantage of writing aphoristically in these notes was that he could trap slippery insights which he did not fully understand and could not have substantiated discursively. In these paradoxes are the seeds of his later philosophy. He was laying an almost insane strain on himself, rejecting Hegelian optimism and moving gradually away from Schopenhauerian pessimism towards a negativism which would have no bounds.

Pessimism is possible only in the realm of *concepts*. Existence would be intolerable without faith in the necessity of the historical process. This is the great illusion: the will holds us gripped inside existence, turning each of our convictions into an opinion that makes existence possible. This is the reason that faith in providence is so ineradicable. It tides us over evil. Hence belief in immortality.[56]

To identify Absolute Spirit with the inner logic of history, Hegel had argued that cruelty, destruction and decadence were integral to the process by which the past had worked its way towards the revelation of spirit in the present. But his view of consciousness was discordantly pessimistic. Though synthesis was positive, the movement of thought towards it was negation of negation. The German word *aufheben* means both 'cancel' and 'preserve'; Hegel used it in both senses simultaneously. Just as Adam, when he coined names for the animals, had deprived them of their reality as separate existing beings, the mind could become perfect thought, annihilating the reality of the world in the variety of its determinations. So consciousness became a negating force. Early in his unpublished notes of 1870 Nietzsche arrived at a similar position:

Complete understanding kills activity: indeed if it is directed inwards on the faculty of understanding, it kills itself. If one is fully aware of what is involved in moving a limb, one can no longer move it. But full awareness is *impossible*, so activity remains possible. Consciousness is a screw with no end: at each moment it is applied, an infinity begins, so it can never be brought into action. . . .

The object of knowledge is the annihilation of the world. Conversely, the immediate effect of a small dose of opium is to intensify one's affirmation of the world. Politically we are now at this stage. . . .

The task of art is to annihilate the state. This happened in Greece. Later, knowledge dissolves art. (So for a time it seems as though state and knowledge collaborate – age of the sophists, our age.)

There must be no war, so that the newly awakened feeling for the state can go back to sleep.[57]

In the thinking of the mature Nietzsche there is nothing that can accurately be described as Fascist, but at this phase of his development Wagner's racist nationalism was undeniably influencing him more than Schopenhauer's had, and he began to use the word 'German' as Wagner did, implying the possibility of a heroic future in line with the legendary past:

I always keep two thoughts in mind. The incredible seriousness and the German profundity in Wagner's attitude to life and art, which well up out of each note he writes, are to most people of 'today' as much of an abomination as Schopenhauer's ascetism and negation of the will. Our 'Jews' – and you know how wide-ranging that concept is – are especially hostile to Wagner's idealistic manner, which gives him his strongest affinity with Schiller; this glowing, high-minded struggle for the 'day of nobility' ['*Tag der Edlen*'][58] finally to arrive – in short the chivalric, which would hardly be more opposed to our daily diet of plebeian political hullaballoo.[59]

Writing in this Wagnerian style to von Gersdorff, Nietzsche tried to encourage him, as previously he had encouraged Rohde, to communicate with the Master by letter. *Die Meistersinger* was to be premièred in Berlin on 1 April 1870, and if von Gersdorff felt inclined, afterwards, 'to write a detailed letter to R. Wagner . . . it will be a source of great delight, and he will already have been informed about who the writer of the letter is'.[60] Nietzsche succeeded in establishing communication between them, and in a letter written at the beginning of July he promised von Gersdorff that he would soon receive a photograph of Wagner.[61]

At the end of May, Rohde, who had not seen his friend for nearly three years, came to Basel. He had planned to spend a week there, but Nietzsche, whose mother and sister were coming for the Whit weekend, persuaded him to stay on. Together they made expeditions to the Bernese Oberland, to Interlaken, Wengernalp and Lauterbrunnen. After returning to Basel, Rohde wrote:

Here we are living very happily in the past. It is a resumption of those blissful days in Leipzig, when, cocooned from the whole world, we gave ourselves to mutual stimulation, strengthening each other. Unfortunately Nietzsche is so inordinately overburdened with work this term that only a few hours of the day remain over for us.[62]

They spent an evening with Jacob Burckhardt, and they went to Tribschen. For Rohde, Nietzsche reported, this visit had been 'the high point of all his fifteen months of travelling "into the blue" '.[63] He had admired 'the whole way of life there, which is imbued with something religious. The presence of the gods in the house of genius awakens the religious mood I am describing.' Nietzsche had lost his faith but not his need to worship. To Rohde he was able to report that Cosima had written: 'We have a very pleasant memory of these days; the Master took a great liking to your friend. His manly seriousness, his committed involvement, and the genuine friendliness which sometimes lit up his stern features, he found thoroughly likeable.'

Nietzsche was half-way through writing this letter to Rohde when he heard that France had declared war on Prussia. 'A frightful thunderclap . . . our whole threadbare culture is toppling, with the ghastliest demon at its throat.'[64] At least Switzerland was neutral. 'If your life now becomes intolerable, come back to me here. We may already be at the beginning of the end. What a wilderness it is!'[65] He signed the letter 'The loyal Swiss'. But the same day, writing to his mother, he said: 'I am distressed to be Swiss! Our culture is at stake! So no sacrifice could be great enough!'[66] In thinking of culture he was thinking partly of Wagner's bid for a reunification of the arts, but one of his main anxieties was whether war might destroy cultural traditions.[67]

Though there was popular support for the war in France, it could have been avoided but for Bismarck's determination not to miss the opportunity. As he said, 'Politics is not a logical science; it is a capacity for choosing, at each moment, in constantly changing situations, the least harmful, the most useful.' He had not planned for this war as he had for the Austrian war, but he knew that nationalism had to be boosted if Germany was to be unified, and that in any case he would not be able to incorporate the southern states into the *Reich* without opposition from France. Already Napoleon III was anxious about the balance of European power, though he would have preferred to adjust it by peaceful negotiation.

Nearly four years had elapsed without any major eruption of violence, and though Nietzsche had been aware, only two years earlier, that another war was inevitable, he had lapsed into assuming that the situation was stable. The quarrel between France and Prussia over the Spanish succession was not the real cause of the war, though it provided a pretext. The Queen of Spain, Isabella II, had fled into exile in September 1869. One of the candidates for the throne was Prince Leopold of Hohenzollern-Sigmaringen, a relation of Wilhelm I, and when news reached France that Leopold had accepted the throne, French public opinion was in favour of seizing an opportunity to avenge the humiliation of Sadowa. Even after Leopold had given up his claim, mutual diplomatic provocations continued quite loudly, but they would not have led to war if Bismarck had not exploited the influence of the newspapers to make it inevitable. 'A statesman can create nothing for himself,' he said. 'He must wait attentively until he hears the steps of God sounding through events, then leap up and grasp the hem of his garment.' Having now heard the steps, he had leapt boldly, and taken a firm grip.

When war was declared, the immediate problem for Nietzsche was what to do with his sister. In the middle of June their mother had gone back to Germany to help a bedridden sister, and since the declaration of war the railway system had been in chaos, with constant crowds of arrivals at the Swiss stations, and German trains requisitioned for moving troops. He could not send Elisabeth back to Naumburg on her own, and, wanting to withdraw into the mountains for a few days, he took her with him from Lucerne to Brunnen on a steamer, then on to Morschach-Axenstein, above Lake Vierwaldstätt, where they stayed in a large hotel. After a week there, he took her to Tribschen for her first meeting with Wagner and Cosima, who had just been divorced from von Bülow. Nietzsche and Elisabeth went on into the Maderaner Valley, staying at a hotel 1,300 metres above sea level. Here he wrote an essay, 'Die dionysische Weltanschauung' ('The Dionysian Attitude'), going a step beyond his public lectures towards *Die Geburt der Tragödie*. Thanks to Schopenhauer, he argued, it was now possible to come closer to the spirit of Greek tragedy than ever before.[68]

Staying at the same hotel was a German landscape painter, Adolf Mosengel, who appears to have catalysed Nietzsche's decision not to take advantage of his Swiss citizenship. According to Elisabeth's melodramatic narrative, the two men had been walking to and fro for a long time before her brother, pale and solemn, came to ask her what she would do if she were a man. She would go to the war, she said, sobbing, but her life mattered less than his. It was his duty, he said, to volunteer for service, and if the university authorities would not allow him to become a soldier, he could serve as an ambulance attendant. Accordingly, he wrote to Vischer-Bilfinger. 'To the Swiss education authorities it will no doubt seem natural and proper that I *must* contribute my small share to the

Fatherland's alms-box, according to my ability. . . . After the great appeal from Germany that each man should do his *German* duty, it could be only under painful compulsion – and to little real effect – that I could allow myself to be kept in Basel by my commitments.'

He was given leave of absence to serve as a medical orderly, and together with Mosengel, he was sent to Erlangen for a ten-day training course, which started on 13 August 1870. (Nietzsche was undeterred by a letter from Cosima pointing out that the ambulance corps was as well organized as the army, and that a gift of a hundred cigars would have been of more value than the presence of a dilettante, which would most likely be a hindrance.)[69]

Every morning from eight-thirty till ten, the trainees were taught how to dress and bandage wounds, and they came into close contact with maimed and bleeding bodies when a train arrived on 20 August carrying wounded Prussians, Frenchmen and Turks.

Telegram from the king today about the decisive victory under his leadership. We just chloroformed a Frenchman for a plaster-of-Paris dressing (the hand is shattered; under the anaesthetic he called out '*Mon Dieu mon Dieu* I am coming.') Before that a girl of eleven, to save her leg from amputation. A few days earlier in a house, a boy with a big head-wound chloroformed; great trouble. Yesterday a Prussian died in hospital, shot in the lung, today a second. A Prussian, Liebig, in a good state: healthy appetite, a good night's sleep, but little hope, arm-bone splintered, impossible to dress with plaster of Paris. We like the Turks, good patients.[70]

Better equipped and better organized than the French troops, the Prussians, led by von Moltke, were making their superiority felt. The two French commanders, Macmahon and Bazaine, were not collaborating effectively. On 6 August Macmahon was forced to retreat, while Bazaine's army was encircled at Metz. Instead of withdrawing to defend Paris, Macmahon was sent to relieve Bazaine. He reached Sedan on 30 August, but penetrated no further.

Four days after leaving Erlangen, Nietzsche had an 'eleven-hour march to carry out our missions in Gersdorf and Langensülzbach, and on the battlefield of Wörth. With this letter follows a memory of the fearfully devastated battlefield, mournfully bespattered everywhere with human remains, and reeking pungently of corpses.'[71] Three days later, at the battle of Sedan, the French army was routed, and the next day Napoleon, who was there with Macmahon, gave himself up. The defeat caused a revolt in Paris, where a republic was proclaimed and a provisional government set up. The new foreign minister, Jules Favre, announced: 'We will not surrender an inch of our territory, or a stone of our fortresses.'

On 2 September, Nietzsche and Mosengel, who had been together all this time, were sent to Ars-sur-Moselle, where they were put on a hospital train to accompany wounded soldiers to the hospital in Karlsruhe. The journey lasted for two days and two nights. 'I had a wretched cattle-truck, with six severely wounded men in it, and I was alone with them for all that time, bandaging them, nursing them, etc.'[72] 'The weather was bad, and the truck had to be kept shut or the patients would have been soaked.'[73] 'They all had shattered bones; several had four wounds. I could also see that two of them had gangrene. It now seems like a marvel that I could survive those pestilential fumes, even managing to sleep and eat.'[74] Hildebrandt conjectures that the syphilitic infection could have originated from contact with the wounded men, but it is not probable. By the time he arrived in Karlsruhe he was feeling very ill. With difficulty he went on to Erlangen, where he was put in bed. A doctor diagnosed both severe dysentery and diphtheria. 'They have so enfeebled and incapacitated me in this short time that I must first of all give up my plans to work as a medical auxiliary.'[75] After a week in bed he was sent to convalesce in Naumburg, but for several days he had been treated with silver nitrate, opium and tannic acid enemas – the normal treatment at this time. And after the training at Erlangen, which had given him an elementary knowledge of drugs and their uses, he took to giving himself doses whenever he felt they would do him good.

By the middle of October he was using work as a means of clearing gruesome memories from his mind. He involved himself in questions of rhythm and metre in Greek verse, preparing lectures for the coming term.[76] He left Naumburg on 21 October. 'All through the second day of the journey I had to battle against vomiting. On the first day I arrived in Frankfurt about midnight, frozen through. I arrived at my lodgings about eight o'clock in the evening of the second day, and immediately ordered lime-blossom tea. Even today I am not yet feeling well.'[77] But he applied himself to work as if it were therapeutic. 'I have plunged into the sciences with true greed, and my professional routine has begun again. My only wish would be for better health. But my whole constitution suffered a great deal under the attack of dysentery, and it is still a long way from having regained what it lost.' After leaving this letter to von Gersdorff unfinished for a few days, he resumed: 'The new term began as usual with a torrent of work which was both deafening and blinding.' He was teaching two new courses – one on Hesiod and the other on Greek rhythm and metre 'according to my own system'. In the middle of October he had had the insight he was to describe as 'the best philological inspiration I have ever had'.[78] He had become convinced that there was no stress accent in Greek verse: word accents were retained, and time quantities were variable. In the long term this was to be one of his main contributions to classical studies.[79]

He now had an audience of twelve. He continued his seminars, his Greek lessons at the Pädagogium, going to meetings and the social occasions he could not avoid. At Burckhardt's weekly lectures on the study of history, Nietzsche believed himself to be the only one of the sixty listeners who fully understood them.[80] 'This elderly, highly idiosyncratic man is inclined not to falsify the truth, but to be silent about it. But in confidential conversations when we go out walking, he calls Schopenhauer "our philosopher".' Listening to him lecture on Hegel's philosophy of history, Nietzsche felt that he was hearing a lecture he might himself have given, had he been older.[81]

The character of the war had changed. France was struggling to defend her frontiers; Prussia was fighting with predatory aggressiveness. At the end of October Bazaine and his army surrendered at Metz and the Germans advanced irresistibly through the north of France, but Paris held out against siege for much longer than Bismarck had expected. There was no serious danger of intervention from Russia, Great Britain, Italy, or even Austria-Hungary, but he wanted a quick peace, and he would have been satisfied if the provisional French government had agreed to give up Metz, together with Strasbourg, which surrendered to the Prussian army a day later.

Nietzsche, who had been so happy about the victory over Austria in 1866, felt very anxious now, especially about cultural continuity. 'Confidentially, I consider the Prussia of today to be one of the powers most dangerous of all to culture. . . . We must be sufficiently philosophical to keep calm in the general pandemonium, so that no thief comes to steal or damage what, in my view, cannot be compared with great military deeds or even with any nationalistic outpouring.'[82] He advised Rohde to escape from 'that fatal, anti-cultural Prussia, where slaves and priests sprout like mushrooms. Soon they will darken the whole of Germany for us with their vapours.'[83] He wrote notes for a play to be called *Empedokles*. His memories of Hölderlin's *Empedokles* had been refreshed by references to him in Diogenes Laertius, and an earlier entry in his notebooks singles out Empedocles as the pure tragic man, helplessly divided between the religious promptings of his soul and the rational promptings of his mind. 'His leap into Etna out of – thirst for knowledge. He longed for art and found only knowledge. But knowledge makes Fausts.'[84] The conception is sub-Wagnerian, simultaneously intellectualizing and melodramatizing the myth. Empedocles' pleasure in art is soured by his awareness of the people's suffering, but after studying suffering like an anatomist, he becomes a tyrant. In a mad scene, staged at the edge of a crater on Mount Etna, he preaches to the assembled crowds about resurrection. They worship him as Dionysus, and, hoping to be resurrected, he throws himself into the volcano. In the final act, he and Korinna, the heroine, are two streams of lava. (The closeness of Korinna's name to Cosima's cannot be accidental.)

After five weeks in Basel, Nietzsche paid his first visit to Tribschen since her marriage to Wagner, which had quickly followed her divorce. Nietzsche had already read Wagner's essay 'Beethoven', and his reaction to it had been to equate 'your philosophy of music' with '*the* philosophy of music'.[85] He was especially excited about the affinity between Wagner's ideas and his own essay on the Dionysian attitude: 'Through this preliminary study I have arrived at the point of understanding – completely and with profound pleasure – the necessity of your line of argument. . . . I feel that to contemporary aestheticians you will seem like a somnambulist. . . . I should think that to follow you, as thinker, in this case is possible only for those to whom *Tristan* has yielded up its secrets.'[86]

What Nietzsche needed, above all, was to feel that a new movement was under way, connecting music, philosophy and classical philology within a triangular field of forces. At one point of the triangle was the revaluation of Schopenhauer, which was long overdue. At another was Wagner's music, which was bound, sooner or later, to win recognition. The third point Nietzsche aimed to occupy himself. 'Give me a few more vears,' he wrote to von Gersdorff, 'and then you should also notice a new influence on classical studies, connected, I hope, with a new spirit in the scientific and ethical *education* of our nation.'[87] His vocation was to teach, but he did not intend to go on indefinitely working in a university. 'Nothing truly revolutionary can start here. We can become real *teachers* only afterwards, by making every effort to lever ourselves out of this atmosphere, becoming not only wiser but, above all, *better* men. Here, too, I feel, above all, the need to be *true*. . . . So one day we will cast off this yoke – for *me* that is quite certain. And then we shall create a new Greek academy.'[88] The project was extremely vague. It was partly modelled on Germania, partly on Wagner's plans for Bayreuth, but Nietzsche was thinking of 'a monastic and artistic community. We shall love, work, enjoy for each other – perhaps this is the only way we can work for the *whole*.'[89] Like D.H.Lawrence half a century later, he had the fantasy of living in a small community with like-minded friends, insulated from the vulgarities and frustrations of life among the philistines. But he was no more realistic than Lawrence was about bringing the ideal into existence. 'I have already begun to keep my needs in check, so as to accumulate a little capital. We will also try our "luck" in lotteries.'[90]

He was again invited to spend Christmas at Tribschen, where he stayed from Christmas Eve until New Year's Day. Christmas Day was Cosima's birthday, so Nietzsche was present when Wagner sprang a well-prepared birthday surprise on his young wife.

When I woke up, I could hear a sound which was growing steadily louder. I could no longer imagine myself to be dreaming. Music was playing, and what music! As the sounds died away, Richard came in with the five children to put the score of his Symphonic Birthday Greeting into my hands. I was in tears, but so was the whole household. Richard had put his orchestra on the stairs, and thus consecrated our Tribschen for ever! The work is called The Tribschen Idyll.

Hans Richter, who had recruited the fifteen musicians and conducted the first rehearsal, had learned the trumpet specially to be able to play himself: 'He blazed out the Siegfried theme splendidly.' The children called the piece 'staircase music', and later it became the *Siegfried Idyll*. Nietzsche had been in on the secret and attended the second rehearsal, which Wagner conducted, in Lucerne. After breakfast the orchestra played it again, followed by the wedding procession from *Lohengrin*, and seven of the musicians played Beethoven's Septet, 'the work I can never hear often enough'.

Nietzsche's present to Wagner was Dürer's 'Knight, Death and Devil'; to Cosima he gave a manuscript copy of his essay on the Dionysian attitude. He also bought toys for the children. He was given a special edition of Wagner's Beethoven essay, a luxurious edition of Montaigne's complete works, and the first copy of *Siegfried* scored for piano. In the evening Wagner read out his libretto for *Die Meistersinger*, and on the following evening Nietzsche read out his essay on the Dionysian attitude, which they then discussed.

Returning to start the new year in Basel, Nietzsche began to lose touch with contemporary politics. On 18 January 1871, in the Hall of Mirrors at Versailles, with the support of all the princes ruling over the German states (except Austria), King Wilhelm was proclaimed Emperor of Germany. Ludwig II of Bavaria was especially active in urging him to accept the imperial throne, and Wagner cannot have been hostile to the idea. On 28 January, when Paris finally capitulated, an armistice was signed. It is puzzling that Nietzsche's letters and notebooks barely refer to events so crucial in the history of Prussia and Germany. He felt no less embattled than he had when war was declared, but, convinced that the cultural issue was the important one, he was channelling most of his energy into his notes.

Between the autumn of 1870 and the spring of 1871, despite his poor health, Nietzsche was working concentratedly on what could be read as a series of footnotes to *Die Welt als Wille und Vorstellung*. Unconsciously, perhaps, he was trying to break free from Schopenhauer, but the questions he was asking himself and the answers he was giving himself were still couched in Schopenhauerian terms, while he was developing both Schopenhauer's idea of consciousness as a fabric of illusions and Wagner's association of the decline of Greek tragedy with the dissolution of the *polis*. 'The disintegration of Aeschylean drama', wrote Nietzsche, 'was not only the symptom but also the *means* for the disintegration of Athenian democracy.'[91] Wagner had explained the dissociation between art and public in Hegelian and Marxian terms. Contemporary theatre was 'a blossom in the morass of the modern bourgeoisie'. Borrowing from Wagner, Nietzsche did not realize he was borrowing indirectly from Hegel and Marx, and it was uncritical faith in Wagner which made it possible for him to believe that Germany, in moving towards a renaissance of tragic music-drama, was moving towards a new golden age. 'Germany as Greece striding backwards: we have reached the period of the Persian Wars.'[92] 'The new artistic phase was not reached by the Greeks: it is the German mission.'[93] This was Wagner's development of a Hegelian idea. Like Winckelmann and Goethe, Hegel had glorified the Greek past, praising classical art for its perfection in unifying inner meaning and outer form. This, he said, was lacking in Romantic art.[94] Wagner, with his unlimited faith in his own powers, aimed to elicit from the modern audience a disciplined unity of response comparable to that of the Athenian audience to performances of tragedy. But he did not feel as much nostalgia for the classical past as Nietzsche, who was looking back to a golden age, free from dualism, rather as T. S. Eliot was when he invented the phrase 'dissociation of sensibility'. Eliot dated the cultural decline from the seventeenth century: Nietzsche laid the blame for it on Socrates and Euripides. Art and philosophy had suddenly taken separate paths. The artist could no longer think and feel at the same time. The Apollonian or shaping principle had become separated from the energetic Dionysian affirmation of unity between man and nature. As in most myths of a golden age, including the Garden of Eden story, nostalgia postulated a primal unity fractured by a fall from grace. Nietzsche was intending to call the final chapter of his book 'Socrates Expels Music'.[95] The charac-

terization of Apollonian and Dionysiac as opposing tendencies
derives partly from dualism in Schopenhauer and Wagner, but
more specifically from Jules Michelet's study of the origins and
evolution of religious belief, *La Bible de l'humanité*, published in
1864. Malwida von Meysenbug, who had known Michelet,
introduced Wagner to his work, and it was probably discussions of
his Apollo–Dionysus polarity that made Nietzsche start thinking
in these terms, while Genelli's picture in Wagner's drawing-room
kept reminding him of Dionysus. Lecturing on Greek music-
drama in January 1870, Nietzsche had mentioned Dionysus, but
not Apollo.

Taken individually as aphorisms, many of Nietzsche's notes are
pleasingly provocative. 'In each art the beautiful begins only when
the purely logical is defeated.'[96] 'Beauty enters when the individual
drives for once run parallel, but not against each other.'[97] 'The
only way to understand Greek tragedy is to be Sophocles.'[98]
'In one half of existence we are artists – as dreamers. This entirely
active world is necessary to us.'[99] But, unlike Schopenhauer, he
was taking it for granted that all his insights were arising from 'a
single foundation', while, unlike Schopenhauer, he was trying to
rally philosophical and psychological propositions under a
philological banner. Really he was less interested in the birth
of tragedy than in its death, and less interested in either than
in the plight of nineteenth-century man. Nor would it be misleading to describe the notes as a series of unposted love letters to
Wagner. In the 'Foreword to Richard Wagner' (which he wrote at
the end of 1871), Nietzsche said of himself: 'As he hatched these
ideas he was communicating with you as if you were present.' It
was no coincidence that he wrote fewer letters than usual during
the winter of 1870–1: the literary energy was going into the notes.
He was sublimating his need for human contact at the same time
as storing ammunition for the cultural campaign he wanted to
launch with the publication of the book.

He had fantasies of 'a new cultural sect as judge and master over
the bedraggled and disgusting culture of today. To engage with the
true cultural elements – enthusiasm for pure science, strict
military hierarchy, deep emotional needs of women etc. and with
the Christianity that still survives etc.'[100] Under the heading
'Delusions of the individual', he listed patriotism, confession, sex,

science, freedom of the will, and piety.[101] The war Prussia was fighting reminded him of the Jews, who, unlike the Greeks, had a national god. Using his name in their warfare with other tribes, they had evolved strict religious customs, and the demand that a father should sacrifice his son had been typical of the ideas they imputed to him. (The New Testament God had sacrificed his own.) The Greeks had been more generous than either Jews or Christians. Their mythology had 'deified *all* forms into a significant humanity'.[102] There was no asceticism in their religion. The Olympian gods sanctified everything – good and evil. The modern artist should have the same freedom and control over religion and its myths as the Athenian tragedians had had, without being pathologically involved. Attic tragedy had declined when the characters had lost their relationship with the gods. In the plays of Aeschylus and Sophocles the hero had always, symbolically, been Dionysus confronting Apollo; in the plays of Euripides one private individual confronted another. Schopenhauer had said that music was at the furthest remove from the principle of individuation; for Nietzsche, Apollo epitomized the spirit of individuation, and when Dionysian music had been expelled from drama by Socrates and Euripides the spirit of individuation had triumphed.

One note prefigures both Nietzsche's pronouncement about the death of God and his doctrine of Eternal Recurrence:

> Individuation – the hope for rebirth of a Dionysus. Then everything will be Dionysus. Individuation is the *martyrdom* of the god – no initiate ever goes on mourning. Empirical existence is something that should not be. Joy is possible in the hope of this reaction. – Art is one such beautiful hope.[103]

Several notes refer to the death of gods. One quotes the primitive German idea that 'All gods must die. . . . The death of Sigurd, the scion of Odin, could not avert the death of Balder, Odin's son. Soon after Balder's death followed the death of Odin and the other gods.'[104] There are also several references to the death of Pan.

The function of art, as Nietzsche saw it, was to create an alternative myth. Recognition of the truth was unfruitful. Art inhibited understanding. Architecture, for instance, proclaimed the greatness and immortality of man.[105] In art the aim was to overcome dissonance. The aim of illusion and imagination was to produce a painless view of things. 'My philosophy – inverted Platonism: the further away from True Being, the purer, more beautiful and better it is. Life of illusion as objective.'[106] This was a variation on Schopenhauer's idea of artistic vision as temporary deliverance from the toils of the will. But whereas Schopenhauer assumed that the artist could shake off the veil of illusion to see the world undistorted by will, Nietzsche suggested that we ourselves are only illusory figments in the consciousness of a greater entity. 'Our thinking is only a picture of the primal intellect, a thinking that arises from the ideas of the single will. . . . I believe in the incomprehensibility of the will.'[107]

Not that this should be an excuse for leaving contemporary culture to take care of itself. In another note, Nietzsche defined the three main tasks that lay ahead: 'Annihilation of all those feeble libertinistic manifestations; education towards seriousness and towards terror, like travellers in the desert; caution against Apollonianism in learning.'[108] And when the Professor of Philosophy at Basel, Gustav Teichmüller, accepted a post in Dorlap, it seemed to Nietzsche that he would be in a better position to create a new cultural sect if he could have the empty chair. It was probably in January 1871 that he wrote to Vischer-Bilfinger, applying for it. He said it was in the interests of the university that he was making the suggestion. His poor health was due to excessive strain, the result of dividing himself, as he had for so long, between philology and philosophy. His real task, 'to which I *would have* if necessary to *sacrifice any career*', was his philosophical task. To prove that he was qualified in the subject, he gave an account of his longstanding interest in philosophical, ethical and aesthetic problems. Two of the courses he had already announced for the coming year were on the pre-Platonic philosophers and on the Platonic dialogues. 'Of more recent philosophers I have studied Kant and Schopenhauer with especial partiality.'[109] The letter went on to suggest that Rohde would be a suitable successor for the chair in philology. At the same time as planning, in the long-term, to withdraw from academic life, Nietzsche was hoping, in the short term, to make Basel University the headquarters for a cultural campaign with Rohde as his adjutant. 'We *perhaps* have a prospect of working together next term,' he wrote.[110] Germania was still his model for fantasies of intellectual activity centring on close friendship. But he had little chance of realizing them: both his championship of Schopenhauer and his deteriorating health would have been strong deterrents against appointing him to the chair. About 21 January he complained that his stomach was troubling him, that he was sleeping badly, getting too little exercise, feeling exhausted. 'I yearn for recuperation and better air, above all, for *less* work.'[111] By 6 February he was feeling very much worse: 'dreadful sleeplessness, haemorrhoidal discomfort, extreme exhaustion etc.' The doctors had diagnosed inflammation of the stomach and intestines resulting from overwork, and they insisted he should have complete rest in a warm climate. As a German lecturer in Basel, he told his mother and his sister, one was irresponsibly exploited for a very poor salary. As soon as he had an opportunity to leave, he would take it. Meanwhile would either of them like to travel south with him?[112] When he heard that neither of them could, he fainted. In response to a letter from his doctor, Elisabeth changed her plans so that she could join him, and she left Naumburg in the middle of a freezing night.

On the first day of travelling they were delayed by snow, which disrupted the stage-coach service, and they had to stop at Flüelen, where Giuseppe Mazzini was spending the night at the same hotel. He had been in exile ever since the overthrow of the Italian republic in 1849 and he was calling himself Mr Brown. Elisabeth struck up a conversation with him in French, but Nietzsche was feeling too ill to join in. They made the journey across the St Gotthard Pass in horse-drawn sleighs large enough for only two people, so Mazzini and the young man travelling with him could not accompany them, but the four of them met at each stopping-point. On 16 February the Nietzsches arrived in Lugano to stay six weeks at the Hôtel du Parc. They made friends with General von Moltke's brother and his family, and they all spent a good deal of time in the open air. By the beginning of March Nietzsche's haemorrhoids were much better, but even after strenuous walking, or a whole day in the open air, he was unable to sleep.[113] Nevertheless, they enjoyed themselves in Lugano. Elisabeth writes lyrically about the scent of the violets, the sunshine and the beautiful mountain air. They were there for the carnival: 'In my mind's eye I can vividly see Fritz dancing a round-dance merrily.'[114] His hotel bill for 2 to 9 March shows that during the week he had fourteen glasses of milk, four beers, two camomile teas, and two jugs of barley water.

By the end of the month he was still averaging only one night's sleep in two nights,[115] but he was working hard at the book, which he was planning to call *Ursprung und Ziel der Tragödie* (*The Origin and Aim of Tragedy*). Before he submitted it to a publisher on 26 April[116] he went through another period of trying to turn his back on philology in order to regard himself as primarily a philosopher. He knew that opposition to his appointment was to be expected from the other Professor of Philosophy at Basel, Karl Christian Friedrich, and, writing to Rohde, he described the book as an attempt to legitimize himself as a philosopher. The Chair of Philosophy, he said, attracted him only for Rohde's sake, and in his insomniac state, alternating between depression and elation, he viewed the whole university situation as something incidental and even tiresome. What excited him was the confidence that throughout his life he had been following a 'good demon' who had been leading him towards professional commitment to philosophy. But its appeal for him depended partly on the support it could give to the illusion that the most disparate ideas were rising from what Schopenhauer called a single foundation.

What a strange feeling it is to see one's own world, a pretty ball, growing round and full in front of one. . . . I learn nothing now that does not immediately find a secure place in some corner of what I have learned previously. And the sense that my own world is growing is never stronger than when I consider – not coolly, but restfully – the so-called history of the world during the last ten months, and use it as no more than a means of working towards my own good ends – without any exaggerated respect for this means. The words *pride* and *madness* are really too weak for my spiritual insomnia.[117]

The 'spiritual insomnia' had its effect on the book, which is less impressive than the notes that remained unpublished. The best paragraphs retain something of the original aphoristic force, and in places the argument is excitingly provocative, but Nietzsche was overrating his ability to integrate everything he learned into everything he knew. He told Elisabeth: 'Science, art and philosophy are growing so closely side by side in me that one day

I shall certainly give birth to centaurs.'[118] Between themselves they then referred to the book as 'The Centaurs'. Its structure also suffers from his eagerness to prove himself as a philosopher at the same time as creaming off the results of more than ten years' work as a philologist.

'Indeed,' he wrote to Rohde, 'even if I should still become a poet, I am prepared for it.' *Die Geburt der Tragödie* is more poetic than scholarly. Though there is genuine insight in the account Nietzsche gives of the tragic chorus, his Wagnerian emphasis on music was misleading: the music in Greek tragedy was not operatic, and it was decisively subordinated to the dialogue. But the book contains some admirably perceptive pre-Freudian remarks about the importance of dreams and their value in satisfying our longing for redemption through illusion.[119] Some of his deductions are far ahead of their time, but the mixture of philosophy and poetic paradox with classical philology is confusing, while the polemic about German culture unbalances the serious study of Greek tragedy. The brilliance of the writing is undeniable, but the strategy is misguided. Nietzsche tells us that we are all images, works of art, projections from the consciousness of the supreme artist: 'It is only as an aesthetic phenomenon that existence can be justified.' Such propositions are intended to be provocative, but they provoke an unintended scepticism about the author's sobriety and reliability as a classical scholar.

On his way back from Lugano he stayed at Tribschen from 3 to 8 April, while Elisabeth went on to Basel. Confident that a German victory over France would enhance the popularity of his music, Wagner was at work on his patriotic *Kaisermarsch*, basing it on a folk song. The children were singing the melody all over the house, much to the irritation of the Comtesse d'Agoult, who was staying there. Nietzsche was eager to read some of *Die Geburt der Tragödie* to Wagner and Cosima before they left on a concert tour, and, according to Elisabeth, her brother's sensitive nature was 'deeply wounded when he realized that Wagner wanted the book, in some way, to be a glorification of his own art'. This is obviously a distortion. In 1870 Nietzsche was incapable of writing a book that was not a glorification of Wagner and his art, but it would have been in character for Wagner and Cosima to consider how the book could best serve their cause, and to put some pressure on

Nietzsche, who possibly did make some final revisions based on their suggestions before he sent the first part of the manuscript to the publisher Engelmann on 26 April under the title *Musik und Tragödie*. The draft of the letter he enclosed contains the sentence: 'But the real function [of the book] is to illuminate Richard Wagner, that extraordinary enigma of our age, in his relation to Greek tragedy.'[120]

In May, events in Paris gave Nietzsche what he called 'the worst day of my life'.[121] Bismarck had refused to make peace with Adolphe Thiers's provisional government until elections had been held for a new national assembly. It met at Bordeaux in February, and on 18 March Paris rebelled against its peacemaking efforts. The city had become an international centre for revolutionaries, and power quickly fell into the hands of the extremists. After the long siege and after the humiliation of seeing German troops march triumphantly down the Champs-Elysées, the Parisians were easily inflamed. The revolutionary government, which took the name 'Commune' when it set itself up on 29 March, was still in control of Paris on 10 May when Thiers signed the Peace of Frankfurt ceding Alsace-Lorraine to Germany. Before the Commune surrendered to the national forces, there was a week of ferocious fighting in the streets. The *communards* shot hostages, including the Archbishop of Paris, and burned the Tuileries and the Hôtel de Ville; in Germany it was reported that the Louvre had been destroyed. The army's reprisals were equally savage. Prisoners were massacred. 'What use is an intellectual', Nietzsche asked, 'faced with such a cultural earthquake? One feels like an atom! One uses one's whole life and the greatest part of one's strength to come to a better understanding of one cultural period, and to expound it. How is this profession to be regarded when in a single wretched day the most precious documents of such periods are burned to ashes?'[122] Karl Marx's reaction could hardly have been more different. There were two Marxists in the Commune, and he was in direct touch with one of them, Leo Franckel. Afterwards he wrote that a new era of direct proletarian revolutionary action was dawning: the Commune represented a triumph for international Marxism.[123]

For Nietzsche the battleground was cultural, not political, but he wanted to be militant. He praised von Gersdorff for leading a 'vigorous cultural life as if you were still fundamentally a soldier, and striving to transpose your military attitude into the realm of philosophy and art. And that is correct: only as fighters can we, in our time, have a right to exist, as fighters in the vanguard for a new spirit.'[124] Like the Nazis sixty years later, he tended illogically to bracket the Jews with any other enemy of Germany. 'Not everything has yet been destroyed by Franco-Jewish trivialization and "elegance" or by the greedy pressures of the "present age".'[125] As his health improved, he became more preoccupied with rallying his friends to fight with him. Forced to abandon hope of moving over to the philosophical chair, with Rohde succeeding to his, he did his best to arrange a job for his friend in Zürich, where the philological professor was due to leave in the autumn. At the same time Nietzsche tried to procure a school-teaching job in Bern for Heinrich Romundt, who had been a philosophy student at Leipzig.[126] 'In all my plans,' he told Rohde, 'especially the educational ones, I am counting on you more than anyone, and, at first, on you alone. It occurs to me, among other points, that for such matters nothing is more important than for us to live our way into them *together*.'[127] To Paul Deussen, who had accepted a position in Marburg, divided, like Nietzsche's, between university lecturing and school-teaching, he wrote that nothing was more important for the future than school-teaching.[128]

At Whitsun he went with Elisabeth to stay at Tribschen. The Wagners had been touring through Germany. Bayreuth had struck Wagner as the ideal place for a festival, though the baroque opera house was too small for his music-dramas. The citizens had been very well disposed, and the prospects of making the town his headquarters must have bulked large in the Whitsuntide conversations. On the last evening, when the four of them went for a walk, Cosima was wearing what Elisabeth described as 'a semi-negligée of rose-coloured cashmere, with broad reveres of real lace falling to the hem of the garment', and she was carrying 'a large flower-trimmed hat of Florentine straw'. In the conversation she was not eclipsed by Wagner or Nietzsche. 'Each one of those three rare natures was at its best; each shone in its own brilliance.'[129]

Though Nietzsche failed to secure jobs for any of his friends in Switzerland, he did at least see three of them before the end of the year. In July, when von Gersdorff came to Basel, they travelled with Elisabeth to Gimmelwald, near Mürren, and Nietzsche took him to Tribschen, where he made a favourable impression. Writing to him in September, Nietzsche said that five years of separation had made no difference to their friendship. 'Together we have once again drawn the net of culture over our heads.'[130] In October they met again, together with Rohde, first at Leipzig, where they went to the fair, and then in Naumburg, where they celebrated Nietzsche's twenty-seventh birthday. Writing to them both, five days later, he proposed a ritual to celebrate the reunion. A simultaneous thanks-offering should be made to the friendly demons. At exactly ten o'clock in the evening of Monday 23 October, Rohde in Kiel, von Gersdorff in Berlin, and Nietzsche in Basel should raise a glass of dark red wine, pour half of it out into the night, pronouncing the words *chairete daemones* in greeting to the demons, and then drink the other half. Both Rohde and von Gersdorff complied. Nietzsche was in Burckhardt's room on the Monday evening: together they poured two beer glasses of Rhône wine down into the street below. 'In earlier centuries we might have been suspected of witchcraft. As I then came home, somewhat demonically, at 11.30, I was astonished to find friend Deussen there.' They strolled through the streets till two o'clock. 'I have an almost ghostly memory of him because I saw him only by pale lamplight and moonlight.'[131] Though Nietzsche was not serious about propitiating the demons, he had since August been associating the idea with seeing his friends again. Suggesting they should meet at a Wagner concert in Mannheim, he said: 'Let us quickly make a sacrifice to the demons, so that they do not frustrate me over this wish.'[132] It was as if magical good luck must be involved in reunions. Romundt had come to Basel on his way to Nice. In Naumburg, Nietzsche had met Wilhelm Pinder and Gustav Krug, and in Leipzig, the Ritschls and the Brockhauses. It then seemed as though Deussen had been conjured up by the ritual.

At the beginning of September, Cosima wrote to ask whether Nietzsche could recommend someone to accompany a young prince, whose mother, Princess Hatzfeldt-Trachenberg, wanted to send him to Italy, Greece, the East, and America.[133] Having never seen Greece, and yearning for prolonged travels,[134] Nietzsche proposed himself, but to Cosima it was unthinkable that he should give up his chair.[135] He submitted meekly when she expressed surprise, though he had been so excited at the prospect that he had been saying he might give up his job. When he announced his decision to stay on, his salary was raised by 500 francs to 3,500.

Irritated that Engelmann had kept the manuscript of *Die Geburt der Tragödie* from April to June without making a decision, Nietzsche withdrew it from him and let himself be persuaded by Rohde and von Gersdorff to submit the book to Wagner's publisher, Ernst Wilhelm Fritzsch, who was primarily a publisher of music but had also brought out Wagner's tracts. Wagner, who had not been consulted, was annoyed. The reason he gave was concern that Nietzsche should make a creditable literary debut;[136] the real reason was probably that as propaganda the book would have been more valuable if it had come out under the imprint of a disinterested publisher. In November Fritzsch accepted the book.

The news set the seal on Nietzsche's happiness. The visit to Naumburg had produced a *rapprochement* with his mother; humorously he threatened to resume the habit of going home each holiday.[137] His health had improved, though he was still not satisfied with it. Perhaps the Basel air did not suit him.[138] He had made a new friendship with Franz Overbeck, the Professor of Theology, a man seven years his senior, who had come to the university in April 1870 and taken lodgings in the same house. Their friendship ripened slowly, but by now they were talking to each other in the second person singular, and for Overbeck's birthday on 16 November 1871 he wrote a short choral piece.

He also wrote a twenty-minute piano duet. That he had broken his musical silence was, in his own opinion, a symptom of the well-being he felt after the autumn reunion with his friends. He played the duet with Overbeck, and he decided to send it to Cosima on Christmas Day as a birthday present.

In November, once again dramatizing his own movements at the moment of writing, he started a letter to Rohde with a description of sinking down exhaustedly on a sofa, covering his eyes with his hands, and then jumping up to seize a pen as his friend came suddenly into his mind. He described his return to composition, mentioning that the second act of *Götterdämmerung* had been completed three days earlier. The main point of the letter was to ask Rohde whether he would write a review of *Die Geburt der Tragödie*.[139]

Wagner had been right to predict that the victory over France would create a nationalistic mood which would make him more popular. At Bayreuth the town council had passed a resolution to support Wagner's festival project: he was to be given a piece of land just outside the city where he could build a new opera-house. Wagner societies were sprouting in several of the bigger cities, and in December, invited by the society in Mannheim to conduct a concert there, he was fêted and cheered when his train arrived at the station. Nietzsche was with him: he had taken four days off. He stayed in the same hotel as the Wagners and acted as escort to Cosima while the Master was busy with rehearsals. 'It seemed to me', he wrote to Rohde, 'as though a deep presentiment was finally fulfilled. For this – and nothing else – is exactly what music is! And that is exactly what I mean by the word "music" when I call it Dionysian! But I think that if only a few hundred people get from this music what I get from it, then we will have a completely new culture.'[140] His theories were conditioning his reactions to his experiences.

He was invited to Tribschen for Christmas again, but he stayed in Basel, ostensibly to work on the six public lectures he was to give in the new year on the future of German educational institutions. The real reason was probably that he was nervous of his audacity in offering Cosima a musical present. He could scarcely have hoped to please her better than Wagner had with the *Siegfried Idyll*, but he may have entertained Oedipal fantasies of temporarily ousting the potent father by sitting down to play a duet with Cosima. In Nietzsche's absence it was Hans Richter who sat down at the piano with Cosima, while Wagner listened restlessly, and then laughed out loud. She was pleased with the 'fine' letter Nietzsche sent her, but annoyed when she discovered that his dedication of his new composition to her had not prevented him from sending it as a Christmas present to his mother and sister, saying it was dedicated to them. He also sent curtains and carved salad servers for his mother and a new edition of an art history book by Lübke for Elisabeth. She had asked for one by Springer, but he would have had to order it 'from a scandalous

Jewish second-hand bookshop'. How could she have expected him to do that?[141]

He should have received copies of *Die Geburt der Tragödie* in time to send them to his friends for Christmas, but the package, despatched from Leipzig on 29 December, reached Basel on 2 January. He immediately sent a copy to Wagner. In the draft of the accompanying letter he promised not to admit in the presence of his 'honoured friend and master' that 'everything I have to say here about the birth of Greek tragedy has been said by you more beautifully, lucidly and convincingly'.[142] In the actual letter, headed 'Most honoured Master', he was less explicit: 'And if I myself believe that the fundamental statement is right, this means no more than that *you* must be eternally right with *your art*. . . . God have mercy on my philologists if they refuse to learn anything now.'[143] But to Gustav Krug, writing before he had a copy to enclose, Nietzsche said: 'Oh! It is wicked and provocative. Closet yourself in a secret place to read it.'[144]

Ritschl, who received a copy from the publisher without any accompanying note from his ex-pupil, wrote in his diary: 'Ingenious vertigo.'[145] At the end of January, still having heard nothing from the sixty-five-year-old professor, Nietzsche wrote: 'I thought that if ever you had come across anything promising in your life, it would be this book – promising for our classical studies, promising for Germany, even if a few individuals might be destroyed.'[146] Ritschl's diary entry on receiving the letter was 'Megalomania'.[147] He replied at length on 14 February, saying that he did not regard the individualization of life as retrogressive. The alternative extreme was a dissolving sense of self-oblivion.[148] There was also a danger that Nietzsche's approach would foment disrespect for learning. Burckhardt was less dismissive. According to Nietzsche, he was 'so fascinated by the light thrown on Greece by the book's discoveries that he thinks about it day and night, and in a thousand ways he is making a most fruitful historical application of it'.[149]

Wagner's reaction was ecstatic: 'Dear Friend! I have read nothing more beautiful than your book. Everything is superb! I am now writing to you hastily because reading it excites me inordinately, and to read it *properly* I must wait till I come back to my senses.'[150] He wrote again on 10 January 1872 to say that he and Cosima were quarrelling for possession of the copy. 'I always need it to put myself into the right mood between breakfast and work, for since reading it I have gone back to composing my last act.'[151] Cosima wrote eight days later: 'Oh, how beautiful your book is! How beautiful, and how profound, and how daring! ... Like poetry I have read your text ... for it gives me an answer to all the unconscious questions of my inner life.'[152] And at the beginning of March Nietzsche received a letter from Liszt, who said he had read the book twice. 'Surging and flaming in it is a powerful spirit that profoundly stirred me.' He had never found a better definition of art, he said, than 'the fulfilment and completion of existence tending to permanence'. The other sentence he quoted was: 'A people – like an individual – is of value only insofar as it has power to set the seal of eternity on its experience.' He was responding to the element in the book of which Nietzsche himself was least aware – a lingering remnant of childhood faith, a hankering after immortality.

6   The Superior Tribunal

For Nietzsche 1872 began as well as 1871 had ended, though of the six public lectures he had announced he delivered only five. *Die Zukunft unserer Bildungsanstalten* was a misleading title, in that it was not the future of the Swiss educational institutions that concerned him: he spoke about the German and especially the Prussian system, concentrating more on the present than the future. But the audience was large and appreciative. For each of the five lectures he claimed to have had about three hundred people in the main hall of the museum.[1] Burckhardt, who attended the lectures, reported that 'in places they were quite enchanting, but then a profound melancholy would make itself heard'.[2] The Wagners came to the second lecture, and there were many other distinguished visitors.

Though no reviews of *Die Geburt der Tragödie* were to appear until April, it was not only locally that word of mouth was contributing to the young professor's fame. He was offered a position at a university in Pomerania, Greifswald, and the news reached Basel that he had rejected it. On his way back from a visit to Tribschen, he was met by a deputation of students wanting to give him a torchlight procession: 'I had difficulty in declining this honour.'[3] The university authorities showed their appreciation by giving him another salary increase of five hundred francs on 27 January, so within three months his basic income had risen from three thousand to four.

In spite of his animadversions against Socrates, Nietzsche imitated Platonic dialogue in his lectures, presenting what he had to say as an extended dialogue, with an elderly philosopher as his Socratic spokesman. To link the conversations he used a narrative, partly fictional, with a higher ratio of fiction to autobiography than the audience would have suspected. He drew on memories of Germania, of schoolboy holidaying in the Rhineland, and of his year at Bonn, and he even introduced a torchlight procession. But he consistently altered details, merging Krug and Pinder into an imaginary friend who had shared the Bonn experience with him. His philosopher, who has a prolonged conversation with the two friends, is less partial to the interrogatory method than Plato's Socrates and more inclined to lose his temper, but the lectures are entertainingly unconventional, and, at the end of each one Nietzsche tried to create suspense with some such forward-looking sentence as 'At that moment something new appeared,' or 'Now I will tell you something comforting.'

Like Marx, Nietzsche understood that education could be a powerful weapon in the hands of a state ostensibly concerned with raising cultural standards but covertly wanting to lower them. The common assumption that collective interests coincided with individual interests had survived from the eighteenth century, but Nietzsche could see that far from wanting to improve the intellectual acuity of its citizens, the modern state needed uncritical subservience and complaisance. So specialization was in its interests: an academic or a scientist, proficient in his own subject without being generally cultured, was like a factory-worker operating only one machine. Unlike Marx, Nietzsche did not believe that the problem could be solved by democratizing education. 'Universal education is only a preliminary for Communism: education will in this way be so diluted as not to confer any privilege.' As he said in the first lecture, journalism was a means of disseminating and diluting culture. 'The journalist, the time-server has made his debut, in place of the great genius, as the all-the-year-round leader, the Saviour of the moment.' What can the genuine philosopher do against 'pseudo-culture'? How can the teacher give students access to the authentic culture of the Greeks?

Nietzsche was too clever to put his pessimism into the mouth of his philosopher. It is one of the students who is full of misgivings; the philosopher makes constructive proposals. 'Our philosophy must start here, not with astonishment but with terror; those who cannot bring it to the subject should stay away from educational affairs.' Much depended on the use of language. In the schools, standards of speaking and writing German were extremely low: this was 'the century of journalistic German'. The high schools were promoting pedantry, not true culture, while boys were conditioned to mediocrity by the conventional standards they were encouraged to apply. Higher education should join battle, should inculcate linguistic self-discipline: 'Culture begins with the mother-tongue.'

The fourth lecture is reminiscent of the letter to Elisabeth presenting faith as a comfortable alternative to the quest for truth. Germany was now at the crossroads: educational reform and cultural enlightenment constituted the only means of averting a relapse into barbarism and slavery in which the individual would stand no chance of realizing his potential. Instead of resisting journalism's tendency to corrupt the reader, scholarship was offering only 'an escape from the self, an ascetic murder of the cultural impulse, desperate annihilation of individuality'. Having launched an attack in his book on the sterility of post-Socratic scholarship in Athens, Nietzsche was now firing a broadside at contemporary academics, on Ritschl's values, on the philosophy that had no connection with either philosophy or art. Standing on a professorial rostrum and publicly denouncing professorial narrowness, Nietzsche achieved detumescence after years of frustration.

Following this climacteric outburst, the final invocation of Wagner as the messianic genius must have disappointed the audience. The fifth lecture had slipped from prophetic philosophy into polemic; the sixth remained an unfulfilled promise, an inconclusive silence. But since Wagner's reaction to his book, Nietzsche felt more committed to him than ever. On 24 January 1872 the Master, on his way to inspect the site he was being offered in Bayreuth, called on Nietzsche in Basel. In the spring he would leave Tribschen to settle in Bayreuth. The moment had come 'in which the bow is finally tensed, after hanging a long time with a slack string'.[4] Just after Wagner had left, Nietzsche wrote to him: 'I consider my present existence to be a reproach, and sincerely ask you whether you can use me.' He told Rohde: 'I have formed an alliance with Wagner. You cannot imagine how close we now are to each other, or how our plans interconnect.'[5] But either Wagner was hesitant about accepting such a sacrifice or possibly he thought that Nietzsche would be more useful if he kept his professorial status, and it was not until the middle of April that he was once again asking Rohde to be his successor at Basel. 'I will move back to the German fatherland in the winter, i.e. at the invitation of the Wagner societies . . . to hold lectures on the *Ring* festival. We must all do our duty, and, in cases of conflict, our *greater* duty.'[6] He would then go on to spend two years in the south, he said. But this time he told the Basel authorities nothing about his intentions of quitting.

Sincere though it was, the sense of where his greater duty lay was not his only motive for volunteering to serve Wagner. Nietzsche's love for him and for Cosima was inseparable from his commitment to his cultural mission, and without having the Wagners in the neighbourhood, he was going to find little compensation for the frustrations of university life. He had ten students in the audience for his lecture on the pre-Platonic philosophers and six for his lectures on *The Choephorae* – 'It is deplorable!'[7]

It would have been pleasant to escape for a holiday in Athens, Crete and Naxos, but, tantalizingly, the opportunity that presented itself was an invitation from a Jewish professor of history, Karl Mendelssohn Bartholdy, son of the composer. He could not have accepted without offending Wagner and Cosima, who made a display of their contempt for such Jewish composers as Mendelssohn and Meyerbeer.

It was some consolation to be invited to Tribschen for Easter. He arrived on Good Friday, 29 March, with a hundred-franc piece for Daniela as a present from her father. Von Bülow, deeply impressed with *Die Geburt der Tragödie*, had visited Nietzsche in Basel, asking him to accept the dedication of his Leopardi translations. On Easter Sunday Nietzsche helped Cosima to hide Easter eggs in the garden, and in the afternoon he played duets with her at the piano. After Easter he went on to spend a week at Vernex, near Montreux, on Lake Geneva.

On 22 April Wagner left Tribschen, never to return, but Cosima and the children were still there, and three days later Nietzsche paid his final visit.

It was like walking among ruins. The feeling was everywhere – in the air, in the clouds. The dog would not eat. Each time one spoke to the family of servants, they started sobbing. We packed the manuscripts, letters and books together – oh, it was so miserable! In these three years I have spent close to Tribschen, I have made 23 visits, which mean so much to me! Without them, what would have become of me? I am so happy to have crystallized that Tribschen world for myself in my book.[8]

At the core of Nietzsche's dependence on his friends was a suppressed hysteria. Though attracted by the idea of hermit-like asceticism, he was terrified of isolation. He was not so much prophesying his own future as betraying his interpenetrating hopes and fears when, in the first of the five public lectures, he made the professor rebuke one of the students for underestimating the gravity of the teacher's task: 'You think you can jump straight to what I could achieve only after a long, obstinate fight simply to live as a philosopher? And you are not afraid that loneliness will wreak vengeance on you? Just try it – being a cultural anchorite. To live entirely off yourself, you need to be abundantly rich!' Nietzsche's two lifelines were commitment to cultural warfare and contact, by letter, with his friends. Not that the two lines were separate: 'It makes me shudder', he wrote to Rohde, 'when I imagine how infinitely lonely I would feel if I were *not* able to think of you in forming all my hopes and plans.'[9]

While lecturing on the future of cultural institutions he was preparing a memorandum on Strasbourg University to submit as a question to the *Reichsrat*, earmarked for the attention of Bismarck. 'I will show you how ignominiously we have missed a gigantic opportunity of founding an authentic German educational establishment for the regeneration of the German spirit, and the annihilation of what has so far been called "culture". We must have war with knives, or cannons.' He signed this letter to Rohde 'The mounted artillery soldier with the heaviest cannon'.[10] He believed himself to be 'among the first to fight and work in a cultural movement which will reach the masses, perhaps in the next generation, perhaps still later,'[11] and he felt entitled to count on his book's having 'a quiet, slow effect, over the centuries.'[12] Inhospitable editors were enemies. Zarncke, who rejected the review Rohde had written of the book, was 'stupid', and to have any further dealings with him would be 'prostitution'.[13] An accumulation of favourable reactions to the book, from friends and strangers, gave him the illusion that it was forming 'a small community'.[14] This is in line with the earlier fantasies of withdrawing into a private society composed entirely of friends, and creating a new cultural sect to impose values and standards on the rest of German society. To the Wagners it was obvious that if no reviews of the book appeared either in the newspapers or in the scholarly reviews, the silence would effectively 'kill' it, but Nietzsche tried to cheer himself up by vilifying the philologists: 'Decades will have to elapse before they can understand a book which is so esoteric and in the true sense scientific.'[15]

Cosima understood better than he did that he had put his academic reputation at risk. In reply to a letter which has not survived, she wrote: 'What you tell me about your situation scarcely surprises me; but I believe that with a long metaphysical silence and with the publication of a specifically philological work you can put everything in order again, as soon as you feel the desire.'[16]

On 26 May a review by Rohde appeared in the *Norddeutsche Allgemeine Zeitung*. His original review had been too metaphysical to please Nietzsche, who was anxious to be taken seriously by philologists; the new review praised the book as 'philosophical art criticism' and as enriching aesthetics philosophically. Nietzsche was delighted: 'Friend, friend, friend, what have you done! There can be no one else like E.R.' He had started to read the review without noticing the initials at the end of it, 'and finally I hear that the voice which sounds so impressive and profound belongs to my friend. Oh my dearest friend, you have done that for me! . . . Victory, victory, victory! I need war!' His jubilation was all the greater for the fact that Rohde was now a professor at Kiel. He had sent Nietzsche a telegram on the last day of April, telling him the news. The appointment had come just in time to give extra weight to his review. But only six days later a scathingly hostile pamphlet was published under the title *Zukunftsphilologie* by Ulrich von Wilamowitz-Möllendorf, who pointed out some unscholarly inaccuracies and omissions. There was no mention of Aeschylus' trilogy on Lycurgus, in which Orpheus led the followers of Apollo in a clash with devotees of Dionysus, and Wilamowitz cited Euripides' *Hippolytus* in a cogent attack on Nietzsche's assumption that the playwright took his ideas from Socrates. (More recent scholarship tends to support the view that Phaedra's speech in *Hippolytus* constitutes an attack on Socrates, while Euripides' *Medea* may have provoked Socrates into formulating a reply.)[17] Instead of answering the pamphlet himself, Nietzsche strategically decided to give Rohde ammunition for a counter-attack.

On 22 May 1872, Wagner's fifty-ninth birthday, the foundation stone was to be laid for the new opera house in Bayreuth. Ten days before the ceremony Nietzsche was suffering from shingles on his neck. This was the first of many physical indispositions which, over the next four years, were to interfere with his attendances at Wagnerian events. 'But I hope a peace will be concluded at the right time between skin infection and brain functioning: for I *must* go to Bayreuth in spite of the *cingulum*.'[18] 'The two Wagnerian professors must not be absent.'[19] They were both present at the second rehearsal of the concert Wagner was to conduct at the old opera house, where they met Malwida von Meysenbug, a fifty-six-year old Wagnerian who had read Nietzsche's book and written to him from her home in Florence. A friend of Alexander Herzen's, she had brought up his children after the death of his wife. His youngest daughter, Olga, became her foster-child.

It was raining as Nietzsche drove in the carriage with the Wagners to the site on a spur of the hills on the north side of Bayreuth. The town was full of supporters from all over Europe, festival patrons and members of the various Wagner societies; carriages being in short supply, many of them had to walk to the ceremony. King Ludwig, angry that his protégé no longer needed his protection, stayed away, but he sent a congratulatory telegram which was put into a metal casket and lowered into the muddy ground with the foundation stone. A military band played Wagner's *Huldigungsmarsch*, but, because of the rain, and because the spectators who had carriages preferred to remain inside them, Wagner postponed the speech he had intended to deliver. Striking three hammer-blows at the foundation stone, he merely said: 'Bless you, my stone. Stand long and hold firm.' As he turned away, tears in his eyes, other dignitaries queued up to hit at the stone with the hammer. He was pale when he climbed back into the carriage, and silent as they drove back to the town, 'turning inward on himself a look which is indescribable'.[20] At the concert he conducted his *Kaisermarsch* and Beethoven's Ninth Symphony, with Cosima and the children on the platform.

In the middle of April, before leaving for Lake Geneva, Nietzsche had developed material from his piano duet.[21] into a new duet, his '*Manfred* Meditation', musically repudiating and satirizing his earlier allegiances to Schumann and to Byron. He later described it as 'an anti-overture to *Manfred*'.[22] After attending two performances of *Tristan* in Munich at the end of June, impressively conducted by von Bülow, he decided to dedicate his own composition to the friendly musician who had dedicated his Leopardi translation to him. Modestly, in the letter accompanying the manuscript, he called his composition 'such dubious music. Laugh your fill. I deserve it.'[23] Von Bülow's answer was written only four days later: 'Your *Manfred* Meditation is the most extreme fantastical extravagance, the most irritating and anti-musical set of notes on manuscript paper I have seen for a long time.' He had wondered whether it was a joke, a parody of the so-called *Zukunftsmusik.* 'Apart from psychological interest ... your meditation has, from the musical viewpoint, only the value of a crime in the moral world.' If Nietzsche had intended the composition seriously, he should, in future, limit himself to vocal music, so that he would have words to guide him. 'Incidentally, you designated your music as "frightful" – it truly is.'[24]

The immediate effect was profoundly depressing. In a letter about Gustav Krug's compositions – also dated 24 July 1872 but obviously written after receiving von Bülow's – Nietzsche said: 'Do not expect anything critical from me – my taste is not good, and as a connoisseur of music, I have been brought very low. . . . I am now no more a musician than is domestically necessary to me as a philosopher.'[25] He also found himself staying away from the piano. He did not reply to von Bülow's letter until October. If the conductor had heard him playing the music, he suggested, his reaction might have been less negative. 'Just consider that until now, from my *earliest* youth, I have lived under the most absurd illusion and had a *very great deal* of joy from my music!'[26]

Nietzsche was never going to stop thinking of himself as an artist, but the conductor's rebuff probably strengthened the feeling that he should concentrate on areas of work where he could not be accused of dilettantism, and he made an effort towards reinstating himself academically. Ritschl's reaction to the book did not preclude the possibility of *rapprochement*, and during the summer Nietzsche set to work seriously on a continuation of the essay Ritschl had published in September 1870: 'Florentinischern Traktat über Homer und Hesiod, ihr Geschlecht und ihr Wettkampf' ('Florentine Tract on Homer and Hesiod, Their Ancestry and Their Competition'). He had been intending to revisit Munich during the first half of August to hear *Tristan* again, together with *Lohengrin* and *Der fliegende Holländer* (*The Flying Dutchman*), but – partly, perhaps, to avoid an encounter with von Bülow – he changed his mind, staying in Basel despite the midsummer heat to do more work on what he had written about educational institutions, on the Homer–Hesiod essay, and on the pre-Platonic philosophers. On 12 August he sent the essay to Ritschl, who was glad to welcome his prodigal pupil back to the philological fold, but the piece did not appear in the *Rheinisches Museum* until February. At the end of August 1872 Malwida von Meysenbug came to Basel with Olga Herzen and her fiancé, and at the beginning of September Nietzsche's mother arrived for a week. Together with Elisabeth, who had been in Basel with him for nearly four months, he took them all into the mountains.

Though he had promised to go home for the autumn holidays, he found that he wanted to be alone. He started out for Italy, but, feeling ill en route, spent the first night at a hotel overlooking the Wallensee, a small lake east of Lake Zürich. His head was still aching when he woke up, and, in increasing discomfort, he went on to spend the second night at Chur. From there, enjoying the mountain scenery, he walked to Passugg, where three glasses of water from the saline soda spring helped to clear his head. Sitting, isolated, in the conductor's seat, high in the post-coach, he travelled for the first time along the Via Mala, the mountain road famous for its views. 'This is *my* nature,' he wrote.[27] Arriving at Splügen, in a valley about five thousand feet above sea level, he knew that this was where he wanted to stay. He went for long walks along country roads towards the San Bernhardino Pass and the Splügen Pass. 'I never need to speak: nobody knows me. I am entirely alone, and I could stay here for weeks on end, going for walks.'[28] The only human contacts he had, or wanted, were by letter. 'Wonderfully rich loneliness, with the most superb roads. I can walk for hours, sunk in my thoughts, without falling into an abyss. Whenever I look around, there is something great and unfamiliar. People come through only in post-coaches. My one contact with them is eating in the dining-room. They are like Platonic shadows in front of my cave.'[29]

Returning to Basel for the winter term, he was aghast to find that no students had enrolled for his seminar or for his course of lectures on Homer and Homeric problems. All he could do was proceed with his three-hour lectures on Greek and Roman rhetoric with an audience of two students who were not philologists.

I have suddenly acquired such a bad reputation in my field of study that it is damaging our small university. This grieves me, because I am really very devoted and grateful to it, and want nothing less than to harm it. . . . In Bonn a philological professor whom I respect very highly has simply advised his students that my book is 'utter nonsense' and totally useless: someone who produces such work is as good as dead, so far as scholarship is concerned. I have also been told of a student who at first wanted to come to Basel, but was made to stay in Bonn, and has now written to a relative here to say he thanks God he did not come to a university where *I* am teaching.[30]

The Bonn professor was Usener.

Rohde's pamphlet *Afterphilologie*, a counterblast to Wilamowitz's *Zukunftsphilologie*, appeared in the middle of October. Already, on 23 June, Wagner had published a letter in the *Norddeutsche Allgemeine Zeitung* attacking Wilamowitz, but some of the newspapers had been hostile, especially the *Nationalzeitung*, which called Nietzsche one of 'Wagner's literary lackeys'. Rohde's pamphlet, which was longer than Wilamowitz's, exposed his misquotations of *Die Geburt der Tragödie*, while incorporating all the philological ammunition Nietzsche had provided. Once again he felt a pang of gratitude to Rohde. 'It is as if I had committed a crime; for ten months people have kept silent. . . . Now your work, with its generosity and its brave comradeship in arms, falls into the midst of the crackling tribe. . . . Above all I like to hear the deep resonant ground-bass, like a waterfall, which is necessary to any polemic, to sanctify it.'[31]

At the end of November 1872 Nietzsche spent three days with the Wagners when they came to Strasbourg. They were touring German opera houses to find singers for the *Ring*. They invited him to spend Christmas at their new home in Bayreuth, but with the pleasure of seclusion still so fresh in his memory, he pleaded exhaustion, preferring to spend the days quietly in Naumburg – his first Christmas there for four years. His Christmas present to Cosima was five prefaces to unwritten books. Having made detailed notes of his afterthoughts on points that had occurred in conversation with her and Wagner, he developed them, especially for her, into five essays. So while Burckhardt was lecturing on Greek civilization to a large audience of students – fifty-three of the 168 students at the university had enrolled at the beginning of the summer term – Nietzsche, lecturing to an audience of two, was working on these fragments of books, conceived hardly less privately than his letters.

In the first, 'Über das Pathos der Wahrheit' ('On the Pathos of Truth'), he postulated a 'feelingless demon' who would say nothing about what we call truth and the history of the world except by telling a story. Once there was a star on which the clever animals found the truth. Nature had taken only a few breaths before the star went numb and the clever animals had to die. It was also high time, for though they had prided themselves on knowing a great deal, they had discovered, finally, that all their previous knowledge was spurious, and they died cursing the truth, as man would if he ever found it. He would be driven to despair and annihilation by the fact of being condemned to eternal falsification. 'He is locked inside his own consciousness, and Nature has thrown away the key.' Only the philosopher has inklings of what is disgusting and murderous in human nature. Indifference to ignorance of all this is like being balanced, asleep and dreaming, on the back of a tiger. Art says: 'Let him dream'; philosophy says: 'Wake him up.' But the philosopher himself is still more deeply asleep, dreaming about 'ideas' or immortality.

The second preface was on the future of German educational institutions, and the third was about the Greek state. Having long believed that the survival of slavery was necessary to the survival of culture, he went on to argue that in modern times it was not the cultured elite but the slaves who determined the names for prevailing conditions. 'Dignity of labour' and 'equal rights' were examples of the fictions necessary to civilization. The truth about the necessity of slavery was 'the vulture which gnaws at the liver of the Promethean culture-monger'.

The state had originated from the tendency that puts the strongest individual, the conqueror, in the dominant position. The law of warfare was that everything belonging to the defeated passed to the victor, and, in a military society, the structure is pyramidal, with uniformed slaves at the base and high-ranking officers at the top. The dignity of the soldier-citizen does not depend on his labour:

In his total activity, each individual has no more dignity than he acquires, consciously or unconsciously, from being the tool of the genius. . . . Man in himself, the absolute man, has neither dignity nor rights. Nor has he any duties. Only as a wholly determined being serving unconscious purposes can he excuse his existence.

The first and the third prefaces form a new nadir in Nietzsche's pessimism, but also an important step towards philosophical independence. The fourth preface is on the relationship of Schopenhauer's philosophy to present-day German culture, which is derogatorily characterized, and the question of whether life is worth living recurs in the last preface, on Homer's treatment of conflict. The pre-Homeric world is characterized as savage and comfortless. According to Orphic thought, life would not be worth living if the basic instincts were destructive; the Hellenic genius was founded on acceptance of this destructiveness. The assumption that conflict was the gift of a benevolent deity made it possible to view one set of instincts as countered by another, and Greek education, unlike modern education, had recognized that contest was the best way of developing every natural gift.

After presenting Cosima with such a careful distillation of the ideas uppermost in his mind – an act of love in line with dedicating music to girls – Nietzsche did not even receive a reply. From 17 to 20 January, von Gersdorff, who had spent Christmas in Bayreuth, came to Basel, but he did not tell Nietzsche that he had offended the Wagners by refusing to share their first Christmas in their new home. After sending a telegram on 23 January 1873, Cosima finally wrote on 12 February to explain that she had decided 'to leave time to repair the insignificant breach'. Her opinion was that the ideas sketched out in two of the prefaces – the ones on Homeric conflict and on the Greek state – should be developed into a book.[32]

Towards the end of the month he was unwell. 'Annoying cold and cough and exhaustion, in sum extreme trivialities, but enough to give one the feeling of being ill.'[33] Not wanting to stay in Basel for the three carnival nights, he withdrew to Gersau. He had still not completely recovered when he wrote to von Gersdorff on 24 February. 'By the way, God knows how often I give offence to the Master. . . . I cannot think how anyone could be more loyal to Wagner than I am in all important matters, or more devoted to him . . . but I must keep a certain freedom for myself in small, subordinate matters. A certain detachment from *frequent* personal togetherness is necessary for me and can almost be called sanitary.'[34]

He spent a great deal of time alone in his room; his pupil, Ludwig Wilhelm Kelterborn, conveys the impression of a hygienic fastidiousness in his teacher's behaviour there:

Here too one is immediately impressed by the combination of exceptional courteousness and refinement in manner and behaviour with the most charming and natural kindliness, so that one soon feels elevated directly and automatically to a finer and nobler, cleaner and higher spiritual atmosphere. . . . In full harmony with the tastefulness of his demeanour and his clothing, and with the almost military precision, are all the furnishings of the apartment contained in the pleasant middle-class house. In light-coloured breeches and a brown frock-coat or jacket, and, out of doors, wearing a top-hat – this is how he lives in my memory. On hot summer days he tried to lower the temperature in his room with blocks of ice.[35]

In April 1873 he went to visit the Wagners in Bayreuth, taking his long essay on 'Die Philosophie im tragischen Zeitalter der Griechen' ('Philosophy in the Tragic Age of the Greeks'), which he read to them with long pauses for discussion – reading and discussion being spread over several evenings. The essay grouped Socrates with Anaximander, Heraclitus, Parmenides, Anaxagoras, Empedocles and Democritus, characterizing them all as 'hewn out of one stone. Between their ideas and their character a firm necessity holds sway. . . . In magnificent isolation they are the only ones who devoted their lives exclusively to knowledge.' Nietzsche intended to emulate them; later he would claim an affinity with Spinoza while praising him for 'making knowledge into the most powerful affect'.[36]

It was one of these discussions with the Wagners that prompted Nietzsche to write about David Strauss, who had published little since the 1864 version of *Das Leben Jesu*, but in 1872 had brought out a naive and facile statement of patriotic optimism, *Der alte und der neue Glaube* (*The Old and the New Faith*). Wagner, who had been involved in a public quarrel with Strauss, directing three satirical sonnets at him in 1868, found the new book 'terribly superficial',[37] and Nietzsche, who had previously admired Strauss, was told he should read it. As eager as ever to be of use to Wagner, he had had the impression that the Master was still displeased with him. 'If you seemed not satisfied with me when I was there', he wrote humbly after returning to Basel,

I understand it only too well, without being able to do anything about it, for I learn and perceive very slowly, and each moment I am with you, I experience something that had never occurred to me, which I wish to impress on my mind. . . . I have often wished to give at least the appearance of greater freedom and independence, but in vain. Enough. I ask you to take me simply as a pupil.[38]

He had finished reading Strauss's book and was 'amazed at his obtuseness and vulgarity as a writer and as a thinker'. Already he was at work on a counterblast, applying the polemical technique he had learned from working with Rohde on *Afterphilologie*. 'A nice selection of his stylistic enormities should show the public once and for all what this supposed classic really is.'[39]

In one of his unpublished notes Nietzsche had written: 'The philosopher of the future? He must become the superior tribunal of artistic culture, comparable to the security officials controlling disorderliness.'[40] In the new essay on Strauss he assumed this role, beginning with an attack on the 'pseudo-culture'. Victory in war was more dangerous than defeat: the conquest of France had not been a triumph for German culture. On the contrary, there was a danger of 'the defeat – indeed the extirpation of the German spirit in favour of the "German *Reich*".'[41] Culture, he said, was 'above all, unity of artistic style in all the expressions of a people's life. But quantity of knowledge and erudition is neither the necessary medium for culture nor a symptom of it. If necessary it can accommodate itself very well with the antithesis of culture – barbarism, i.e. stylelessness or the chaotic confusion of all styles.'

Nietzsche's attitude to the Prussian victory over France was more perspicacious than Gustav Freytag's. In 1871 the novelist wrote: 'No struggle was ever fought for a greater ideal than this . . . never, perhaps, did divine providence apportion rewards and punishments with such human justice and logic. Hundreds of thousands of people saw this as the poetry of the historical process.'[42] In 1873, after reading Nietzsche's indictment of the war's cultural backwash, Freytag retorted: 'When has Germany been greater or healthier than today, or better deserved the reputation of a cultured nation?'[43]

While working on the Strauss essay, Nietzsche was having trouble with his eyes, and he was treated with atropine (deadly nightshade) to keep the pupils dilated, making it impossible for him to focus them. He suffered a great deal of pain, and he had to start dictating his essay. On 22 May the doctor forbade him to do any reading; for two weeks he had to lecture without notes or books. He had intended to send Wagner a complete manuscript of the essay for his birthday on 22 May. The first draft was ready by the 5th, but the eye trouble slowed him down. Fortunately von Gersdorff arrived in Basel on 18 May, and he helped Nietzsche by taking dictation for the text of *David Strauss der Bekenner und der Schriftsteller* (*David Strauss the Confessor and the Writer*) which was to be published by Fritzsch as the first in a series of pamphlets titled *Unzeitgemässe Betrachtungen* (*Untimely Reflections*). Nietzsche had previously used the word '*unzeitgemäss*' *à propos* Wagner, praising him in an 1869 letter to Rohde for standing on his own feet, independent of his century. The essay was sent off on 25 June and published in August. There was no reply from Strauss, and Nietzsche never discovered whether he had read it (as, in fact, he had). When he died six months later, Nietzsche wrote to von Gersdorff: 'I very much hope that I have not aggravated the end of his life.'[44]

In July, working from notes, Nietzsche dictated another essay: *Über Wahrheit und Lüge im aussermoralischen Sinn* (*On Truth and Falsehood in an Extra-moral Sense*). It began with the fable he had created for 'Pathos der Wahrheit' about the clever animals. He also repeated the images of Nature's throwing away the key, and of hanging onto the back of a tiger, lost in dreams. Starting from the same premises, the new essay developed a more forceful argument. Against the perspective of universal history, human intellect can have no great value. Aeons had existed before it, but we think of it as cognate with the central consciousness of the universe, just as a gnat must assume itself to be the flying centre of the world. Perhaps intellect is given to us only to delude us into thinking existence worthwhile: cognition is deceptive because a flattering image of itself is built into it. We know virtually nothing about the interior functioning of our body, but, fluttering around the central flame of our vanity, we have unlimited capacity for deception, dissimulation and display.

Usually it is assumed that linguistic philosophy dates back no further than the twentieth century. A. J. Ayer, for instance, maintains that there was no 'extreme, conscious preoccupation with language' until Wittgenstein and Russell began to take an 'interest in the relation between language and the world'. [45] But in this 1873 essay the twenty-eight-year-old Nietzsche arrived at an insight which was to prove crucial. Previously it had been taken for granted that words could convey the objective truth about external reality; Nietzsche saw that there can be no question of objectivity. Since we cannot help being defrauded, we have evolved linguistic conventions to defraud ourselves reassuringly. Language is like an umbrella we can hold up against awareness that the universe is hostile to us. But words can never be transparent,

for between two absolutely disparate spheres such as subject and object there can be no connections which are causal, precise or expressive, but nothing more than an *aesthetic* interaction,[46] I mean, the transmission of hints, a stumbling translation into a wholly foreign language, for which we invariably need a freely poeticizing and freely inventive intermediate faculty and intermediate area.

So language can at most designate our relationship to the thing, never the thing-in-itself. The thing is divided from the name we give it first by the nervous stimulus it produces and then by the percept we form. The insect and the bird perceive a different world from ours, and we are not entitled to the comfortable assumption that our perceptions are more accurate, for there is no standard of comparison. A poor man may be said to be lying if he claims to be rich, but what does 'rich' mean? All our words are based on the equation of unequal things. One rich man may be richer than another, one leaf bear little resemblance to another. Why should a tree be masculine in German and a plant feminine? The word 'Schlange' suggests the sinuosity of the snake, but none of its other attributes. Words can never have more than a tenuous relationship to what they represent.

So what is truth? A mobile army of metaphors, metonyms, anthropomorphisms – in short an aggregate of human relationships which, poetically and rhetorically heightened, became transposed and elaborated, and which, after protracted popular usage, poses as fixed, canonical, obligatory. Truths are illusions whose illusoriness is overlooked.

Nietzsche is still placing a Schopenhauerian emphasis on the aesthetic mode. What differentiates us from the animals is our 'capacity for volatilizing plastic metaphors into a scheme, and so dissolving a picture into an idea'. The essay goes on to compare human truth with a complex dome of ideas on a movable base, floating on running water. The impulse towards the formation of metaphors, which is central to our functioning, leads us into myth-making and into artistic activity.

Intellect, that master of dissembling, is released from his former slavery, so long as he can deceive without doing *damage*, and then he celebrates his Saturnalia. Never is he more exuberant, richer, prouder, more skilful or daring. . . . Indigent man had his life saved by clinging to an elaborate framework of concepts, but now the emancipated intellect uses it only as a stage for its most daring performance or as a toy.

The imagery of game-playing also extends into the comparison of concepts with dice, 'made of hard bone . . . octagonal and negotiable'. But they are the residue of metaphors.

Nietzsche was going a long way beyond Schopenhauer towards Saussure and Wittgenstein. What he was doing, fundamentally, was applying to the whole territory of language the radical scepticism he had learned from his philological research. The parables he had invented about the feelingless demon and the clever animals had led him to the Kantian idea that Nature had thrown away the key of the consciousness into which humanity was locked. Kant apologized for having to abolish knowledge in order to make way for faith; Nietzsche taught the truth that we have to live without truth.

The insistence that language cannot connect the subject to the object points forward to Saussure's principle that language is form, not substance. It is a system of elements which cannot be described physically, which can be defined only by their relations to each other within the system. It was Nietzsche's insight – since he was not going to baulk at exploring its implications – that would make it necessary for him to overturn the whole tradition of Western metaphysics. Not that it came suddenly to an end. Residue from it is still to be found in Wittgenstein's *Tractatus Logico-Philosophicus* in the doctrine that propositions are meaningful insofar as they depict a state of affairs, a relationship between things in the world. Nietzsche has a great affinity with Wittgenstein, but the Wittgenstein of the 1920s had still not caught up with this essay of 1873, though his *Philosophical Investigations* makes it axiomatic that no statement about the world can be true in the metaphysical sense. Nothing can *mean* anything. Philosophy should not be a theory but an activity which consists partly in demonstrating how false assumptions about language can produce false impressions of the world. Hence the prominence of language games and the Nietzschean insistence on the extent to which language can be a prison-house (Nietzsche's word) or a net (Nietzsche's word) or a 'bewitchment of our intelligence' (Wittgenstein's phrase). He spoke also of 'bruises which the understanding has suffered by bumping its head against the limits of language'.[47]

After suffering a great deal of pain in his eyes while dictating the essay, Nietzsche spent his summer holidays at the Hotel Segnes in Flims with Heinrich Romundt and von Gersdorff, who wrote: 'I hope our friend's eyes and nerves will benefit from the clockwork regularity of life, from inhalation of the best, most fragrant forest air, from daily bathing in the beautiful green Caumansee, from good food and relaxing company, from intercourse with the greatest and best authors – Wagner, Goethe, Plutarch – good conversation, etc. The so-called accommodative pains of the eye muscles recur periodically, but his eyes are significantly stronger.'[48] The water in the lake was said to have healing properties: Nietzsche made compresses for his eyes with it.

Elisabeth, who came to Flims for the last day or two of the holiday, travelled with von Gersdorff and her brother to Basel, where she may have stayed from mid-August till about 21 October, helping him through a period of enforced rest. Von Gersdorff had to leave on 17 September, ten days before the end of term, when Nietzsche wrote to him: 'My health has been changeable, so I hope the holidays will be restful and productive. For it is only when I am producing something that I can be really healthy and feel well. The rest is bad *entr'acte* music.' Romundt, who was now lecturing at the university in Basel, and later moved into the house, took most of Nietzsche's dictation, including the jaundiced letter written on 18 October to Rohde: 'Everything that is new is terrible.'[49]

To raise money for the Bayreuth project, Nietzsche had been

asked to write an appeal to the German nation, which he did reluctantly; he was convinced there was an international Communist plot to muzzle Wagner and him. 'F [Fritzsch], we are afraid, is already compromised, and probably he has received money by now.'[50] Nietzsche's fears were unfounded, though by now two radical groups were at work, Lassalle's General Union of German Workers, founded in 1863, and the Social Democratic Workers' Party, founded on more Marxist lines in 1869. But the agitation had no effect on Fritsch except to foment strikes among the typesetters, causing delay in the printing of work by Wagner and Nietzsche.

In November and December Nietzsche was working on the second in his series of *Unzeitgemässe Betrachtungen vom Nützen und Nachteil der Historie im Leben* (*On the Uses and Disadvantages of History for Life*). After the essay about the falsifications of language, it was natural that Nietzsche should go on to challenge the view that historical objectivity was possible. Goethe, though alert to the need for world history to be rewritten from time to time, had praised an account of the Ostrogoths in Italy for proving to us that 'such things really happened in those days'.[51] Nietzsche, still oriented towards the aesthetic, wanted to show that what we require from the historian is an artist's ability to recreate past reality. 'But it is no more than superstition to suppose that the picture which things reflect on such a man corresponds to their empirical reality.'[52] The past could be explained only in relation to the present. The great historian is always forced to say something universal or to repeat something already known, transforming it in the process.[53]

Although the essay on truth and falsehood was still unpublished, he did not devote very much of the essay on history to the impossibility of objectivity; but his scepticism about 'truth' made him more critical towards the activities of scholars who were under the illusion that what they were doing was in pursuit of 'the truth'. Goethe had said: 'I hate everything that merely reaches me without increasing or directly enlivening my activity,' but since the beginning of the century the study of history had become more widespread, more intensive and more academic. To Nietzsche this seemed a cultural phenomenon of some importance. Taken beyond a certain point, historical awareness is destructive of the present. By destroying illusions, historical justice deprives things of the only atmosphere in which they can survive.[54]

There are three kinds of history – monumental, antiquarian and critical.[55] The value of the monumental is in the knowledge that greatness which was possible once may be possible again. Schopenhauer had believed in the continuity of the great in every age: he had spoken of a republic of genius, believing that the greatest men formed 'a kind of bridge across the turbulent stream of becoming'.[56] It was absurd to believe in a *Weltgeist* that moved autonomously forward, particularizing itself in progressively purer forms. 'For Hegel the highest and ultimate phase of the historical process was attained in his own Berlin existence.'[57] Darwinism had contributed to the conviction that the quality of life was steadily improving. 'No, the *goal of humanity* cannot be located in its end but *in its finest specimens*.'[58] Two more years of Goethe's life would have been worth more than 'cartloads of fresh modern existences'. Only the greatest spirits can learn from history the lesson which matters most – how to live.[59] 'Only strong personalities can withstand history; the feeble are extinguished by it.'[60]

The virtuous man is the one who will rise up against the blind force of facts, against the tyranny of the actual, submitting only to laws that are not those of historical volatility. He always swims against the waves of history, whether by fighting his own passions, as being the nearest brute facts of his existence, or by committing himself to honesty, while falsehood weaves its glittering nets around him.[61]

Nietzsche was preparing his anti-Hegelian path towards hermit-like isolation, but he was echoing Hegel in contrasting the unity of Greek culture with the fragmentation that is characteristic of modernity. Schoolboys and students were being pumped full of ideas taken second-hand from past cultures, not from immediate contact with life.[62] If a modern student could be transported, magically, back to ancient Greece, the Greeks would strike him as very uneducated.[63] But their culture was not split between internal and external. The chaos of elements taken from foreign cultures – Semitic, Babylonian, Egyptian and Lydian – had been organized as people arrived at self-possession by thinking their way into their true needs, and letting go of everything superfluous.[64]

In modern Germany no one lived philosophically, in the sense that the Stoics had, with a single-hearted virile faith. In the suggestion, which is made twice,[65] that a hundred men could deliver the death-blow to the sham education that was currently prevalent, we can recognize Nietzsche's old idea of an elite – himself and his friends – to inaugurate educational reform.

The critical historian sits in judgement on the past, which must always be condemned, though we ourselves are the result of errors perpetrated by our ancestors. 'It takes great strength to go on living, remembering that life and injustice are synonymous.'[66] Historical movements had invariably been activated by the egoism of individuals, groups or masses, but, far from being disturbed by this discovery, people seemed content to make egoism into their god.[67] Here, as in the essay on Strauss, Nietzsche was glancing uneasily at the task lying ineluctably ahead. What was needed was a new ethic.

On 20 December he left Basel to spend Christmas in Naumburg, with the idea of coming back via Bayreuth. Ill again, he was in bed over Christmas, and changed his mind about visiting the Wagners, though he went to see Fritzsch in Leipzig about a second edition of the pamphlet on Strauss, which had been in demand since the outright attack on it in the October issue of *Grenzboten* under the title 'Herr Friedrich Nietzsche und die deutsche Kultur'. *Die Geburt der Tragödie* was also in demand, and the second edition went to press in January 1874, though it did not appear in the bookshops until 1878. While he was in Leipzig, Nietzsche went to see Ritschl, but differences of opinion were more in evidence than feelings of friendship. Ritschl wrote: 'Quarrelsome conversation about principles.'[68]

As soon as the essay on history was printed, Nietzsche sent a copy to Burckhardt, whose position was closer to Goethe's than to Nietzsche's, and his response, phrased politely enough, was that his intention had never been to 'breed scholars and men of learning in the narrow sense'. He had always encouraged his students to form their own view of the past.[69]

Nietzsche had been trying to maintain his health by dieting. He was breakfasting at eleven-thirty on soup and two ham sandwiches, which usually kept him going until the evening, when he would eat a vegetarian supper in his room, though sometimes he would have lunch with meat.[70] In February 1874, writing to congratulate his mother on her birthday, and wishing her good health in the coming year – her forty-ninth – he warned her 'not to follow the absurd example of your esteemed son, who has started ailing far too early in life, and already, like a little old man, is grateful for each day when he is not reminded of indigestion and pains. . . . In any case I must certainly do something about it. Infirmity is gaining ground too quickly.' If only he had a country estate, he would give up his job. 'I have now been a professor for five years – almost long enough, I should think.'[71] But at least he had stopped dosing himself with his own prescriptions. In the middle of the month he reported that he had not taken any medicine since Christmas.[72] At the end of March, after three months of 'being very careful and regular in my routine', he decided not to take another cure. He was almost resigned to the probability that his health would never improve. 'I really suffer too much and feel glad when I am physically ill, because then I can give myself the illusion that something can be done to help me, which now, without illness as a pretext, I cannot believe. But there is nothing to be done. One's life must go on. I can vent my rage in printed maledictions, and am now starting on number 3 of my *Unzeitgemässen.*'[73]

Since Christmas he had written nothing, though since the middle of February he had had regular secretarial help from a student, Adolf Baumgartner, who came regularly on Wednesday afternoons to take dictation and read to him. Developing a taste for polemic and the publicity it was bringing him, he was planning to write thirteen *Unzeitgemässe Betrachtungen*. 'I want to sing my way energetically up and down the whole scale of my antipathies. . . . Later, five years later, I will give up polemics and think of a "good work". But now my chest is really congested with pure aversion and distress, so I must expectorate, with or without propriety, but conclusively.'[74]

He was worried, though, about the amount of energy he would need to work through negative material: 'The goal is so remote, and, even if one reaches it, most often one's strength has been used up in the long quest and struggle. One reaches freedom exhausted, like a fly in the evening of its only day of life.'[75] An equally depressed letter arrived in Bayreuth on 4 April. Wagner, who had not seen him for nearly a year, concluded: 'He must either marry or write an opera.'[76]

In February 1874, when the essay on history was published, the Wagners were piqued to receive their copy, not from him but from Fritsch. Unlike the first of the *Unzeitgemässe Betrachtungen* it had nothing to do with Wagner, and Nietzsche had been right to anticipate that this would displease him. He wrote, briefly but amiably,[77] while Cosima wrote at length, praising the essay for its profundity and the completeness of its 'mastery over the manifold phenomena of life', but suggesting that it could appeal only to a small public, and venturing some stylistic criticisms: Nietzsche occasionally lapsed into carelessly familiar expressions (such as 'Where did he get that?') and often seemed anxious to avoid the relative pronoun 'which'.[78] He felt tempted to tell her that her husband's prose was more in need than his of her critical attention, and he was still more annoyed when he found that their comments to Fritsch had been much less favourable than their comments to him.

The disenchantment was mutual. Nietzsche was already planning to include an essay on Wagner in his series. The name occurs among a list of fourteen subjects under the heading *Unzeitgemässe Betrachtungen* in a notebook dated 'Beginning of 1874 – spring 1874', and the title he was to use, 'Richard Wagner in Bayreuth', appears a few pages later. The surrounding notes are more critical than anything he had previously written about 'the Master', who was histrionic by disposition, he said, and understood his sources only insofar as he could use them. Nor could he understand why anything should fail to have the same impact on the public that it had on him, or should succeed in having more. He was insensitive about his contemporaries, both musicians and poets. He had a feeling of 'spurious omnipotence' and a tyrant's love of the colossal. 'It is fortunate that Wagner was not born on a higher level, as a nobleman, and did not take a fancy to the political sphere.' Believing himself to be without heirs, he was trying to disseminate his ideas as widely as possible, reproducing himself through them. 'No one is more honestly against himself than the man who believes only in himself. Wagner gets rid of all his weaknesses by charging his period and his enemies with them. . . . He measures state, society, virtue, people – everything – against his art and, in his refusal to be appeased, he wants the whole world to be destroyed.' He was no longer in touch with his earlier, socialist self. His art was conceived 'not to improve reality, but to deny the actual or conjure it away. . . . As an actor he wants to imitate men only at their most effective and most outgoing – in extreme emotion. The intoxicating, the sensually ecstatic, suddenness and rapture at all costs – fearful tendencies.'

In the spring of 1874 Wagner's new house Wahnfried was completed, and in June, after Nietzsche had declined an invitation, he wrote back, in brief paragraphs, parodying the young professor's usual demurs: 'Oh friend: /Why do you not come to us?/ I can find an excuse for everything – or whatever you care to call it./ Only do not hold yourself so aloof! If you persist, I can do nothing for you./ Your room is ready./ However – or, on the contrary:/ Nevertheless!/ or yet:/ "if it must be"!'[79]

At the same time von Gersdorff, who had been planning to visit Switzerland in the autumn, threatened not to come unless Nietzsche visited Wahnfried first. 'Just remember that I have obligations towards myself, which are difficult to fulfil with my health in such a fragile state. Really, nobody should use coercion on me.'[80]

At the beginning of July he was still working on the third of the *Unzeitgemässe Betrachtungen*, *Schopenhauer als Erzieher* (*Schopenhauer as Educator*), which he had begun at the end of March, but without any hope of finishing it before the holidays. 'The body is obstructive, and needs to be cheered up a little.'[81] Nor was Fritsch encouraging. He agreed to publish the essay, 'but with the sourest and sulkiest face in the world,'[82] making Nietzsche assume that the series would come to a premature end. But on 8 July another publisher, Ernst Schmeitzner, approached him, and within a week Nietzsche had invited him to take over the series, starting with the Schopenhauer essay. Schmeitzner accepted eagerly, and Fritsch was almost disappointingly agreeable.

Wanting to spend his summer holidays in the mountains again, Nietzsche went to Bergun, which he liked better than Flims, though he missed the bathing. At first he suffered from 'a little constipation, caused by the good Veltliner wine'[83] but by the end of the month he had gone back to work on the Schopenhauer essay, finding the mountain air conducive to concentration. 'A great deal comes to mind which would never have occurred to me in the depths and the sweltering summer heat of the towns.'[84]

The high altitude accorded with his definition of the philosopher's function – to sit in a higher tribunal passing judgement on contemporary culture: 'I know of no better objective I can have than somehow or other to become an "educator" in a wide sense.'[85] But he no longer wanted to use the university as headquarters for his campaign. On 14 May 1874 he was hoping 'to withdraw into the most shameless solitary existence, miserably simple but dignified.'[86] He was thinking of establishing his 'private citadel and hermitage' in the unspoiled medieval Bavarian town of Rothenburg. 'I hate the characterless mixed cities that are no longer whole.'[87]

Schopenhauer als Erzieher is in line with the impatience he had shown as a boy with Deussen and other schoolfriends for apparently failing to realize their potential. Instead of exulting in their individuality, most people let inertia and conventionality deafen them to the voice of their own conscience when it said: 'Be yourself! Everything you are doing, thinking, wanting is not really you!'[88] We all discover limitations in our talent and in our moral will, but our sense of sin makes us yearn for the holy, while our intellect makes us long for contact with our latent genius. 'These are the roots of all real culture, by which I mean man's longing to be reborn as saint and "genius".'[89]

The educator should help his student to discover the fundamental laws of his own character. 'Your true being does not lie hidden deep inside you, but incalculably high above you.'[90] The question to ask yourself, looking back on your life, is 'What have I really loved?' Objects have formed a ladder on which you have climbed up to your present self. The true educator gives you access to something in yourself which is quite incapable of being educated. He does not shape it for you, but helps you to unchain it.

The tempo of life was increasing. Amid the general bustle, the waters of religion were receding, leaving swamps and stagnant pools, while the sciences were disrupting and dissolving all firm beliefs. But three images of man had been set up which could provide incentive: Rousseauian man, Goethean man and Schopenhauerean man. The spirit behind the contemporary revolutions was Rousseauian – longing for something beyond himself, oppressed and humiliated man calls on holy nature, crying for light, fighting for freedom. Goethean man abhors violence, clings to moderation, gradual change. This liberal spirit can degenerate into philistinism, as Goethe must have realized when he made Jarno tell Wilhelm Meister that irritation and bitterness were all very well, but real anger was better.[91]

Nietzsche's anger was real, and he fuelled it with thoughts of emulating his favourite philosopher. His characterization of Schopenhauerian man is like a letter written to himself about his unhappy future. Despite his Franconia experience, he still believed that he could have opted for comfortable gregariousness, but

'Schopenhauerian man voluntarily takes on himself the pain of truthfulness.'[92] To his myopic contemporaries, 'who always take negation as a symptom of evil',[93] he appears more Mephistophelean than Faustian. But 'all existence that can be denied deserves to be denied; to be truthful is to believe in an existence which could never be negated or flawed with falsehood. So the truthful man feels a metaphysical meaning in his activity, explicable according to the laws of a higher life, and profoundly affirmative, though everything he does seems to violate and destroy the laws of that life.'[94]

Magnetically drawn towards the negative principle, Nietzsche was tentatively formulating a reductionist morality: if it was proper to test the positive by applying the negative, he was justified in being as consistently negative as he could. At the same time he was proposing for himself nothing less than a heroic striving towards the level he had characterized (in his essay on history) as suprahistorical. To be content to understand your life as a point in the evolution of a race, a state, or a science is to belong among the history of becoming. 'This eternal becoming is a mendacious puppet-play in which man forgets himself, essentially the diversion which scatters the individual to all the winds, an endless, mindless game which that overgrown child, Time, plays for us and with us. This heroism of truthfulness consists in desisting, one day, from being his plaything.'[95] Instead of 'conserving himself and enjoying the multiplicity of things', the heroic man sets himself 'a huge task . . . that of destroying everything that is becoming, and exposing all the spuriousness of things'. It was to this task that Nietzsche would devote the fifteen remaining years of his sanity.

One problem he was ignoring was the relationship between nature and culture. I am formulating it in eighteenth-century terms because Nietzsche himself, despite his advanced thinking about language, was still taking it for granted that nature had a purpose in raising us above the animals, and that without understanding it, we can help towards its consummation if we contribute to the work of the philosopher, the artist and the saint. Hegel too had held philosophy, art and religion to be the most sublime of human pursuits, but for Nietzsche the crucial issue was nonconformity. Controlled by despots who were indifferent to the truth, the state was using military methods to organize the herd, while demanding

from it the same obedience and devotion it formerly gave to the
Church.[96] The state is concerned not with truth, but only with
what is useful to it, whether true, half-true, or false.[97] Schopenhauerian man would have no time for politicians or even for reading
the newspapers: in a well-organized state only statesmen need to
concern themselves with politics.[98] But, Nietzsche insisted, everyone had a cultural obligation: to contribute to the work of the
philosopher, the artist and the saint.[99] It is only in this way that we
can 'work towards the fulfilment of nature'.[100] So he was writing as
if there was a consciousness in nature that was taking an interest in
the best works of art and philosophy. At the same time he was
generalizing out of his private compulsion towards self-transcend-
ance. Temperamentally he had an affinity with Kant, who gauged
moral goodness according to the amount of effort that went into
conquering personal inclination.

For Nietzsche a philosopher's ideas were less important than the
quality of his striving towards existence on a philosophical or suprahistorical plane. In short, he must be a hero, as Schopenhauer had
been. This attitude, implicit in the essay, is explicit in one of
Nietzsche's unpublished notes. 'A man's character is worth a hundred systems. . . . There is something in a philosopher there can
never be in a philosophy: the origin of many philosophies – the
great man. . . . To take on ourselves the voluntary pains of truthfulness, the personal injuries. Suffering is the object of life.'

In June his inclination to think more critically of Wagner was
encouraged when Brahms came to conduct the Basel *Gesangverein*
in a performance of his *Triumphlied* – a celebration of the German
victory over the French, written for baritone solo, eight-part choir
and orchestra. 'For me it was one of the most difficult aesthetic
problems of conscience to come to a confrontation with Brahms. I
have now some little opinion of this man.'[101] The problem was that
Wagner, regarding all contemporary German composers as rivals,
derided them, but Nietzsche bought a piano score of the *Triumphlied*
and took it with him in August, when he finally went from Bergun
to Bayreuth together with Elisabeth. After arriving at the Hotel
Sonne he sent a message to the Wagners that he was feeling too
unwell to visit them. Wagner came straight to the hotel and persuaded him to go back to Wahnfried, which was even more sumptu-
ously decorated than Tribschen. Damask and satin wallhangings

predominated. The huge drawing-room, which looked out on the garden, contained Wagner's piano, his big writing-desk and a smaller one for Cosima, his pictures and his souvenirs. Among the marble busts in the hall was one of himself. The Scandinavian snake motif along the frieze framed pictures by Echter of the *Ring der Nibelungen* copied from frescoes in the Munich Residenz. Nietzsche was not so easily overawed as when he paid his first visit to Tribschen in 1869. He provoked Wagner by saying that he had lost interest in the German language, preferring to express himself in Latin, and he left the red-bound score of Brahms's *Triumphlied* on Wagner's piano. 'You see, here is someone else who can write good music!' When the Master lost his temper, Nietzsche merely blushed, looking at him with modest dignity. In his notebook he had already made the point: 'The tyrant admits no individuality other than his own and that of his most intimate friends. Wagner runs a great risk in granting nothing either to Brahms or to the Jews.'[102] (Wagner's 1850 article 'Das Judentum in der Musik' had argued that Jews are lacking in 'true passion' of the sort requisite to artistic creativity.)[103] The *Triumphlied* incident is mentioned in none of Nietzsche's letters, and Elisabeth heard about it from Wagner. When she asked her brother why he had never mentioned it, his answer was: 'On that occasion Wagner was not great.'[104]

On 19 August Nietzsche posted part of the Schopenhauer essay to Schmeitzner, though a long section needed to be rewritten. He had it ready in time to post it on 9 September, but a fortnight later he had still not recovered from 'the unavoidable exhaustion and nervous upheaval'.[105] Needing rest, he left for the mountains with Romundt and Baumgartner when term ended on 26 September. At Rigi he put himself on a milk diet, but slept badly and left after three days for Lucerne, where he took the waters, went for long walks, and resigned himself to being at the end of his twenties. 'At the age of thirty one counts one's treasure and asks oneself whether one can cope with life – it seems I can.'[106] But he was not one to miss the chance of making resolutions for the next decade in his life. He wanted to be 'more masculine and equable and not so damnably up-and-down'.[107] He condemned himself for being too despondent and not sufficiently grateful for what he owed to his friends. 'The truth is that I live through you. I make progress by leaning on you.

My idea of myself is weak and pitiable and *you* have incessantly to guarantee me to myself.'[108]

He had been hoping to see both Rohde and von Gersdorff in Basel during October, but Rohde had come in September, while Nietzsche's struggle with *Schopenhauer als Erzieher* was at its most painful; and when von Gersdorff came for a week in the middle of October, Nietzsche was busy from eight in the morning till eleven at night. He had seven hours of teaching in the university and six in the Pädagogium, together with preparatory work for lectures on new subjects, including Greek literary history.

None of Nietzsche's books was selling well. About five hundred copies of the essay on David Strauss had been sold and two hundred of the history essay, but the second edition of *Die Geburt der Tragödie* had not come out because there were still two hundred unsold copies of the first. Habituated to self-conquest, Nietzsche tried to take pleasure in adversity. 'Even hostile counter-measures I now find useful and favourable, for they often enlighten me more quickly than friendly collaboration, and there is nothing I want more than to become enlightened about the whole highly complicated system of antagonisms that constitute the "modern world".'

For the third time he rejected the invitation to spend Christmas with the Wagners, and on the second day of the holiday the Master sat down to pen a rebuke: 'When we built our house, we made arrangements to offer you accommodation at any time – no such offer was ever made to me at the time I most needed it. . . . We could be most helpful to you. Why must you always scorn our help? . . . For Heaven's sake, marry a rich woman! Why was von Gersdorff born a man?'[109]

This barbed question must have helped to make Nietzsche feel remoter than ever from his boyhood friendship with Wilhelm Pinder and Gustav Krug, who had both got married during the year. Back in the family home for Christmas, he found a pretext for brooding on past emotion: instead of working at another essay for his series, he devoted his leisure to his old musical compositions. 'Turning my back on thinking and reverie, I made music. Many thousands of notes were written down.'[110] He was revising and rearranging his earlier work, partly to see whether anything could be made of it, and he wrote a solo version of his latest duet, *Hymnus an die Freundschaft*. 'I am *very* satisfied with it. . . . I should like my music to prove that it is possible to forget one's century, and that ideality consists in this!'[111] He was thirty – the age at which Hegel had arrived at the opposite conclusion. Without being suicidal, his feelings at the beginning of 1875 could scarcely have been more negative. 'I looked into the future with real terror. To be alive is frightful and dangerous – I envy those who can die in some honest way. However, I am determined to grow *old*, for otherwise it can be brought to nothing. But it is not enjoyment of living that will keep me alive.'[112]

A letter to von Bülow shows how he was beginning to think negatively. The conductor had suggested he should translate some Leopardi, and he declined, partly because of being a bad linguist but also, he said, because he was likely to be too healthy. It was only during vacations and illnesses that he could write, 'and since my daily cold baths preclude the probability of any illness, my future as a writer is almost hopeless'.[113] Behind the literary relish for the paradoxical is an unmistakably masochistic pleasure in the cold metallic hardness of the negative.

When he returned to Basel, external events joined forces with his unconcealed inclination to withdraw into greater isolation. After his hymn to friendship he began work on a hymn to loneliness, *Hymnus an die Einsamkeit*, but it remained unfinished.[114] The prospect of the mid-February carnival once again drove him out of Basel: 'I must at all costs avoid the festivities.'[115] He went to Lucerne for a couple of days. He was lucky to have an opportunity of continuing his relationship with the Wagners vicariously: it would have been hard to continue it in any other way. In January Cosima had written to say that they were going to be away on a concert tour from 15 February, and to ask whether Elisabeth would be able to visit Wahnfried from the beginning of the month, staying on after they left, to take charge of the household, including the children, their governess, the housekeeper, her sister, the gardener and the man-servant. After copying out Cosima's letter verbatim, Nietzsche added: 'urgently ask you to comply with this request. Our good mother will say yes with pleasure.' She did say yes, but grudgingly. To lose her daughter to her son during the summer months was bad enough; to lose her to strangers for part of the winter was almost intolerable.

On 6 March 1875, while Elisabeth was in Bayreuth, von Gersdorff came to spend the rest of the month in Basel, and Nietzsche started to dictate *Wir Philologen* (*We Philologists*), the essay he intended as the fourth in his *Unzeitgemässe Betrachtungen*. Out of every hundred philologists, he maintained, only one should have joined the profession; the motives of the others had been imitation of their teachers, expediency, and the need to earn a living. Deceived into regarding life merely as preparation for life in another world, most people were content, like ants, to invest labour in projects that could be important only as a preliminary for something else, as philology was for philosophy. He went on to combine the argument of the third preface for Cosima with a point he had made in his essay on history. 'Without *leadership*, the *greatest* part of our ant-like labours are simply *nonsensical* and superfluous.' Modern culture allowed no one to remain an individual except the philosopher, the saint and the artist. Greek culture had been quite different, but most classical philologists had no interest in using their knowledge to put the current situation in perspective. 'My object is to generate relentless hostility between antiquity and our contemporary "culture". Whoever wants to serve the latter must hate the former.' Nietzsche thought he would have the essay finished in the early summer, but after dictating less than three thousand words, he left it in abeyance.

He was about to lose both the friends who had been living with him at the house in Schützengraben. Romundt's lectures had been going so badly that Nietzsche and Rohde were calling him 'the classroom-emptier'.[116] He had been through a spiritual crisis which precipitated a decision to join the Catholic Church and work in Germany as a priest. Nietzsche took this as a personal rebuff. 'I sometimes feel it is the most evil thing anyone could do to me. . . . Our good, clean, Protestant atmosphere! . . . Does the wretch want to turn his back on all these liberating influences? Is he still in his right mind or should he be treated with cold baths?'[117] Attempts at dissuasion were predictably futile. 'He knows and he kept repeating that all the good things – the best things in his experience – were at an end, and, weeping uncontrollably, he begged for forgiveness.'[118] On 10 April 1875, a few hours before his train was due to leave, he was saying that he did not want to go, and at the last minute, after the guard had shut the doors of the compartment, he wanted to say something else to Nietzsche and Overbeck. Failing to wind the window down, he became desperate, but the friends could communicate only by signs as the train steamed out of the station. 'Incidentally I was in bed the next day with a headache that lasted for thirty hours, and I was vomiting a great deal of bile.'[119]

Nietzsche had intended to go off by himself for several days on a walking tour, but he was not well enough. Four months later he was still feeling that he had not fully recovered from the upset caused by Romundt.[120] In March he had already been needing to rest his eyes, which, after the strenuous winter term, were intermittently painful.[121] At the end of April, after feeling ill, and having twice to take to his bed, he gave himself a week's holiday in Bern, staying at the Hotel Victoria, where, as the only guest, he had the best bedroom — on the first floor, with a balcony. Each day he went for long walks outside the town, admiring the scenery.[122] Coming back to Basel at the beginning of May, he felt much healthier. He was expecting to be alone in the house, for Overbeck was leaving on 10 May to take a long cure in Karlsbad, but on the 9th, Nietzsche heard that Elisabeth would be arriving on the 13th.[123] He moved into Overbeck's room to give her his, but recurrent pains in his stomach, his head and his eyes prevented him from taking much pleasure in her company, useful though it was to have her there to look after him.[124] He was still having to cope with thirteen hours of teaching each week, staying in bed only on the worst days, and there was no prospect of doing any more work on *Wir Philologen* until the end of term. In the letter he wrote to Wagner on 24 May for his birthday, Nietzsche suggested that illness forced people to think only of themselves; Wagner was to be congratulated on the good health that was cognate with generosity and genius.[125] Nietzsche sometimes took the opposite view, claiming sickness as an aid to understanding.

In June it was already becoming apparent that he would not be well enough to attend the rehearsals for the *Ring* at Bayreuth in August.

The stomach would no longer be subdued even by the most absurdly rigorous diet. Recurrent headaches of the most violent sort, lasting for several days. Vomiting that lasted for hours even when I had eaten nothing. In short the machine looked as if it wanted to break down, and I will not deny that I have several times wished that this could be the end.[126]

Since Professor Immermann, the head of the Medical Faculty, could not diagnose what was wrong, all his prescriptions were experimental. 'God help Immermann, and then he will be able to help me. Meanwhile *dubito*.'[127]

Elisabeth, who had always been at least half in love with her brother and at twenty-eight was no closer to marrying than he was, suggested that they should set up house together. He was delighted: 'My fine plans for the next seven years are feasible only on the basis of some such order and stability in my everyday life. . . . I did not utter a single word of persuasion: she arrived quite voluntarily at the decision.'[128] Their mother, who objected vehemently to the arrangement, was persuaded, in the end, only by Nietzsche's insistence that he would otherwise have to resign from his professorship. After finding a new flat around the corner in Spalentorweg, he ordered new furniture, but did not move in before the summer holidays, which he decided to spend at the clinic of a well-known specialist in diseases of the stomach, Dr Wiel, at Steinabad in the Black Forest. Perhaps he would even feel well enough to go on to Bayreuth before returning to Basel.

Dr Wiel's diagnosis was that he had 'gastric catarrh' with significant dilation of the organ, causing vascular engorgements which kept the brain from being supplied with sufficient blood. 'Now we should be able to bring the fellow down to a manageable size again. We have carefully mapped out his former territory and hope, after a time, to see that he has withdrawn modestly to his frontiers.'[129] After starting the day with a self-administered enema and taking a coffee-spoonful of Karlsbad mineral salt at seven, he breakfasted on beefsteak and rusks, ate roast meat at midday, two raw eggs at four with white coffee, and roast meat again at eight. He was given a glass of red wine both at lunch and at dinner. Attributing the abnormal acidity of the stomach to mental and nervous pressures, the doctor applied leeches to Nietzsche's head. It was obvious to Nietzsche that he was eating too much, and when he asked to be put on a smaller diet, the doctor complied. For a man of sceptical habits, he was quaintly credulous about doctors, and his faith in Wiel remained unshaken. He abandoned the idea of going to Bayreuth: even to leave the clinic at the end of four weeks would be to leave sooner than he wanted to.[130]

By the end of July his stomach seemed better, but Wiel promised no such quick results with the nervous disorder.[131] Thinking constantly about the *Ring*, Nietzsche imagined himself conducting the music during the long walks he took in the forest, humming passages he knew by heart.[132] But by the second week in August the acidity in his stomach was no better, and he was still liable to be kept in bed by agonizing headaches and vomiting.[133] He was convinced that all the physical symptoms 'were deeply intertwined with spiritual crises, so that I have no idea how medicine and diet could ever be enough to restore my health'.[134] The secret was 'to acquire a certain hardness of the skin, because of the great inner vulnerability and capacity for suffering'.[135] Living with his sister he would be inside a 'snail's shell',[136] and the prospect suddenly attracted him so much that he left Steinabad on 12 August 1875, three days before his treatment was due to finish, knowing that Elisabeth had been preparing the home they were to share.

It consisted of seven rooms, including the kitchen. They had the whole ground floor of the house, part of the first floor, a cellar and an attic. Settling in, Nietzsche felt more hopeful than he had for years.[137] At first he was feeling not only well but optimistic about his health. Following Dr Wiel's advice he ate regularly at four-hour intervals: an egg, a rusk and cocoa at eight; meat at twelve; soup, meat and vegetables at four, cold meat and tea at eight. 'Everyone should do the same!'[138] He was ill in the middle of September, when he had to stay in bed for two days. He had recovered before the term ended on the 25th, but he was no longer feeling young. 'Almost from each day to the next I am accompanied by a certain sense of disillusion, but of a sort that spurs one to activity, like a fresh autumn wind.'[139] Having exiled himself, as he felt, 'from everything that pleases other people', he was glad to have his own stronghold, where he would 'no longer feel so vexed by life'.[140] Towards Rohde, whose life was now revolving around a woman's, Nietzsche could feel only compassion: 'Heaven preserve you and me from such a fate,' he wrote to von Gersdorff. [141]

Richard Wagner in Bayreuth was almost finished, but Nietzsche did not intend to publish it.[142] Nor did he want anything else to appear in print. 'The disgust I feel towards publication increases daily.'[143] It was impossible to be totally honest in print. The Wagner essay, he told Rohde, had pointed him towards 'a new attitude to the most problematic issue in our previous experience. But I have not resolved it, and if I cannot succeed in crystallizing the attitude for myself, I must keep silent instead of trying to help other people.'[144] Instead, he would give a seven-year 'cycle' of lectures on Greek civilization.[145] Starting from literary history he wanted to range over works of art, mythology, political history, rhetoric, rhythm and metre, philosophy and ethics. He loved to draw up long-term plans.

Unable to meet Rohde, he took three days' holiday at the end of September with Overbeck, who had returned from Karlsbad feeling better. They went to the Burgenstock, where they found themselves alone in the hotel, but Nietzsche was too restless for such tranquillity: 'The quietness can drive one mad.'[146] Soon after returning to Basel he had company: von Gersdorff, who arrived on 12 October, stayed till the 21st, and Malwida von Meysenbug arrived on the 15th. One topic of conversation was the newly published book *Psychologische Beobachtungen* (*Psychological Observations*) by Paul Rée, a Jewish friend of Romundt's whom Nietzsche had met two years before, when Rée, five years his junior, had been working on a thesis for his doctorate. The day after von Gersdorff left Basel Nietzsche wrote to tell Rée how much he and his friends had enjoyed the book.

In November it became clear that he had been over-optimistic to expect that the new routine of living with Elisabeth would make a difference to his health.

Each two or three weeks I spend about thirty-six hours in bed in real torment of the sort you know. . . . With new courses etc. the day is so exhausting that by the evening I have no appetite left for living, and feel surprised at how hard life is. It really does not seem worthwhile, all this torture.[147]

He took some comfort from a book of Indian proverbs von Gersdorff sent him, and from an English translation of a Buddhist book lent to him by a friend of Schmeitzner's. 'That life is worthless and all objectives deceptive is a conviction which often impresses itself on me so strongly – especially when I am ill in bed – that I need to hear more about it, but not adulterated with Judaeo-Christian terminology.'[148] While coming to think of the will to knowledge as an 'intermediate region between willing and ceasing to will', he was trying to temper his greed for knowledge: it was haste that deprived scholars of the glorious Nirvana-like calm of gaining insight. 'Then my health, too, will become more stable, but I shall not achieve this until I also *deserve* it, until I have found the state of soul which is, as it were, promised to me, the state of health in which the soul's only drive is towards knowledge.'[149]

Again he went to Naumburg for Christmas, but on Christmas Day he collapsed. 'I could no longer doubt that I am afflicted with a serious brain disease and that pains in the stomach and eyes are only symptomatic.'[150] Following Professor Immermann's advice, he used ice compresses and had cold water poured over his head in the early morning, but after a painful week in bed he was still not better. Returning to Basel he asked to be released from his teaching at the Pädagogium until Easter, but he went on teaching the eleven students he now had at the university. 'I am living almost entirely on milk, and I am sleeping decently. . . . If only the fearful day-long attacks would stop. Without them I can at least drag myself from one day to the next.'[151]

Early in February 1876 he had to give up all reading and writing: on the 7th he stopped lecturing in the university. On the 18th his mother, alarmed at the news, arrived in Basel, but he was recovering sufficiently to think of going to Vienna for a performance of *Lohengrin* on the 24th. He was not well enough to make the journey, but after von Gersdorff arrived in Basel on 6 March, they went off together to a boarding house in Veytaux near Montreux, leaving his mother with his sister. 'The air is strong: all the way here I could feel its refreshing power.'[152] Undeterred by rain and snow, they went for walks that often lasted five or six hours. Nietzsche stayed on in Veytaux after von Gersdorff had to leave on 29 March, and, the next day, his mother left Basel without waiting to see him again. His headaches were still recurrent, but for part of the time he felt quite happy.[153]

On 6 April he left for Geneva, to stay with Hugo von Senger, a conductor he had met at Bayreuth. He added Berlioz's *Benvenuto Cellini* overture to a concert programme specially to please Nietzsche. Von Senger also introduced him to two of his piano pupils, Mathilde Trampedach, a slim, twenty-three-year-old green-eyed blonde, and her younger sister. When, during a discussion about poetry, Nietzsche mentioned that he did not know the German translation of Longfellow's 'Excelsior', she offered to copy it out for him. A few days later, the men invited the two girls out for a walk, with their landlady as their chaperone. At their third meeting with Nietzsche, he improvised at the piano, and on the day he was leaving Geneva, 11 April, von Senger called to say that the following morning Mathilde would receive an important letter from Professor Nietzsche. The letter proposed marriage. 'Do you not think that together each of us will be better and more free than either of us could be alone – and so *excelsior*? Will you dare to come with me . . . on all the paths of living and thinking?'[154] She refused: she may already have been too attracted to von Senger, a married man nine years older than Nietzsche and eighteen years older than she was. Two years later he divorced his wife and eleven months after that he married Mathilde.

It was at about the end of April 1876 that Heinrich Köselitz, a twenty-two-year-old musician who had come to Basel for Nietzsche's lectures, began to take an active interest in the essay on Wagner. When Nietzsche let him read it, Köselitz tried to persuade him not to leave it unfinished. The essay still seemed to Nietzsche too personal to be publishable, but, thinking of giving it to Wagner in May as a birthday present, he let Köselitz make a fair copy. When he read this he changed his mind about publication. In June he dictated the three final chapters to Köselitz, who began to help him regularly, reading to him, taking dictation from him and correcting proofs with him. After appealing publicly for the German nation to support the Bayreuth festival, Nietzsche could not have attempted to resolve his ambivalence towards Wagner in print, just at the moment that the long-laid plans were culminating in a festival.

But it is surprising that such an honest man as Nietzsche should be willing to stand his own arguments on their head and that he should be so adept in doing so. In the notes the comparison with the legislator was pejorative; in the published essay 'Wagner is never more Wagner than when difficulties proliferate and he can take charge. On a grand scale, with all the joy of a law-giver, he unites violently conflicting forces in a simple rhythm, asserting his will through a bewildering heterogeneity of claims and demands – these are the tasks he was born for, and in performing them he finds his freedom.'[155] The essay concedes that Wagner 'simplifies the universe', but justifies the simplification as the result of 'concentrating on past and present life the illumination of an intelligence strong enough to span the remotest areas'.[156] Instead of attacking Wagner's art for wanting 'to deny the actual or conjure it away', Nietzsche praises it for making us 'feel that the whole visible world wishes to be spiritualized, absorbed and lost in the world of sounds'.[157] And whereas the unpublished notes criticize Wagner for losing touch with his earlier socialism, for having no remaining interest in improving reality, the essay praises him in the perspective it creates by defining the task of philosophy as 'to proceed courageously and unhesitatingly with the task of reforming that part of reality which has been recognized as susceptible of change'.[158] As a philosopher, Wagner had gone through different systems, always keeping faith with his higher self, and implicitly Nietzsche is endorsing the most grandiose claims Wagner had made about the redemption of society through art. His understanding of the past, says Nietzsche, is superior to that of the scholars who connive in the use of history as an opiate against anything novel.[159] It would be impossible to reinstate the art of drama in its purest, highest form without precipitating change in manners, politics and education. Battle must be joined with modern culture, which is the outworks of the loathsome organization that is nourished by the violence and injustice of state and society. 'For us Bayreuth is the sacred fire at dawn before the battle.'[160]

Having denounced Wagner in the notes as a tyrant, Nietzsche now represented him as having passed through a phase of falling prey to his 'gloomy, insatiable, demanding, personal drive towards *power and glory*. . . . He wanted to conquer and dominate as no artist ever had before, and, if possible, to rise at one stroke to that tyrannical omnipotence he so obscurely yearned for.'[161] He had understood that through theatre 'an incomparable influence can be wielded, the greatest influence of any art', and this had become the ruling notion of his life.[162] 'I doubt whether there has been any great artist in history who has clung to such monstrous fallacies in approaching his art or, with naive sincerity, used such crude forms.'[163] But, seeing his mistake, he had gained great insight into 'modern success, the modern public, modern artistic deception'. From then on, 'as if he were coming out into the light after a long illness', Wagner found that his higher self no longer grudged the service it had to give its baser brother.[164] Making his own experience of illness into a simile, Nietzsche used it not to gain insight into

Wagner's development but to take the potency out of a misgiving. Still envying Wagner's good health, and unable to attack the qualities that had enabled him to convert the Bayreuth fantasy into a reality, Nietzsche found a way of pushing his stowaway criticisms on board the vessel of praise. But the main statement is vehemently positive. 'The first to recognize the inner deficiency in spoken drama, he had provided a threefold clarification of each dramatic step – in word, gesture and music. The music conveys the inner emotions of the *dramatis personae* directly to the souls of the specta- tors.'[165] Wagner has a demoniac power of articulating his most inward, intimate experiences. 'His début in the history of art resembles a volcanic eruption of the combined artistic forces of nature herself.'[166] Wagner endows everything in nature with the power of speech – dawn, forest, mist, cliff, hills. Previous music had been concerned with *ethos* – permanent states of mind. Beethoven had broken through to the language of feeling, but only in his last and greatest works had he been unconstrained by the conventions of *ethos*. By comparison with Wagner, all previous music seemed stiff and uncertain, alien and faltering.[167]

On 30 May 1876 Nietzsche sent most of *Richard Wagner in Bayreuth* to Schmeitzner, and over the weekend of 17–18 June he drafted the remainder at Badenweiler, near Müllheim. By sup- pressing his misgivings he was creating a tension that took its toll on his health. 'For three or four weeks', he wrote on 7 July, 'I have been feeling wretched again, and I must see to it that I can force myself along *until* – and above all *through* – Bayreuth.'[168]

The essay was published on 10 July, and in one of the drafts he prepared for his letter to Wagner he wrote: 'This time there is no alternative but to ask you: read this text as if it were not about you and not by me. . . . When I think about my audacity on this occasion, I feel retrospectively dizzy and overcome.'[169] But his anxiety was allayed by return of post. 'Friend! Your book is prodigious! How did you come to know me so well? Now come soon and acclimatize yourself to the impacts through the rehears- als.'[170] And Wagner sent a copy of the essay to King Ludwig.

On 21 July Nietzsche wrote: 'Health from day to day deplorable! If only I knew what will happen! Otherwise no wishes, no illu- sions!'[171] But on the 23rd, without waiting for term to end on the 28th, he left for Bayreuth. After breaking the journey to spend a night in Heidelberg he arrived on Monday the 29th. Not having seen the Wagners since the summer of 1874 he must have been disappointed that, preoccupied with aristocratic patrons, temperamental singers, technical hitches, the takings at the box office, the dangers of having to recast singers or replace technicians, they could not spend much time with him. After mentioning the visit he paid them on arriving in Bayreuth, Cosima's diary makes no reference to his presence there, and according to Edouard Schuré (author of *Le Drame musical*), Nietzsche was 'timid, embarrassed and nearly always silent' when in Wagner's company.

Without consulting Wagner, the management committee had advertised a public rehearsal of *Götterdämmerung* in three parts, and on his first evening Nietzsche attended the first part. He had had a headache since midday on Sunday, and his feeling of exhaustion was exacerbated by the sultriness of the weather. He did not stay till the end of the rehearsal. But on Tuesday he began to feel better. 'For three days', he wrote on Friday, 'I have not had to look after myself: I have been living at Frl. von Meysenbug's, go out into the garden early, drink milk, bathe in the stream, and eat only what agrees with me.'[172] He had seen the rest of *Götterdämmerung* in rehearsal. On Wednesday there had been a row on stage between Wagner, the choreographer, and the designer, who was disaffected and had been threatening to leave when he found himself described in the programme as a machinist. But Nietzsche's feelings about the performance were changing. 'It is good to become familiar with it. Now I am in my element.'[173] Not that the Wagners themselves were happy with the production. 'Throughout', wrote Cosima, 'the costumes remind one of Red Indian chieftains and, together with their ethnographical absurdity, they bear all the marks of provincial tastelessness.'[174] Wotan was wearing 'a veritable musketeer's hat!' But Nietzsche did not see enough of the Wagners to know what their feelings were.

On the 31st he heard a complete rehearsal of *Die Walküre*, but he did not see all of it: his eyes were so painful that he had to close them. 'I long to be away from here. It is too nonsensical if I stay. I dread each of these long art-evenings; yet I do not stay away. . . . I have had quite enough. Nor shall I be at the first performance. Anywhere else, but not here, where it is nothing but torture for me.'[175] Without waiting for Elisabeth, who was due to arrive on 5 August, he left for the Bavarian Forest on the 3rd or 4th, staying at a boarding house in Klingenbrunn. 'I am so wearied and exhausted after my short stay there [Bayreuth] that I do not feel myself. Had a *bad* day here, lying in bed; but *persistent* headaches, as sometimes in Basel. . . . I will stay here perhaps ten days, but will not come back through Bayreuth.'[176] When he felt well enough, he did some work on an essay he had begun to dictate, almost improvisationally, at the end of June, intending to call it *Die Pflugschar* (*The Plough-share*) and to make it the fifth of his *Unzeitgemässe Betrachtungen*. After making some headway with it he did feel strong enough to return to Bayreuth on 12 August, the day the Kaiser and the Archduke of Weimar arrived. Wanting to avoid contact with the other monarchs, Ludwig 11 had already come in secret to attend the dress rehearsals, arriving at midnight on 5 August. The Emperor of Brazil, Dom Pedro 11, arrived in time for the official opening on Sunday 13 August.

The performance of *Das Rheingold* was disaster-ridden. Franz Betz, who played Wotan, lost the ring and ran into the wings twice during the curse. In the first scene-change a stagehand raised the backdrop too early, revealing men in shirtsleeves and the back wall of the theatre. According to Nietzsche, the Kaiser, who stayed only for the first two operas, 'clapped with his hands while calling out to his adjutants: "Frightful! Frightful!"'[177] The first-night audience shouted for Wagner to take a bow, but he refused to appear. His demands on stage machinery had been exorbitant and the dragon for *Siegfried* had been ordered from London because no German firm could cope with the specifications. It was transported in sections. The head had failed to arrive in time for the public rehearsal on 2 August, and the neck failed to arrive at all – apparently it had been sent to Beirut – so the head had to be fitted squatly onto the body.

In his essay Nietzsche had praised the symbiosis Wagner had achieved between his higher self and his lower self after going through a phase of gaining insight into 'modern success, the modern public, modern artistic deception'. In reality, confronted with the Bayreuth public, Nietzsche found it impossible to be tolerant. Having believed in Wagner as a cultural redeemer, he found himself participating in a philistine festival.

Even to those most intimately concerned, the 'ideal' was not what mattered most. . . . Then there was the pathetic crowd of patrons . . . all very spoilt, very bored and unmusical as yowling cats. . . . The whole idle riff-raff of Europe had been brought together, and any prince who pleased could go in and out of Wagner's house as if it were a sporting event. And fundamentally it was nothing more.[178]

The main consolation for Nietzsche was sudden friendship with a woman who had been living in Paris, Louise Ott. He knew she was married, but the discovery that she had a son seems to have acted as a deterrent. She left on 23 August, and their correspondence began when he wrote to her from Basel: 'It grew dark around me when you went away from Bayreuth: to me it was as if someone had taken the light away from me.' But he made it clear that he had no wish for a liaison. 'I think of you with such brotherly affection that I could love your spouse because he is *your* spouse.'[179]

When Nietzsche left Bayreuth on 27 August it was in the company of Paul Rée. According to Cosima's diary, it was not until 1 November that the Wagners discovered Rée was Jewish, but after rejecting an opportunity of a visit to Greece for fear of offending them by going with Mendelssohn's son, Nietzsche would never have allowed the friendship with Rée to develop at Bayreuth if he had still wanted their good will. But he did not refuse to buy underclothes for Wagner when the Master wrote to him from Rome, asking for some from a Basel shop, C. C. Rumpf. Replying, Nietzsche described how the atropine treatment to his eyes had made it necessary for him to sit in a darkened room, where he had been 'thinking of things past, far and near. . . . After *this* summer the autumn is for me – and probably not only for me – more autumnal than ever before. Behind the great events is a streak of the blackest melancholy, from which, certainly, one cannot escape quickly enough, whether to Italy or into work or both.'[180]

One of Nietzsche's best comments on the breach between them was made anonymously four years later. 'They both wanted to break off their friendship at the same time, one because he felt misunderstood, the other because he thought his friend understood him too well. Both were deceived, for neither of them understood himself well enough. . . .'[181]

7 Volte-Face

If the inevitable breach with Wagner had not come so soon, it might have taken Nietzsche longer to emancipate himself from Schopenhauer and the tradition of idealism. He had proved his capacity for originality, especially in the five prefaces, the essay on truth and falsehood, and the essay on history, but in all these his imagination had set the pace: his lightning-like verbal talent for paradoxes, parables and images had flashed into areas he could not have illuminated discursively, one hindrance being emotional loyalty – more unconscious than conscious – to the living composer and the dead philosopher who had been his mentors. An emotional wrench had to precede intellectual liberation. Preparing for the breach with Wagner the crucial experience was the acute discomfort at Bayreuth – such a disillusioning sequel to the happiness at Tribschen. But it was not a matter of making a choice. The discomfort was more physical than mental: at the crossroads of Nietzsche's development it was nearly always illness that took charge. But he was so confident it had pushed him in the right direction that Wagner and the job at Basel began to look like 'symptoms' of 'a total instinctual aberration',[1] while the symptoms of illness seemed beneficial – allies in his battle to win possession of himself. They enabled him to obtain a year's leave of absence from the university without giving up his job or even his salary: only the fees of teachers standing in for him were deducted from it. Retrospectively he was even grateful for the eye-trouble that stopped him reading. 'I was saved from the "book" . . . the greatest benefit I ever conferred on myself.'[2] To read is to submit oneself silently, repressively, to other selves. 'I have never felt happier with myself than in the sickest periods of my life, periods of the greatest pain.'[3] He believed he had at last taken possession of himself after a protracted period of belonging to other people. But this was also the decisive moment of submitting to a habit he would never throw off – generalizing on the basis of inadequate research.

In April 1876, Malwida von Meysenbug had invited him to the Adriatic coast for a year: 'You *must* come away from Basel next winter. You must rest under a sunnier sky among sympathetic people.'[4] She had intended to take a villa at Fano for her protégé, Nietzsche's student Albert Brenner, Nietzsche and herself. But she opted for the Bay of Naples, where the Wagners were due to come for a month, and she took a villa close to their lodgings. Nietzsche was not expecting to be confronted with them, while she was not expecting him to bring Rée. 'It will be a sort of cloister for free spirits.'[5] If he could not fulfil his earlier fantasy of a private community, at least he could surround himself with a few friends.

At the beginning of October 1876 he spent eighteen days in Bex, near Veytaux, with Rée, who wrote: 'It was to some extent the honeymoon of our friendship.'[6] Once Nietzsche had recovered from the train journey he felt well, and it was here that he completed the essay which had originally been called *Die Pflugschar*, and retitled it *Der Freigeist*. They left on the 19th. Nietzsche made a detour to visit Pisa with Isabella von Pahlen, a girl he had met on the train. Together with Rée and Brenner, he went from Genoa to Naples by steamer. On the last day there was a storm. 'One after another people got up from the lunch table. . . . Nietzsche held out for a long time.'[7] They docked in Naples at one in the morning. Malwida took them to a boarding house she had found in Sorrento. From the lounge they could see Naples, Ischia and Vesuvius; there was an olive grove in front of the house. Watching evening fall over the Bay of Naples, the thirty-two-year-old Nietzsche realized that he had spent his entire youth in the north, and could have died without ever seeing the Mediterranean. 'I shuddered, sorry for myself at having been old at the beginning of my life, and I shed tears at the thought of being saved at the last moment.'

According to Malwida, Wagner and Nietzsche 'hurried towards each other' each time they met.[8] Though Wagner objected to spending time with Rée, Malwida's party went to the Wagners' hotel about half a dozen times, and the Wagners came to the boarding house. Both Nietzsche's correspondence and Cosima's diary make significantly little reference to the meetings, and the last time Nietzsche and Wagner saw each other was when they went for a walk together on the evening before the Wagners' departure. Wagner, who was working on *Parsifal*, talked enthusiastically about his religious experiences and the new pleasure he was taking in Protestant ceremonial. Elisabeth, who was not even in Sorrento, has given an implausibly detailed account of the last meeting between the two men. Melancholy in the light betokening the approach of winter, she tells us, Wagner remarked: 'A valedictory mood!' The sun was sinking into the sea, and a light mist was coming up as he asked: 'Why are you so silent, my friend?'[9] Unable to believe in the sincerity of his religious emotion, Nietzsche may well have been silent, and he may partly have misunderstood Wagner's explanation of his position. He had not come to believe that mankind could be saved through the Church. 'When religion becomes artificial,' he wrote, 'it is for art to perform the function of religion.'[10] Wagner was planning *Parsifal* as a *Bühnenweihfestspiel* (stage dedication play) and he did not want it to be performed in ordinary opera houses. In January 1878, when Wagner sent Nietzsche the completed text, his immediate reaction was: 'More Liszt than Wagner – spirit of the Counter-Reformation . . . it is all too Christian, time-bound, limited; purely fantastic psychology; no flesh and far too much blood (especially at the Holy Communion). . . . The dialogue sounds like a translation from a foreign language.'[11]

Rée was glad when the Wagners left for Rome on 7 November: 'We are more relaxed, especially in the evenings, and we go to bed early.'[12] The men would get up at six-thirty and go for a walk before having breakfast. At nine Nietzsche would dictate for an hour before they went out walking again. Lunch would be followed by a siesta, and then they would take another walk, or, if it was raining, work. The evening meal was followed by readings from Burckhardt's lectures on Greek culture – a student had given Nietzsche his notes on the lectures – from Herodotus and Thucydides, with interpolations from Nietzsche. Later they went on to Montaigne, La Rochefoucauld, Vauvenargues, La Bruyère, Stendhal – who made an enormous impact on Nietzsche – and the New Testament. Rée did most of the reading, sitting at a table next to the lamp. Nietzsche sat in an armchair, wearing an eye-shield.

One evening, when Brenner was helping Malwida to peel oranges for supper, she said: 'We really look like an ideal family.'[13] Gradually they evolved the idea of founding a sort of cultural mission-house to encourage adults of both sexes to develop a fuller mental life, so that they could help to disseminate a new culture.

Once again Nietzsche was indulging in his fantasy of combining his gift for friendship with his vocation for cultural reform, while Malwida's ambition was to 'groom female students into the noblest representatives of women's emancipation'.[14]

With her to look after him, Nietzsche felt much better. 'As soon as he feels a headache coming on, I have a foot-bath prepared with ashes and salt, give him bromide powder, put a plaster behind his ear to raise a blister, give him food at regular intervals, etc. So the demon is subdued. Already it has stopped coming regularly every week, and it is less violent.'[15] There was a setback in the middle of December, but on Christmas Eve he could write home that he was having no trouble with his stomach, though he was still expecting weekly headaches. By then, half-way through a five-week treatment involving snuff and nasal douches, he was almost persuaded that catarrh in the head was the source of all his suffering.[16] In January 1877, when he had two days in bed, he cheered himself up with unrealistic plans. 'The "school for educators" (also called modern cloister, ideal colony, *université libre*) is floating before our eyes. Who knows what will happen?'[17] He was thinking of involving about forty people, including his sister, who was instructed to learn Italian.[18]

At the end of January he thought he was making progress, but in February he had a relapse, spending two days in bed within a week. On the 13th the three of them accompanied him to Naples for a consultation with Professor Schrön of the university's medical faculty, who reassured him that he had no tumour on the brain, only neuralgia, which he could treat.[19] For two days they stayed in Naples, where the carnival was in full swing. In March they went to Pompeii and to Capri. But on 10 April Rée and Brenner had to go back north, leaving Nietzsche with Malwida, who, with eye troubles of her own, could neither read to him nor take dictation. Her advice was that he should find a wife, 'good but rich'. Here was another pretext for making plans, and he wrote to Elisabeth discussing candidates, including Natalie Herzen, Alexander's daughter, who was 'the most suitable so far as intellectual qualities are concerned'.[20] Malwida was suffering from rheumatism and Nietzsche was bored, despite a visit from the writer Reinhardt von Seydlitz and his attractive wife Irene. 'In the evenings we play *Mühle* [nine men's morris, a board-game]. There is no reading.

Seydlitz is in bed. We might as well be taking it in turns to nurse each other, as we are taking turns to stay in bed.'[21]

He left Sorrento on 8 May, crossing to Genoa by steamer, not without being seasick. 'Everything on board was rolling about noisily. Crockery leaped around, came to life, children shrieked, the wind howled: "eternal sleeplessness was my lot", as the poet would say. Disembarkation brought new agonies: brimful with a splitting headache, I wore my strongest glasses, mistrusting everybody.'[22] Always bold on trains, he struck up an acquaintance with a ballerina who was also travelling from Genoa to Milan. 'Now and then I still feel a bit angry with myself for not staying on at least a few days in Milan for her sake.'[23] But he went on to Lugano. 'The closer I came to the mountains, the better I felt. . . . This morning I can see all my beloved mountains in front of me – the mountains I remember.'[24] He had been thinking of taking a cure at Pfafers, but the clinic there was not yet open, so he went instead to Bad Ragaz, arriving on the 14th or 15th.

He stayed for four weeks, taking remedial baths daily and seeing the doctor every three days. Yet another of his friends was now married – Overbeck, who came to see him over the Whit weekend. Nietzsche said he was feeling better than in Sorrento, but that it would have been irresponsible to resume his professorial duties in the autumn. 'My head is in a far worse state than we thought . . . any mental strain immediately harmful. . . . You cannot believe how weary and unwilling to work head and eyes are. . . . Marriage, though indeed very desirable, is the most *improbable* thing – I know that *very* clearly.'[25]

Expecting to feel better in the mountains, he went on to Rosenlauibad, which is 1,328 metres above sea level in the Bernese Oberland. 'Here I am the only remaining guest as usual. Very beautiful, without exaggeration. No wind, pine forest.'[26] He soon came to believe that, provided he was released from teaching at the Pädagogium, it would not be irresponsible to resume his professorial life. He even managed to persuade himself that it was in the interests of his health: 'My very problematical cerebrations and writings have so far always made me ill; so long as I was really an academician I was healthy.'[27] He would obviously have been better off in Rosenlauibad if he had had someone to look after him: 'Atmosphere mild and pleasant from early in the day till night. But

I must be careful of long walks, which twice already I have had to atone for (it took two days for me to feel all right again . . .). Each time there is a storm in the air I get a headache. Perhaps it is not high enough. . . . In the long run the stay here must be good. It is *my* kind of nature.'[28] He also tried drinking the St Moritz waters 'as a remedy against deeply entrenched nervous illness'.

A book he read there was *Der entfesselte Prometheus* (*Prometheus Unbound*) by his Viennese admirer, Siegfried Lipiner. Nietzsche had heard about him from Rée, who said that he was 'not an appetizing creature', and Rohde, who called him 'the most bow-legged of Jews'.[29] But the book aroused Nietzsche's enthusiasm: 'If the poet is not a "genius", I no longer know what genius is.'[30] To Lipiner he wrote: 'From now on I believe we have a poet amongst us. . . . Tell me frankly whether in respect of origin you have any connection with the Jews. The fact is that I have recently had many experiences which have aroused in me the highest expectations from young men of this origin.'[31] His rebound from Wagnerian anti-Semitism could hardly have been more extreme. When Wagner sent him the text of *Parsifal*, his comment to von Seydlitz was that he almost wished Lipiner would rewrite it.[32]

Nietzsche stayed in Rosenlauibad till the end of August, walking for six to eight hours nearly every day. 'I am always on the road two hours before the sun comes over the mountains, and especially in the long shadows of afternoon and evening.'[33] Disregarding his own theory that cerebration made him ill, he was thinking his way towards his next book. His sight had deteriorated so badly that his eyes had to be within about two inches of the paper he was writing on. He had no one to take dictation, but he made notes almost every day. 'My thoughts are now pushing me forwards . . . it feels as though the old layers of moss formed by daily philological work needed only to be peeled away – everything is still green and full of sap.'[34]

His twelve years of dependence on Schopenhauer had ended abruptly. He advised the musician and musicologist Carl Fuchs: 'When writing your "Musical Letters", try to avoid using terms from Schopenhauer's metaphysics. The fact is that I believe – forgive me, I think I *know* – that it is false, and that writings which bear the stamp of it may soon become incomprehensible.'[35] And on receiving Paul Deussen's Schopenhauerian *Die Elemente der*

Metaphysik, Nietzsche's response was that a few years ago he would have been more grateful for it. 'But, the way human thought is developing, your book serves me in a strange way – as a felicitous compilation of everything *I* no longer believe to be true.'[36]

It was inevitable, living when he did, that he should try to find in science an ally against the 'conventional exaggerations of popular or metaphysical interpretations. . . . All we need – and it is available only since the separate sciences have attained their present level – is a *chemistry* of the moral, religious and aesthetic ideas and sentiments, and of all the inner agitations we experience in cultural and social intercourse, and indeed even in solitude.'[37] This is no more unacceptable than the scientific piety of his contemporaries. Anton Chekhov maintained that 'A writer must be as objective as a chemist,' while Emile Zola held that a work of art's only merit was 'that of exact observation, of the more or less profound penetration of analysis, of the logical concatenation of the facts'. But in the essay on truth and falsehood, Nietzsche had not exempted scientific language from his strictures. If words could function only metaphorically, how could they serve adequately in a chemical analysis of moral ideas and emotional upheavals?

Nietzsche's dilemma is apparent in his treatment of oppositions. His instinct was to disbelieve in contrasts, to assume that in every conventional antithesis lay a mistake in reasoning. He was able to expose many of the fallacies underlying commonplace moral discriminations when he showed that what looks like altruism is not generically dissimilar to egoism. When a mother subordinates her own needs to her baby's, she is not activated by philanthropy: 'in ethics one considers oneself not as an *individuum* but as a *dividuum*'.[38] We are all motivated by an innate interest in self-preservation and an innate preference of pleasure to pain.[39] None of us is responsible either for his predispositions or his actions.[40] Between good and evil actions there is no difference in kind, only in degree. The individual's drive towards self-gratification never stops,[41] while the sensation we mistake for love is pleasure in the gratifications other people provide. But, since all these points are made in the conventional language of morality, Nietzsche cannot escape the assumption, which is intrinsic to language, that moral contrasts refer to generic differences. Even when he argues that 'good actions are sublimated evil ones, evil ones coarsened or brutalized good ones',[42] the sentence see-saws between the concepts of good and evil as if they derived from opposing principles. He may have convinced us that the words 'good' and 'evil' are misleading, but he will neither be able to manage without them nor to redefine them with any precision.

Nietzsche's linguistic dilemma was complicated by the religious (and linguistic) conditioning he had received in childhood, while the violence of the distaste he felt for the reverential language of Lutheran religiosity did not liberate him from mental habits that can be described only as religious. His scepticism was radical enough to make him invert some of the main tenets of Christianity. 'He that humbleth himself shall be exalted,' said St Luke;[43] 'He that humbleth himself wants to be exalted,' said Nietzsche, making a valid point, though he is not moralizing any less than St Luke was.[44] As an immoralist, all he could do was suggest an alternative set of standards. Nothing angered him more than Christianity's habit of encouraging false humility and the self-abasement prompted by covert vanity. 'The whole morality of the Sermon on the Mount belongs here: man takes genuine pleasure in doing violence to himself with these exaggerated objectives, and then deifying that tyrannically exacting element in his soul.'[45] So Nietzsche was no longer willing to bracket the saint with the artist and the philosopher, as he had in the *Unzeitgemässe Betrachtungen*. Whereas regular sexual intercourse can assuage the sensual imagination, abstinence provokes it. 'The imagination of many Christian saints was dirty to an extraordinary degree; thanks to the theory that those desires raging inside them were actually demons, they did not feel too much to blame for them.'[46] He goes on to quote Novalis: 'It is strange that the association of lust, religion and cruelty did not alert men long ago to their intimate relationship and to their common tendency.'[47]

One way of looking at *Menschliches, Allzumenschliches* is to see it as a stepping-stone between La Rochefoucauld and Freud. Nietzsche was becoming the most Gallic of German philosophers: in Sorrento, Paul Rée had catalysed the process by reading from the work of Montaigne, La Rochefoucauld and Vauvenargues. It struck Nietzsche forcibly that in the German tradition the philosophical dogmatists – not only idealists, but materialists and realists – had all been concerned with problems irrelevant to everyday living.[48]

He now made it his objective to concentrate on 'the small inconspicuous truths'.[49] Without mentioning Rée by name, he cited his
work as an example of what can be achieved when human actions
are observed 'scientifically'. La Rochefoucauld had produced
psychological observations, but more with the desire to give literary
pleasure than to turn the subject into a science. If Rée had not pre-
empted *Psychologische Beobachtungen* (*Psychological Observations*)
as the title for his first book, perhaps Nietzsche would have used it.
Menschliches, Allzumenschliches was intended to convey the same
idea. 'The title means: "Where *you* see ideals – *I* see what is –
human, alas, all too human!"'[50]

The discontinuity of the argument in the book corresponds not
only to Nietzsche's idea of concentrating on the psychological
observation of small, inconspicuous truths, but also to the method
of composition. When he was able to write his own notes he had felt
compelled to work them into a coherent structure, though in *Die
Geburt der Tragödie* much was lost in the process. Dictating notes
to Köselitz and working with him on the new book, Nietzsche
realized that it was best to keep the notes as notes, selecting and
regrouping, but not rewriting much. He structured the book into
638 brief sections, which mostly consisted of a single paragraph, and
which were arranged under nine headings. But, as with his first
book, he might have organized his material quite differently if he
had been more aware of the undercurrents that were pulling at him.
To him it probably seemed that the impulse towards self-conquest,
which was essentially a compulsion towards self-transcendence, had
nothing to do with the anti-transcendentalism in his philosophy,
though he did seem quite regretful when he conceded that rejection
of the metaphysical might prove more of a curse to mankind than a
blessing. But probably our 'metaphysical need' would be cut off at
the root when 'historical philosophy' had confirmed Rée's contention that moral man was 'no closer to the intelligible (metaphysical)
world than physical man'. As soon as it was recognized that the
origins of religion, morality and art were not supra-human, there
would be much less interest in the old philosophical problem of the
relationship between the phenomenon and the thing-in-itself.
'Religion, art and morality do not touch on the "inner reality of the
world". We are in the realm of representation, and no inspiration is
going to carry us further.'[51]

But what would be the consequences of cutting off 'our meta-physical need' at the root? He was aware that unbridled scepticism would slide into nihilism, and he wanted 'historical philosophy' to act as a brake. In his essay on history he had said that only great artistic spirits can learn from history the one real lesson – how to live.[52] He had faith in himself as a great artistic spirit, but here too he was caught in a dilemma, for he also believed that 'the unre-strained historical sense, pushed to its logical extreme, uproots the future . . . undermines and ruins the living thing – its judgement always means annihilation.'[53] Though he would soon have doubts about whether the pursuit of truth was intrinsically admirable or valuable, he was caught in the vicious circle of truthful enquiry. His historical impulse was too strong for him to resist.

Where it joined forces with his scientism was in the urge to apply Darwinist evolutionism to history, and especially to the history of morality. If the various injunctions and vetoes had not come from God, how had they evolved? Nietzsche's phrase 'genealogy of morals' aptly describes the analysis he excelled in, and his 1887 book *Zur Genealogie der Moral* has its roots in *Menschliches, Allzumen-schliches*. His main point is that there are no absolute values, no transcendental criteria, no divine commandments, no categorical opposition between superhuman principles. Good and evil did not precede the existence of the human race: notions of each evolved from the other. It is from cruel people that we can see what everyone used to be like, before moral restraints were imposed on them, but the cruel are no more responsible for their cruelty than granite is for being granite.[54] Even for murder the real guilt lies with educators, parents, surroundings.[55] Nietzsche defends injustice on the grounds that the men with power do not realize what suffering they are inflicting, any more than the rich man can understand the value a poor man sets on his few possessions.[56] The idea of justice originated out of exchange and recompense based on the concept of equal power. Judicious self-preservation was the original motive, but God has appointed forgetfulness as gatekeeper at the temple of human dignity.[57] The social instincts grew out of shared pleasures and common aversion to danger.[58] The Christian religion was coarser and more powerful than the Greek philosophy it replaced.[59] What is especially un-Greek about Christianity is the idea of God as master.[60]

In practice, Nietzsche moves away from his declared objective of concentrating on small, inconspicuous truths. Many of his statements centre moralizingly on major developments in the history of morality, but many of his psychological insights are radical and important. He saw that the brain function most affected by sleep is memory: in dreams we resemble the savage. Our cognition is unreliable, and we make erroneous comparisons, seeking and representing the causes of excitement as related sensations and moods are echoed.[61] And no previous explanation of laughter had been as plausible as Nietzsche's is. After centuries of conditioning to extreme danger, the human animal reacts with exhilaration to an abrupt transition from fear to reassurance. The tragic phenomenon is the opposite – a transition from exuberance to fear.[62] We also take pleasure in nonsense, when experience is harmlessly transformed into its opposite. The yoke of the obligatory is removed. Like slaves at Saturnalian feasts, we laugh at the innocuousness of what is normally dangerous or oppressive.[63] It was not for nothing that Freud said Nietzsche's 'premonitions and insights often agree in the most amazing way with the laborious findings of psycho-analysis'.

Few of the observations in *Menschliches, Allzumenschliches* refer even obliquely to Nietzsche's private situation, but there is one which is obviously prompted by his deteriorating health. 'The thinker – and similarly the artist – who has put the best of himself into his work experiences an almost malicious joy as he watches the erosion of his body and spirit by time. It is as if he were in a corner watching a thief at his safe, while knowing that it is empty, his treasure being elsewhere.'[64] Nietzsche must have come to feel that his writing constituted a higher self, that his physical existence was no more than a stepping-stone towards it. He was also commenting obliquely on his own situation when he condemned the literary journalists who kept up a flow of chatter to distract their audience from 'the solemn chimes of great events. . . . If a man *is* something, there is no true need for him to do anything, though in fact he does a good deal.'[65] Genuine free-thinkers plan to live without much revenue or much social involvement: they reserve their energy for the pursuit of knowledge.[66] Slavery still exists, and anyone who does not have two-thirds of his day for himself is a slave, even if he is a statesman, tradesman, official or scholar.[67]

Addressing his reader in categorical imperatives, Nietzsche was talking to himself:

Whatever state you are in, serve yourself as a source of experience! ... You have inside you a ladder with a hundred rungs which you can scale towards knowledge. Do not undervalue the fact of having been religious; appreciate how you have been given real access to art.... No one can become wise without having loved religion and art like a mother and a nurse. ... It is within your power to ensure that all your experiences – trials, false starts, mistakes, deception, suffering, passion, loving, hoping – can be subsumed totally in your objective. This objective is to make yourself into a necessary chain of culture links, and from this necessity to draw general conclusions about current cultural needs.[68]

His priorities were still aesthetic, as in his Schopenhauerian period, and this is one reason that his philosophical position was so remote from Karl Marx's. Socialists demanded the best possible living conditions for the greatest possible number of people. But genius thrives on hardship. 'The highest intelligence and the warmest heart cannot exist side by side in the same person. ... The wise man must *resist* those extravagant wishes of unintelligent philanthropy because he has a vested interest in the continuance of his type and in the eventual emergence of the highest intelligence.'[69] Christ had the warmest of hearts, but 'he tended to make mankind more stupid, siding with the mentally weak and retarding intellectual progress'.[70] Aghast at having to recognize that Socialism and democracy were on the advance, Nietzsche quoted Voltaire: 'When the populace tries to become involved in thinking, all is lost.'[71] Though still valued in the army and the bureaucracy, hierarchic subordination would soon be extinct, and the world would be poorer without it. Governments would no longer be regarded as superior to the governed, but only as organs of the people.[72] It was all very well for socialists to point out that the current division of property was based on historical violence and injustice, but 'The whole of the old culture has been built up on force, slavery, deception, error. As heirs of all these conditions, resultants of the total past, we cannot repudiate ourselves, and we should not wish to withdraw any of it.'[73]

The least impressive part of the book is the one titled 'Wife and Child'. Pontificating about marriage, Nietzsche revealed his inexperience of it, but he made some perceptive remarks about the parent–child relationship. 'Usually a mother loves *herself* in her son more than she loves him.'[74] Freud's theories are prefigured in the pronouncement: 'The unresolved dissonances in personality and opinion between the parents go on echoing in the child's character, forming the history of his inner sufferings.'[75] Nietzsche also gives himself advice on the subject of choosing a wife. 'Before going into a marriage, one should ask oneself: "Do you think you could have a good conversation with this woman, continuing into old age?" All else in marriage is transitory; it is conversational intercourse that occupies most of the time.'[76] In any case marriage was incompatible with the image he was evolving of himself as a wanderer. 'The man who has achieved intellectual freedom is not so much a traveller towards a goal as a wanderer on the face of the earth.'[77]

In the final draft of *Menschliches, Allzumenschliches* Wagner is not mentioned by name. Intending to publish the book anonymously – Schmeitzner later dissuaded him[78] – Nietzsche referred to Wagner several times in the draft; the references are retained, but 'the artist' is substituted for 'Wagner'. The artist, Nietzsche argues, stands still at the point in his development when he was overcome by his devotion to art. 'Without knowing why, he gives himself the task of infantilizing humanity. That is his glory and his limitation.'[79] Wagnerian music is implicitly disparaged by the contention that 'The noblest kind of beauty is that which does not carry us off our feet, which does not make a thunderous or intoxicating assault on us – this can easily become disgusting – but seeps into us gradually.'[80] Nietzsche must also have been thinking of Wagner when he made the point that genius is liable to regard itself as superhuman. Without the restraint of self-criticism, the famous man gradually becomes irresponsible; convinced that he is conferring a favour by talking to us, he is enraged by any comparison with other artists.[81] There is another anti-Wagnerian point in the sentences added at the end of Section 109 condemning 'any form of approach to Christianity'.[82] When Hans von Wolzogen, editor of *Bayreuther Blätter*, had rejected an article Köselitz had submitted for the first issue, Nietzsche had felt no less resentful – and vengeful – than when Ritschl or Zarncke had rejected Rohde's work.

For six weeks after Nietzsche's return to Basel on 1 September he was free from academic duties, and he used the time to work with Köselitz on preparing the first volume of *Menschliches, Allzumen-*

schliches for submission to Schmeitzner. Writing to him at the beginning of December Nietzsche called it his 'principal book' and asked to be forgiven for writing it in numbered sections.[83] Once again Nietzsche had Elisabeth to act as his housekeeper, and from the beginning of September they were living in a new flat in Gellertstrasse. Malwida came to Basel for a few days from 6 September, and the Overbecks came to Zürich, where Nietzsche visited them.

Still impressed easily by doctors and continuing his haphazard voyage from one to another, he had placed himself in the hands of Dr Otto Eiser, an admirer of his writings. After being consulted at Meiringen and visiting Nietzsche in Rosenlauibad, Eiser arranged a joint consultation in Frankfurt with the ophthalmologist Dr Otto Kruger. Their verdict was that the headaches were due partly to severe damage sustained by the retinas in both eyes – choroido-retinitis is frequently syphilitic in origin – and partly to 'a predisposition in the irritability of the central organ', originating out of excessive mental activity.[84] The patient could not be allowed to read or write for several years. He should avoid bright light and extreme exertion, mental or physical. He must alternate methodically between work and relaxation, avoiding spicy or indigestible food, strong coffee, tea and heavy wines.[85] Kruger prescribed dark blue sun-glasses and Eiser prescribed quinine, but their treatment produced no results, and, defying etiquette, Eiser began corresponding about the case with Wagner, whose theory was that Nietzsche's malady was due to excessive masturbation.[86] Later, when Eiser visited Wagner, he gave his opinion that *Menschliches, Allzumenschliches* marked the beginning of Nietzche's mental derangement.[87] Eleven days after Dr Eiser and Dr Kruger had written their report, Nietzsche applied to the university authorities to be relieved of his duties for a further six months.

The complete text of *Menschliches, Allzumenschliches* was sent to Schmeitzner in the middle of January 1878, and when the proofs came, Nietzsche worked on them with Köselitz and his friend, Paul Widemann. In February Nietzsche paid another visit to Eiser, whose new prognosis was pessimistic. He had not wanted to depress his patient, he told Overbeck, but he had never discounted the possibility of brain disease, and the observations of his Basel colleague, Rudolf Massini, made it seem probable.[88] Massini, recommending that Nietzsche should be released from his duties at the Pädagogium, gave the opinion that he was suffering from 'intense over-stimulation of the nervous system'. Both doctors, probably, were now suspecting *dementia paralytica*.

At the beginning of March he went to Baden-Baden for a hydropathic cure, and on the 7th he was formally discharged from his commitments at the Pädagogium. He stayed in Baden-Baden till 5 April and then went on to convalesce in Naumburg. When Köselitz left Basel five days later to settle in Venice, it was partly to escape from Nietzsche. Throughout the winter he had been at his disposal for dictation, and he had collaborated in arranging the material for *Menschliches, Allzumenschliches*. Though he was reluctant to abandon his demanding friend, it seemed the only way to advance his career as a musician and to regain his independence. When Nietzsche returned to Basel on 24 April, he must have realized the extent of his loss, though Widemann did what he could to compensate.

Nietzsche received printed copies of *Menschliches, Allzumenschliches* in time to send them to his friends by the end of the month. For Rée, who said that he threw himself on it like a beast of prey, it was 'the book of books'; for Rohde it was full of unpleasant surprises. 'Is it possible to divest oneself so completely of one's soul and substitute another? Suddenly to become Rée instead of Nietzsche?'[89] Overbeck was surprised at Nietzsche's *volte-face*, and for Cosima, who claimed to have read little of the book, it represented the culmination of a process she had long been trying to resist. 'Finally Israel intervened in the form of a Dr Rée, very sleek, very cool, at the same time as being wrapped up in Nietzsche and dominated by him, though actually outwitting him – the relationship between Judaea and Germany in miniature.'[90]

Most of Nietzsche's friends blamed Rée's influence for the reorientation. 'Unlike Rée', wrote Malwida, 'you were not born for analysis. Your approach must be artistic.'[91] 'The ideal you speak of', objected von Seydlitz, 'I cannot find. Indeed everything is very reeal.'[92] Marie Baumgartner felt as though something inside her had been killed,[93] while Heinrich Romundt, who had abandoned his priestly ambition to resume teaching, suggested that the title should have been simply 'Allzumenschlich' ('All Too Human').[94] Lipiner, too, disapproved of the turn against Wagner,[95] and

Nietzsche wrote to Rée: '*All* my friends are now unanimous in the opinion that my book was originated and written *by you*. . . . Long live Reealism and my good friend!'[96]

Nietzsche had no sooner learned how to survive in Basel without help from Köselitz than he found that he would have to manage from the end of June without any help from Elisabeth. Disagreements over religion and a general deterioration in their relationship seem to have combined with pressure from their mother to regain possession of her daughter, though there is no recrimination in Nietzsche's letters to Naumburg. Unable to keep the flat going, Nietzsche sent most of the furniture to his mother and gave some away. He found furnished lodgings in Bachlettenstrasse on the outskirts of the town, giving himself a long walk to the university. He moved in July. He had not, in effect, lived on his own since Overbeck had moved into the same house, but he was not too dispirited to go on taking pleasure in laying plans. Wanting a regular routine, he tried to timetable his life:

200 weeks. Each week a *Weekly Programme*. Decisions on diet, reading, walking and times for reading and walks. Sunday a.m. report on the week with *crosses* and *new week* – revision every *month*. 6–7 walk, 7–8 breakfast, 8–9 preparation, 9–10 walk, 10–11 teaching, 11–12 Pfaltz or Burckhardt, 12.30–1.30 meal, 1.30–4 to friends. Sleep. Reading. 4–7 out. 7–8 meal, 8–9.30 rest – Luncheon: Liebig bouillon, $\frac{1}{4}$ teaspoon before the meal. 2 ham sandwiches and one egg. 6–8 nuts with bread, 2 apples, 2 gingerbread, 2 biscuits. Supper: 1 egg with bread. 5 nuts. Sweet milk with 1 rusk or 3 biscuits.[97]

He had not thrown off the habit of time-conservancy inculcated at Pforta, where he had learned to use Greek culture as a standard. Of all the reasons for his breach with Wagner none was more important than the realization that tragedy was not going to be reborn through his music-drama. To call *Parsifal* 'the spirit of the Counter-Reformation' was to anathematize it.[98] According to *Menschliches, Allzumenschliches*, the Counter-Reformation had blocked all the progressive forces launched by the Renaissance, permanently frustrating all hope of interpenetration between antiquity and the modern spirit.[99] Having arrived at this equation of Wagner with baroque medievalism, Nietzsche felt that he was himself 'a hundred paces closer to the Greeks than ever before'.

That metaphysical befogging of everything true and simple, the battle *of* reason *against* reason, seeing each single detail as both wonderful and absurd – this opposed to a baroque art of overstimulation and glorified exaggeration – I mean the art of Wagner – it was both these things that finally made me ill and still more ill, almost alienating me from all my good humour and from my talent.[100]

He desperately wanted to believe that the disease had been attacking him on a front where he could defend himself.

He was in Interlaken, trying to convalesce with the aid of long walks and therapeutic baths, as in Baden-Baden, when he read Wagner's attack, written without mentioning him by name, in *Bayreuther Blätter*.[101] 'Furious and almost vindictive pages', Nietzsche called them. 'Heavens, what clumsy polemics!'[102] 'It caused me pain, but *not on the spot* Wagner wanted to.'[103] By the middle of September Nietzsche felt too ill to stay in Interlaken. 'I feel as if I were on the run, and scarcely know where to lay my head.'[104] On the 17th he travelled back to Basel, and on the 20th to Zürich to be with the Overbecks. Four days later he was in Naumburg, where Schmeitzner visited him on the 29th. 'Nietzsche had broken down, and he looked frightful. He was in a state of collapse.'[105]

He stayed for three weeks, convalescing. He was there for his thirty-fourth birthday on 15 October, when he received letters from Rée and his old friend Gustav Krug, but he seems to have been in no condition to write letters. He arrived in Basel on the 18th, three days before term began, and by 1 November he was cancelling lectures. On the 14th he wrote belatedly to Krug: 'It was like having to swim through treacherous straits this year, and not only in respect of my health.'[106] His mother and sister sent him ham and sausages, while Frau Overbeck sent venison and roast chicken, and Frau Baumgartner brought grapes and rusks.

The meticulous accounts he kept from October 1878 to March 1879 show how cautious he was being over expenses. He kept a record of his outlay on ham, tongue, meat extract, eggs, tea, bread, rusks, milk, biscuits, sugar, mustard, nuts, figs, postage stamps, nutcrackers, having his hair cut, having his spectacles repaired, and so on. He carried the totals neatly forward from page to page, and at the end of 1878 he calculated that since 19 October he had spent 497 francs. 'So I began the year 1879', he noted, 'with 2,186 francs.'

He made monthly totals of his expenditure and elaborate calculations about weekly spending. In one week, for instance, he spent 1 franc 95 centimes on milk and 1 franc 27 centimes on eggs (three on Wednesday and two every other day). When he abandoned the notebook in the middle of March, he had spent 494.80 since the beginning of the year, including 60 francs on rent, 28.45, 11.20, and 29.50 on restaurants where he had accounts, 12.00 on boots, 15.50 on the *Hamburger Post* and 18.40 at Detloff's second-hand bookshop.[107]

Headaches were now liable to spread over nine successive days; lecturing was such a strain that he sometimes had to spend the following day in bed. Changes of temperature affected him badly, and he had many sleepless nights. But he was eager to publish the second part of *Menschliches, Allzumenschliches*, a series of 408 *Vermischte Meinungen und Sprüche* (*Miscellaneous Opinions and Sayings*). Some of the material derived from notes written the previous year; some was new. 'You see how wretched your friend is,' he told Marie Baumgartner, who prepared the fair copy for him, 'how *unfree* his body is, and *why* he is so thirsty for mental freedom.'[108] Or, as he wrote to Seydlitz, 'I have to live my *position* and my *task* – a lord and a mistress and a goddess at the same time: much too much for my feeble strength and shattered health. Seen from outside it is the life of a senile recluse. . . . But I am of good spirit. Forward, Excelsior!'[109] By the end of December the manuscript was ready for Schmeitzner.

He said later that *Menschliches, Allzumenschliches* had cost him so much effort 'that given the option, nobody would have written it at such a price.'[110] If he did not have the option, it was partly because his consciousness seemed to have become a battleground for a conflict between his disease and all the mental forces he could muster to oppose it. Still unwilling to believe that his formidable intellect was impotent against it, he manoeuvred to convince himself that his body did not matter, that his real treasure was elsewhere. Developing his earlier aphorism about the thief at the safe, he celebrated the self-knowledge that makes us 'richer than we were before' when 'life has stolen everything it can from us by way of honours, pleasures, connections, health and possessions'.[111] '*To make himself superfluous*', he wrote, ' – that is the glory of each great man.'[112] Another compulsion was to believe that the disease was something he could conquer. 'Writing should always indicate a conquest of oneself, though there are dyspeptic authors who write only because they find something indigestible.'[113] Or as he put it in one of the last aphorisms in the book, 'You find the burden of life too heavy? Then you must increase the burden of your life. If the sufferer is finally longing to drink from the River Lethe, he must become a *hero* to be certain of finding it.'[114]

Though he was no longer using his illness to camouflage his apostasy, he was still feeling a need to defend it. 'Belief in truth', he asserted, 'begins with scepticism about everything previously held to be true.'[115] This is not far from what Wittgenstein was to say in his *Investigations* about his repudiation of his earlier philosophy: 'the axis of our examination must be rotated, but about the fixed point of our real need.' Nietzsche's dicta about his intellectual reorientation are not grouped together, but he keeps returning to the subject, directly and indirectly. 'The more one lets oneself go, the less other people let one go.'[116] 'Our supporters never forgive us if we take sides against ourselves, because it seems to them that we are not only rejecting their love but impugning their intelligence.' [117] (This is why Bertrand Russell was so shrill in his refusal to forgive Wittgenstein.) 'So long as you go on being praised, you must believe that you are not yet on your own course, but on someone else's.'[118] 'It cannot be helped – each master has only *one* pupil – who will betray him – for he too is marked out for mastery.'[119] '"Forgive us our virtues" should be our prayer to humanity.'[120] 'When someone secedes from us, it is not we but our supporters who are offended.'[121] But with the apostasy, as with the illness, Nietzsche was able to move out from private experience to generalization. 'Good conscience always has bad conscience as its stepping-stone, not as its opposite, for everything good was once new and consequently unfamiliar, unconventional, *immoral*, gnawing like a worm in the heart of its fortunate discoverer.'[122]

He probably had a bad conscience about attacking Schopenhauer, but at last he felt free to apply the principles of his essay about truth and falsehood to the philosopher's use of the word 'will'. Not only had he used it for different mental actions, he had used it metaphorically as if all the elements in nature possessed willpower, and as if all natural willpower tended in the same direction. 'The description generally given of this Single Will has the effect of making it seem we want the *stupid devil* for our god.'[123] Nietzsche also saw that Schopenhauer had had 'a prejudice in common with the moral man'. He had maintained that 'The ultimate and true explanation of the inner reality of the entirety of things must necessarily be closely connected with that of the ethical significance of human actions.' As Nietzsche saw, there is no necessity to make this connection.[124] At the same time Wagner came under attack for his idealization of the unfamiliar gods and heroes from the sagas – 'sovereign beasts of prey with spasms of thoughtfulness, generosity and boredom with life'.[125] The Wagnerian spirit was hostile to the enlightenment that had passed into the nineteenth century from the eighteenth, hostile to the supra-national ideals of French revolutionary Romanticism, and to Anglo-American sobriety in the reconstruction of state and society.[126]

But Nietzsche was less interested in condemning retrogressiveness than in analysing how 'surplus poetic energy' could help to point the way towards the future. Where could greatness of soul still be 'incarnated in harmonic, equable conditions, so that it can become visible, permanent and exemplary, helping to create the future through emulation and envy?'[127] Several of Nietzsche's critical aphorisms are about the civilizing effects of great art. Romanticism comes implicitly under attack in his dismissal of 'that barbaric though enchanting outpouring from an undisciplined and chaotic soul of hot and highly coloured things, which is what we understood by art when we were young'.[128] It is only when we have 'become wiser and more harmonious' that we appreciate the art of Homer, Sophocles, Theocritus, Calderón, Racine and Goethe, 'the overflow from a wise and harmonious way of living'.[129] Nietzsche's definition of originality is in keeping with his rejection of Romanticism: 'It is not being the first to see something new that indicates a genuinely original mind, but seeing the old, the familiar, the commonplace *as if it were* new.'[130] He had also developed an aversion to signs of exertion in art: 'To give an impression of health, a work of art should seem to involve at most three-quarters of its author's strength. . . . All good things have something idle about them: they lie around like cows in a field.'[131]

The complete text of *Menschliches, Allzumenschliches* was sent to Schmeitzner on 31 December 1878, after Nietzsche's loneliest Christmas since leaving Bonn.[132] It was an exceptionally severe winter, and he had a septic inflammation under a fingernail. He had thought of going home for Christmas, but, too depressed, he stayed in Basel, unable even to oblige Elisabeth with the Christmas presents she had asked for – a book about the world fair and a silk neckerchief. Instead he sent a pair of gloves and a copy of *Buch der Erfindungen usw.* (*Book of Inventions, etc.*) 'with good illustrations of architecture. . . . If only I could be with you!'[133] From Sunday the 22nd until Friday the 27th he had 'one *attack* after *another*. You see, I cannot write.'[134] He would still have liked to leave Basel, if only for a few days, before term began, but he was too ill, and in the second week of January 1879 his finger was getting worse. His letters home had become brief and telegraphic in style: '*Worst* winter weeks behind me! Monday bad, Tuesday the *attack*, Wednesday bad, Thursday *and* Friday new, very violent attack not wanting to stop, today shattered and exhausted. Now it must get better again, I hope!'[135] One afternoon during a December snow-storm he arrived, almost breathless, in Kelterborn's Basel office, asking to borrow his scarf. He was afraid of catching cold on the way back to Binningen. Kelterborn sent him a scarf as a New Year's gift, and, later in the month, called to see him. 'After having settled himself, earlier, into a certain comfortable elegance, he was now living far from the noise of the town in a small, modest, furnished room on the upper floor of a small village house. I found him lying on the couch; he was pale and he had lost weight. The first glance gave me an idea of the frightful suffering and pain the poor man must have been through.'[136]

Schmeitzner had gone to press with the second part of *Menschliches, Allzumenschliches* as soon as the manuscript reached him, and Köselitz, who was now using the pseudonym Peter Gast, offered to correct the proofs in Florence. 'On the whole,' Nietzsche wrote to him, 'I am living almost like a complete saint, but almost with the mental habits of a complete, genuine Epicurean – at peace and patient, yet watching life joyfully.'[137] He was becoming aware, though, that he would not be able to continue in his job much longer. 'Teaching causes me too much mental strain, though I am doing *nothing* else *at all*. Never have I spent a winter concentrating so exclusively on convalescence. . . . With the stomach it has been brilliantly successful. But the eye trouble has got worse; on the worst days the attacks of *cramp* (which made me keep my right eye half closed for several hours) spread over my whole body. . . *Everything* has to be expiated.'[138] This is one of the very few references Nietzsche ever makes to feeling more pain on one side of his head than on the other. If he had been suffering from migraine it would almost certainly have been unilateral, at least in the early stages, and the pain would not have lasted so long. By the middle of February he was losing all desire to go into details about what he was suffering. 'The eyes are no longer good enough for teaching, to say nothing of the head. (I had a headache that lasted for six days except when I was asleep.)'[139] During the second half of February he had two violent 'attacks' with vomiting, one lasting for four days, the other for six. He lectured only once. And at the end of February there was a night when he thought he was dying.

He was glad to have completed the second part of *Menschliches, Allzumenschliches*. 'Dear Heaven, perhaps it is my last work,' he wrote to Peter Gast. 'There is, it occurs to me, a daring imperturbability in it.'[140] The letter drove Gast into the hills outside Florence. 'I felt moved all day. . . . I wept like a child, I believe. . . . I felt strongly that I was entitled to feel related to you, to love you more than anyone, more than father and mother – although at the same time I was entitled only to revere you!'[141]

But Nietzsche had neither given up hope nor stopped taking cures. A cold-water treatment was doing him good, he believed, and he was considering another course of remedial baths.[142] He even thought of trying to rest continuously for five years. 'You can have no idea of the convulsions in my head or the fading in my eyes.'[143] He was tempted by an invitation from Gast to visit Venice, but Burckhardt dissuaded him from risking such a long journey. He was determined to leave Basel on 21 March, but on the 19th he still did not know where he was going. Not feeling well enough to travel beyond the mountains, he settled for Geneva, staying first at a hotel near the railway station and then moving to another overlooking the lake. 'My life is more torture than convalescence. . . . "If only I were blind!" This stupid wish is now my philosophy. Because I should not *read* and I do – just as I should not *think* – and I do.'[144]

On 6 April he received a letter from Burckhardt about the second part of *Menschliches, Allzumenschliches*: 'Where I cannot accompany you, I watch with a mixture of fear and pleasure as you safely climb the giddying mountain ridges, and I try to form a picture of what you must see, looking down and around. . . . In the meantime I know a great many sayings would provoke the serious envy of La Rochefoucauld, for instance.'[145] Von Seydlitz, who found the second part spoke to him more directly than the first, underwent something of a conversion: 'I have decided . . . not to go to Bayreuth. I woke up to this last idea with the sense of having narrowly escaped a danger . . . I cannot abide absolutism.'[146] Cosima, who had now read more of the first part, pronounced it 'pretentious and slipshod. . . . On almost each page of this book I believe I could point out superficiality and childish sophistry.'[147]

The summer term of 1870 began on 15 April. Though he had announced, through Overbeck, that his first lecture would be given at nine o'clock on the 26th, he had almost decided to resign. 'I have the opinion of all sorts of men from all over Switzerland. They are unanimous about Basel's having a badly depressing atmosphere, conducive to headaches. . . . Ergo: Academia derelinquenda est.'[148] The next day he complained to his mother and sister about 'abominable, noxious Basel, where I have lost my health and will lose my life'.[149] What he wanted to believe was that by leaving he could redeem his health. 'I cannot deny that my existence is purgatorial torment. *Probably* this will cease with my academic activity; perhaps with activity in general; possibly with – .'[150]

He returned to Basel on the 21st, and on the 24th he consulted the oculist, Professor Schiess, who found that his eyesight had deteriorated badly. Massini confirmed that he could not continue lecturing, and he submitted his resignation to the President of the Board of Education. It is dated 2 May 1879 and signed as if he were in Basel, though by then he was back in Geneva. He returned to Basel on the 7th, and his sister, summoned by Overbeck, arrived on the 10th. 'I hardly recognized my dear brother: with deep emotion, an exhausted man, prematurely aged, gave me his hand.'[151] He had already sold some of his books and given away others, but the majority were to be packed in cases and stored with friends, except for two trunk-loads which were to accompany him on his travels. He was too nearly blind to be concerned about his notebooks or manuscripts, and he let Elisabeth take charge of them, though he was no longer entrusting her with the management of his financial affairs, which were in the hands of the Overbecks. He was awarded an annual pension of three thousand francs to be paid partly by the government and partly by the university. He and Elisabeth left Basel on the 11th, travelling through Geneva to a clinic at a castle in Bremgarten, near Bern. He stayed barely a week. She went back to Basel to take possession of everything he had left there while he travelled on, uncertain of where to go or what to do. He spent a few days in Zürich, and at the end of the month he was in Wiesen, near Davos, 1,400 metres above sea level. For four nights he had no sleep.[152] He spent three weeks there: 'Pain, loneliness, walks, bad weather – that is my routine. No trace of excitement. Rather a kind of mindless, stupefied indisposition.'[153]

Schmeitzner, who had expected to sell at least a thousand copies of *Menschliches, Allzumenschliches* Part 1, sold only a hundred and twenty. He did what he could to publicize the book, working in liaison with Gast, who, without telling Nietzsche what he was doing, wrote a series of anonymous reviews, one of which appeared in the *Grazer Tageblatt*.

Released from commitments to Basel, Nietzsche was unaware of what life would be like without an anchorage. For ten years, from now until he went mad, he would want to stay away from Basel, stay away from Naumburg, stay away from Germany, but all the magnetic forces working on him were negative. His life was not going to revolve around one city, one woman or one doctor. His sufferings would have been alleviated if there had been someone to look after him, as his mother would have done if he had gone home, but he could not afford to pay for attention, and Elisabeth was the only other person who might conceivably have devoted her life to nursing him. But after the experiment in living together at Basel they never tried again.

His last years of sanity were to be spent shifting joylessly from place to place in search of propitious climatic conditions, rather in the way that he moved from one doctor to another, always hopeful that he had made the right decision but seldom making one he did not later regret. Mostly he spent his summers in the Upper Engadin, believing the altitude to be good for him, and his winters near the Mediterranean, where it was not so cold, if not warm enough to live comfortably in unheated rooms, as he mostly did, feeling too poor to pay for heating.

On 21 June 1879 he moved to St Moritz – 1,800 metres above sea level – where, at last, he began to feel better. 'I live in complete isolation, eating in my room (as in Basel, and almost the same things, only no figs), very little meat but a lot of milk. It does me good. I will stay here a long time.'[154] After spending four successive days in bed, he could get up, on average, one day out of two, and when he did he went for long walks, spending seven to eight hours of each day in the open air.[155] Thinking of going south for the winter, he asked Elisabeth to find out as much as she could about the timing of Wagner's winter visit to Naples: he had no wish for a repetition of the Sorrento encounter.[156] At least he could take pleasure in making plans. On the rampart of the old city of Naumburg, quite near his mother's house, there was a tower with a large garden adjoining it. Perhaps he would be able to rent both, live in the tower and cultivate the garden. 'You know that my preference is for a simple, natural way of life, and I am becoming increasingly eager for it. There is no other cure for me. I need real *work*, which takes time and induces *tiredness* without *mental* strain.'[157]

He wanted to spend a few days in the Lower Engadin from 3 August, but within an hour and a half of his arrival, he took to his bed and stayed there for three days. Back in St Moritz on 14 August, he began drinking the waters 'so as not to feel there is nothing I can do.'[158] Overbeck, who came to visit him, was alarmed both by his condition and by his growing addiction to isolation. 'I can only repeat my urgent advice that you should not commit yourself to any plan that condemns you to loneliness.'[159]

It must have cost him a series of enormous efforts to write *Der Wanderer und sein Schatten* (*The Wanderer and His Shadow*), the third and final part of *Menschliches, Allzumenschliches*, but nothing seemed more important than to finish the book. Like Dante, he felt 'surrounded by death' in the middle of life. He was approaching his thirty-fifth birthday, believing he might well die, like his father, in his thirty-sixth year. In July he had already written: 'Escaped the gates of death a few times, but tortured frightfully. And so my life goes on from day to day.'[160] And on 11 September, the day after sending his manuscript – two exercise-books – to Peter Gast, he wrote:

The nature of my illness forces me to consider the possibility of a *sudden* death (though I should a hundred times rather have a slow lucid one . . .). In some ways I feel like the oldest of men – but also in that I have done my *life's work*. A good drop of *oil* has been poured out through me, I know that, and it will not be forgotten. Fundamentally I have already *tested* my view of life: many yet will test it. . . .[161]

Once again Gast was deeply disturbed by the fear of losing his friend. 'I broke out into loud sobbing and wailing. A fearful premonition of death is hanging over him, and I myself need him to be alive. It is as if I must lay my head against his breast and weep, weep. I love him more than I have ever loved any man, even my father. . . . It feels as though my most beautiful duty were to die *with him*. I cannot explain this feeling; I am betraying it by express-ing it.'[162]

Nietzsche told Gast how he had written the book in the teeth of his awareness that mental effort was liable to induce agonizing and long-lasting headaches. 'Except for a few lines, it was all thought out *while I was walking*, and drafted in pencil in six small notebooks.'[163] Transcribing it in ink into the two exercise-books made him ill almost each time he set about it.

Reading it now, especially the longer sections, I often shudder at the unpleasant memories. . . . About 20 of the *longer* thought sequences – unfortunately really essential ones – had to be left out because I never found time to extricate them from my frightful pencil scrawl. It was the same the previous summer. In the meantime my memory loses the connections between the thoughts. I have to steal and collect minutes and quarters of an hour of 'brain energy' as you call it, steal them *from* a suffering brain.[164]

The style of the book had been determined partly by physical pain: both his eyes and his head compelled him to write tersely, tele-graphically.[165]

But for his devotion to Schopenhauer, Nietzsche might have arrived earlier at a rejection of the idealist tradition of German philosophy in favour of the more pragmatic approach of the French. He now complained that the philosophical dogmatists – not only idealists but materialists and realists – had all been concerned with problems irrelevant to everyday living.[166] Thanks to metaphysicians and priests, language had been used hypocritically, as if our thoughts should be focused on higher things than food, clothes, sexual inter-course or domestic activities.[167] The moralism of Kant was rooted in Rousseau and in Roman stoicism,[168] while the whole of German philosophy since Kant could be regarded as a semi-theological attack on the eighteenth-century *philosophe* Helvetius and on the laboriously accumulated wisdom he expressed so well – the wisdom of the Enlightenment.[169]

As always, Nietzsche was concerned about cultural continuity. In one aphorism the argument against Romanticism is that while there have always been classical and romantic visions of the future, the former derive from the strength of their period, the latter from its weakness.[170] Nietzsche's explanation for his hermit-like reclusion is that it was based not on a rejection of current social and political conditions, but on an understanding of the need to conserve forces that culture would one day need.[171] There is another veiled apology for his mode of life in the aphorism that explains sociability as inability to get on with oneself: 'Society's stomach is stronger than mine is,' says the sociable man, 'it can put up with me.' The same uneasiness about isolation can be discerned behind the anecdote about the man who used to undervalue himself and over-value other people. When he corrected this mistake, he found that there was no one to share the enjoyment that his intellect could offer. 'But to *give* is more blessed than to *have*: and what is the richest man in the loneliness of the desert ?'[172]

Nietzsche's best known story – about the man who proclaimed 'God is dead' – is prefigured in a story about prisoners who one day found there was no warder in the yard to supervise their work. Some carried on as usual; others stood idle. One of them said it would make no difference whether they worked or not. In a few days' time, a terrible judgement would be passed on them, but he was the warder's son and he would save those of them who believed what he told them. One prisoner said that if he was really the warder's son, it shouldn't matter to him whether they believed him or not – he should put in a good word for them anyway. Just then a prisoner came into the yard with the news that the warder had died suddenly. The man who claimed to be his son was undeterred. 'I will set free each one who believes in me as surely as my father still lives.'[173]

In the second part of *Menschliches, Allzumenschliches* Nietzsche had bracketed Jesus with Socrates: the two greatest judicial murders in the history of the world, he said, were covert suicides – each of them, wanting to die, had let his breast be pierced by a sword in the hand of human injustice.[174] In this part Nietzsche compared Jesus unfavourably with Socrates, who had been superior in intelligence, and 'by virtue of that joyful style of seriousness and that *roguish wisdom* which goes to the making of the best state in the human soul'.[175]

Neither the classical Greek philosopher nor the eighteenth-century *philosophe* had required divine sanctions for his ethical argument, but as the first moralist in the German tradition to dispense with them, Nietzsche was revolutionary. We must not trust our conscience, he maintained: 'The bite of conscience is like the biting of a dog at a stone – sheer stupidity.'[176] 'The contents of our conscience are the total residue of everything that was regularly and unreasoningly *demanded* of us in childhood by people we feared or respected.'[177] Like the *philosophes*, he argued that 'Morality is primarily a means of protecting and preserving the community.'[178] But 'the robber and the powerful man who undertakes to protect the community against robbers are probably, at root, very similar beings. . . . Even now all commercial morality is really no more than a *refinement* of pirate-morality: buying cheaply – paying nothing but overhead expenses if possible – and selling dearly.'[179] But the survival of society is guaranteed because 'the powerful man promises to maintain a *balance* against the robbers: this affords the weak man a possibility of survival'.[180] The community is fundamentally an alliance between the weak against the strong aggressor, and disgrace is an important defensive weapon. Punishment is not merely retaliation. Treated as an inferior or outsider by the group, the offender is implicitly and threateningly reminded of natural ferocity, of conditions prevailing at less advanced stages of civilization.[181]

Nietzsche's psychological observations were leading him to a radical reassessment of conventional assumptions about virtues and vices. The pejorative connotation attached to the word 'vanity', for instance, dated from the period when the most commonplace natural impulses were denigrated, so one of the most substantial and significant of human qualities was represented by a word that suggested it was empty and negative.[182] Vanity originated from the powerful man's realization that his power depended not on his strength but on his reputation. In primitive conditions, living from hand to mouth, the predator robs and kills more than is necessary for his survival. Having gained power by inspiring fear, he goes on trying to consolidate other people's faith in his power. Those who become dependent on him stand or fall not according to what they are but according to what he thinks them to be. So vanity became a means of self-preservation.[183]

According to Nietzsche, none of the human virtues could survive without vanity and self-seeking. Plato, who had believed there was a difference in kind both between good and bad men, and between good and bad qualities, had maintained that humanity could be cured of selfishness by the abolition of property.[184] Marxism was based on the same fallacy. The socialists would have liked to substitute 'Thou shalt not possess' for the commandment 'Thou shalt not steal.' But state ownership of the land would have a deleterious effect on agriculture. 'For man is hostile to everything he possesses only temporarily. Ruthlessly and recklessly, he treats all such property like a robber, a pirate and spendthrift.'[185] But the existence of extreme poverty and great accumulations of private wealth are genuinely against the interests of society. Transport and the money market should therefore be taken out of private hands.[186]

On 17 September Nietzsche left St Moritz to meet Elisabeth in Chur. In March she had been appalled at his appearance; now she was amazed at how much better he seemed. 'He looked so fresh and resilient, with such a healthy complexion, and he had regained his firm, upright deportment.'[187] They stayed in the same hotel for three nights, spending much of the day going out for walks, and then on the 20th he went on to Naumburg while she returned to Tamins, where she was working as companion to a lady who was mentally ill.

He succeeded in renting the tower and the garden, but they were both larger than he had remembered: he was not fit enough to cope with the work, though he was feeling relatively well.[188] His eyes were too weak for the gardening, while the constant bending was a strain on his back.[189] Within three weeks he was eager to abandon the experiment. In September he received more than half of the *Wanderer und sein Schatten* text in Gast's fair copy, and the remainder arrived on 3 October. 'I cannot fathom how you could complete this frightful work in such a short time.'[190] Gast had made some alterations and proposed others; Nietzsche rejected some of his suggestions but accepted many. His first reaction to the book had pleased Nietzsche. It 'corresponds to my most inward wish so closely that our spiritual relationship must be at work'.[191] Schmeitzner produced proofs before the end of October, and Gast worked on them for Nietzsche, making creative suggestions as well as corrections.

About the beginning of November Nietzsche's condition began to deteriorate, 'though the pain has not yet passed a certain threshold of the "tolerable"'.[192] By the middle of the month he felt that the beneficial effects of his summer in St Moritz had worn off.[193] Overcast skies and persistent rain seemed to intensify his discomfort. Since mid-November, he wrote on 11 December, he had been 'constantly ill, the attacks frightful (with vomiting etc.), many days in bed'.[194] 'I am suffering extraordinarily and constantly, attack after attack.'[195] He was keeping count of the days spoiled by headaches, and he did not quite wait for the end of the year to report a total of 118.[196]

He wanted to leave for Italy before Christmas, but he was not well enough to travel. On 18 December he received his copies of *Der Wanderer und sein Schatten*, and the book reached his friends on the 20th. Erwin Rohde, who had not written to him for exactly a year, broke the silence to say: 'You live in your own spirit; the rest of us *never* hear such voices, either speaking or in print . . . for a time I feel lifted onto a higher plane, as if spiritually ennobled.'[197]

Yet again Nietzsche's health was at a nadir over Christmas, and this was the worst Christmas yet. After three days and nights of vomiting, he fell into a coma on the 27th.[198] Before it, he had been longing for death,[199] and afterwards he thought death was near: 'If I cannot escape into better, warmer air, the worst will happen.'[200]

In reply to New Year greetings from Dr Eiser he wrote:

My existence is a fearful burden. I would have thrown it off long ago if I had not been making the most instructive tests and experiments on mental and moral questions in precisely this condition of suffering and almost complete renunciation. . . . On the whole I am happier than ever before. And yet, continual pain; for many hours of the day a feeling closely akin to sea-sickness, a semi-paralysis which makes it difficult to speak, alternating with furious attacks. . . . My consolation is my thoughts and perspectives. I write nothing at a desk, but on my way here and there I scribble on a scrap of paper.[201]

The Marquis de Sade, after six and a half years of imprisonment at Vincennes, had found that he valued nothing more than what was going on in his mind: 'My way of thinking is the fruit of my reflections; it is part of my existence, my constitution. . . . [It] is my only comfort; it alleviates all my sufferings in prison, creates all the pleasure I have in the world, and I value it more highly than life.' Nietzsche, in the mobile torture-chamber of his disease, had arrived at the same self-sufficiency. So long as he survived, his reflections provided his main nourishment, but they reminded him that everyone was a prisoner inside the concentric circles of limited vision and limited experience.

According to these horizons, which confine our senses like prison walls, we *measure* the world, calling this near and that remote, this big and that small. . . . This measuring, which we call perception, is quite erratic. . . . The habits of our senses have implicated us in the lies and deceptions of perception, and these form the basis of all our judgements and our 'knowledge' – there is no escape, no secret passage or crooked path into the real world.[202]

To him, as to de Sade, the luxury of free thinking was a necessity.

ABOVE The parsonage at Röcken in Prussian Saxony where Nietzsche was born on 15 October 1844

LEFT Nietzsche's mother Franziska (*née* Oehler)

LEFT The sixteen-year-old
Nietzsche, who was confirmed
in March 1861

TOP RIGHT Undated pencil
sketch from Nietzsche's
juvenilia

RIGHT Friedrich Ritschl

OPPOSITE ABOVE Franconia,
the student fraternity at Bonn
University in the summer of
1865. Nietzsche is the third
from the left in the sitting row,
leaning on his hand.

OPPOSITE BELOW The Philo-
logical Society at Leipzig
University (1866–7) with
Nietzsche sitting on the extreme
left and Rohde sitting on the
extreme right

ABOVE Richard Wagner in 1862, aged forty-nine

ABOVE RIGHT Pastor Carl Ludwig Nietzsche

RIGHT Wagner's house Tribschen. Of his first years at Basel University Nietzsche said: 'In these three years I have spent close to Tribschen, I have made twenty-three visits, which mean so much to me.'
See page 151.

ABOVE LEFT Cosima von
Bülow. When Wagner died in
1883 Nietzsche wrote to tell her
she was still 'the woman my
heart most honours'.
See page 261.

ABOVE RIGHT Nietzsche in the
autumn of 1868. He was discharged from the army on his
twenty-fourth birthday,
15 October. See page 96.

LEFT Elisabeth Nietzsche

TOP LEFT Carl von Gersdorff

TOP RIGHT Franz Overbeck

RIGHT Lou Salomé (holding the whip), Paul Rée (centre) and Nietzsche photographed in Lucerne by Jules Bonnet in 1882. The idea for the grouping was Nietzsche's. See page 246.

OPPOSITE ABOVE The house at Sils-Maria where Nietzsche spent the summers of 1881 and 1883–8

OPPOSITE BELOW Nietzsche's small, simply furnished room at Sils-Maria still contains the bed, the writing-table, the sofa and the wash-stand that he used.

TOP LEFT A page from the hand-written volume of poems by the thirteen-year-old Nietzsche given to his mother for a Christmas present in 1857. See page 24.

TOP RIGHT Crayon scrawl including two attempts at a signature and at writing the names of his mother and sister. Probably 1892. See page 344.

BELOW Hans Olde's charcoal sketch of Nietzsche during the final bed-ridden year of his illness

8   Mediterranean Sunrise

Early in the morning of 26 January 1880, Peter Gast received an unexpected payment of 250 francs through the post; the explanation arrived at midday in a letter from Paul Rée. Nietzsche was coming to Italy, probably to Riva on Lake Garda. The money was to cover the railway fare from Venice and the expenses Gast would incur in looking after him. Though irked by Rée's high-handedness, Gast waited impatiently for news, wanting to be at Riva in time to welcome Nietzsche and install him in a hotel.

It was warm in Riva, but in Naumburg it was too cold for Nietzsche to set out before 10 February. Again illness interrupted his journey. After two bedridden days in Bolzano, he arrived in Riva on the 14th, staying at the Hôtel du Lac. Gast heard nothing from him until five days later, when he said he would travel to Venice – a distance of two hundred kilometres – on 13 March. But on 23 February Gast left for Riva, arriving at eleven o'clock at night and taking a room at the same hotel. At five-thirty Nietzsche woke him to say that it was probably going to rain, so if they were going out for a walk they had better start now. It turned out to be a fine day, and, far from feeling resentful, Gast was 'extraordinarily happy. Again I am fully experiencing the exalted mood which somehow surrounds Nietzsche. You can have . . . *no* impression of it, although you have sensed what is magical and unique about this man: his personal presence is part of it.'[1]

Gast wrote to his Austrian girlfriend Cäcilie Gusselbauer: 'If Nietzsche were a girl, with only a quarter as much brightness and spirit as he possesses, I cannot deny that I would marry this girl on the spot. . . . He must be very strict with himself, living by rules of his own invention to regulate speaking and thinking, seeing and hearing. Only in bodily movement can he afford to be quite un-disciplined.'[2] Naturally, Cäcilie became jealous.

After three weeks of what he called 'strenuous Samaritan

service'[3] Gast still had no regrets about the time he spent in Riva: 'I will always think of it with pleasure.'[4] Nietzsche could not have said the same: 'I am very disappointed. My condition has deteriorated during the three weeks, and the pain continues to be very troublesome.'[5] During the second week, together with Count Pappenheim, Gast played the third act of *Götterdämmerung* as a piano duet. Nietzsche was frightfully upset. 'He went quite pale and solemnly warned me that I must never again let him hear this mad, distorted music of Wagner's.'[6] Nietzsche went on seeming deeply hurt and for the whole of the following week he was feeling ill, which made Gast feel guilty.

On 13 March they left for Venice, where Nietzsche found himself a room looking out on the Island of the Dead. There was no rain until 2 April, and soon he began to feel better: 'On the whole the place is doing me more good than Riva. . . . I will probably stay here for the summer. . . . With the high rooms and the silence I sleep well, and the sea air reaches me before it has been spoiled by going through Venice. . . . I feel a calming influence.'[7] 'The whole city has been decorated with flags, and the doves of St Mark are flying peacefully all around.'[8] Gast was coming twice a day, at two-fifteen and seven-thirty, to read to him for an hour or an hour and a half. Gast was also taking dictation and transcribing his notes, but what killed the pleasure Gast took in his company was the sense of responsibility for his wellbeing. 'You have no idea of the strain Nietzsche's presence causes me, and the self-control it necessitates.'[9] He had to ask Cäcilie for forbearance: 'I will do everything I can for Nietzsche, because I cannot look on while such an excellent man is left helpless and abandoned.'[10]

In April Gast's patience was tried even more severely when an Italian friend of his, Minutti, arrived in Venice. He was eager to meet Nietzsche, but soon fell ill himself, so Gast had to look after both of them. 'If my impatience with this dog's life grows any worse, I shall leave Venice in two weeks and let the sick take care of the sick.'[11]

The first half of April was rainy, windy and sultry; the second half was warmer, but the heat brought the mosquitoes, while the rain continued intermittently. Nietzsche believed that the combination of rain and heat was bad for his headaches, and possibly the belief had more effect on them than the weather. At the end of the month he had the worst attack since Gast had been with him.

The longer he stayed in Venice, the more resentful Gast became about the time he was losing, though he also felt guilty about feeling resentful: 'I again thought of how indebted I am to Nietzsche for so much emotional stimulation, and how isolated the poor blind man has been ... since all his former friends broke with him out of intolerance towards his free thinking.'[12] Gast would often give up five or six hours of his day: 'I would lie down at night, wanting to sleep, and when I thought about the day's events, seeing that I had done nothing for myself and everything for other people, I would go into convulsions of rage, consigning Nietzsche to death and damnation. ... Then, after I had fallen wearily to sleep at four or five in the morning, Nietzsche would often come along at nine or ten, asking me to play Chopin for him.'[13] He was trying to wean himself fully off Wagnerian music.

Nor did he realize until later that he was upsetting Gast with the anti-Christian tenor of the notes he was dictating under the title *L'Ombra di Venezia*. Much of this material was to be absorbed into *Morgenröte* (*Sunrise*), which was subtitled *Thoughts on Moral Prejudices*. The first of the five books launches a powerful attack on Christian doctrines about sin. 'The passions become evil and vicious when regarded from an evil and vicious viewpoint. Christianity has succeeded in making Eros and Aphrodite – great, ennobling ideals – into goblins and phantoms, by means of the torment that each sexual impulse was made to arouse in the conscience of the believer.'[14] Thanks to the vetoes of the Church, the devil had become more interesting than angels or saints, and the love story was now the one interest that all social classes had in common.[15] Doubt, too, had been proclaimed sinful: 'What are wanted are blindness and ecstasy and an eternal song over the waters in which intelligence is drowned.'[16] The Jews had loved life too much to think about doing penance after death: their idea of punishment for the sinner was forfeiture of immortality. The Romans had conceived the notion of purgatorial punishment. Epicurus had attacked it, but Christianity had revived it.[17] Altogether too much stress had been laid on sin and punishment. With the doctrine of Original Sin, Christianity had at once denied the innocence of fortuitous events and stigmatized the whole of human existence as a punishment.[18] 'It is as if human education had until now been determined by the fantasies of gaolers and executioners.'[19]

The first Christian had been St Paul, an ambitious and officious man, superstitious and cunning. But for him, the Christians would have remained an obscure sect. The reason he wanted to jettison so much Jewish ballast from the Christian ship was that as a young man he had not come to terms with the Jewish law, transgressing not so much from sensuality as because the law itself seemed so demanding: it was provoking him into disobedience. His sins may have included murder, witchcraft, idolatry, debauchery and drunkenness. Nietzsche compares him with Luther, whose frustration while striving towards monastic perfection exploded into a bitter hatred for pope, saints, priesthood and the ecclesiastical ideal. When Saul became Paul, he started preaching against the law. 'To become one with Christ meant to be with him as an annihilator of the law . . . with the thought of sharing his identity, all shame, all subjection, all inhibitions were removed, and the unruly thirst for domination revealed itself in an anticipatory revelling in *divine* supremacy.'[20]

It was because custom had been so continuously oppressive that madness had a bearing on the history of morality. 'Plato was speaking for the whole of antiquity when he said: "From madness Greece has derived its greatest benefits." For those superior intellects who were irresistibly driven to break the yoke of a convention and make new laws, there was no alternative, *if they were not really mad*, but to feign madness.'[21] If they were not brave enough to feign it, they must induce it. Almost all the best minds of the older civilization yielded to this terrible logic, and the recipe Nietzsche offers is like a distorting mirror focused on his life: 'inordinate fasting, continual sexual abstinence, withdrawal into the wilderness, or climbing a mountain, or onto a pillar, or "sitting on an ancient willow facing a lake", and thinking resolutely of nothing except what provokes ecstasy and mental derangement'.[22] In all periods of history, most creative men have suffered the greatest mental agony, and, haunted by the law they have killed, they have prayed for the convulsions and the delirium that will empower them to think themselves above it.[23] So Nietzsche's diatribe against St Paul was based at least partly on empathetic identification with him as a law-killer, just as later, when he writes about the death of God, he will be thinking about the death of divine law, and, to some extent, blaming himself for its demise.

The recipe tends to strengthen one's suspicions that there was an element of self-destructiveness, mainly unconscious but at least partly conscious, in Nietzsche's life-style. His sexual abstinence was largely involuntary, but his eccentric and inadequate diet was determined partly by poverty, partly by masochistic self-discipline. Physical comfort was of less importance to him than ambition to be one of the great law-killers who was also one of the great creators. Insofar as he thought about madness as a price he might have to pay, he does not seem to have been scared of it. On one level he genuinely believed that his incessant wanderings were in search of the climate in which he would suffer least, but he was also, in his way, withdrawing into the wilderness, climbing mountains, cultivating solitude. When he decided to spend the winter in Genoa, Elisabeth wrote to ask whether he would like one of his friends to join him;[24] his answer was: 'I want to be my own doctor, and so I must be true to myself in the deepest sense, and no longer listen to anyone else. I cannot tell you how much good *solitude* is doing me.'[25]

Unable, since his stay in Venice, to go on believing that humidity was bad for him, he was drawn magnetically towards mountains, forests, lakes, the sea. On 22 June, wanting shade for his eyes, he decided to leave Venice, possibly for Carniola in Yugoslavia.[26] A week later he started the journey northwards, ending up in Marienbad. 'I had a very bad journey, looking for woods and mountains: *everything* was disappointing, or rather it was *impossible* for my *eyes*. . . . I can find nowhere that suits me, as I did in Venice. But it was too hot there. Even the woods are not yet thick enough. . . . I shall not be able to bear it here for more than four weeks. Then I shall go to the Thuringian forest, which is the thickest.'[27] In fact he stayed on in Marienbad for two months, feeling too ill to travel in August. He spent September in Naumburg, but when he left on 8 October he did not return for two years. The journey to Stresa was even worse than the one from Marienbad to Naumburg. He had an attack of vomiting in Frankfurt, retired to bed in Heidelberg, and again in Locarno.[28] He stayed for nearly a month at Stresa, on the Lago Maggiore, before moving on to Genoa, where he decided to spend the winter.

The long train journeys were an ordeal. Arriving in Marienbad, he wrote to Gast: 'The journey seriously damaged my health. A few times I was almost in despair. The mountains seemed to me pointless and "nonsensical". . . . Think carefully before leaving Venice. The people are so ugly here, and a steak costs 80 kreuzer. It is like being in an evil world.'[29] He was drinking the local waters and walking for as much as ten hours a day, as well as working at *Morgenröte*: 'I am digging eagerly in my moral mine, which sometimes makes me feel like a subterranean creature. I *think* I have now found the main gallery and the way out.'[30] In the preface he wrote for the book six years later he developed the image of digging into a conceit about undermining the public's faith in morals.[31] The mineworking metaphor may have been suggested by the attempts he made in Book 11 to explore the unconscious workings of the mind. He had already suggested in *Menschliches, Allzumenschliches* that our motives are not what we think they are; but what are they? 'We are impelled by the habitual play of our energy; or by a slight encouragement from someone we fear or honour or love; or by the convenience of taking action on something that is to hand; or by the fantasy, stimulated at the decisive moment by some minor detail. We are affected by unpredictable physical factors, moods, and the movements of passions which happen to be on the point of coming to a head.'[32]

As before, his psychological investigations were fuelled by anger at the falsifications of the old morality. What really activates us when we think we are behaving altruistically? Why, for instance, do we jump into the water to save a stranger's life? 'Other people's accidents offend us, testifying as they do to our impotence or even to our cowardice unless we come to the rescue.'[33] Motivation is hardly ever simple, but 'as surely as we wish to free ourselves from suffering, we submit to an *impulse of pleasure* – pleasure at glimpsing a contrast to our own situation, at the possibility of being helpful if only we want to, at the prospect of praise and gratitude, at the activity of helping . . . but mainly in the sensation that our action sets a limit to an appalling injustice – already the release of indignation is refreshing.'[34]

Nietzsche's emphasis on unconscious motives was complementary to his denial of free will. Our belief in it was born out of our pride and our sense of power.[35] To the sceptic who professes ignorance both of what he is doing and of what he should be doing, Nietzsche's answer is: 'You are right, but have no doubt that *you are being done*! Humanity has always confused the active with the passive – its constant grammatical blunder.'[36] 'At each moment of our lives, some polypus arms of our nature grow, others wither, according to the nourishment conveyed by that moment.'[37] Our development, therefore, depends on chance. 'Perhaps this cruelty of fortune would be more conspicuous if all impulses were as rudimentary as *hunger*, which is not to be fobbed off with *imaginary food*, while most impulses, especially the so-called moral ones, *do precisely that* – if I am right in conjecturing that to some extent the value and purpose of our *dreams* is to *compensate* for the "nourishment" that chance fails to produce during the day.'[38]

In Marienbad, Nietzsche was having dreams about Wagner. 'How often I dream about him, and always in the spirit of our former intimacy! Never was an angry word spoken between us ... the conversation was encouraging and cheerful. I do not think I have laughed so much with anyone else. All that is now over, and what use is it to know that in many respects he was in the wrong?'[39] Although Nietzsche had chosen to spend very little time in Wagner's company ever since he left Tribschen in 1872, it was only now that the pangs of loss seem to have become really persistent. A letter written to Gast over a month earlier contains the sentence: 'One ceases to love oneself *properly* when one *ceases* to exercise one's capacity for love towards other people; which means that the latter (ceasing to love) is highly inadvisable.'[40]

For three months Nietzsche was deeply depressed. 'Since that August letter. ... I have not dipped my pen into the ink, so disgusting was my condition, so trying, as it still is.'[41] He was disappointed with the Lago Maggiore, which struck him as quite unlike Lake Garda and more like a Swiss lake.[42] For the first time in his life he forgot his birthday, his thirty-sixth: he was concentrating on *Morgenröte* again. Writing to thank Overbeck for remembering the birthday that he had forgotten, he said: 'Probably my head is too full of other thoughts which make me ask myself ten times daily: "What is the matter with you?" '[43]

It is in the fourth book that the idea of the will to power

surfaces. 'The first result of happiness is a sense of power . . . its most usual ways of expressing itself are presents, derision, destruction.'[44] One means of raising oneself above one's insignificance is to dominate a wife, a dog, a friend, a party or a century.[45] Humanity is bedevilled by love of power, which contributes more to happiness than health, nourishment, home, entertainment.[46] Even charity and self-sacrifice are motivated, paradoxically, by the same fixation. The philanthropist is gratifying a need of his own: the stronger it is, the less concern he has for the feelings of the beneficiary.[47] Self-sacrifice is encouraged by the notion of being one with the power – human or divine – that inspires it. 'You exult in the feeling of his strength . . . in short you want rapture and excess.'[48] Reacting in *Menschliches*, *Allzumenschliches* against the simplifications and distortions involved in Schopenhauer's notion of will, Nietzsche set up no rival thesis, and now, evolving the idea of the will to power, he lays himself open to the charge he had made against Schopenhauer. Nietzsche too is applying the word to heterogeneous mental actions, and later he will begin to use it metaphorically, as if natural forces possessed willpower.

At the end of October 1880 Nietzsche was intending to stay on in Stresa for another two weeks,[49] but by 7 November he was in Genoa. Gast, who had been sending manuscripts of his compositions, was told that he had been cheering himself up by singing and whistling his melodies. It had been 'an inconceivable, extremely agonizing period, over whelming me with every physical and spiritual evil. Oh, the deepest melancholy in Stresa!'[50] In Genoa he had to move three times within the first ten days. He settled in an attic. 'I have to climb a hundred and sixty-four steps inside the house, which is itself situated high up in a steep street of palaces. Being so steep, and ending in a great flight of steps, the street is very quiet, with grass growing between the stones. My health is in *terrible* disorder, my stomach too. But the sea air is indescribably beneficial.'[51] Sometimes he lived for days on dried fruit, but he did some cooking for himself on a spirit stove and his landlady sometimes helped him to prepare dishes. But the room was unheated, and the winter was a cold one, especially after Christmas. 'When the sun shines, I always go to a lonely cliff by the sea and lie there in the open under my parasol, motionless as a lizard. That has often helped my head. I wash my whole body every day, especially my whole head, giving it a brisk rub.'[52] Though he had no option but to take his sufferings seriously, he could see that they had a comic aspect: 'The daily battle against headaches and the ridiculous complexity of my troubles occupy so much attention that I am in danger of becoming *petty*.'[53] Generally he was not much concerned with the impression he was making on other people, but *Morgenröte* contains an indirect reference to his big moustache: 'The most placid, most reasonable man, so long as he has a big moustache, can quietly sit in its shade – as the accessory of a big moustache he will give most people the impression of being military, irascible and sometimes violent, so they will behave accordingly.'[54] Other people might dismiss his philosophy as invalidated by his physical condition: 'That man thinks his illness is an argument, and his feebleness is proof of everybody else's. He is vain enough to fall ill in order to feel the superiority of the sufferer.'

The final book of *Morgenröte*, which was mostly written in Genoa, showed that he believed his suffering had taught him to understand himself. 'The man who is genuinely in possession of himself, i.e. who has finally *conquered himself*, regards it as his special privilege to punish, pardon or pity himself. He need never delegate this privilege, but may confer it on someone else – a friend, for instance.'[55]

In *Menschliches, Allzumenschliches* he had written: 'To improve your style means to improve your ideas, and nothing else.'[56] He had now improved his style so much that verbal felicity is sometimes indistinguishable from self-satisfaction: 'You glorify that as my *creation*? All I have done is cast off what was burdensome to me! My soul has risen above the vanity of creation. You glorify that as my *resignation*? All I have done is cast off what was burdensome to me! My soul is above the vanity of resignation.'[57] The implicit identification with God on the seventh day anticipates the delusions of grandeur which overtook him before the breakdown.

What he valued most in himself was his capacity for knowledge. He could infallibly penetrate to the bottom of things. In one of the brief dialogues he writes in *Morgenröte* a character says: 'The helplessness of a thing pulls me so far and so deeply into it that I finally reach the bottom, and see that it is not really worth so much.'[58] Using underground imagery again, he implicitly compares himself (in another dialogue) with a worm, though he claims not to have turned into one. 'B: Precisely. You have *stopped* being a sceptic! Because you *negate*! A: 'Which is how I have learned to *affirm* once again!'[59] He thought he had put an end to idealism, especially German idealism,[60] and he compares Kant and Schopenhauer unfavourably with the writers 'whose thinking constitutes the involuntary biography of a soul' – Plato, Spinoza, Pascal, Rousseau and Goethe,[61] though Plato, Spinoza and Goethe were men 'whose intellect could soar away from their temper and character'.[62] It is obvious that Nietzsche wanted to resemble them in both respects. He was still compulsively interpreting his earlier philosophical mistakes as the source of his illness: 'thinking against the grain' is defined as 'failing to follow the thoughts that offer themselves to a thinker from inside'; if he lets himself be taken over by other ideas, 'he will eventually fall ill, for what may appear to be virtuous self-control saps his nervous energy no less profoundly than regular debauchery'.[63] Confused by his commitment to the ideal of self-mastery, he had failed to be sufficiently kind to himself. Without making any autobiographical statement, he formulated his new conviction: the man who 'runs away from himself, hates himself, damages himself is certainly not a good man. For he finds refuge from himself only *in other people*.'[64] Despite his disbelief, the Wagnerian Nietzsche had been living in accordance with Christian principles. 'To shun and hate the ego, to live for others, through others – until now this has mindlessly but confidently been proclaimed as "unselfish" and therefore "good".'[65] But now he had graduated out of these errors, which still held his contemporaries captive. Earlier philosophers, themselves victims of the lust for intellectual power, had not provided enough help. 'When we evaluate what has hitherto been worshipped as super-human (*übermenschlicher*) intellect, as genius, we come to the sad conclusion that the intellectuality of mankind must on the whole have been very low and wretched: so little intellect was required to feel considerably superior! . . . People kneel down – like slaves – before *power*, and the *degree of intellectual power* will determine the degree of *veneration*.'[66] But the most beautiful manifestations of genius do not inspire mass worship – 'I mean the spectacle of that power which a genius directs *not into his works* but *into himself as a work*, i.e. into self-mastery, purification of his imagination, control and selection of his tasks and insights.'[67] Nietzsche was not immune to desire for power, but it was for power over himself that he lusted. Was his writing perhaps no more than a formulation of how he wanted to live, a sketch for a critical biography of his anti-social soul?

Where is this whole philosophy going, with all its deviations? Does it do any more than, as it were, rationalize a steady, powerful craving for mild sunlight, a bright and bracing atmosphere, Mediterranean vegetation, sea breezes, quick snacks of meat, eggs, fruits and glasses of hot water, quiet walks that last all day, a paucity of conversation, occasional careful reading, solitary living, hygienic, simple and almost military habits – in short all the things I find most enjoyable and most wholesome?[68]

The final instalment of Nietzsche's manuscript was sent on 19 February 1881 to Gast, who sent back a fair copy within ten days. Nietzsche's first plan was to divide it into four books, but the final version has five. On 14 March the revised manuscript was sent back to Gast, who set to work on it immediately, despatching the first part to Schmeitzner the next day. Generously, despite all memories of strain and resentment, Gast then invited Nietzsche back to Venice. He did not want to go there, but accepted promptly when Gast proposed a reunion in Recoaro, near Vicenza.[69] Meeting in Vicenza on 1 May they stayed in a hotel, but the next day Nietzsche was too ill for the forty-four-kilometre journey, so he stayed on an extra night while Gast went on ahead to prepare things for his friend's arrival. Nietzsche was 'full of gaiety, enthusiasm and generosity',[70] and, though he was not feeling well, there was nothing forced or insincere about his reactions to the score of Gast's comic opera. 'He is a musician of *the front rank* and what he can do no one alive can do better. I can also take a personal pleasure in what is precisely the music that belongs to *my* philosophy.'[71]

Nevertheless, it was a relief when Gast left Recoaro at the end of the month. 'In spite of being careful, my health can no longer take the strain of such companionship. I had attacks of the worst Basel variety.'[72] If he stayed on in Recoaro, it was mainly because he had nowhere else to go. By 19 June he had decided on St Moritz.[73] He made the journey on 2 July, but the place now seemed repulsive, a 'crystallization of what he had suffered there two years earlier'.[74] He stayed only three hours, leaving without knowing where he was going. But on the overnight train he met 'a serious, kindly Swiss' who described Sils-Maria in terms that made him want to go there. It struck him as 'the loveliest corner of the earth. . . . I have never found anywhere so quiet.'[75] But it took him three days of headaches and vomiting to recover from the double journey and the indecision. He felt that he had been very close to death.[76]

He now believed 'atmospheric electricity' to be the decisive climatic factor for him. 'Basel, Naumburg, Genoa, Baden-Baden, almost all the mountain resorts I know, Marienbad, the Italian lakes etc. are places for going to ground. Winter by the sea is tolerable; but the changeableness of the clouds makes spring [in Sorrento and Genoa] an incessant torment . . . The Engadin is the best place in the world for me.'[77] But within a fortnight he had three more bad bouts of headaches, each lasting two or three days.[78] The main pleasure of the first month in Sils-Maria was the discovery of Spinoza: 'I have a precursor, and *what* a precursor!'[79] Nietzsche found that 'this most abnormal and lonely thinker' had five points of affinity with him: they were both sceptical about free will, intentions, the moral world-order, altruism and evil. 'My isolation, which has often made me gasp for breath, and lose blood, as if I were on a very high mountain, has at last become a solitude to be shared.'[80]

Together with the feeling of having narrowly escaped death and the abnormal quantity of physical suffering during July, this new sense of solidarity may have contributed to the new mental experiences of August. In the middle of the month he wrote: 'On my horizon thoughts have arisen, the like of which I have never seen before. . . Sometimes I think the life I am living is really dangerous because I am one of those machines that could *explode*.'[81] Several times he had found his eyes were so inflamed that he could not leave his room. 'Each time I had wept too much the previous day while I was walking, and not tears of sentimentality but jubilation. I sang and talked nonsense, possessed by a new attitude. I am the first man to arrive at it.'[82]

This letter is itself an attempt at administering the remedy it prescribes. 'If I could not collect strength from myself . . . where would I be? What would I be?' There had been periods in his life (e.g. the year 1878) 'when an encouraging remark, an approving handshake, would have been the best of tonics',[83] but he had come to expect nothing. He was locked into the fortress of his solitude. 'I regard everyone who breaks into my Engadin working summer . . . as my enemy . . . and if I cannot be sure of my isolation, I will go away from Europe for several years, I swear it!'[84] When Rée, who was travelling with his mother, proposed a visit to Sils-Maria, Nietzsche excused himself. 'I need *complete* solitude, not as a luxury but as indispensable to my *possibly* enduring life for a few more years.'[85]

In none of these letters to Gast and Elisabeth did he describe the new attitude, but the first notes relevant to *Also sprach Zarathustra* contain the jotting: 'Beginning of August 1881 in Sils-Maria, 6,000 feet above the sea, and much higher above all human things.'[86] Exactly what happened he never tells us, but he appears to have asked himself how he would react if given the chance of repeating the whole of his life exactly as it had been. He had suffered so much that it would have been natural to reject the option, but the elation he now felt was sufficient to convince him that he would accept it. In *Die fröhliche Wissenschaft* (*The Joyful Wisdom*), the book he developed out of material originally intended for a continuation of *Morgenröte*, he imagines a demon who breaks the news that we will have to go through everything 'once again and countless times after that, with nothing new in it, but each pain, each pleasure, each thought and sigh . . . everything in the same sequence. . . . The eternal hourglass of existence is turned around, again and again – and you with it, you grain of dust.'[87] Would you curse the demon, asks Nietzsche, 'Or have you ever experienced a tremendous moment when you would have answered: "You are a god, and never have I heard anything more divine"? . . . Or how benevolent would you have to feel towards yourself and life to *demand* nothing more than this ultimate eternal confirmation and approval?'[88] Despite the torments of July, Nietzsche felt as optimistic as this in August 1881.

Among his books he had a copy of Heine's *Letzte Gedichte und Gedanken* (*Last Poems and Thoughts*) which contains the passage:

For time is infinite, but things in time, concrete objects, are not. They may separate into minute particles, but these, the atoms, have their determinate number, as do the configurations that can be formed with them. According to the law of the eternal play of repetitions, which governs combinations, all configurations that have ever existed on the earth will again meet, attract, repel, embrace and corrupt each other.[89]

Nietzsche may have been reminded of this passage by Julius Nobert Mayer's book *Mechanik der Wärme* (*Mechanics of Heat*), which Gast had sent to him in April and which they must have discussed in May. As formulated by Mayer, the principle of conservation of energy is that its power is variable in quality but quantitatively indestructible. Heat is only a form of movement. Each can be converted into the other, but the law of the invariable quantitative relationship between them can be expressed numerically. Nietzsche was later to call eternal recurrence 'the most *scientific* of all possible hypotheses',[90] and though he never attempted to prove it scientifically, his unpublished notes contain the statements: 'The law of the conservation of energy demands *eternal recurrence*';[91] and 'The two most extreme modes of thought, the mechanistic and the Platonic, are reconciled in the law of *eternal recurrence* – both as ideals.'[92] He also referred to 'the energy of knowledge and strength',[93] as though intellectual resources, like mineral resources, could be made to undergo chemical change but could not be destroyed. His later intellectual elaborations of his idea could not have occurred without the emotional experience of August 1881, but the experience would probably not have taken the form it did if his mind had not been tingling with the impact of Heine's and Mayer's formulations. The reading Nietzsche did at Sils-Maria was dependent mainly on the books he asked Overbeck to send him. These included *Die Thomsonsche Hypothese* by the Darwinist Otto Caspari, *Versuch über Ursache und Wirkung* (*Essay on Origin and Effect*) by Adolf Fick, and J. G. Vogt's *Die Kraft* (*Energy*), a book which applied E. A. Hackel's monistic assumptions.[94]

One reason for the idea's appeal to Nietzsche is that it restores to life itself the eternalizing capacity which Romantic aesthetics had claimed for art: nothing need be done to perpetuate the moment if it is in any case indestructible. The idea also serves

Nietzsche as a quasi-scientific coefficient of the Dionysus myth: human experience becomes as indestructible as the god.

No one but Nietzsche would have been able to evolve a theory like this at a time like the summer of 1882, when he had only ten days free from pain:[95] 'Five times I have asked Death to be my doctor, and yesterday I hoped it was the end – in vain.'[96] Later he told Dr Paneth that he had got rid of his pessimism by defying his illness, in order not to let it tyrannize over him, and even if the idea had been conceived in a moment of euphoria, painful defiance of pain was the other side of the dialectic in which it evolved.

The question of whether his aching brain was functioning 'normally' would be almost meaningless, and he still believed he was absorbing electricity from the atmosphere. 'Each cloud contains some form of electric charge which suddenly takes hold of me, reducing me to utter misery.'[97] This illusion about absorbing electricity is common in schizophrenia, but Nietzsche was *in extremis*. He ought to be an exhibit, he said, at the Paris electricity exhibition: 'Perhaps I am more receptive on this point, unfortunately for me, than any other man on earth.'[98] Sometimes he felt 'like a zig-zag doodle drawn on paper by a superior power wanting to try out a *new pen*'.[99]

Though Schmeitzner said that his readers wanted no more aphorisms from him,[100] he was not deterred from planning the continuation of *Morgenröte*. And if Wagner had been the musically potent father-substitute, Gast, having proved himself, to Nietzsche's satisfaction, as a composer, became a surrogate son. He must be encouraged to bring his art to maturity: 'That is what I feel when I think about you, enjoying in this prospect a fulfilment of my own nature as in a picture.'[101] Nietzsche even brought himself to believe that Gast's music could help him to survive long enough to complete his new task without any appreciation from friends or readers. 'If humanity gives me no joy, I will give it to myself! But *your* music must retune me. I *need* that, I now see.'[102]

Delayed by another bout of illness, he could not leave Sils-Maria until 1 October. 'I travelled with almost the energy of a madman. The change in my condition and the torment my half-blindness causes me on journeys have gone beyond all measure.'[103] It was a relief to be in Genoa again. He enjoyed going to the opera: he saw Bellini's *I Capuleti ed i Montecchi* four times,[104] and became enthusiastic about *Carmen*, which was new to him. The French had written better dramatic music, he decided, than the Germans: passion did not seem so far-fetched as it did in Wagner.[105] 'I almost think *Carmen* is the best opera there is,'[106] and within seven years he had seen it twenty times.[107]

But he was not writing much:

> I do not trust the thoughts that occur when my soul is oppressed and my intestine afflicted, and even what might get written when I have a headache will certainly be torn up. On the other hand I am well aware of being tremendously indebted to this inconstancy in my health ... this magical feeling of getting better – a wonderful condition and the source of the most elevated and courageous perceptions. ... As in the Engadin I go for walks in the hills, exultantly happy, and looking into the future as no one before me has dared to.[108]

In a letter T. S. Eliot wrote in 1931 about Beethoven's quartets, he said: 'There is a sort of heavenly or at least more than human gaiety about some of his later things which one imagines might come to oneself as the fruit of reconciliation and relief after immense suffering.'[109] Nietzsche's gaiety in what became *Die fröhliche Wissenschaft* reflects his elation at being able to write again. In November 1881 he could hardly even read: 'Extraordinary pain after using my eyes for even the briefest period.'[110] But within just over two months he completed the first three books of *Die fröhliche Wissenschaft*, stretching his literary wings like a bird that has been lying feebly in a corner, and in rediscovering how large the cage is, forgets about the bars. Delighted to find he could go further than he had in *Menschliches, Allzumenschliches* towards redefining good and evil, he forgot to ask himself whether the project of redefinition was compatible with the belief that there is no generic difference between them and that no contradistinctions can be valid. Intuitively he may have become aware that he had been putting himself into an untenable position: towards the end of the third book, he introduces a defensive paradox: ' "Good and evil are the prejudices of God", said the serpent.' Conditioned as we are to disbelieve the serpent, we interpret this as meaning that good and evil cannot merely be prejudices in the mind of a dead God. So what are they? Nietzsche was too much of a moralist to stop himself from trying to explain. He may have thought he was merely exposing the viciousness in what seems virtuous and the positive value in what seems evil, but without having the linguistic equipment he needed, he embarked on the kind of redefinition that implies alternative principles of good and evil.

Developing his schoolboy insight into the constructive value of conflict, he demonstrates that hatred, *Schadenfreude*, the compulsions to steal and to dominate can all contribute to the preservation of the species: without these impulses humanity would have become feeble and rotten.[111] In a peaceful, well-organized society, the passions can go to sleep until violence, warfare or moral innovation reawaken them.[112] 'What is new is invariably *evil*, wanting as it does to break through the old limits and subvert the old pieties, while only what is old is good. . . . The exhausted soil will inevitably need the ploughshare of evil again and again.'[113]

We are conditioned to admire such virtues as industriousness, submissiveness, chastity, filial piety, and a sense of justice because society benefits from them, but the 'virtuous' man invariably suffers: his capacity for self-preservation and self-assertion has been undermined.[114] Needing a word for the alternative virtues he wants to champion, Nietzsche resorts to 'noble' ('*edel*'). The noble individual does not proceed according to reason: when he is magnanimous or self-sacrificing, it is his instincts he is following, and when he is brave it is not for the sake of winning honours. His overflowing self-sufficiency empowers him to be generous.[115] Not that magnanimity is any more altruistic than vengefulness, but it is different in quality.[116]

Nietzsche introduced the subject of madness long before he came to the madman who proclaimed the death of God. Nobility may seem close to madness because it can lead to 'the divinization of values which cannot be weighed in any existing balance'.[117] Like the Romantics, Nietzsche believed that the most authentic experience was the most individual, while his prejudice against institutions that claimed canonical authority was intensified by the compulsion to justify the urge that had made him throw off the Wagnerian yoke – the urge towards independence. Inevitably, he went to the extreme, favouring all deviation from the norm, condemning all subservience to what he called 'the morality of mores'. The man who renounces (*der Entsagende*) 'aspires to a higher world. He wants to fly further and higher than the men who affirm'.[118]

In a passage reminiscent of the letter telling Elisabeth to choose between comfortable faith and the uncomfortable quest for truth, Nietzsche treats madness as the opposite of faith. 'The madman's world has its Antipodes not in truth and certainty, but in the generalities and the general restrictiveness of a faith.'[119] 'So far the greatest bulk of human effort has been invested in building up consensus over many points and establishing a *law of consensus*, regardless of whether the points are true or false.'[120] Not that Nietzsche could afford to commit himself unequivocally to supporting madness against conformism: in the same paragraph he warns us that the greatest danger hanging over humanity is an 'eruption of *madness* – an outbreak of arbitrariness in feeling, hearing and seeing; pleasure in mental indiscipline; joy in human unreason'. Like a somnambulist liable to fall if he wakes, we must go on dreaming that there is a reality behind appearances.[121] (This echoes the image of clinging to the tiger's back.) What things are called is more important than what they are.[122] Humanity would not have survived but for its ingrained habit of preferring commitment to uncertainty, error and fiction to doubt, assent to denial, passing judgement to being just.[123] The choice was between disorienting scepticism and stabilizing faith.

It is after this ambivalent approach to madness that Nietzsche makes his most famous pronouncement, using a madman as his mouthpiece. By lighting a lantern in broad daylight and looking for God in the market-place, the man makes himself an object of ridicule. But once he has accused the people and himself of murdering God, his questions rapidly cease to be absurd, while the bludgeoning rhythm and the nightmarish imagery make it harder for us to sidestep them:

Who gave us the sponge to wipe away the entire horizon? What were we doing when we unchained this earth from its sun? Where is it orbiting? Where are we orbiting? Away from all suns? Are we hurtling straight downwards? And backwards, sideways, forwards, in all directions? Is there still an up and a down? Aren't we drifting through infinite nothing? Isn't empty space breathing on us? Hasn't it grown colder? Isn't night after night closing in on us? Don't we need lanterns in the morning? Are we still deaf to the noise of the gravediggers digging God's grave? Has the smell of divine putrefaction not reached our nostrils? . . . The holiest and mightiest being in the world bled to death

under our knives. . . . No greater deed was ever done, and whoever is
born after us will, thanks to this deed, live in a higher history than there
has ever been.[124]

Finally the madman smashes his lantern, saying he has come too
early. 'This tremendous event is still on its way, meandering –
it has not yet reached the ears of men. . . . This deed is still further
from them than the furthest star; *yet they have done it themselves*.'[125] Nietzsche was borrowing from Christianity not only the
language and the rhythms of Biblical parable but the crucifixion
story, writing a daring sequel about the death of the father. He
may simultaneously have been thinking of the assassination in
Julius Caesar, which he considered to be Shakespeare's best
tragedy: he may have thought of himself as playing Brutus to
Wagner's Caesar. He may also have been indebted to Heine's *Zur
Geschichte der Philosophie und Religion in Deutschland* (*On the
History of Philosophy and Religion in Germany*), 1852: 'Our heart
is filled with fearful pity. The old Jehovah is preparing for death.
. . . Do you hear the bell tolling? Down on your knees. They are
bringing the sacraments to a dying God.' Both the idea and the
rhythm seem to have had their effect on Nietzsche.

While the madman explicitly associates himself with the killers
of God, Nietzsche associates himself with the madman. We may
not be ready for the news, but we are not allowed to dismiss it as
insane babbling. Like Dostoevskian epilepsy or Dionysiac rapture,
or like the inspiration of an Old Testament prophet, the madness
is inducing a clarity of vision denied to the majority, addicted as it
is to sane fictions. Any doubt about Nietzsche's identification
with his madman is dispelled by a passage that links madness with
isolation, rather in the way that Hegel had. In the past it would
have seemed insane if a man had opted for isolation: to be excluded
from the herd, to be 'condemned to individuality', had been one of
the harshest punishments.[126] In those days, any inclination 'to be
a self and to value oneself according to one's own size and weight'
was equated with madness.[127] Having lived his way towards the
anti-Hegelian idea that the only way of coming fully to life was to
take permanent refuge in a private world, Nietzsche had to justify
his position. The last section of Book III is obsessively full of
references to personal isolation. 'The Man who lives alone neither

speaks nor writes too loudly: he is afraid of the hollow resonance—criticism from the nymph Echo. And in solitude all voices sound different.'[128] Some of the disguised autobiography is in dialogue: ' "You are moving away faster and faster from the living. Soon they will cross you off their list." "It is the only way to share the privilege of the dead." "Which privilege?" "Not to die any more." '[129]

Originally the three books were planned as a continuation of *Morgenröte*, and he intended to complete it with two more books, but on 25 January 1882 he told Gast: 'I am not yet *mature* enough to deal with the elementary ideas I want to present in these final books.'[130] He wanted to postpone them until the winter, knowing that he must soon come to grips with the idea of eternal recurrence and with Zarathustra. 'There is one idea which really needs thousands of years to develop properly. Where will I find the strength to express it?'[131] But eleven days later the fourth book was in draft,[132] which probably means that he had not only been working very rapidly but drawing more heavily than he had expected on material in his notebooks.

Titled *Sanctus Januarius*, the book begins with a new year's resolution: 'I want to learn progressively to regard the necessary as beautiful, so shall be one of those who make things beautiful. *Amor fati*: let that be my love from now on . . . sooner or later I want to be someone who says nothing but yes.'[133] Eleven years earlier, working on the *Unzeitgemässe Betrachtungen*, he was already feeling impatient to arrive at an affirmative position, as if merely by expressing negative feelings he would get rid of them, but now the idea of *amor fati* was associated in his mind with eternal recurrence. To envisage existence as 'an eternal hourglass' he had to feel not only that he could bear repetition of all the pain he had suffered, but that he could restrain himself from doing anything he would not want to repeat: 'If that thought enforced itself on you, it would transform you and possibly crush you. Every single thing would have to take the great weight of the question "Do you want this repeated again and then again *ad infinitum*?" '[134] The moral implications of this question bring Nietzsche's idea dangerously close to Kant's categorical imperative: everything is to be done as if one's will were a legislator with universal powers.

The compensation for the repetition of pain was the conviction that his work was supremely important. What would have been intolerable – unlike the pain – was to think that his life would make no difference to other people. 'Every philosopher has probably had bad moments of asking: "What do I matter unless they accept even my bad arguments?" And then a malicious little bird flew by, twittering: "What do you matter? What do you matter?"'[135]

If he had known that he would never see any positive public reaction to his books, never collect any disciples, never find an alternative to solitude, he might have been glad to know that he would eventually find the escape-route into madness, but in 1882 it was still possible to entertain more heroic fantasies. If only the masses would once again become respectfully involved with ideas, as they had been during the religious wars,[136] they would need leaders like him. If he relished the prospect of war, it was primarily ideological war that he was envisaging. He could not help wishing for a situation that created a need for 'men who understand how to be silent, lonely, resolute, steadfast and content to be involved in intangible activity: men with a strong proclivity to seek in all things for what needs *to be conquered*'.[137] Such men would take risks happily and productively. 'For, believe me! – the secret of harvesting the greatest fruitfulness and happiness from existence is – *live dangerously*. ... Live at war with your equals and yourselves!'[138] These men, in other words, would be like him. They would wish for 'the eternal recurrence of war and peace' without needing to believe that every occurrence can be explained, without needing the comforts of faith and worship.[139] Perhaps it was only by jettisoning these reassurances that humanity could fulfil its potential: perhaps man, like a lake that has been dammed where it flowed off, 'will rise higher than ever before when he no longer *flows out* into a god'.[140] Though he does not yet use the word '*Übermenschen*' for the men who will lead the way upwards, he observes that most people are in an elevated state of mind only rarely and briefly, but that 'history may one day give birth to men more like those few who know from experience elevated feelings of longer duration'.[141]

These ideas helped to cheer Nietzsche up, but not quite sufficiently. The man who has achieved greatness through self-control, he admits, is 'impoverished and cut off from the most beautiful vagaries of the soul', and from what he might still have been capable of learning from things unlike himself.[142] And in a brief narrative about 'the wanderer', Nietzsche makes him say: 'I often look back angrily at the most beautiful things which could not detain me – *because* they could not detain me.'[143] Writing the book produced a mood in which he wanted to be detained by friends. Having rejected Rée in Sils-Maria, he now organized his itinerary around the possibility of receiving him: 'Nothing has kept me in Genoa', he wrote on 25 January, 'except the news from my family that Dr Rée's long-expected visit is imminent.'[144] Otherwise he might have paid a surprise visit, he said, to Gast. Rée arrived on 4 February, bringing a typewriter from Naumburg. He was surprised to find Nietzsche looking so healthy. 'The first day, very good things; the second, I held out only with frequent recourse to tonics; the third, exhaustion, and I fainted in the afternoon; the attack came in the night; the fourth, in bed; the fifth, I got up again, to lie down again in the afternoon; the sixth and until now, constant headache and debility. In short we must still *learn* how to be together.'[145] They went to see Sarah Bernhardt playing in *La Dame aux Camélias*. 'She reminds me, in appearance and manner, of Frau Wagner.'[146] But at the end of the first act Bernhardt collapsed. The interval lasted for an hour, and during the second act the performance came to a stop when she burst a blood vessel on stage.

The typewriter had been damaged in transit, but once it was repaired, Nietzsche used it to send seven two-line rhymes to Gast, who liked them. With minor emendations Nietzsche included all but two of them in the sixty-three that form a prelude – in lighter verse than he had written before – to *Die fröhliche Wissenschaft*.

Nietzsche and Rée went to the opera, and spent two days in Monaco. Before they parted on 13 March they had agreed to meet again in the summer and go to Africa together next year. Nietzsche was still taking pleasure in unrealistic plans. And after Rée's departure he went on to draft some of the poems which were to appear in the June issue of Schmeitzner's *Internationale Zeitschrift* under the title *Idyllen aus Messina*. Messina, where he arrived on 29 March, is in the north-east of Sicily, 150 miles from Palermo, where Wagner had been ensconced since November, as Nietzsche must have known – if only from the newspapers. He could hardly have known that for his last four days in Sicily (10–14 April) Wagner was going to be in Messina, but after he had taken so much care the previous summer to avoid the Wagners, it was odd that he should venture so close, unless he was half-hoping for a chance encounter. They were never to meet again, but the ambivalence continued into Nietzsche's relationship with the music. In 1887, when he finally experienced the *Parsifal* Prelude in a performance at Monte Carlo, he enthused about the 'psychological knowingness and precision of the music', its clarity, and the 'sublime and extraordinary adventure of the soul' in it: 'There is something similar in Dante, but nowhere else.'[147]

9 Lou Salomé

When Paul Rée left Genoa on 13 March 1882 he was on his way to Rome, where Malwida von Meysenbug had partly realized the fantasy Nietzsche had shared with her in Sorrento. At a villa overlooking the city she had formed a 'Roman Club', surrounding herself with idealistic young girls. The most outstanding was Lou Salomé, a highly intelligent, good-looking, ambitious twenty-one-year-old Russian, daughter of a general. She had been studying at Zürich University, where the poet Gottfried Kinkel was a professor, but she had become ill, running a constant temperature, and when she started coughing blood her mother had brought her to Italy. Kinkel had introduced her to Malwida, who was reminded of herself when young.

Invited to expound his moral philosophy to the girls, Rée was fascinated by Lou and the quickness of her mind: 'it is almost exasperating that she always knows what is coming next, and where it is going to lead'.[1] Lou was not living at Malwida's villa in the Via della Polveriera, but at a boarding house with her mother, who was half Danish, half German. At midnight Rée would see Lou home – but not straight home. They would walk arm-in-arm through the streets for a couple of hours, provoking more disapproval from the emancipated Malwida than from Lou's mother.[2] According to Lou, whose testimony is no more reliable than Elisabeth's, Rée professed himself to be 'disgusted' by sex but in love with her. After her experiences with a pulpit orator attached to the Dutch legation in St Petersburg, she was going through a phase of revulsion against sex, but she persuaded Rée into the idea of sexless cohabitation with her. They would set up a salon *à deux*. But the magnetism that pulled great men to her – she was to become Rilke's mistress and, later, a close friend of Freud – was already active. She had heard about Nietzsche from Malwida before Rée described him to her, and the salon fantasy became triangular. Lou, Rée and Nietzsche could live Platonically together.

Rée's descriptions of Lou made Nietzsche eager to meet her: she sounded like a girl who had dedicated herself since childhood to the quest for knowledge. 'People like this are so exceedingly rare that I would circle the earth to meet one.'[3] When he went to Sicily, Lou felt snubbed. 'She wanted to return via Genoa and was very angry you were so far away. She is forceful and incredibly clever, but with the most girlish, even childlike qualities.'[4] It was not the prospect of meeting her but the sirocco that drove him back northwards.[5] He went to Naples first, and on his second day in Rome the long-delayed encounter took place, as Rée proposed, in St Peter's.[6] According to Lou, Nietzsche's first words were 'What stars have sent us orbiting towards each other?'[7] She was impressed by his 'noiseless way of talking', his 'neat style of dressing', and his 'cautious, wistful gait, shoulders slightly rounded'.[8] His hands were 'incomparably beautiful and nobly moulded'; his ears were 'unusually small and delicately shaped', while she noticed his 'fine, highly expressive mouth lines, almost entirely hidden by the ample moustache combed over them. . . . His failing eyesight gave his face a special magic because they reflected not outward impressions but only what was going on inside. They looked . . . inwards as if into the distance.'[9] If the moustache and the near-blindness curtained him off from other people, the effect was compounded by his illness, which kept him in bed most of the time he was in Rome. He was planning to visit the Italian lakes with Rée, and the wilful Lou persuaded her mother to synchronize their return to the north with this journey, but before leaving Rome he came out with what she took to be a proposal of marriage: 'I would feel obliged, in order to protect you from gossip, to offer you my hand.'[10]

The three of them met again at Orta on 5 May. The next day Lou and Nietzsche together climbed the Sacro Monte, while Rée stayed with her mother. Nietzsche spoke to her about eternal recurrence and Zarathustra, who had been conceived, he told her, partly as a substitute for the son he would never have. (A few days later he told the Overbecks about the possibility of 'creating a filial figure artistically'.)[11] The original impulse, according to Ida Overbeck, was to revalue Zoroaster, 'whom he regarded as a representative of the values of good and evil in the oldest stories of humanity'.[12] Zoroaster had raised the old Aryan folk-religion to a higher level with his doctrine of eternal punishment or eternal death according to the balance between a man's good and evil deeds on earth. The fantasy of Zoroaster as a son may have been inflamed by a new fantasy of Lou as daughter, pupil, and spiritual bride. There was a strong religious eroticism in the incipient relationship between them. She wrote that his nature was essentially religious;[13] he spoke to the Overbecks about the extent to which her religious experiences had conditioned her.[14] When they came down from the mountain, Rée was angry that they had been together for so long, and Lou, writing about the incident later, pretended not to remember whether she had kissed Nietzsche, though he later thanked her 'for the most enchanting dream of my life'.[15] He was now eager that they should live in close proximity, if not together. On 7 May he left to visit the Overbecks, who were delighted at how much healthier he seemed.[16] He had succumbed to 'the hope of having found his *alter ego* in Fräulein Salomé, of working towards his goal with her and through her help'.[17] 'He felt reassured that Rée was to be the third member, and he was expecting a great deal from Rée's helpful, unselfish disposition.'[18] Desperation was making Nietzsche over-optimistic: ailing and almost blind, he had been alone, with no one to look after him, since the *ménage* with his sister had broken up in 1878.

When the 'Trinity' (as Lou called it) met again in Lucerne on 13 May 1882, she wanted to reject Nietzsche's proposal of marriage, while he wanted to explain that he had not made one. But the embarrassment did not last long enough to prevent the three of them from posing for a photograph: the two writers pretended to be hauling a cart with her perching on it, a whip in her hand. The next day they made a pilgrimage to Tribschen. According to Lou, Nietzsche wept. Afterwards he reacted almost ecstatically to her poem 'An den Schmerz' ('To Pain'), and when Gast mistook it for a poem by him[19] he was not offended.

They decided to spend the winter studying natural science in a university town, probably Vienna, and to take a holiday together in the summer. In his euphoria at the new arrangement, Nietzsche felt safe to go home. He arrived in Naumburg on 24 May, to stay till the end of June. Gast had not been well enough to make a fair copy of *Die fröhliche Wissenschaft*, which was now prepared with the aid of Elisabeth and a bankrupt old businessman. On 19 June Nietzsche wrote to ask whether Gast would be able to help with the final corrections, and by the 24th the book was being printed.[20] The first pages were in proof by early July.

In the absence of her two admirers, Lou discovered her power over them. Rée bombarded her with letters, trying to strengthen his hold over her. He claimed to be acting on her mother's behalf in offering her 'membership in our family. It will then be easier for Nietzsche to understand if you are not so much with him as with me.'[21] And on 28 May, just before she was due to leave Zürich for Berlin, Nietzsche wrote that he would come while she was there, 'and withdraw immediately into one of the lovely deep woods . . . so that we can meet, *if* we, if you, like.'[22] Perhaps he would find a house in the forest where she could come to stay for a few days. 'For honestly I should very much like to be quite alone with you for once. Such solitary creatures as I must first accustom themselves very slowly even to the people who are dearest to them.'[23]

On the way back from Zürich, Lou and her mother stopped at Basel to visit the Overbecks – Nietzsche had suggested she should find out from them what kind of man he was – who were kind. Lou was frustrated only in her desire for an introduction to Jacob Burckhardt. The Overbecks were not hostile to the trinity's intention of living together, but Malwida was, and Nietzsche was eager that neither his family nor anyone else should learn of it.[24]

Lou did not want to meet Nietzsche in Berlin; the reason she gave was that it would jeopardize their plans for the winter.[25] Impulsively, on 15 June, he wrote to tell her that he would be in Berlin at eleven-forty the following morning at Anhalter Bahnhof, hoping to see her. He would stay at Grünewald, and could be reached *poste restante* at Charlottenburg. 'Everything went wrong,' he wrote on the 18th. 'I travelled back the following day, slightly more knowing about the Grünewald and myself, laughing rather derisively, and *quite* exhausted.'[26] To Rée he wrote: 'Generally I am in no state to do anything alone. In Berlin I was like a lost *groschen* which I had lost myself, and thanks to my eyes I could not see it was already lying at my feet, so all the passers-by laughed.' He needed all the *amor fati* he could muster, while

hoping at least to be her teacher, her 'guide to scholarly produc-
tiveness . . . I believe the blind are more reliable than the half-
blind. So far as Vienna is concerned it is now my wish to be
deposited like a suitcase in a small room of *the* house you wish to
live in. Or next door, as your faithful friend and neighbour.'[27]

On 25 June he travelled to the Thuringian village of Tautenburg,
near Jena, with Elisabeth, who installed him in a farmhouse with
a young couple, the Hahnemanns. At Malwida's suggestion, Lou
was going to the Bayreuth festival in August, and Nietzsche
suggested: 'My sister would escort you here from Bayreuth and
stay with you in the same house – possibly the parson's.'[28]
Knowing that Elisabeth could introduce her to the Wagners and
probably to plenty of distinguished festival-goers, Lou accepted
with alacrity, but she had no interest in giving Nietzsche what he
needed from her – help in becoming less hermit-like.

Staying with Rée and his mother in the house that now
belonged to his elder brother, Georg, at Stibbe, near Tütz in East
Prussia, Lou submitted to the strategy of making her into a member of the family, a sister. They spoke to each other in baby-talk.
She was '*Schneckli*' (little snail), Rée was her shell ('*Hüsung*').
They kept a log-book of their time together in the 'Stibbe nest',[29]
where he helped to implant the idea that Nietzsche merely wanted
to exploit her sexually and secretarially. 'Never', Nietzsche
protested in his first letter from Tautenburg, 'did I think you
would "read aloud and write" for me, but I very much wanted to
be your teacher. . . . I am carrying around with me something that
is absolutely not to be found in my books, and I am seeking the
finest, most fertile soil for it.'[30]

On 31 July 1882 she left the nest for the Bayreuth festival.
Travelling with Elisabeth from Leipzig, Lou was so charming that
before they arrived they were talking to each other in the second
person singular. Lou was keeping a diary for Rée and posting it to
him in instalments, while, at her suggestion, he kept one for her.
Through Elisabeth she met Cosima, and, briefly, Wagner, but she
had to stand all through the first performance of *Parsifal* on 26
July. It would have been impossible to keep Elisabeth from
becoming suspicious of her and hostile to the idea of her setting
up house with Nietzsche and Rée. But on 1 August, when Elisabeth
returned to Naumburg, Lou was still expecting her to report

favourably: 'Your sister, who is now almost mine too, will tell you everything – her presence was a great help to me and I am heartily grateful to her for it.'[31] She was underestimating both Elisabeth's jealousy and Nietzsche's fear of gossip. He was outraged to learn she had been boasting that he and Rée wanted to study with her, and showing people the photograph of them pulling her along on the cart. His letter cancelling the invitation to Tautenburg was followed by his letter cancelling the plans for holidaying and studying together, but she reacted so touchingly that Nietzsche immediately relented: 'Do come. I am suffering too much from having made you suffer. Together we shall endure it better.'[32]

Elisabeth was sent to meet her in Jena at the house of Professor Heinrich Gelzer of Basel University. It was probably Elisabeth who provoked the hostilities while the two women were alone together in a bedroom, but Lou soon launched into a flood of loud invective: Nietzsche was a madman who wanted to shame her by exploiting her body and her mind. Why should she sacrifice herself? She'd already been in situations like that with men.[33] Extremely embarrassed both by Lou's language and by the impression they must be making, Elisabeth could only apologize to Frau Gelzer. On the way to Tautenburg Lou was calmer, but there was another outburst while Nietzsche went out to find accommodation for them. They spent the night at the house of a clergyman called Stolten. In the morning Elisabeth's expurgated account of what Lou had said made Nietzsche extremely angry. His natural *pudeur* was affronted, and if the Gelzers started a scandal in Basel his pension would be jeopardized. He asked Lou to leave the next day but she did not want to, and Nietzsche was only too vulnerable to her charm. At the end of her fourth or fifth day in Tautenburg he kept coming back to the clergyman's house, 'and in the evening took my hand and kissed it twice and began to say something which would not come out'.[34] When she retired to bed for several days, genuinely or strategically ill, he wrote letters to her, and spoke to her through the door of the room. 'I believe the only difference between us is in age,' he said. 'We have lived alike and thought alike.' When she got up on 13 August she and Nietzsche spent the whole day together. Nor did he seem perturbed by the photograph of Rée on her desk.[35] On the 14th they again spent the day 'in the quiet dark pine forest alone with the sunlight and squirrels . . . we can almost communicate with half-words . . . our conversation really consists in what is not quite spoken but emerges on its own from our meeting each other half-way'.[36]

Their talks, he said, were 'most profitable'.[37] He rated her as 'the most intelligent of all women'.[38] Religion, he said later, was 'really our only topic'.[39] 'One day,' Lou wrote to Rée, 'he will reveal himself to be the prophet of a new religion, a religion that will recruit initiates from among heroes.'[40] They were spending ten hours a day in conversation, she reported. 'And we are led involuntarily by our conversation to the abyss, to those giddying spots where you have the impression of having climbed in solitude for a vantage-point to view the depths. We have always chosen the paths the chamois take, and anyone who overheard us would have thought he was listening to a conversation between two demons.'[41] But it is hard to gauge whether the conversations influenced *Also sprach Zarathustra*. 'In mentality and taste,' he wrote, 'there is a deep affinity between us, together with so many dissonances that each of us is most instructive to the other. . . . I wonder whether such philosophical openness as there is between us has ever existed before.'[42] He was saying that it was thanks to Lou he was having new ideas, or so Elisabeth told Frau Gelzer,[43] but he may have been exaggerating to make Lou sound indispensable. He also tried to make himself indispensable to her, helping her with her writing while she, eager to establish herself as a writer, shelved her book on woman to undertake the first full-scale book about Nietzsche. Accordingly, she began taking notes on him: 'From merely romanticizing his every sign of fondness for her', comments Rudolf Binion, 'she had gone on to divinize Nietzsche in her own image.'[44] But privately she was aware that physical pain had played a more decisive role in his life than in hers. 'With Nietzsche pain was always the origin of each new phase of development. . . . The passivity of his suffering is also peculiarly expressed in that he must suffer so much physically, while my earlier experience made pain synonymous with conflict. In this endowment of Nietzsche's is the reason he has embraced and abandoned so many different objectives. His abandon appears to him as a kind of self-annihilation, but it is only a self-redemption, and it is intended as such.'[45]

Elisabeth was daily growing more hostile to Lou. 'I cannot deny that she really personifies my brother's philosophy: that rabid egotism which tramples on anything in its way, and that complete indifference to morality.'[46] She had ruined Fritz. Before she left on 26 August, they had agreed to study in Paris. He went back to Naumburg the same day, leaving Elisabeth in Tautenburg: 'I told him I . . . did not want mama to see my grief or my tear-reddened eyes. He should tell her everything first.'[47] In Naumburg he felt moved to start writing music again. He set the poem Lou had given him just before leaving, 'Lebensgebet' ('Life Prayer').[48] But with Elisabeth inciting their mother against him by letter and refusing to come home while he was there, it was impossible for him to stay long, and when his mother called him 'a disgrace to his father's grave',[49] he left the next morning for Leipzig.

Rée conceded that Lou had grown 'a few inches taller in Tautenburg',[50] but to Nietzsche it seemed that his attempt 'to return "to people" was resulting in my *losing* the few I still in any sense possessed'.[51] Rée offered to withdraw completely: 'Let us go our separate ways to death.'[52] But Lou and Nietzsche held the trinity together. He wrote to Rée, conciliatingly, and when Rée wrote to tell Lou that she was the greatest loss he could ever suffer, and that, for this reason, he, as a pessimist, did not expect her to stay with him long, she annotated the letter triumphantly: 'Now you are mine.'[53] Cynically aware that Rée's cynicism, with the licence it gave him to condemn everyone else, was a means not merely of flagellating his own ego but also of gratifying it, she wrote to Nietzsche suggesting 'the reduction of philosophical systems to personal records of their authors'.[54] He replied that this was 'truly the notion of a sister-soul. This is how I taught the history of ancient philosophy at Basel. I would tell my students: "This system is dead, but the personality behind it is irrefutable and immortal. Plato, for instance." '[55]

She spent September at Stibbe with Rée but fixed her mind on Nietzsche, reading his *Menschliches*, *Allzumenschliches*, drafting a characterization of him and composing aphorisms in his manner. She even adopted his way of writing a capital N.[56] 'Latest news,' he wrote to Gast from Leipzig in mid-September, 'on 2 October Lou comes here; a few weeks later we go away – to Paris, and we stay there, perhaps for years. *My* proposal!'[57] Meanwhile he was using what influence and contacts he had in Leipzig to promote Gast's opera, hoping to arrange for a performance. 'Here is a new Mozart ... beauty, warmth, serenity, amplitude, overflowing inventiveness and masterful lightness of touch in counterpoint – a unique combination of qualities. Already I want to hear no other music.'[58]

Die fröhliche Wissenschaft had been published on 26 August, and Nietzsche sent a copy to Rohde, but it merely set the seal on their estrangement. Burckhardt's reaction was characteristically perceptive: 'Fundamentally, perhaps, you are always teaching history and in this book you have opened up many astonishing historical perspectives.' He would have liked to see Nietzschean illumination applied consistently to world history. Proudly Nietzsche sent Lou a copy of the letter.

Lou arrived in Leipzig with Rée on 1 October, to stay for five weeks (not three, as she recorded). Nietzsche took them to a séance; they went to the theatre; they met friends including Romundt and Gast, who called Lou a genius. Nietzsche corrected and revised her aphorisms, even contributing to them. The most trenchant were the most personal: 'Women do not die of love but waste away without it'; 'The worst torture is self-hatred'; and 'Nietsche's flaw: oversubtlety'. She had summed up the three of them but misspelt Nietzsche's name.

'I have perhaps never endured such melancholy as in Leipzig this autumn,' he wrote, 'though *surrounded* by reasons for being cheerful.'[59] When, on his way to meet Lou and Rée, he visited Gast, he seemed off-balance.[60] His fear of gossip in Basel as a result of her indiscretions in Bayreuth and Jena exacerbated the triangular tensions of the relationship. It must have become increasingly difficult for the two men to sublimate or disguise their rivalry, while Lou's feelings towards Nietzsche were changing. Her diary is ambiguous in its comparison of mysticism 'which is transformed into crude religious sensuality' with ideal love, which becomes sensual again 'because of the great pressure of emotion. Unattractive, the way the human element revenges itself – I dislike feelings which short-circuit, for this is the moment of *false pathos*, when truth and emotional integrity are lost. Is it this that is alienating me from Nietzsche?'[61] Talking to Rée, she could be very coarse; writing about Nietzsche she was compulsively delicate. Was it her feelings or his that were becoming sensual? The impending arrival of Rée's mother put extra pressure on both Lou and Rée, who kept the old lady at bay by arranging to spend some time with her in Berlin. Before leaving with him, Lou told Nietzsche she had something further to say to him. 'I was full of hope.'[62] But the something remained unsaid, and on 5 November they left. Nietzsche did not immediately break off the relationship. At her request, he had written to St Petersburg to obviate any family pressure that might be put on her to return, and he started inquiring for a large furnished flat in Paris. On 8 November he wrote to tell her what he had done. The only hint of rebuke in his letter was in the question 'You had something further to tell me?'[63] Her reply, which is not extant, was disappointing enough to make him leave Leipzig. He spent three days in Basel, where he told Frau Overbeck that 'it was probably all over between them. He was still expecting letters and pinning hopes on them, asked whether I had received none for him, even seemed afraid I might be keeping something back. Though deeply upset, he would neither be comforted nor take comfort from talking about it.'[64] Nevertheless, he was so full of praise for Rée that Ida Overbeck accused him of describing Daniel Deronda.[65] After a few days in Genoa, he went on to Rapallo, twenty miles away. 'I hope your life is more successful than mine,' he wrote to Gast. 'Even here I am not yet over the nightmare this year has brought. ... Cold. Sick. I am suffering.'[66]

Rée wrote to admonish him for leaving, and before the end of the month he brought himself to reply: 'I belong to you both with my deepest feelings – as I believe my absence indicates better than my presence. Proximity makes one so demanding.'[67] He decided to enclose the letter in one to Lou: 'I feel all the stirrings of the higher soul in you – and love nothing else about you. I gladly renounce all intimacy and closeness if only I can feel certain that where we feel *united* is where ordinary souls cannot reach.'[68] He needed to feel that he had made a heroic sacrifice. 'As soon as we come to love something totally, the tyrant in us (which we are only too glad to call "our higher self") says "Sacrifice just *that* to me." And we do, but it is torture, like being roasted over a slow fire. It is almost a straightforward problem of *cruelty* ... and I have too much of this "tragic" complexion not to execrate it often.'[69]

There was no chance of a quick recovery. 'Fearful pity, fearful disillusion, fearful sense of wounded dignity – how can I bear it any longer?. . . Each morning I despair of surviving the day. . . . This evening I'll take enough opium to send me insane.'[70] He told Lou and Rée that if he one day took his own life it would 'not altogether be something to mourn'.[71] He reviled Lou violently in drafts of letters – probably less violently in the letters he sent – and at the end of November he broke off his correspondence with Elisabeth: 'Souls like yours, my dear sister, I do not like, especially when they are morally bloated.'[72] To Overbeck he later wrote: '*I do not like my mother, and it is painful for me to hear my sister's voice. I always became ill when I was with them. We have hardly ever quarrelled, even last summer. I know how to get on with them, but it does not suit me.*'[73]

In one draft letter he fantasized about how differently he would have moulded Lou if he had been her creator: he could no longer think of her as either mother or sister to his fantasy son Zarathustra. On Christmas Eve he returned his mother's letter, unopened, and on Christmas Day he wrote: 'This last *mouthful of life* was the toughest I have ever had to chew, and it is still possible I shall choke on it. . . . I am straining every fibre of my self-control, but I have lived alone too long, fed too long on my own fat, so now I am being broken as no one else could be on the wheel of my own passions. . . . The strongest doses of my sleeping draught are no more help to me than my six or eight hours of walking every day.'[74] He was using fifty grammes of chloral-hydrate and for fourteen months – until April 1884 – he went on dosing himself with it every night.[75] 'Unless I can learn the alchemist's trick of turning this filth into gold,' he told Overbeck, 'I am lost. Several times I have thought of renting a room in Basel, visiting you occasionally and attending lectures. Several times, too, I have considered the opposite: to continue in my solitude and renunciation until I reach the point of no return and —.'[76] Without some such alchemy he would have been unable to go on answering yes to the question of wanting to relive the whole of his experience.

shortest route is from peak to peak, but for that one needs long legs . . . I am looking down because I am elevated. . . . He who climbs the greatest mountains can laugh at all tragedies and all tragic seriousness.'[5] It is a crucial test for the totality of his previous thinking and writing. Is its summit high enough for him to look down on everything that has been depressing him? And even if it is, can he stay on top without overbalancing into solipsistic megalomania? Can he keep his sanity while identifying with his alter ego, who used to believe that a mad god created the world to distract himself from his troubles?

> Drunken delight it is for the sufferer to look away from his sorrows and lose himself. Drunken delight and self-oblivion the world once seemed to me.
> This world, eternally unperfected, always a contradictory and imperfect image – a drunken delight to its imperfect creator – this seemed the world.
> Oh my brother, this god I created was human madness, like all gods.[6]

Nietzsche is developing his idea that existence can be validated only as an aesthetic phenomenon, and he is using his analogical device: because he can cheer himself up by writing creatively, God, if he had existed, would have distractedly created the world to distract himself from depression.

Zarathustra is Nietzsche's first sustained attempt at fiction. In his lectures on educational institutions he had intermittently resorted to narrative and to dialogues in the Platonic manner. In both *Morgenröte* and *Die fröhliche Wissenschaft* he had sometimes made statements through a persona. Now he needed a mask more than ever before, but, like an actor, found that with his features hidden he could reveal more of himself. As he said on completing the book, it 'contains the most sharply focused image of me as I am *after* I have fully unburdened myself.'[7] But it is not a novel. In form and style it probably derives from Carl Spitteler's *Prometheus und Epimetheus* (1880–1), which is similar in its biblically inspired syntax and in its strongly rhythmic prose set out in short paragraphs. It also uses a mountain landscape as background for a heroic story in which Prometheus represents the fulfilment of human potential, while Epimetheus personifies the backsliding into a mediocrity representing that of the contemporary bour-

Nietzsche 'celebrated the New Year' with 'one of the most violently painful attacks of my illness'.[1] But it was a sign of progress that he could describe Lou as 'almost a caricature of the ideal I revere'.[2] His mind was his only alchemical retort, and in ten days, working from sketches made in August, he wrote the first book of *Also sprach Zarathustra* (*Thus Spoke Zarathustra*), partly as therapy for his depression. ('It is not anger but laughter that is lethal,' says Zarathustra. 'Let us kill this gravity.'[3] Having been insulted, he is entitled to revenge. 'Take care not to insult the hermit! But if you do so, then kill him too!' There is no question of repressing the urge for vengeance, but the main drive is towards gaiety, as in *Die fröhliche Wissenschaft*, which ends, as *Also sprach Zarathustra* begins, with the paragraphs about Zarathustra's decision to come down from the mountains so as to be among men. When the saint tells Zarathustra, 'You carried your ashes into the mountain, now you carry your fire into the valley,'[4] Nietzsche is introducing only an alternative image for the conversion of filth into gold. Having taken something negative, he must transform it into something so positive that it can inflame other people. He has never been in greater need of the survival tactic used previously against physical pain. Can an emotional wound be staunched with nothing but a wad-like determination to send the blood coursing in the opposite direction? Can Nietzsche look down into the abyss and make it ring with defiant laughter? If he had overcome his pessimism by sheer effort of will, to prove that illness was not going to master him, he must now prove that an imaginary son can be a match for the real girl who had defected. But the atmosphere of the new book is more rarefied than its predecessors', the tendency more anti-social, as if Lou and Rée are being equated with life in the big city, while high altitude represents withdrawal, meditation, peace. The writing is almost like an act of levitation: 'In the mountains the geoisie. Nietzsche had already had frequent recourse to parable, as in the story about the madman, but without Spitteler's example he might never have arrived at the notion of using biblical syntax and biblical cadences, and without these, his central figure would perhaps have been conceived differently. As it is, Zarathustra emerges as an anti-Jesus, a saviour who preaches self-transcendence and prophesies a future in which humanity will have redeemed itself without divine help. At its worst the style is hollowly portentous; at its best it is impressive in both a negative and a positive way, savaging the New Testament in a parody that exposes its mannerisms, though the rhetoric sometimes helps to enlist sympathy for the prophet who is using parable and quasi-biblical paradox to expound his reversal of Judaeo-Christian values. Zarathustra advises the adder to take its poison back because it is not rich enough to give it away. So the reptile falls around his neck to lick the wound.

But if you have an enemy, do not repay evil with good: for that is shaming. Rather show that he did something good to you.

And rather feel anger than shame. And if you are cursed, it is displeasing to me if you want to bless. It is better to join in the cursing a little.

And if you are greatly wronged, commit five small wrongs quickly. It is not pleasant to see all the wrong on one side. . . .

A little revenge is more human than no revenge. And unless a penalty is also a privilege for the transgressor, I do not like your punishment.

It is nobler to declare oneself wrong than right, especially when one is right, only one must be rich enough for that. I do not like your cold justice. The eye of the judge glints with the cold steel of the executioner.[8]

This hits a psychologically shrewd balance between Mosaic vengeance and Christian forgiveness.

The biblical style also helps Nietzsche towards a confrontation with the residue from his childhood faith: he can adapt some elements, while inverting others. Instead of blessing the poor in spirit, the meek, the merciful, the pure in heart or the peacelovers, Zarathustra favours the great despisers, those who live for knowledge, those who 'do not want to have too many virtues', those who do not hold back one drop of spirit for themselves.[9] Impertinently, Nietzsche was listing his own qualities, as he saw them, but the experience with Lou had jeopardized his ability to think well of himself, and *Also sprach Zarathustra* is not merely the record of an attempt to build himself up again, but the tool for making the attempt. All Nietzsche's skill in the art of self-conquest is directed into a therapeutic characterization of a prophet who feels disgusted at what arouses happiness and preaches that happiness should arouse disgust. 'What is the greatest experience? It is the hour of great contempt . . . when you say "What does my happiness matter? It is poverty and filth and pitiful contentment." '[10] 'I love those who do not know how to live except by going under, for they are the ones who go over. I love the great despisers, for they are the great reverers, arrows of longing for the other shore. . . . I love him who makes his virtue into his bent and his fate: then his virtue makes him want both to live on and to live no more.'[11]

But the condemnation of happiness and physical contentment did not make Nietzsche hostile towards the body. All faith in the beyond, he insists, has been the outcome of suffering and incapacity: 'Believe me, my brothers! The body it was that despaired of the body, that touched the furthest walls with the fingers of a deluded spirit.'[12] But Zarathustra condemns those who despise the body. 'The mature and the enlightened say "I am wholly body and nothing else; soul is only a word for something about the body." . . . Behind your thoughts and feelings, my brother, stands a mighty ruler, an unknown sage called Self. He inhabits your body, he is your body.'[13] This is a counterblast to the assumption basic in Western philosophy that the body is irrelevant, that existence centres on mental activity. The self-transcendence that Nietzsche advocates is by no means anti-physical. Zarathustra teaches that man must be overcome, that man is a bridge between the beast and the superior man (*Übermensch*): 'I love all those who are as heavy drops, falling singly out of a dark cloud. . . . Behold, I am a prophet of the lightning and a heavy drop from the cloud: but this lightning is called superior man (*Übermensch*).'[14]

Still taking a heroic view of himself, Nietzsche made a heroic effort to metamorphose his private humiliation into a literary triumph. There could be no question of putting Lou out of his mind, so he used her, but unrecognizably. He had often compared her with an eagle. 'Sharp-witted as an eagle', he wrote to Gast in one letter, and in another, disillusioned, 'I thought I had seen an eagle.'[15] The two animals which befriend Zarathustra are an eagle and a snake, which is coiled round its neck, suggesting both strangulation and temptation in the Garden of Eden. Zarathustra's observations about women are generalizations provoked by a particular experience. 'Is it not better to fall into the hands of a murderer than into the fantasies of a woman on heat?'[16] 'How charmingly the bitch sensuality knows how to beg for a chunk of spirit when refused a chunk of flesh.'[17] 'Everything about women has one solution: pregnancy. Men are for women the means, the end is always the child.'[18] 'A real man wants danger and sport, so he wants the most dangerous plaything there is – woman.'[19] 'You are going to see women? Do not forget your whip.'[20] In *Morgenröte* and *Die fröhliche Wissenschaft* Nietzsche had written cynically about women, but never so bitterly as this.

His misanthropy is almost equally inflamed. Social life is vilified with the imagery of flies in the market-place: 'Escape, my friend, into your solitude! Here you are dazed by the noise of the big men and stung all over by the stings of the small men. . . . Escape, my friend, into your solitude, where the air is fresh and strong. It is not for you to chase flies.'[21] Nietzsche had already, involuntarily, escaped – but by surrounding himself with imaginary characters, Zarathustra and his disciples, he felt less isolated, and he knew it was isolation that had made him so vulnerable: 'The lonely man offers his hand too readily to anyone he meets. Some people should be offered not a hand but a paw, preferably with claws.'[22]

The Christian ideal of neighbourly love is subverted. 'Your love for your neighbour is only love for yourself. You escape from yourself to your neighbour.'[23] Less has been accomplished by neighbourly generosity than by bravery and warfare. 'You say that a good cause justifies even war? . . . I say unto you: it is a good war that justifies any cause.'[24] But, as if sensing the danger that this dictum could be exploited as propaganda by militaristic politicians, Nietzsche launches straight into a denunciation of 'the new idol': 'State is the name of the coldest of cold monsters. Coldly it tells lies . . . in all the tongues of good and evil; all it says is lies, all it has is stolen. Everything about it is false. It bites with stolen teeth, and it bites readily.'[25] In the state, good and evil men all lose themselves: 'The slow suicide of all is called "life".'[26]

For ten days, while writing, Nietzsche was euphoric. 'I feel as if lightning had struck – for a short time I was fully in my element and in my light.'[27] But the feeling could not last. 'I am again surrounded by darkness. . . . I think I shall perforce disintegrate unless something happens . . . with my physical way of thinking I now see myself as victim of a European disturbance, terrestrial and climatic.'[28] As far as he could contrive it, this idea of thinking physically and chaotically is absorbed into the tissue of the narrative. 'Of all there is to read I love only what has been written in blood. Write with blood and you will find that blood is spirit. . . . I have learned to walk: so I let myself run. I have learned to fly: so I do not let myself be pushed.'[29] 'I say unto you: to give birth to a dancing star one must have chaos within oneself.'[30] The hope was to escape the chaos by flying; the fear was that the chaos would overtake him. One of the best written and most resonant sequences in the book is about a jester who kills a tightrope walker performing on a rope stretched between two towers above a market-place. The trapeze artist manages to ignore the taunts and insults of the jester, who has followed him out on the rope, but when the jester jumps over him, he panics, tosses away his pole, and falls, 'like a whirlpool of arms and legs. The market and the people were like the sea when the storm strikes: all fled asunder and among each other, and most of all where the body must fall.'[31] Only Zarathustra stays where he is, and it is next to him that the body hits the ground, maimed and disfigured, but not yet lifeless. He promises to bury the man with his own hands. The sequence can be interpreted in different ways – one is suggested much later when Zarathustra says that while there are many methods of conquering oneself, only a jester thinks that man can be skipped over[32] – but the vividness and urgency probably derive from an equation of tightrope-walking with the task Nietzsche had set himself. The fear is that madness will overtake him; the hope is that Zarathustra, his own creation, will come to his aid.

Finishing the book, Nietzsche felt that he would never write again, that it would be his 'last will and testament'.[33] He made the fair copy himself, and on 14 February it was ready to be sent off to Schmeitzner. In the afternoon, when he was in Genoa, he read in a newspaper that Richard Wagner had died the day before. His first reaction was physical illness: he was in bed for several days. His second reaction was relief – unmistakably filial. 'It was hard, having for six years to be against the man one has most revered. . . . Finally it was the senescent Wagner that I had to resist; as for the real Wagner, I shall to some extent become his *heir*.'[34] To Cosima he wrote: 'The only way I know of pouring out my feelings is by directing them entirely and exclusively to you. I regard you today, even from far away, as I have always regarded you – as the woman my heart most honours.'

The winter on the Riviera was abnormally severe, and Nietzsche failed to find a stove for his room. Feeling cold, unwell, and ill at ease in Rapallo, he went back to Genoa at the beginning of the last week in February, but almost immediately fell ill: 'Fever, chill, sweating at night, acute headaches, constant chronic exhaustion, no appetite, dull palate.'[35] By the middle of March he was no better: 'The headache is at work every day from 11.30 till 7 in the evening. I spend nearly all the time in bed, apart from a couple of hours in the morning.'[36] There was still snow on the ground in Genoa, and the doctor was advising him to leave for the south of Spain. He was thinking of 'disappearing from the world for a decade',[37] and of going to Barcelona in the autumn, which would not conflict with this plan.[38] In Genoa there were such distractions as performances of *Carmen*, and conversations with acquaintances about music or 'Physica and Medica'.[39] He was also writing poems or 'Dionysus Songs in which I arrogate freedom. . . . This is the latest form of my madness.'[40] But he was at a nadir of despondency: 'I no longer see *why* I should go on living for another six months – everything is tedious, hurtful, *dégoûtant*. . . . It is now too late to make things good. I shall never again do anything good.'[41] He called *Zarathustra* his 'latest folly': 'Only lethargy has stopped me from sending a telegram to cancel the whole printing.'[42] He was still blaming the weather for his sufferings: in Barcelona it would be better, but commitment to the idea of eternal recurrence could not stop him from saying he would kill himself rather than live through another winter like the last one.[43]

By the beginning of April 1883 he was less depressed, but not expecting to live much longer.[44] His mainstay was still friendship in which the only contact was correspondence. 'Perhaps I have had no greater pleasure in my life than your letter,' he wrote after Gast's encomiastic reaction to *Zarathustra*.[45] Overbeck, meanwhile, was trying, by letter, to coax him into settling in Basel again and teaching German at the Pädagogium. Though Burckhardt's presence there was an attraction, 'my objections are considerations of weather and wind etc.'[46]

When Elisabeth wrote a conciliatory letter from Rome, he made a quick decision to join her there, leaving Rapallo at the end of the month. Soon he was feeling so much better that some of his worst experiences seemed like hallucinations.[47] 'Life is *very eventful*, and I am spending a good deal of time in lively company; as soon as I am alone I feel more shattered than ever in my life.'[48] They visited museums and explored the countryside around Rome, but he was too unsettled to collect the trunk containing his books from the railway station,[49] though Elisabeth wanted him to spend the rest of the summer with her. The intention of 'disappearing for a few years', which he had shelved, is mentioned again in a letter written on 28 May: 'I want to make things *as hard* for myself as they have ever been for anybody: only under this pressure do I have a *clear* enough *conscience* to possess something few men have or have ever had – *wings*, so to speak.'[50] He stayed on in Rome until about 12 June. He thought of settling in Aquila, 'the very antithesis of Rome',[51] but, dissuaded by the sirocco, he left on the 14th for the Engadin, where it was cold and wet. After a few days of headaches in a hotel, he rented an unheated room in Sils-Maria for three months, waiting impatiently for it to become warmer[52] and preparing to write the second book of *Zarathustra*. On 21 June he addressed a letter jointly to his mother and sister – the first for eight months – asking them to send sausages.

In *Morgenröte* he had ridiculed the notion of a god who punishes men for not believing in him, and in the first book of *Zarathustra* he had scoffed at the pettiness of legal justice. In the second book he contradicted all conventional ideas of retributive justice. '*That man will be delivered from vengeance:* that is the bridge to my highest hope, and a rainbow after prolonged storminess.'[53] Virtue should not need recompense as an incentive or retribution as a deterrent. 'And verily I do not even teach that virtue is its own reward. . . . You are *too pure* to be sullied with the words revenge, punishment, reward, retribution. You love your virtue, as a mother does her child, and whoever heard of a mother wanting to be paid for her love? Your virtue is your self, not something alien.'[54]

The most direct inversion of New Testament material occurs in Zarathustra's revulsion at the idea of performing miracles to cure the deformed, the blind and the lame. 'If one takes the hump from the hunchback, one takes away his spirit – thus teach the people. And if one gives sight to the blind, he sees so much evil on earth that he curses the healer. But he that makes the lame man run does the greatest harm, for no sooner can he run than his vices run away with him.'[55] To Zarathustra, no one alive seems undamaged. 'I find man in ruins and scattered, as after a battle or a slaughter. And when my eyes fly from the present to the past, they see the same – fragments and limbs and gruesome accidents, but no men. . . . I walk among men as among fragments of the future, the future of my vision.'[56] This is as close as Nietzsche can come to abolishing the present, reducing it in fantasy to a mere bridge towards a better future that can be created through exertion of the will. Once the will has been liberated from the idea of retributive justice, it will be capable of 'something higher than reconciliation'.[57] Where Schopenhauer took a negative view of will, Nietzsche is presenting it in a favourable light, but he also slips into the fallacy he had exposed in Schopenhauer's work: it is now Nietzsche who is not only applying the word to different mental actions, but using it metaphorically, as if all the elements in nature possessed willpower, and as if all natural willpower could tend in the same direction. This is one of the drawbacks of Nietzsche's analogical method: the operations of personal willpower to achieve self-conquest are confused with operations of cosmic willpower towards a better future. 'And life itself did tell me this secret: "Behold," it said, "I am that *which must always conquer itself*. Indeed, you call it will to procreation or drive to a purpose, higher, further, more manifold: but all this is one, and *one* secret. Rather would I go under than forswear this one thing: and verily, where there is decline and the falling of leaves, behold, life is sacrificing itself – for power." '[58] This is to personalize nature as involved in constant conflict with itself, will to power being the animating force. Certainly, Nietzsche is writing more poetically than scientifically, but it is as if he had forgotten his own essay on truth and falsehood. Wearing the Zarathustra mask, he believes himself to be telling the truth. The great danger of this method is that it becomes hard to retain firm artistic control. Intent on using biblical language to forge a new morality for a world that will have, sooner or later, to recognize that God is dead, Nietzsche fails to notice when he is slipping back into echoing Wagner. Wotan said: 'Whatever I love I have to abandon, those whom I woo I murder, deceitfully betray whoever trusts me ... destroy what I have built.' Zarathustra says: 'Whatever I create and however much I love it, I must soon be an adversary to it and to my love: my will wills it to be thus.'[59] The reader is caught in the cross-fire of Nietzsche's battle against himself. As Zarathustra warns him, 'And you too, truth-seeker, are only a path and a footprint of my will: verily, my will to power treads in the steps of your will to truth.'[60]

So we have no right to complain about contradictions, but it is troubling to find Nietzsche trapped so helplessly in categories he wants to reject. 'Verily I say unto you: good and evil that are not transitory do not exist.'[61] But at the beginning of the book Zarathustra dreams about a child who holds up a mirror to him, and when he looks into it he sees the face of a devil. He interprets the dream as meaning that his teachings will be twisted by his enemies, but Nietzsche sees himself as a 'creator in good and evil', and, as we have been told in Part I, 'Zarathustra has found no greater power on earth than good and evil.'[62] Nietzsche's whole procédé is evaluative, but, like a self-destroying machine, the teaching is constantly undoing itself. While value judgements are being pronounced, the concept of value is being undermined.

The superior man is used, vaguely, as a personification of the future in which human potential will be more fully realized, but the closest Nietzsche comes to defining him is by using his phrase 'all too human' antonymously: 'Verily, even the greatest men I found all-too-human.'[63] Having rejected the Hegelian dialectic, he is proffering a dialectic of his own – a process of conflict and self-conquest that culminates in self-transcendence. 'When power becomes gracious and descends into visibility, beauty is my name for this descent. And from no one do I want beauty so much as from you who have power: let your goodness be your ultimate self-conquest. All evil is within your reach: therefore I want good from you. Verily, I have often laughed at those who are weak and think themselves good because there is no strength in their claws.'[64] This is the argument that had been used almost a century earlier by William Blake, who had put it into the devil's mouth: 'Those who restrain desire do so because theirs is weak enough to be restrained. . . . And being restrained, it by degrees becomes passive, till it is only the shadow of desire.'[65] Those with strength, says Zarathustra, should imitate the virtue of a marble column, which becomes finer and gentler but internally harder as it ascends. Those who are elevated will one day become beautiful and shudder with godlike desires, their vanity imbued with adoration. 'For this is the soul's secret: only when the hero has abandoned it does the superior hero, in dream, approach it.'[66]

Blake had many affinities with Nietzsche. Both were appalled by the gulf between human potential and human attainment, between the fullness of living they believed the Greeks to have achieved and the paltriness of their contemporaries. Both used themselves as a psychological model; both confronted the problem of guilt with the assumption that no innate tendency could be evil.

> Mutual Forgiveness of each Vice,
> Such are the Gates of Paradise.[67]

'Believe me, my friends', says Zarathustra,

the bite of conscience trains you to bite. But the worst of all is petty thoughts. Verily, it is better to do evil than to think pettily. . . . An evil deed is like a boil: it itches, irritates and bursts. It speaks honestly. 'Look, I am disease.' . . . But a petty thought is like a fungus: it creeps and stoops and evades – until the whole body is flabby and decayed with little fungi.[68]

This is quite close to Blake's *Proverbs of Hell*: 'He who desires but acts not breeds pestilence.' 'The cistern contains: the fountain overflows.' 'The eagle never lost so much time as when he submitted to learn of the crow.' 'Sooner murder an infant in its cradle than nurse unacted desires.'[69] What if this tolerance towards evil is abused? It was awareness of this danger that made Blake speak through a diabolical persona and Nietzsche make Zarathustra see a diabolical reflection in the mirror.

But was Nietzsche to some extent activated by a desire for vengeance not merely against Lou and Rée but against humanity? Or was he, in his disaffected state, at least willing to be less careful, less scrupulous, than he might otherwise have been? Lou had opened a channel that had been blocked, and the flow of erotic energy had to find an outlet. If a certain proportion of it went into erotic prose, the unfamiliar experience of writing it must have been more arousing that satisfying. 'Night has fallen: only now do the songs of lovers come to life. My soul too is the song of a lover. ... Light am I. Would I were night! But this is my loneliness, to be girdled with light. Would I were dark, nocturnal. How I wanted to suck at the breasts of light.'[70] Like Blake's prose, Nietzsche's is simultaneously moving towards the biblical and towards verse, while the memory of humiliation adds a sado-masochistic piquancy to the literary experience. 'But I live in my own light. The flames that break out of me I drink back into myself. I do not know the bliss of receiving and I have often dreamed it must be still more blessed to steal than to receive. That is my poverty: my hand never rests from giving. ... Hunger grows out of my beauty: I wish to hurt those I enlighten, steal from those who benefit – this is my evil appetite.'[71] Here the mask is slipping: Zarathustra is speaking directly out of Nietzsche's experience, as he does in the next section, which dithyrambically characterizes both life and wisdom as flirtatious girls. 'Whole-heartedly I love only life – and, verily, never more than when I hate it.'[72] He is well disposed to Wisdom, but she is so much like life: 'She has her eyes, her smile and even her little golden fishing-rod. ... One's thirst for her is never slaked, one glimpses her through veils, reaches through nets. ... She is volatile and way-ward. I have often seen her bite her lip and comb her hair the wrong way.'[73] Obliquely, perversely, he is declaring his love for Lou, provoking himself in order to subdue himself, and when he asks whether it is not foolish still to be alive,[74] he is reaffirming the burden of his depression. 'In the details [of the book] there is an incredible amount of personal experience and suffering, intelligible only to me. Many pages struck me as almost *bloodstained*.'[75] At the end of the book his sense of isolation is visible behind the stratagem of consoling himself with the voice that reassures Zarathustra: 'What does their mockery matter? You are one who has grown away from the habit of obedience: now you must take command. ... To do great things is difficult; to command great things more difficult still. What is most unforgivable in you is having the power to rule and not wishing to.'[76]

The euphoria induced by writing could not last long. The 'cold, gloomy, rainy summer'[77] intensified his depression, and his letters allude repeatedly to the danger of insanity. 'You cannot imagine how this madness is raging inside me, day and night. . . . I *need* to survive *through next year*. Help me to *hold out* for another fifteen months.'[78] 'That I lapsed, last winter, against all expectation, into a real, prolonged *nervous fever* . . . could mean that something else will happen to me that I would *never* have believed possible – mental breakdown.'[79] He dated the mental imbalance from his attempts to put the Lou experience behind him. 'It was my worst, sickest winter, with experiences that could have turned one overnight into a Timon of Athens. . . . It has done me irreparable harm that my imagination has had to wade through the slime of these experiences for about a year.'[80]

His confusion was exacerbated by Elisabeth's persistent interference: 'My sister regards Lou as a poisonous vermin which must be exterminated at any price.'[81] 'My sister wants her revenge on that Russian girl – well, fine, but so far I have been the victim of everything she has done about it.'[82] Elisabeth's letter to Georg Rée was virulent enough to make him ask Malwida to put pressure on Lou's mother so that she would take her daughter back to Russia. Elisabeth also wrote, venomously, to Rée's mother, but provoked Nietzsche into writing to her and to Georg Rée, 'who threatened to sue him for slander'. Nietzsche was beginning to feel 'a real hatred' towards Elisabeth.[83] She had sabotaged all his efforts at self-conquest, inflaming his lust for revenge. 'This internal conflict is pushing me, step by step, closer to madness.'[84] His philosophizing, as always, reflected his mood. While sketching out the third part of *Zarathustra*, he reported that 'poor Zarathustra is sinking into real gloom – so much so that in comparison with his "pessimism", Schopenhauer and Leopardi will seem mere beginners and novices.'[85] Depression was beginning to lead to puffery.

It would have been wiser to stay away from Elisabeth, but in September, after his spirits had been boosted by a three-day visit from the Overbecks and depressed by their departure, he spent four weeks in Naumburg, which involved him in the unexpected strain of having to join in family arguments about Elisabeth's growing friendship with Bernhard Förster, an ex-teacher whom she had known, and liked, since the beginning of 1877. In 1880, convinced that German culture was threatened by the manoeuvrings of 'international Jewry', he had provoked a fight in a Berlin tram by making loud anti-Semitic remarks, and he had helped to organize a petition for Jewish immigration to be curtailed, for Jews to be barred from the stock exchange, and for their financial and journalistic activities to be restricted. Elisabeth had helped to collect signatures, and 250,000 people signed the petition before it was submitted to Bismarck.

Of all the German states Prussia had the best reputation for religious tolerance, and anti-Semitism had been quiescent since the 1820s. But in the early seventies resistance to the virus was weakened by the so-called *Kulturkampf*, a campaign against the Catholics. Bismarck was suspicious of the Zentrum, the Catholic political party, which might, he thought, ally itself with anti-Prussian forces in Austria or even in France. With a new Minister of Culture, Adalbert Falk, who was appointed in 1871, and with encouragement from Rudolf von Delbrück, the head of the *Reichskanzleramt* (Chancellor's Office), a man who professed allegiance to the Lutheran tradition and the Hegelian political ethic, Bismarck enacted a series of measures against the Catholics. In 1873, when the state assumed control of the schools, all members of religious orders were debarred from teaching in them; stringent legislation against the Jesuits followed later in the year. By a law passed in 1874 the Prussian government was empowered to expel all clerics who failed to conform with state regulations, and by 1876 nearly a third of the parishes in Prussia were left without incumbents.

The economic crisis of 1873, which had its effect on confidence in the government and on anti-clericalism, led directly to a revival of anti-Semitism. The economy had been overheated ever since 1871, when the French payment of a five-billion-franc indemnity coincided with currency reforms that put an extra 762,000,000 marks into circulation. Industrial expansion was unhealthily rapid. The laws controlling joint-stock companies were liberalized, and thousands of investors, beneficiaries of the nation's prosperity, put their faith and their savings into hastily formed companies. A Jew, Eduard Lasker, one of the leaders of the National Liberal Party, made a speech in the *Reichstag* denouncing the unscrupulous speculators who were swindling their investors, and he exposed some corrupt politicians and civil servants who had benefited personally from the granting of railway concessions. The revelations caused a scandal and a collapse of confidence. Those who lost money wanted scapegoats, and it was easy for anti-Semitic writers in the press to make out that the stock market, the banks and the speculative companies were all dominated by Jews.

When Bismarck rejected the anti-Semitic petition, Bernhard Förster went on to found a German People's Party, partly to protect himself against protests in the Berlin papers about schoolmasters who fomented anti-Semitism in the classroom. The party's activities caused so much controversy and litigation that he had to give up teaching; he then decided to found a 'New Germany' on soil uncontaminated by Jews. In February 1883 he left to found an Aryan colony in Paraguay. Elisabeth had spoken of joining him there, and her mother, nervous of losing her, asked Nietzsche to intervene. Disillusionment with Rée had done nothing to make anti-Semitism more palatable to Nietzsche, who was appalled that she should have become so involved with such a man.

Nietzsche left Naumburg on 5 October 1883. After staying the night at Frankfurt he set out for Basel, but he had to interrupt his journey at Freiburg, where he had a night of vomiting. At Basel he stayed with the Overbecks. On the 9th he was feeling well enough to leave for Genoa, only to find that his room would not be available until the 15th. Hearing that Malwida was in La Spezia, sixty-five miles away, he went there, but failed to find her. He stayed on, looking, until the 13th, when he went back to Genoa, still being overtaken by one 'attack' after another, but hoping to recuperate steadily, as he had in the city three years earlier. 'I am not short of energy. . . . I have a task and *no time* to lose.' But he could not settle. Hearing that Nice was brighter and less cloudy, he left Genoa on 23 November to spend nine transitional days in Villefranche, installing himself in Nice on 2 December. Again he rented an unheated room, and it was not even carpeted, though he was paying twenty-five francs a month. It was on the second floor of a house in rue Ségurance, ten minutes from the sea. At first he found the town too noisy, too fashionable, too cool and too windy, but for a while he believed that the sunlight was having an 'electrifying influence . . . on my whole system. The constant, painful pressure on my brain, which I was feeling in Naumburg, has disappeared, and I eat twice as much, without any protest from my stomach.'[86] But he soon found he could eat only once every two or three days; he was suffering from catarrh, sleeplessness, headaches and shooting pains in his eyes. 'Nor have I ever suffered so much from the cold as here; at night it usually freezes.'[87] Before Christmas he bought a small stove, but it produced more smoke than heat.[88]

By the beginning of 1884 he was feeling that *Zarathustra* might be no more than a gateway to a straightforwardly discursive philosophical book, and he was impatient to write it.[89] During January, in another burst of intensive writing, he completed the second book of *Zarathustra*, which was intended to be the last. Once again the experience of writing was euphoric: 'I have *never* sailed with such sails across such a sea, and the tremendous presumptuousness of this whole mariner's story ... has arrived at its climax.'[90]

This self-induced excitement permeates the book, which exudes the feeling he had often had of hardening himself against himself. The audience that Zarathustra addresses – 'Oh my brothers', he keeps saying – consists of phantoms called up to dispel the overwhelming solitude. But wintry solitude is the doctrine he preaches. Even Zarathustra's children – his works – must learn to stand alone. Where they are together there are islands of happiness, but each one will be dug up, transplanted. 'Gnarled and crooked but hard and supple, it will stand for me by the sea, a living lighthouse of invincible life.'[91]

'Become hard'[92] is his crucial injunction – to his readers and himself: 'Your greatest gentleness must become your greatest hardness. Those who are consistently protective towards themselves will thereby make themselves sickly. ... To see *much*, one must learn to look away from oneself – every mountain-climber needs this hardness.'[93] And the lover of knowledge must learn to climb over himself and above himself: 'I have not reached my peak until I can look down on myself and on my stars.'[94] The idea of the superior man may derive from the recurrent metaphor of mountain-climbing.

One of the weaknesses of this book is that it makes less sense outside its biographical context. It is the unhappy Nietzsche,

freezing in his underheated room, who is recommending unhappiness and discomfort, while anathematizing overheating as one
of the detrimental characteristics of city life. 'For the sake of those
who may one day become companions and collaborators and
celebrants of Zarathustra I must perfect myself: therefore I sidestep my happiness and offer myself to every adversity – for *my*
ultimate trial and judgement.'[95] 'I am Zarathustra the godless. I
boil every misfortune in my pot, and only when it has been
thoroughly cooked do I welcome it as *my* food.'[96] 'Winter, an evil
guest, is sitting in my home; my hands are blue from his friendly
handshake. . . . A narrow bed warms me better than a rich one,
for I am jealous of my poverty. And it is never more faithful to me
than in winter. I begin each day spitefully: I mock the winter with
a cold bath, which makes my harsh house-mate grumble.'[97]
Unwilling to be an object of pity, Nietzsche makes Zarathustra
insist that all his misfortunes are voluntary: 'They still sympathize
over my accidents – but *I* say: "Let misfortunes come to me: they
are as innocent as little children. How *could* they endure my
happiness if I did not surround it with mishaps and wintry
severity . . . if I myself did not take pity on their pity?'[98] The
attack on the overheated city is put into the mouth of a fool who
apes Zarathustra: 'This is the great city, where you can gain
nothing and lose everything. . . . Spit on the city of narrow chests
and constricted souls, beady eyes and sticky fingers, the city of
the importunate, the shameless, scribblers, screamers, overheated
fortune-hunters. . . .'[99] Zarathustra is less intolerant but no more
enamoured of urban life: 'Where we can no longer love, there we
must pass on.'[100]

The most vivid sequence introduces a dog howling in a dream
or vision which leads Zarathustra to a young shepherd, writhing,
choking, jerking about, with a heavy black snake hanging from his
mouth. Zarathustra saves his life by telling him to bite off the
snake's head.[101] Later in the book, Nietzsche implicitly associates
the snake with the nausea and weariness that humanity induces in
Zarathustra: 'This was choking me. It had crept into my gullet.
And what the soothsayer said: All is the same, nothing is worthwhile, knowledge sticks in the throat. . . . He recurs eternally, the
man who wearies you, the small man." ' In this respect Nietzsche
remains incurably Wagnerian; nothing that falls short of the

heroic can be admirable. His contempt for quotidian contentment intensifies his distaste for the morality evolved to protect it. 'He who one day teaches men to fly, he has dislocated all milestones; all milestones will themselves fly up in the air for him.'[102] The compulsion to revalue all values, then, was rooted in Nietzsche's lifelong impatience with mediocrity: he found madness more attractive than resignation to the impossibility of teaching men to fly. Zarathustra's arch-enemy, the spirit of gravity, is accused of creating constraint, law, necessity, purpose, consequence, will, good and evil.[103] The old commandments are no longer valid. What has caused more killing and theft than the biblical vetoes on killing and theft?[104] The good must be Pharisees: they have no option but to crucify the man who creates his own virtue.[105] But how can virtue be created without reference to earlier ideas of good and evil? Like Jesus, Nietzsche could only refine on existing ethical ideas.

As a moralist he was too much of a revolutionary to accept this. But he does reconcile himself, in the course of writing this third book, with the idea that humanity will never be able to discard pettiness and vulgarity, which must recur endlessly, like everything else. The affirmation at the end of the book grows out of accepting the eternal recurrence of the small man. Zarathustra sees that he is entangled in a knot of causes which will recur and recreate him. He belongs to the causes.[106] It is as if Nietzsche finds lust for eternity preferable to sexual desire. 'Never yet have I found the woman from whom I wanted children. It must be this woman, whom I love, for I love you, oh Eternity. *For I love you*, oh Eternity.'[107] This refrain occurs seven times in the final section.

The manuscript was ready on 18 January 1884, when he wrote to Schmeitzner about it, immediately beginning on the preparation of a fair copy, and by 8 February it was being printed. 'By the way, the *whole* of *Zarathustra* is an explosion of forces that have been building up over decades. And the originator of such explosions can easily blow himself up. I have often wanted to.'[108] Pride in his achievement made him write another letter to Rohde: 'I fancy that with this Zarathustra I have brought the German language to its full realization. After *Luther* and Goethe a third step had to be taken – tell me, my old friend, whether there has ever been such a combination of strength, resilience and euphony. Read Goethe after a page of my book ... my line is tougher, more virile, without ever lapsing into coarseness, like Luther's. My style is a *dance*, playing with symmetries of every kind, jumping over them and mocking them. This enters the very vowels.'[109] It would be pointless to deny that *Also sprach Zarathustra* is one of the finest pieces of prose in the German language; it would be pointless to pretend that Nietzsche was still capable of objectivity about his work. By now he was unmistakably suffering from delusions of grandeur that dulled his sense of reality, reducing his capacity for self-criticism. 'It is possible', he had written ten days earlier, 'that I am a fatality for all the coming generations of mankind, that I am their doom. Consequently it is very possible that I will one day fall silent; out of love for humanity!!!'[110] His determination to believe in his own importance was joining forces with the disease. 'This is certain,' he wrote in May 1884, over four years before the final breakdown, 'I will push humanity to decisions which will determine its whole future.'[111] Nor was he any more realistic, on re-reading *Morgenröte* and *Die fröhliche Wissenschaft*, to claim that 'hardly a line in them does not serve as introduction, preparation and commentary' on *Zarathustra*.[112] It is only towards the end of *Die fröhliche Wissenschaft* that he swings away from psychological observation in the manner of *Menschliches*, *Allzumenschliches* towards the quasi-metaphysical dogmatism of *Zarathustra*.

His breach with his sister seems to have dated from the beginning of the year, when she sent him 'a letter full of venomous insinuations about my character'.[113] In May he wrote: 'There can be no question of reconciliation with a vengeful anti-Semitic goose.'[114] After that, so many of his letters failed to reach his mother that he began to suspect Elisabeth of intercepting them. At the beginning of June he enclosed a letter for his mother in a letter to Overbeck, who was asked to forward it and to write the address on the envelope.[115] His sister's persecution of Rée and Lou was making him feel better disposed towards them: in April, again toying with the fantasy of forming a small community, he thought of inviting them to join it.[116]

He had come to believe, quite unrealistically, that his ancestry was Polish. This is what he told Resa von Schirnhofer, a girl of twenty-nine, introduced to him vicariously by Malwida. Resa was in Nice from 3 to 13 April 1884, and he was delighted when she told him that the shape of his head and the growth of his moustache reminded her of a historical painting by Jan Matjekos she had seen in Vienna. He also gave her the impression that he felt an affinity with Napoleon, seeing him, if not as a superior man, at least as a transitional type. He had abnormally strong will-power, and, like Nietzsche, an exceptionally slow pulse-beat. Wanting to visit Corsica, Nietzsche asked her to accompany him. If Gast had accepted the invitation to go with them,[117] Nietzsche might have become involved in another triangular relationship; as it was, the expedition was never made.

On 21 April 1884, a week after Resa's departure from Nice, Nietzsche left to stay in Venice, where Peter Gast was finishing his opera *Il Matrimonio Segreto*. Nietzsche did his best to help, making suggestions, both strategic and musical, but he expected Gast to take a reciprocal interest in his compositions. 'Nietzsche comes home and plays his heavy music, which I cannot bear. Devil take this dreadful noise.'[118] His piano-playing must have reflected his predominant mood, 'a distress so profound that I am wondering whether anyone has ever suffered so much. Indeed, who else has had the experience of feeling with every fibre in his body that "the values of all things must be reassessed"?'[119] He had formed the habit of writing about moods and emotions in super-latives: whatever he felt could never have been felt more in-tensely by himself or by anyone else.

After six weeks in Venice, he surprised the Overbecks by reappearing in Basel on 15 June.[120] 'It is now only in the world of his visions', Overbeck wrote, 'that he can sometimes feel happy, until it comes over him that he is, for the time being, alone in his understanding of them.'[121] Burckhardt, embarrassed at having to comment on *Zarathustra*, asked whether he had ever thought of trying his hand at drama, and he failed to gather reassurance from his other ex-colleagues: 'It was like being surrounded by cows.'[122] For sympathetic interest he again had to depend on a stranger. After spending a few days at Piora, which is even higher than Sils-Maria, he left for Zürich, where he met a twenty-nine-year-old friend of Resa's and Malwida's – Meta von Salis:

An acute self-consciousness made posing superfluous. ... A quiet melodious voice, and his extreme soft-spokenness, made an immediate impact. . . . When a smile illumined his face, bronzed in the fresh Mediterranean air, the expression was movingly childish, inviting involvement. . . . He spoke better and more vividly than almost anyone I knew, but by no means avoided commonplace subjects, merely gave them significance through his wholly individual approach. . . . We went on conversing for about two hours. . . . Saying goodbye, Nietzsche took both my hands in his and expressed the wish that we should see each other again.[123]

On 18 July he returned to Sils-Maria, where he began to lead a less isolated existence, lunching every day at the Hôtel des Alpes and enjoying long conversations with acquaintances. Re-reading *Schopenhauer als Erzieher*, he felt satisfied that he had been living in accordance with his own precepts.[124] He claimed to have a clear view of his future philosophical task: he would need six years to fulfil it.[125] But there was cholera in Nice, and it was hard to make any headway in Sils. 'Here, without a stove, frozen through, with blue hands, I can hardly hold out for long – I would have to buy a stove. . . . My health is unsteady . . . one *good* day in every ten, those are my statistics, devil take them! Nobody to read to me. Every evening depressed in the low-ceilinged room, teeth chattering, waiting three or four hours for permission to go to bed.'[126] Permission, he meant, from himself. His eyesight was again deteriorating, and he could no longer hold his back straight or walk as he used to.[127] Resa, who came to visit him, found him much worse than in April. 'He spoke a great deal about himself and his suffering, and he had a bad attack.' For thirty-six hours he could not receive her; then she was admitted to a modest diningroom.

I stood waiting by the table as the door of the adjoining room opened, and Nietzsche appeared. He leaned wearily on the jamb of the half-opened door, a stricken expression on his pale face, and began immediately to say how unbearable his sufferings were. He described how, as soon as he closed his eyes, he saw a profusion of fantastic flowers, twining round each other and constantly growing, changing in shape and colour with exotic opulence, one sprouting wildly out of another. 'They never give me any peace,' he complained – words which made an impact on me. Then suddenly, with his great, dark eyes fixed on me anxiously, and with disturbing urgency in his soft voice, he asked: 'Don't you believe this condition is a symptom of incipient madness? My father died of a brain disease.'[128]

He treated the young Austrian woman like an old friend, and when the time came for her to leave Sils he accompanied her to the post-coach, tears in his eyes. 'I was hoping you would stay here longer. How long will it be before I again hear that refreshing laughter of yours?'[129]

But what Nietzsche was to describe as 'the experience of the summer' was a visit at the end of August from Baron Heinrich von Stein, the twenty-seven-year-old Wagnerite aesthetician who had first written to him two years previously. He professed to understand only twelve sentences of *Zarathustra*, but he had learned one of the dance-songs by heart. 'In the narrow peasant's room in Sils I found a man who arouses compassion at one's first glimpse of him.'[130] The day they met Nietzsche was ill, and a sleepless night ensued for him, but the next day they spent eight hours together, deep in conversation. 'In the evening he was fresh and bright-eyed. . . . I left Sils with the sincere wish to do something for Nietzsche. There is a fatality hanging over him.'[131] Von Stein promised that he would move 'to Nice to be with me as soon as his father's life is over'.[132] Once again Nietzsche was left feeling that his practical task was to gather around him 'enough young people of a very particular quality'.[133]

Hoping to effect a reconciliation between him and Elisabeth, his mother urged him to come home, but he refused; if he agreed to meet his sister in Zürich, it was partly because it might be his last chance to see her before she left Europe with Förster. He had two other objects in breaking his journey from Sils to Nice at Zürich: to meet Gottfried Keller, who lived there, and to persuade the conductor, Friedrich Hegar, whom he had met at Tribschen, to consider Gast's music.

Nietzsche was in Zürich from 25 September till 31 October; Elisabeth was there from the weekend of 27–8 September till 14 October. 'Your children are being nice to each other, and things are good in every way.'[134] 'So far there has been plenty of sunshine between us and all round us.'[135] Förster, who was in San Bernardino, had advertised in a German newspaper that he planned to be in Buenos Aires at the beginning of 1885, returning to Naumburg at the end of March. (Nietzsche pasted the announcement into his address book.) When Förster went back to South America, Elisabeth would go with him as his wife, and at least they would be too far away for Förster's activities to damage his brother-in-law's reputation. Meanwhile, Elisabeth's companionship was enjoyable. 'I had not expected to rediscover the old cordiality undiminished, and perhaps I had not deserved to.'[136]

In fact Schmeitzner's anti-Semitism was more immediately dangerous than Förster's. As immoderate in his activities as in his attitudes, the publisher had brought his company so close to bankruptcy that Nietzsche found himself offered for sale: 'Schmeitzner wants to sell "me" for 20,000 marks, but he can find no publisher brave enough to take "me".'[137] The market for Nietzsche's books was still extremely small.

In September 1882 he had sent Gottfried Keller a copy of *Die fröhliche Wissenschaft*. 'Despite its gay title, this book will perhaps hurt you, and truly, whom do I less want to hurt than you, who give so much pleasure?'[138] After receiving a copy of *Zarathustra* Keller invited Nietzsche to his home.[139] He was small, shy, and sixty-five years old. When they met on 30 September they were extremely polite to each other, and Elisabeth had never seen a face change so much as Keller's did when it smiled: 'The eyes sparkled roguishly, and the whole face took on an expression of animated slyness.'[140] The two men went for several walks together, and Keller introduced Nietzsche to some of the local *literati*.

Friedrich Hegar was now conductor of the local orchestra, and after Nietzsche had paid for orchestral scores of Gast's overture to his opera *Der Löwe von Venedig*, Hegar tried it out at the concert hall on 18 October with Nietzsche sitting alone in the auditorium. After the first rehearsal, four days earlier, Hegar had told Nietzsche that Gast's intentions were subtler than his realization of them, and he could not have had an accurate impression of how the music would sound when performed by the orchestra.[141] Nevertheless, Gast was invited to conduct a performance of the overture at a concert given by Hegar's *Gesangverein* in December, after Nietzsche had left Zürich. Overbeck, who made the eighty-five kilometre journey from Basel, found the overture naive but pleasing. 'The audience enjoyed the music, and I had the pleasure of seeing my applause swallowed up in the rest.'[142]

Nietzsche had gone to Menton, on the Franco-Italian border, not far from Nice. After arriving on 2 November it took him three days to recover from the journey. He liked the room he found, but hated the landlady's cooking.[143] 'Menton is splendid, compared with Nice. I have already discovered eight walks.'[144] He thought of going to Corsica to join Paul Lanzky, but they decided instead to stay in Nice at the same boarding house, the Pension de Genève, which Nietzsche had previously used. He was still thinking about 'my future "colony". . . . I mean sympathetic men to whom I can teach my philosophy'.[145] But Lanzky, who arrived on 3 December, disappointed him: 'the old story: while I need someone to entertain me, what happens is that I do the entertaining. He is silent, sighs, looks like a cobbler and neither smiles nor shows any animation. Not tolerable for very long.'[146] Lanzky, who professed to hold Nietzsche 'in reverence',[147] intended to write about him, but Nietzsche made him promise not to.[148] Nice now struck him as highly unattractive. 'I keep myself on the defensive, and as if it were not there.'[149] The weather was exceptionally wintry, and his eyes were troubling him: 'Spots, dimness of vision, floods of tears. I should never come back to Nice: the danger of being run over here is too great.'[150]

He had to have his food served to him, and could not trust himself to eat in a public room. But in this state, thrown back painfully on himself, Nietzsche completed the work he had begun in Zürich and continued in Menton, the final book of *Zarathustra*, in which his alter ego is less isolated than in any of the previous instalments. But the paradox is only superficial: the craving for company induces fantasies, and the greatest need of all was to feel appreciated, loved; the 'higher men' who come to visit Zarathustra are modelled on the friends who were no longer seeing Nietzsche. Insofar as they are tested by the action they all prove inadequate, and at the final climax Zarathustra is surrounded not by men but, like St Francis, by animals who love him. A lion nuzzles him like a cat, licking up the tears that fall on his hands, while doves, unafraid, sit on his shoulders, caressing his hair, which has turned white.[151]

The act of putting words on paper was still more than satisfying: it could dispel depression. Zarathustra preaches on the value of gaiety: 'All good things laugh. A man's gait shows whether he is going *his own* way; so watch my movements. But the man who comes near his goal dances. ... Lift up your hearts, my brothers, high, higher! ... Lift up your legs too, you good dancers, and better still, stand on your head!'[152]

At the beginning Zarathustra has claimed to be concerned only with his work; his happiness is the honey he is sacrificing as bait or spreading out like a net to lure men up to the mountains. 'Biting at my sharp, hidden hooks, they must come up to *my* heights, the lowest and brightest groundlings must come right up to the most perverse of all anglers for human fish.'[153] Here he is parodying the New Testament image of Christ as a fisher of men. The bait attracts two kings, the last pope, the ugly murderer of God, an old magician, a spiritually conscientious man and a beggar who is identified with Jesus of Nazareth by a reference to the Sermon on the Mount. He maintains that we should learn from cows how to chew the cud, patiently. Zarathustra, who is quick to recognize him as a vegetarian, averse to the pleasures of the flesh,[154] invites them all to his cave, going outside when the human smell becomes overpowering. They have been partly enlightened by his doctrines, but as 'higher men' they can serve only as bridges to the superior man. 'For me you are not high or strong enough ... may higher men stride over you.'[155] But if Zarathustra is disappointed not to have better men wanting to learn from him, Nietzsche was dejected at not having any, and the book contains one of his sourest caveats about solitude: 'Solitude is conducive to the growth of whatever one takes into it, including the inner beast. For many, therefore, it is inadvisable. Has there ever been anything filthier on earth than the desert saints?'[156] His anxiety about deteriorating circumstances and impending madness is refracted in the soothsayer's prediction that the waves of distress around his mountain are rising higher: 'Soon they will lift up your boat and carry you away from it.'[157] But self-pity is generalized into an ambivalent compassion for the 'higher man': when Zarathustra hears a long-drawn-out cry of distress, the soothsayer warns him: 'I have come to seduce you to your final sin. The sin will be pity.'[158]

The old pope serves much the same function as the old pope in de Sade's *Juliette*, explicitly raising the question (which de Sade's pope raises implicitly) of whether he is not still more godless than the character who has been epitomizing godlessness. Nietzsche's pope, who served the old god till he died, has sought out the man he calls 'the most pious of all non-believers'.[159] Zarathustra asks whether it is true that God 'saw how *man* was hanging on the cross and could not bear it, that love of man became his hell and finally his death'.[160] Just as Christianity adopted and adapted the pagan myth of the dying God, Nietzsche is adopting and adapting the Christian myth. The old pope denounces the dead god. He was 'full of slyness. He even had to go about getting a son in an underhand way. At the door of his faith stands adultery.'[161] But eventually he became old and soft, more like a grandmother than a grandfather, and in the end he choked on excessive pity. In Dostoevsky's *The Possessed* the bishop tells Stavrogin that he honours the Holy Spirit without knowing it; Nietzsche's pope tells Zarathustra that he is more pious than he believes. 'Some god in you converted you to godlessness. Is it not your piety that no longer lets you believe in a god? And your excessive honesty will yet lead you beyond good and evil.'[162] This is the nearest Nietzsche came to calling himself religious. The phrase which served him as the title of his next book – *Jenseits von Gut und Böse* (*Beyond Good and Evil*) – was one of the titles he considered for this book before deciding to make it the final section of *Zarathustra*.

All Zarathustra's conversations with the 'higher men' correspond to arguments Nietzsche had with himself. The closest correspondence is in the conversation with the homeless shadow, which has followed Zarathustra devotedly all through his pursuit of the forbidden, the worst, the remotest.[163] 'I discarded my faith in words, values, great names. . . . Too often, verily, I followed so close on the heels of truth that she kicked me in the face. . . . Nothing I love is still alive, how can I still love myself?'[164] This echoes Nietzsche's complaint after Lanzky left Nice. 'For me he signifies what I call "overcast weather", "German weather" and the like. Indeed there is no one now alive who means *much* to me; the men I like have been dead for a long time.'[165] The 'higher men' in the book correspond less to his dream of having disciples than to his nightmare of being misunderstood, misrepresented, betrayed. The fear of betrayal is heightened by the knowledge of provoking it, of betraying us by using words, values, names, without having faith in them. He cannot help revenging himself on us for the defection of his friends. The most unforgivable loss was Wagner, and the old magician (*Zauberer*) – 'charmer' (*Bezauberer*) in the drafts – is partly a caricature. Described as 'a trembling old man with vacant eyes',[166] he keeps looking pitifully around as if 'forsaken by the whole world'. His versified moaning expresses the desire for reconciliation Nietzsche felt sure Wagner had harboured:

> All my streaming tears
> Flow towards you!
> And the last flame in my heart
> Is flaring up for *you*!
> Oh come back,
> My unknown God! My torture! My ultimate – happiness![167]

We have little evidence of what Wagner had actually felt towards him after the breach, but, according to Lou Salomé, when Nietzsche's name was mentioned at Wahnfried during the 1882 festival, Wagner left the room in great agitation after demanding that the name should never again be spoken in his presence.

Curt Paul Janz has suggested that the ex-pope may refer to Liszt, and the man with a spiritual conscience to either Overbeck or Rohde.[168] The satire, in any case, is fairly crude; Nietzsche's direct attacks on religiosity were more convincing, as when he wrote to Overbeck accusing St Augustine of hypocrisy: how dishonest to claim that after the death of the best friend, with whom he shared a *single soul*, he 'resolved to go on living so that his friend would not wholly die!'[169]

Nietzsche must have been nervous that his friends would recognize themselves in the new book: he had only forty copies printed. 'I have sent no copy to Burckhardt or to anyone in Basel. Please let us remain silent about the existence of a fourth part.'[170] 'If a man like me sums up his deep and hidden life, it is only for the eyes and consciences of the most select few.'[171] In Zarathustra's absence the higher men worship a donkey, like the children of Israel worshipping the golden calf while Moses was on Sinai, or like the medieval congregation that paraded in church behind a donkey during the feast of fools. The braying of the ass mingles with the worshipful jubilation of the men, and the pope defends their celebration of the animal, arguing that the first man to proclaim that God was a spirit took the greatest possible step towards disbelief.[172]

In the poem sung by the shadow, the image of tinsel skirts probably stems from Nietzsche's experience in the Leipzig brothel, while the Song of Dejection, which is sung by the old magician, contains oblique references to Nietzsche's misgivings about the form in which he is writing. Can he be an emancipator of truth when all he is doing is playing the fool poetically, 'climbing around on mendacious word-bridges'?[173] The next book will be less poetic, more straightforwardly philosophical. 'Resolution: I will speak prose and write no more *Zarathustra*.'[174]

Early in 1885 he had been intending to write two more books, continuing Zarathustra's story to his death, but by 21 March he knew that this fourth part would be the last.[175] In the middle of February he had written to von Gersdorff, asking him to finance the printing of twenty copies,[176] but he did not reply until May, and by then Nietzsche had gone ahead at his own expense. The first proofs reached Gast on 22 March, and the proof-correcting was complete by 13 April. The first copy was sent to Nietzsche early in May.[177] The printing cost him 284 marks, but when the dispute with Schmeitzner came before the courts he guaranteed to pay Nietzsche 5,600 marks in June.[178]

Nietzsche had not been to Naumburg or seen his mother for nearly two years. Writing conciliatingly to her from Zürich in October 1884, he called his 104 kilograms of books a club-foot that hampered his movement, and conceded that she was right to remonstrate with him about dressing more carefully: 'I am rather shabby, and, as a result of moving about so much, somewhat *too* scraped, like a mountain sheep.'[179] But like his pretence of being Polish by descent, his unwillingness to go home was an index of his hostility to everything German. Writing to the musicologist Carl Fuchs from Nice, he bracketed German music with German philosophy, lamenting the distance between the current decadence and 'the *grand style*, to which, for example, the Palazzo Pitti belongs, but *not* the Ninth Symphony. The grand style is the highest form of the melodic art.'[180] *Tristan* was full of rhythmical ambiguity, and this was symptomatic of dissolution. 'The part becomes lord over the whole, the phrase over melody, the moment over time (and tempo), pathos over ethos (character, style, or whatever you care to call it), finally also *esprit* over sense.'[181]

Stripped of his unmistakably German name, Köselitz, Gast was expected to play his part in Nietzsche's private war against Germany by 'ensuring that the actors and pseudo-geniuses will not ruin people's taste for much longer!'[182] Wagner's music was that 'of a *great actor*', whereas Gast was still 'my pupil'.[183] Nietzsche had been intending to stay in Zürich so as to be with him, but in the middle of March he announced that he was about to leave for Venice. Nietzsche's emotional dependence on him became all the greater after von Stein made it clear that he was not, after all, to be dislodged from allegiance to Wagner. When Nietzsche wrote a long personal poem[184] to ask how long it would be before von Stein could join him, his reply was to invite Nietzsche's collaboration on a Wagnerian lexicon.

Tired of Nice and its noises, tired of the other German guests at the boarding house, their boring conversation and their boorish table-manners, he persuaded himself that he wanted nothing more than to revisit Venice, 'the only place I have liked and which has done me good'.[185] But when he arrived there on 10 April 1885, he was disappointed. 'All in all Venice was a torture for me; result – much melancholy and mistrust of everything undertaken.'[186] Gast, who had taken no trouble to find a suitable room for him, seemed listless, unsociable, awkward. But Nietzsche went on admiring his *Löwe von Venedig* as 'the most beautiful music since Mozart, and indeed music that Mozart could not have written'.[187]

The date of Elisabeth's marriage to Förster had been fixed for 22 May, Wagner's birthday, which upset Nietzsche, though they explained the gesture as a tribute to a nationalistic composer. Nietzsche's thoughts turned once again to his own unmarried state: 'Your son is ill-suited to marrying; my need is to remain *independent* to the last.'[188] He was still compulsive about attributing his bad health to staying for too long in the wrong place or believing in the wrong principles or the wrong music, but it is not impossible that he was worrying about whether he had inherited syphilis. After the sensuous love songs in the third part of *Zarathustra*, he had gone on in the fourth to write caustically about male sexual abstinence. Zarathustra says that he always suspects the motives of men who embrace chastity, while Nietzsche took

Hölderlin and Leopardi to task for 'contradicting the simplest facts, e.g. the fact that a man sometimes needs a woman just as he sometimes needs a well-cooked meal'. Nietzsche himself needed neither well-cooked meals nor women as often as most men do, but even if he was suffering—or believed himself to be suffering – from syphilis, he was not shy of mentioning the subject in his notebooks: 'Where is there a noble family with no venereal disease and degeneration in its blood?' There could be no question of racial 'purity' after the wars of the seventeenth century: 'It was probably worst of all with the German nobility, where the damage went deepest. Those who stayed at home suffered from alcoholism, those who ventured forth and came back, from syphilis. Up to the present they have had little to say in intellectual matters.'[189] But he did not recognize that the dissolute nobility had approximated more closely than he had to the sexual abandon of the Dionysiac orgy: in ancient Greece there had been no syphilis – a disease Columbus brought back to Europe. Reacting against his Lutheran upbringing, Nietzsche was torn between puritanic disapproval of self-indulgence and a theoretically Dionysiac affirmation of the libidinous self.

Elisabeth's hostility to Lou had been fortified by this puritanism, but now, unable though he was to forgive her for her vindictive interference, he felt personally betrayed by her marriage. The possibility of suicide is mentioned for the first time since the defection of Lou.

Perhaps all the anxieties about my future could be removed at a single stroke. I can endure life in the mornings, but scarcely any longer in the afternoons and evenings; and it seems to me that I have done enough, under unfavourable circumstances, to withdraw honourably from the dust. And I am becoming too blind to read and write much. Almost every day I have enough ideas for German professors to make two thick books out of them. But I have no one who could use the stuff.[190]

It was still not too late for her to renounce Förster in order to look after Nietzsche again, but preparations for the wedding went ahead.

He did not want to meet Förster and he refused to give his sister away at the ceremony or even to attend it. His wedding present was the Dürer engraving 'Knight, Death and Devil' which had been on loan to the Overbecks: it may have been partly to spite them that she asked for it. The armoured knight riding towards his castle seems unaware of the pig-snouted devil behind him with an axe and of Death beside him with an hourglass.

Two days before the wedding Nietzsche sent her a letter almost entirely about himself and his conviction that he had not yet found himself. She could not realistically have been expected to take much interest in him at this moment, but, losing the one woman who might once have been expected to devote her life to looking after him, he was too desperate to be realistic:

Until now, from childhood onwards, I have found *nobody* with the same needs of heart and conscience. . . . The feeling that there is some-thing remote and alien about me, that my words have different colours from the ones they have when other people use them, that there is in me a bright foreground which is deceptive – this feeling . . . is the subtlest degree of 'understanding' I have yet found. Everything I have so far written is foreground; for me myself it always begins with the dashes. . . . If I have, in a popular manner, now recommended Schopenhauer or Wagner to the Germans, now thought up Zarathustra, these things are for me recreation and, above all, hiding places, in which I can sit down for a while.[191]

On the wedding day he went to the Lido with a Basel family he had met in Nice,[192] but the only evidence of depression in his next letter to his mother is in the understatement of his scepticism about his new brother-in-law's ambitions. Förster's vegetarian diet must predispose him to irritability and gloom, while there is the example of the English to suggest that phlegm and roast beef are prerequisites for success in founding colonies.[193]

Nietzsche left Venice on 6 June 1885, to arrive on the 7th in Sils for his fifth summer there. He set to work on revising *Menschliches, Allzumenschliches* for a new edition, though the first was far from having sold out. He had invited an old German lady from Zürich, an acquaintance of Gast's, Frau Louise Roder-Widerhold, to Sils, where she stayed for four weeks, helping him for two or three hours every day, reading to him and writing to his dictation. But he was not pleased with the results: 'Everything I dictated to her is value-less, and she wept more often than I like. She is spineless . . . but the worst thing is that she has no manners and does not keep her legs still.'[1] He characterized what he had written as 'more or less a fifth *Unzeitgemässe Betrachtung*', but he complained that 'Thinking out the principal problems . . . always brings me back . . . to the same conclusions: they are already there, as veiled and obscure as possible in my *Geburt der Tragödie*, and everything I have since learned has become an ingrown part of them.'[2] After his protracted experiment in parable he was anxious to explicate his ideas as systematically as possible. 'But', he wrote to Overbeck, 'my "philosophy", if I have the right to use this word for what persecutes me right into the roots of my being, is no longer communicable, at least not in print. From time to time I yearn for a clandestine conference with you and Burckhardt, more to ask how you would solve this problem than to tell you news.'[3] He wrote copiously but disconnectedly in his notebooks, outlining possible structures for a new book but making no progress in integrating his heterogeneous material. While he deprecated writing that did not intertwine intimately with the author's experience, he could extrapolate no pattern from his insights except by looking at the uncomfortable consistency of his life. He was a moralist whose criteria of better and worse were inseparable from the pattern of feeling better or worse.

In all my phases of illness, I feel, with alarm, a sort of downward pull towards proletarian weaknesses, proletarian mildness, even proletarian virtues. . . . For instance a constant appearance of *frivolity* is the correct mask for stoic hardness and self-discipline. It is more distinguished to go slowly, in every sense, and to be slow in focusing one's gaze. We seldom display amazement. There are not too many things of value, and these come to us of their own accord, and *want* to. It is better to avoid small honours, and to distrust those who readily give praise. It is distinguished to doubt whether feelings are communicable, and to be solitary, not by choice but by talent . . . to live almost always in disguise, to travel *incognito*, as it were, to spare oneself shame, to be capable of *otium* and not active like a hen, clucking, laying eggs, clucking again, and so on.[4]

His constitution gave him a temperamental inclination towards the qualities associated with social distinction. When the musician Adolf Ruthardt met him in Sils, he thought Nietzsche looked like a Southern French nobleman or a high-ranking Spanish or Italian officer in mufti.[5]

He was ambivalent about whether to see Elisabeth again before she left for Paraguay, and about whether to revisit Naumburg. 'What could perhaps emerge too *clearly* from another meeting is how lonely your Fritz now feels – for I have lost *all* my friends in the last few years *without exception* – and how he is already living in a remoter, stranger, more unapproachable land than all the Paraguays could be.'[6] He even claimed to feel better disposed towards Förster's colonial enterprise 'now he has withdrawn from all that agitation'.[7] When he wrote this letter from Sils on 6 September, he was intending to settle in Florence for the winter, but nine days later he was on his way to Naumburg. A week later he was feeling very nervous about the effect of the Naumburg climate on his health.[8] He did not meet Förster, who was touring Westphalia, lecturing on his colonial plans and fomenting anti-Semitism.[9] After feeling 'continuously dull and overcast' for two weeks[10] – Nietzsche described his health as if it were the weather – he left for Leipzig, and it was only on returning to Naumburg for his forty-first birthday that he met his brother-in-law, who did not strike him as unsympathetic: 'There is something warm and noble about him, and he seems well equipped for action. I was surprised to see how many things he could deal with at the same time, and how easy he found it.'[11] The corresponding disadvantage was that 'everything is done too speedily'.[12]

Schmeitzner's bankruptcy was involving Nietzsche in a turmoil of legal letters and telegrams. By the middle of August the publisher had promised to pay him seven thousand francs in October. The whole firm had been impounded in Nietzsche's name and put under seal, so that Schmeitzner, returning to his office in Chemnitz after a journey, was unable to get in.[13] Trusting the promise, Nietzsche released the hold his lawyers had secured for him on the premises, and he received the money later in the month.[14] After paying his debts to a second-hand bookshop in Leipzig and to his printer for the forty copies of *Zarathustra* Part IV, he ordered a large new marble tombstone for his father's grave, in which his mother wanted eventually to be buried.[15] Obstructively, Schmeitzner was refusing to part with Nietzsche's unsold books. A Jewish publisher, Hermann Credner, wanted to bring out the second edition of *Menschliches, Allzumenschliches*, but when Schmeitzner demanded 2,500 marks compensation for the unsold copies of the first, it merely convinced Nietzsche that a second would be superfluous.[16]

When he went back to Leipzig in mid-October, he side-stepped another meeting with his brother-in-law. He was in Naumburg again on 27 October, but without going to his mother's house he left on the same day for Munich, where he stayed with von Seydlitz and enjoyed the company of his attractive wife, Irene. 'I almost talk to her in the second person singular.'[17] When he left a few days later to meet Paul Lanzky in Florence, she gave him tea and beef-steaks for the journey.[18]

Florence disappointed him, partly because of the noise, the cobblestones and the traffic,[19] partly because he had rainy weather,[20] but this time he enjoyed Lanzky's company, and they planned to go on to Vallombrosa together. Instead Nietzsche went on alone to Nice, staying once again at the Pension de Genève, which had been redecorated, but moving on before the end of November to a room in the rue St François de Paule. The weather was bad, but, in spite of what he had said in March about the folly of coming back to Nice, it was a relief to be there again, and to feel settled for the first time since leaving Sils in September. 'There is no substitute for the Nice air, and the splendid freedom of this cosmopolis. . . . Besides, one can live here cheaply, absurdly cheaply, and if I have not yet managed to do so, it is because of my eyesight and other imperfections.'[21] He even tried to persuade Gast that he, too, should settle in Nice. 'We ourselves, as hard-working and solitary animals, will keep tactfully out of each other's way, except for an occasional celebration of togetherness.'[22] They should both 'let Germany get on with being German. . . . Here one is so un-German.'[23] During his two months in the fatherland Nietzsche had seen quite clearly that 'I should still expect nothing there. It is a different kind of work and worker that is wanted.'[24]

Nietzsche's new room pleased him inordinately. Like his room in Sils it was small and simple. The carpet was dark yellow, the bed twice the size of his bed in Naumburg. There was no bric-à-brac in the room, and nothing superfluous, only a fairly large writing-table and a comfortable chair. He looked out on eucalyptus trees, the Mediterranean, the mountains and the brilliant sky.[25] He had taken to drinking a glass of beer as a nightcap. 'It is precisely in such invigorating climates that beer seems to act like a medicine.'[26]

Jenseits von Gut und Böse: Vorspiel einer Philosophie der Zukunft (*Beyond Good and Evil: Prelude to a Philosophy of the Future*), which he had begun in the summer and completed early in 1886, could not have been written by a man unwilling to put his sanity, or what remained of it, at risk. Previously, despite everything he had said about the inaccessibility of objective truth, Nietzsche had never quite given up the fantasy that the philosopher could stay afloat by clinging to a spar of veracity, by at least telling the truth about the impossibility of telling the truth. Religiously inclined to believe in redemption – if not by faith then by literary works – Nietzsche found it hard to break the habit sanctified by over two thousand years of philosophizing, the habit of worshipping truth as if it were divine. The self-conquest he aimed to achieve in *Jenseits* is suggested in the first paragraph with a stern question that had probably never been formulated before: what is the value of the will to truth? Why should we not prefer untruth or uncertainty or ignorance?[27] The answer is that we do. Our instinct for self-preservation teaches us to be superficial.[28] This book is written by a man in whom the instinct had become abnormally feeble.

Describing himself as an initiate of Dionysus, Nietzsche lets his readers taste 'the philosophy of this god',[29] who often considers how to help man forward, 'and to make him stronger, more evil and more profound than he is'.[30] Realizing that none of his earlier books had gone forward as they might have done from the premises set out in his essay on truth and falsehood, Nietzsche returns to his attack on the assumption that consciousness can report objectively on reality. The point of departure for all our logical procedures is the metaphysical assumption that things of higher value cannot derive 'from this transitory, seductive, deceptive, trivial world, from this tangle of desires and delusions'.[31] There must be another mode of existence, a reality behind the appearance, a *Ding an sich*. Though it might appear to be autonomous, our logic depends on value judgements which stem from this outlook and correspond to a 'physiological demand that a particular kind of life should be maintained'.[32] Most conscious thinking must be counted as an instinctive activity.[33] Falsification is a condition of our existence: to renounce it is to renounce life itself.[34]

One of Nietzsche's main statements is about the impossibility of making any statement. Who is making it? How is it even possible to say 'I think' or 'I will'? The premise from which Descartes – ignoring the body – had deduced existence raises metaphysical questions: 'Where does the concept *thinking* derive from? Why do I believe in cause and effect? What gives me the right to speak of an "I", and even of an "I" as cause, and finally of an "I" as cause of thought?'[35] 'It is falsifying the facts to say that the subject "I" is a condition of the predicate "think". A thought comes when "it" wants, not when "I" want. . . . *It* thinks, but that this "it" is identical with the good old "I" is at best only an assumption.'[36] The point had already been made in the eighteenth century by Lichtenberg, but Nietzsche's formulation of it was to be tremendously influential. When Freud published *Das Ich und das Es* (*The Ego and the Id*) in 1923, he acknowledged that he was taking the term *es* from Georg Groddeck, 'who never tired of insisting that what we call our ego is essentially passive in its behaviour, and that, as he puts it, we are "lived" by unknown and uncontrollable forces'.[37] (It might have been better if Latin had never been introduced into the Englishing of *ich* and *es*, but the translators, who were already committed to *ego*, opted for *id*.) Privately Freud taxed Groddeck – a doctor, the grandson of Nietzsche's old teacher Koberstein – with deriving the term *es* 'in a literary, not an associative way', from Nietzsche, and later Groddeck admitted to

using the word 'in connection with Nietzsche'.[38] Groddeck formulated the point in an essay: 'There is no such thing as an I; it is a lie, a
distortion, to say: "I think, I live." It should be: "it thinks, it
lives". It, that is the great mystery of the universe. . . . Science has
long since proved even to the pedants that this I is made up of
millions of smaller I's.'[39] Indubitably, Freud was indebted to
Nietzsche via Groddeck, but the essential point had already been
made in May 1871 by a boy who was not yet seventeen: 'It is a
mistake to say "I think",' wrote Arthur Rimbaud in a letter. 'One
should say: "I am being thought" – Forgive the wordplay. *I* is
someone else. So much the worse for the wood which finds it is a
violin.'[40]

Rimbaud's letters were not published until 1899, and though
Une saison en Enfer appeared in 1873, there is no reason to think it
had any influence on Nietzsche, who had arrived by a different
route at the experience of self-alienation, and therefore at the idea
that 'our body is only a social structure consisting of many souls'.[41]
Just as Descartes had assumed a coherent self that did the thinking,
Schopenhauer had assumed one that did the willing. But each act
of will involves a complex of sensations, emotions and thoughts,[42]
while thinking is no more than the relationship between the various
drives.[43] Nietzsche could now envisage himself – perhaps masochistically – in a state of Dionysian dispersal.

Dionysus was the god of masks, but Nietzsche's love of masks
was based on need. Without a mask one has no face to present, and
it is only through a mask that one can speak out what one has
learned, obeying Heraclitus' injunction to listen not to the voice of
men but to the voice of being. The mask can never be removed unless
there is another mask behind it, and we write books not to reveal but
to conceal what is inside us. Can a philosopher ever have 'final and
genuine' opinions? We should doubt 'whether, behind each cave,
there is not another deeper cave'.[44] There is something arbitrary
and suspect about each of his decisions to stop digging and lay his
spade aside at a particular point. 'Each philosophy *conceals* another
philosophy; each opinion is also a hiding-place, each word also a
mask.'[45] 'Every profound thinker is more afraid of being understood than of being misunderstood.'[46]

But Nietzsche could not restrain himself from making claims that
are inconsistent with this. A new breed of philosophers is appearing,

he announced, philosophers of the future.[47] Authentic philosophers are commanders and legislators. 'They say "This is how it must be." They are the ones to determine the Whither and Wherefore of mankind ... they reach creatively for the future, and everything that exists or has existed becomes for them a means, an instrument, a hammer. Their "knowledge" is creation, their creation legislation, and their will to truth – will to power. Are there such philosophers today?'[48] Though neither as unbalanced nor as blatantly self-advertising, this prefigures the claims he was going to make in the last few months before his capitulation to madness, when he believed himself to be holding the future of humanity in the palm of his hand.

Not that anyone as perceptive as Nietzsche could have looked at current events without misgivings and a desire to intervene. The prognosis he had made when writing on David Strauss was accurate: delusions of cultural supremacy might lead to 'the defeat – indeed the extirpation – of the German spirit in favour of the "German Reich".' Bismarck valued national prosperity as a means of retaining power, while Delbrück's economic policy tended to increase spending power throughout society. Despite the economic crash of 1873, industrialization continued rapidly as iron ore from Alsace and Lorraine was used in the Ruhr and the Saarland, and trade expanded as the railway system was developed and duties were reduced on imports from foreign iron manufacturers. The feeling of prosperity spread to small tradesmen, waiters, farmers. The big cities grew, and money changed hands rapidly as more and more people could afford to buy quick gratification. Prostitution thrived; entertainment in theatres, vaudevilles and cabarets became more vulgar, more sensational; wine bars and beer-halls luxuriated. The endemic greed for mindless self-indulgence was culturally destructive. As Nietzsche put it, it had become 'almost fashionable and patriotic' to question whether the disappearance of 'German profundity' should not be welcome.[49] Without mentioning Bismarck by name, *Jenseits* makes a caustic comparison between the genuine greatness of the idea which imparts quality to a deed or a thing, and the meretricious greatness of the statesman who builds up a new tower of Babel, 'a monstrosity of imperial power' which impresses the populace.[50] His leadership had forced the German people 'to sacrifice their old, well-tried virtues for the sake of a new and dubious mediocrity'.[51]

In building his monstrosity of imperial power, Bismarck had given Germany a political centre of gravity, but the capital of the *Reich*, Berlin, did not become a centre of artistic activity until much later. It was not Bismarck's policy to encourage freedom of expression. He favoured the newspapers that supported the government, giving them postal concessions and priority when official information was released, but generally the press had less freedom than in other Western countries, and there were numerous libel suits to show how morbidly sensitive he was to personal criticism. He tried to encourage the growth of national consciousness and to abort any public conscience that might have been critical.

To Karl Marx, as to the new Social Democratic Party, which gathered strength as the Liberal Party declined, it seemed that the only possible amelioration was political and economic; to Nietzsche, always primarily concerned with culture, it was obvious that socialism would be detrimental. The Europeans of the future would probably be 'talkative, weak-willed, and highly employable workers, who need masters, leaders, as badly as they need daily bread. The democratization of Europe is conducive to the production of a type prepared for slavery in the finest sense.'[52]

Not that the situation, as Nietzsche saw it, was hopeless for humanity, or even for Germany. He still took a high view of what 'could be cultivated out of man'[53] and he believed that 'man is the animal whose nature has not yet been fixed',[54] but for eighteen centuries one will has dominated Europe 'until finally a diminished, almost absurd species, a herd animal has been bred – ingratiating, sickly and mediocre – the modern European . . .'.[55] As for Germany, Wagner's music was paradigmatic – perhaps the over-full soul, young and antiquated at the same time, was most at home when hiding behind the refinements of decay. The Germans 'belong to the day before yesterday and the day after tomorrow – *they still have no today*'.[56]

The temptation to intervene must have been overwhelming, and the desire to alter the course of history was not merely an assertion of Nietzsche's will to power. If it was inevitable that democratization would breed the slave mentality, it was important that the slaves should have the best possible masters, who would understand the difference between master morality and slave morality – though Nietzsche was here falling into precisely the kind of contradistinction he had abjured when he insisted that two seemingly antithetical things may be the same thing at different stages of development. Christianity, he explained, had inherited slave morality from the Jewish prophets, who had inverted values, using 'world' as a word of abuse, while equating sensuality, violence and wealth with godlessness and evil.[57] Predatory men like Cesare Borgia had subsequently been stigmatized by moralists as 'sick', whereas in fact they were 'the healthiest of all tropical monsters'.[58] The imperatives of the herd morality are based on timidity: 'Sooner or later we would like a world in which there is *nothing left to be afraid of*. In modern Europe everything that tends *in this direction* is called "progress".'[59] The democratic movement was in the Judaeo-Christian tradition of slave morality, tenaciously opposing 'every special claim, every special right and privilege (which means, ultimately *every* right, for once everybody is equal, nobody needs "rights")'.[60]

In this contempt for the compassion and neighbourly love that Christianity advocates, and in this glorification of the ruthlessness typified by the Borgias, Nietzsche is reminiscent of de Sade, who condemned pity as a sin against the inequality decreed by nature. In *Juliette*, Noirceuil mocks at Christianity's hopes of converting tyrants to the precept of brotherliness. Representing the weak, religion has to use the language of the weak.[61] But no one can be expected to love his neighbour:

> To abstain from mutual injury, violence, exploitation, to equate one's will with someone else's . . . reveals itself as will towards the *denial* of life, the principle of dissolution and decay . . . life itself *essentially* consists of dispossessing, injuring, overpowering the foreign and the more feeble, suppression, severity, imposing one's own forms, annexing and – at least and at mildest – exploiting.[62]

This could easily be mistaken for a quotation from *Juliette*, but it is from *Jenseits*. All human refinements, it argues, have been achieved by aristocratic societies, and these have invariably come into existence when one nation, race or culture has been conquered by another – less civilized, probably, but with a stronger lust for power. (Nietzsche hardly ever substantiates his historical generalizations with examples or documentation.) The conquerors 'were more *complete* human beings (which on every level also means "more completely bestial")'.[63] What an aristocracy needs is the faith that society is there to serve it. Once it begins to feel guilty about its privileges, decadence sets in, as it did before the French Revolution, when the nobility sacrificed itself in excesses of sublime disgust.[64] The aristocrat should believe that he has duties only towards his equals.[65] Once the ruling caste relaxes its severity, mediocrity emerges; the debasing virtues canvassed by the slave morality are moderation, industriousness, duty, dignity, patience, neighbourly love.[66] A morality of utility is evolved,[67] while religions such as Christianity and Buddhism teach the lowly to accept hardship and humiliation in their everyday life, deluding themselves that through piety they can simultaneously belong to a higher order.[68]

Nietzsche was to call his book 'frightening . . . very black, almost ink-fish.' And though he mentions Byron, Musset, Poe, Leopardi, Kleist and Gogol, he was probably thinking of himself when he said that poets revenge themselves in their works for an inner pollution, 'often taking flight from an all-too-persistent memory, often bogged down and almost enamoured of the muck, until they become will-o'-the-wisps around the swamp, *pretending* to be stars – people then call them idealists.'[69] But if he felt inwardly polluted, the act of writing was attractive because it combined vengeance with the sensation of self-cleansing. Without trying to establish any intimate relationship with the reader, Nietzsche tells him that he will be unable to guess at what the book's ingredients were like before they were translated into words. When they occurred to him, the ideas were 'colourful, young and mischievous, full of thorns and secret spices that made me sneeze and laugh'; now some of them are 'about to become truths: they already look so immortal, so heartbreakingly honest, so boring'.[70] For the writer the process matters more than the product, the pleasure of making the mask more than the efficacy of the disguise.

So it was not difficult for him to go on writing without any certainty of publication. He offered the book to Hermann Credner, whose reply he found one night, pushed under the door of his room. Credner accepted 'with pleasure, and expressly wishes to be counted among my admirers'.[71] 'What he wrote gave me such pleasure that I could not help doing a little round-dance in my shirt.

Despite the cold, for I have not been heating the room till today.'[72] Förster had given him some woollen shirts, and Nietzsche had been wearing them as if they were vests.[73] He was still intending to publish the book as a continuation of *Morgenröte*,[74] but before the end of the month he had decided on giving it independent status.[75]

Before leaving for Paraguay at the beginning of February 1886, Elisabeth and Förster sent him a gold ring engraved with the words 'Think lovingly of B. and E.' Writing to his mother, he said that he would;[76] writing to Elisabeth he rejected the suggestion that a piece of land in Paraguay should be named after him, but said he would send her everything he possessed if it would help to bring her back soon.[77] Though he had seen little of her since August 1884, when they were in Zürich together, her departure heightened his sense of isolation. Replying to a pre-Christmas letter from Rohde, he wrote: 'It seems to me that you have a better understanding of life, having placed yourself in its midst; while I view it from an ever-increasing distance – perhaps more and more clearly, fearfully, comprehensively, attractively. But woe betide me if I am one day unable to bear this alienation! One grows old, one feels full of longing.'[78] With Overbeck too, Nietzsche could not help feeling envious of married companionship: 'Thanks to your wife, things are a hundred times better for you than for me. You have a nest together. I have, at best, a *cave*. . . . I have spent the winter feeling *profondement triste*, tormented day and night by my problems, really more in hell than in my cave. . . . Occasional contact with people is like a holiday, a redemption from "me".'[79]

His eyes were still worrying him, however ruthlessly he ignored the pain while working. 'Sooner or later my eyes will function only in the shade of forests, but *old friends* must live near these forests.'[80] He was planning to leave Nice on 13 April because of the summer brightness.[81] Gast, who was at his father's house in Annaberg, near Chemnitz, offered his Venetian flat to Nietzsche, whose departure was delayed by bad weather in Nice and the danger that a wave of cholera would reach Venice, but he installed himself in the flat on the last day of the month.[82] Within a week he was planning to move on. 'I myself [am] perhaps on the far side of good and evil, but not of disgust, boredom, *malinconia* and pain in the eyes.'[83] He must have strained them very badly by writing the book: the compulsion had been irresistible, and there was no one to take dictation from him. 'My eyes torment me day and night. The weather is brilliantly bright and fresh, but I must not look at anything, and everything *hurts* me.'[84] He decided to go home, stopping at Munich en route. 'This time your son really needs to let himself be taken care of.'[85] In Munich he tried to convince the conductor Hermann Levi that Gast's opera deserved a production, and, after failing, he left on 11 May. The train was due to arrive at 3.53 a.m. in Leipzig, where he would have to wait at the station for the first train to Naumburg. His one piece of good luck was that he had left Venice just in time to avoid the cholera and the quarantine which was to make it impossible for anyone to leave the city.

The publication of *Jenseits* was delayed by Schmeitzner, who did not want to publish it, but did not want anyone else to either, and had involved Credner in protracted litigation. In the end Nietzsche disappointedly decided to have the book printed at his own expense, but not in such a small edition as the final part of *Zarathustra*. In effect he became his own publisher, with the printer, C. G. Naumann, as his distributor: 'Assuming that 300 copies are sold, I recover my expenses and can repeat the experiment.'[86] But Schmeitzner had sold only about sixty or seventy copies of *Zarathustra*.[87] Nietzsche was trying to arrange for his former publisher, Fritzsch, to take over his earlier books from Schmeitzner. Fritzsch was sufficiently interested to visit Schmeitzner in Chemnitz, but his price was too high – twelve thousand marks.[88]

Erwin Rohde had been offered a professorial chair at Leipzig, where Nietzsche went to visit him and to hear him lecture. It was their last meeting before Nietzsche went mad, and it was mutually disappointing. 'I did not have a single word of intelligent conversation with him,' Nietzsche reported. He was 'sitting there like a martyr in bed, and after six weeks of lecturing he accepted an invitation to Heidelberg'.[89] Writing after Nietzsche's breakdown, Rohde thought he could recall 'an indescribable atmosphere of strangeness, something that seemed quite uncanny . . . as if he came from a country where no one else lived'.[90] When *Jenseits* was published, Rohde's reaction was equally unsympathetic. 'It is no more than the after-dinner discourses of a man who has overeaten – elevated here and there by inebriation, but full of a repulsive disgust with everyone and everything. . . . Viewpoint is dictated by mood, and then everything is made to agree with this viewpoint, as if there were no other.'[91] Aware that the book would tax the good will of his friends, Nietzsche implored Overbeck not to let it alienate him. 'If you find the book insufferable, perhaps a hundred details in it will not be.'[92] Possibly it would also help to illuminate *Zarathustra*, 'an *incomprehensible* book because it is founded on experiences I share with nobody'.[93]

On 5 June Nietzsche moved into lodgings in Leipzig. He sent a telegram to Gast, asking him to come for a week. He arrived with a pleasant surprise, a partita based on Nietzsche's setting of Lou's poem 'Lebensgebet' ('Life Prayer'). Paul Widemann came from Dresden to visit them before Gast left – after keeping Nietzsche company for two weeks – on 20 June.[94] Nietzsche stayed on in Leipzig for another week. He broke his journey to Sils-Maria twice, spending one night (28 June) in Rorschach, on Lake Constance, and the next in Chur. On the 30th he travelled on the post-coach through the Julier Pass, and within a week he had received the last of Gast's proof corrections for *Jenseits*.

The first month in Sils went badly for him: 'constantly indisposed and enervated, sleeping badly, eyes painful. . . . What I lack is the right *nourishment*, which I have in Nice, the right *room*, with good light, and the right company.'[95] But his health and his spirits both improved during August. 'The recipe I prescribed for myself was very strange: to go into the hotel and *eat in company* – the same meals as *everybody else*. This has got me back on my feet. (To feel well I need plenty of nourishment: if only I were rich enough for this "treatment", which suits me. . . .)'[96]

On 5 August a telegram arrived from Fritzsch: 'Finally in possession!'[97] He had come to terms with Schmeitzner. The good news coincided exactly with the publication of *Jenseits*, and therefore with a new sense of freedom. Two weeks earlier he had written: 'The printing of the book is keeping me more occupied than is comfortable; liberty will come (together with authorization to think about something new) when the first copies are ready.'[98] As soon as they were, he wasted little time. By 16 August he had completed a preface for the second part of Fritzsch's new edition of *Menschliches, Allzumenschliches* (having optimistically written a preface for the first part in Nice during the spring) and by the 29th a preface, subtitled 'Attempt at a Self-Criticism', for *Geburt der Tragödie*. 'Retrospectively,' he wrote to Gast, 'it seems to me fortunate that

I did not have either *Menschliches, Allzumenschliches* or *Geburt der Tragödie* to hand when I wrote the prefaces: for, between ourselves, I can no longer bear all this old stuff.'[99]

The preface to the second part of *Menschliches, Allzumenschliches* raises the question of whether his personal experience of illness had any supra-personal relevance. He was addressing himself, he said, to

> those who have the hardest time of it, you rare spirits, the most jeopardized, most intellectual, bravest spirits, who must be the *conscience* of the modern soul, and as such must be possessed of its *consciousness*, concentrating all the disease, poison and danger that only modern times could have produced – you whose lot it is to be more diseased than any individual if only because you are not mere individuals.[100]

By using disease as a metaphor, he had empowered himself to view his private suffering as qualifying him for the place he had assumed in the superior tribunal. And, having seated himself there, he could look back on his battle for self-conquest as if he had won, as if the disease had been routed. 'One should speak only when one cannot remain silent, and only about what one has conquered. . . . The man who is suffering has as yet no right to pessimism.'[101]

'Attempt at a Self-Criticism' is no less outspoken than his letter to Gast: *Geburt der Tragödie* is condemned as 'badly written, turgid, embarrassing, mad and confused in its imagery, sentimental, in places sickly sweet . . .'.[102] Nor was Nietzsche now satisfied with his explanation of how tragedy had emerged. Could it not be said that Dionysian madness had been the source of both comedy and tragedy? Surely the growth of optimism, rationality, utilitarianism and democracy had been symptomatic of decadence?

Without mentioning Christianity, the book, he could now see, had evidenced an inclination to relegate morality to the domain of illusion: Dionysus had been the first name he found for the Antichrist. But his own Dionysian tendencies had been expressed in Schopenhauerian terms, and he had been naively optimistic both about 'the German spirit' and about German music, 'which is steeped in romanticism and as un-Greek as any art form could be . . . doubly dangerous for a people that loves drink and regards obscurity as a virtue'.[103] He was now going further than before towards identifying madness with the Dionysian, and presenting it as the polar alternative to Christianity. Sending the new preface to Gast, Nietzsche wrote: 'You have *carte blanche* to make changes.'[104] He was then to send the fair copy direct to Fritzsch without even telling Nietzsche what his revisions were.

When Meta von Salis arrived in Sils she was amazed at how well Nietzsche looked. 'He seemed younger than when we last met, and he was carrying on a lively conversation with the lady sitting on his right. . . . When he came over to us, and I introduced my mother and my friend, he was enchantingly warm and kind to my mother.' Later he took Meta to the Chasté peninsula, telling her how strongly it reminded him of the Levantine Riviera. To excuse the 'irritated tone' of his writings, he told her that the isolated thinker, whose books provoked no applause or response, automatically raised his voice.

In fact *Jenseits* was producing some favourable reactions. More tolerant than Rohde, the sixty-eight-year-old Burckhardt praised 'your astonishing survey of the whole area of current spiritual movements, and the power and art in your subtle delineation of details'.[105] The anti-Romantic historian Hippolyte Taine, Nietzsche's senior by sixteen years, wrote to congratulate him on the book, and in the Bern newspaper *Der Bund*, J.V.Widmann, a friend of Brahms, published an enthusiastic review: 'Intellectual explosives, like the other kind, can be very useful. . . . But it is as well to put up a warning sign where they are being stored: "There is dynamite here." . . . Nietzsche is the first man who has found an escape route, but it is so terrifying that one feels genuinely frightened to see him treading this lonely, previously untrodden path.'[106] Copying out most of the review for Malwida, Nietzsche underlined the phrase about dynamite and asked her not to read the book: 'Let us assume that people will be permitted to read it in about the year 2000.'[107]

On 25 September he left Sils for Ruta, near Rapallo. 'I have never lain about so much in true Robinson [Crusoe] insularity and oblivion.'[108] He loved the landscape but hated the food served in the Albergo d'Italia. Declining an opportunity to visit Corsica with Paul Lanzky, he went back to Nice on 20 October. 'My three-quarters blindness forced me to return to Nice . . . which my eyes have "learned by heart".'[109] He settled, once again, in the Pension de Genève. During October, he wrote the fifth book of *Die fröhliche*

Wissenschaft, which was added to the new edition of 1886. His epigraph for the new section – about seventy pages – was a saying of the Maréchal de Turenne, a seventeenth-century French general, who must have been as ruthlessly habituated as Nietzsche was to self-conquest: 'Carcasse, tu trembles? Tu tremblerais bien davantage, si tu savais où je te mène.' In what follows it becomes clear that Nietzsche saw himself as leading humanity into a solitude which had never previously been experienced. The believer never believes himself to be alone: God is always there as the silent partner in a dialogue.[110] Faith, therefore, can be seen as an alternative to willpower: 'Buddhism and Christianity perhaps both owed their origin and their rapidly won popularity to a great collapse and *disease of the will.* . . . Both religions taught fanaticism in periods when willpower was exhausted. . . . Once a man arrives at the conviction that he *needs* to be commanded, he becomes "a believer".'[111]

Insofar as the will to truth is founded on the religious assumption that truth is divine, Nietzsche wrote, it is a destructive principle, hostile to life, when life seems to aim at dissemblance, error, self-delusion. Freud's idea of a death-wish is closely prefigured in Nietzsche's conception of a 'covert will to death', which he equates here with the will to truth. What he says about it is similar to what he had said in *Jenseits* about Christian morality: that it is essentially a 'denial of life'. This is similar to the view that Freud adopted towards the end of his life – that civilization is 'founded on the suppression of instincts', that each individual is 'potentially an enemy of civilization', which was 'built up on the coercion and renunciation' of natural impulses.[112] It is a point that Robert Musil makes when his man without qualities, Ulrich, observes that if humanity could dream collectively, it would dream Moosbrugger, the rapist-murderer.[113]

The other point at which Nietzsche's book anticipates Freud is the suggestion that consciousness may be pathological. Leibniz had already distinguished between perception and consciousness, suggesting that consciousness was not a necessary attribute of experience, but an accidental result of instinctual activity, something less fundamental than the drive to reconstitute a diversity as a unity. Nietzsche's summary barely stops short of postulating an unconscious area of the mind: 'what we call consciousness does *not by any means* constitute *the whole* of our spiritual and psychic world, but only one state (perhaps pathological)'.[114] It is against this perspective that Nietzsche now looks, more charitably than before, at Hegel, who had 'dared to explain how one genus of concepts develops out of another'.[115] Without Hegel there could have been no Darwin.

If consciousness is pathological, art and philosophy are therapeutic: 'they always presuppose suffering'.[116] There are two kinds of ailment. Those who suffer from 'the *over-fullness of life*' need a Dionysian art and a tragic outlook; those suffering from 'the *impoverishment of life*' need either tranquillity and redemption through art or 'inebriation, convulsion, anaesthesia and insanity'.[117] Taking Wagner and Schopenhauer as exemplars of Romanticism, Nietzsche defines it as corresponding to the dual needs of the latter type. Dionysian richness in the 'fullness of life' empowers a god or a man to afford any luxury of disintegration or negation: 'the desire for *destruction*, change or development can be an expression of an overflowing energy that is pregnant with future', whereas the anarchist's desire for destruction derives from feeling underprivileged and outraged by everything that exists.[118] Nietzsche is no longer using the word 'Dionysian' as antithetical to 'Apollonian' but as synonymous with extreme plenitude.

He is in a position to characterize himself by contrasting himself with the Romantic, the Epicurean and the Christian: he is a Dionysian pessimist, constantly misunderstood because constantly developing. He is becoming younger, more in touch with the future. 'We are powerfully pushing our roots deeper and deeper into evil, at the same time as embracing the heavens more and more lovingly, expansively, sucking their light in thirstily with our twigs and leaves.'[119] At the same time he gives a new twist to the argument that philosophy must relate to the philosopher's health. Spinoza's interest in the will to life derived from his being a consumptive.[120] All philosophical idealism has been 'something like a disease',[121] unless, as with Plato, it was a prudent attempt to preserve equilibrium against the pressure of 'a dangerously excessive healthiness, *extremely potent* senses'.[122] As for us moderns – Nietzsche was probably thinking of himself – 'Perhaps we are merely not healthy enough to be in need of Plato's idealism. We are not afraid of the senses because – .'[123] The reason is withheld. Nine months later, in a letter to Taine, he explained some of his books in terms of health. *Morgenröte* was written when he was 'most painfully ill . . . face to face with death'; for *Die fröhliche Wissenschaft* he was 'indebted to the first sun-rays of returning health'.[124]

When a letter arrived from Paraguay urging him to invest his money in the colony, he did not find it easy to refuse. He wrote for advice to Overbeck,[125] who reinforced his resistance to sisterly pressure. Nietzsche bolstered his refusal by referring to his friend's advice,[126] with the result that she never forgave Overbeck. Nietzsche tried to expiate the guilt he felt at saying no by writing to tell his mother that he had five hundred francs to spare. What would she like for Christmas? He could afford a little luxury for her, he said.[127] In fact he was in arrears with his rent, and he was suffering from 'permanently blue fingers'[128] in a north-facing room, feeling too poor either to heat it or rent a south-facing room. 'How I have frozen during my seven winters in the south! . . . Reckoning my summers in the Engadin at a monthly average of 10, 11 and 7 degrees Celsius (the last being September) you establish the *frostiest* existence you could possibly have in this life.'[129] These rueful calculations contrast with Zarathustra's habit of mocking the winter with cold baths.

On 3 January 1887 he finally moved into a south-facing room in the rue des Ponchettes, the twenty-first room, he calculated, that he had occupied during his seven winters in Genoa and Nice. He had looked at about forty rooms during the last few months, but nearly all of them had been too dirty.[130] But he was not too self-absorbed to feel anxious about Gast, who, still frustrated as a composer, was reviewing music for the *Süddeutsche Presse* at four pfennigs a line. Nietzsche, apprehensive that he might break down, offered to lend him two thousand marks.[131] Fortunately Gast refused.

It was a severe winter, and in Nietzsche's new room, which he did not heat, his fingers still went blue with cold.[132] In spite of his stringent economies, he could not keep abreast of his rent payments. On 12 February, before the next instalment of his pension fell due, he was already asking Overbeck to send money and to address it to him at the Pension de Genève: at the new boarding house the letter might have been opened before it reached him.[133] Nor was there any pleasure in writing with blue fingers: 'I am amusing myself and recovering my strength with the coldest of rational criticism. . . .

The result will be an attack on the whole idea of causality in philosophy up to the present, and some still worse things.'[134]

Though ill and depressed, coughing, shivering, and irritated by the noisy carnival crowds in the streets,[135] he was delighted at his belated discovery of Dostoevsky.[136] Here, he said, was the only psychologist from whom he could learn anything. He probably never read *The Brothers Karamazov*, the novel with the greatest affinity to his own work, but in 1887, chancing on a French translation of *Notes from the Underground* in a bookshop, he was reminded of the luck that had led him to Schopenhauer at the age of twenty-one. He went on to read Dostoevsky's *The House of the Dead*, 'one of the most human books ever written',[137] and *Insulted and Injured*.

In the early morning of Ash Wednesday, 23 February, six hours after the last *girandola* of the carnival, Nice was shaken by an earthquake. 'How amusing when the old buildings rattle like coffee mills and the ink bottle acquires a life of its own! When the streets fill with half-naked figures and shattered nervous systems!'[138] He walked cheerfully around the streets, observing people's reactions. Muffled in their warmest clothes and surrounded by howling dogs, they were eating and sleeping in the streets, preferring the cold to the risk that their houses could collapse on top of them. Each tremor brought a new wave of conviction that the end was at hand.[139] At the Pension de Genève, the fourth floor, where he had written nearly half of *Zarathustra*, was damaged irreparably. 'I am grieved by the transitoriness of things.'[140]

He left Nice on 3 April for Cannobio, on the Lago Maggiore, where the sunlight was too bright for his eyes,[141] but he stayed for over three weeks: 'This place is more beautiful than anywhere else on the Riviera.'[142] 'Each morning surprised me with the splendour of its colours.'[143] But he was profoundly depressed: 'Nothing comes to me from outside to encourage or stimulate me.'[144] He was forcing himself to go walking each day for between four and six hours, 'but for a year, at the very least, I have not had a single "good day" – a day of feeling fresh, strong, bright, spirited, full of energy.'[145] He felt abandoned by his friends, unloved, unappreciated, even as a writer. It seemed to him that with *Zarathustra* he had 'issued a cry from the depths of the soul',[146] without hearing a single sound in answer, while only 114 copies of *Jenseits* had been sold.[147] He neither expected to live long, nor wanted to. 'I will not conceal a constantly deepening desire for death.'[148] But he would leave something behind, a legacy that would be dangerous for Europe: 'With me a *catastrophe* is being prepared. I know its name, but I will not pronounce it.'[149] With at least part of his mind he may have wanted, vengefully, to expedite the catastrophe. The inner pollution was becoming unbearable: how could he but be a will-o'-the-wisp around the swamp?

He thought of taking a cold-water cure in Switzerland, 'but I am more afraid of the Swiss than of loneliness'.[150] He also thought of going back to Venice, but 'everything protested, especially the eyes and the head: just had four of my frightful attacks; a frightful melancholy and irritability as result; a deep need for *silence*'.[151] Finally he left for Zürich, arriving on the evening of the 28th. He had two meetings with Meta von Salis and one with Resa von Schirnhofer, but the reunion he enjoyed most was with Overbeck, who came from Basel to see him. After a stay of ten days Nietzsche left for Chur and went for walks in the surrounding woods to rest his eyes.[152] He would have to stay for about a month before it was warm enough in a higher altitude. Even walking he found burdensome, 'in that I am really too tired, but have nothing else to do'.[153]

On 8 June he left Chur, hoping to settle in Lenzerheide for the summer – it would have been quieter than Sils – but he stayed only four days. He arrived in Sils with a violent headache, and for twelve hours he could scarcely stop vomiting.[154] Afterwards he found himself with a heavy cold, a temperature, no appetite, sleepless nights, giddiness and lassitude.[155] He could look out of his window at the snow which never melted on the mountains, but it had no effect on his unhealthy sweating.[156] He felt 'mortally wounded: it astonishes me that I am still alive'.[157] Even on days without physical discomfort he was lethargic, perpetually irked by the failure of his books to produce any reactions,[158] though he was aware that 'it will do me no good when people begin to understand me'.[159] It was gratifying to hear from Widmann that Brahms was interested in *Jenseits* and about to read *Die fröhliche Wissenschaft*,[160] but when Nietzsche sent the composer his setting of Lou's poem, he received only a formal acknowledgment.

If it was possible to intensify his sense of isolation, the news of Heinrich von Stein's death had that effect. Barely thirty, he had suddenly had a heart attack. 'I really loved him; it seemed to me that he was being saved up for a later period of my life. He was one of the few men whose *existence* gave me joy.'[161]

When Nietzsche's health improved, during the second half of June, he set to work on what he called a polemic, *Zur Genealogie der Moral* (*On the Genealogy of Morals*). The title is apt. The fifth of the nine sections in *Jenseits* had been called 'On the Natural History of Morals', and now Nietzsche devotes a whole book to this subject, concentrating on the evolution of good and evil as concepts. Without abandoning his method of writing in numbered paragraphs or sections, he organizes them into three essays, developing a coherent argument in each. The first is about the difference between 'bad' and 'evil', and about contrasting meanings of 'good' in master and slave moralities. He overturns the unhistorical assumption of 'English psychologists' that the idea of goodness was originated by those who benefited from altruistic actions. The evolution of language had been determined by the dominant groups, who had used their name-giving prerogative to glorify themselves and their qualities, while denigrating those of other groups.[162] 'Good' had been cognate with 'noble', 'bad' with plebeian. (The association of 'high-born' with 'high-minded' and 'low-born' with 'base' still survives in most languages.) Nietzsche could cite Theognis as the mouthpiece of the Greek nobility in the sixth century BC. The words for good, *esthlos* and *agathos*, had connotations of nobility and bravery, while their antonyms *kakos* and *deilos* suggested plebeian cowardice. In Homer the heroes are always noble, the commoners always feeble, contemptible or cunning. The Latin *malus* (bad) may have derived from the Greek *melas* (black, dark) and from the assumption that the blond Aryan conqueror was morally superior to the dark Italian native, while the Gaelic word *fin*, meaning good, noble, pure, had originally meant blond.[163] In English, fair is both the opposite of dark and the opposite of foul; in German *schlecht* (bad) is related to *schlicht* (plain, simple). Based securely on philological knowledge, and owing nothing to speculative teleology, these etymological paragraphs are richly suggestive.

Turning to the emergence of the priestly sect, Nietzsche suggests that its emphasis on cleanliness made abstinence into a virtue. The various lusts – for power, for conquest, for love-making, for revenge – all came to seem dangerous, and man became an interesting animal because he now had an opportunity denied to other predatory beasts – the opportunity of doing evil.[164] While the values of the warrior-leaders presupposed a healthy interest in fighting, hunting, adventure and dancing, the achievement of the priests was to poison the bloodstream: the Judaeo-Christian morality was a slave morality, the outcome of an ethical revolution fuelled by resentment, 'the *ressentiment* of those who are incapable of taking action and make up for it by means of an imaginary revenge'.[165] The weak can feel superior to the strong if they can look pityingly at them, thinking: "They know not what they do.'[166] Thomas Aquinas had rejoiced malignantly at the idea that the world would be destroyed by fire on the Day of Judgement,[167] while the Apocalypse of St John was 'the most rabid of all the literary outbursts that the spirit of vengeance has on its conscience'.[168]

The idea of evil popularized by the morality of *ressentiment* corresponds to the idea of goodness proposed by the aristocratic morality: the qualities of the good warrior – audacious pride, courageous pugnacity, destructiveness, cruelty, contempt for safety and moderation – must be contested if the priests were to achieve power. It is in this context that Nietzsche introduces his much-misunderstood phrase 'the blond beast'.[169] From the examples he gives, which include Arabian and Japanese aristocracies, it is clear that he is not referring to the Nordic race. His argument is that the noble human animal is naturally rapacious, but from the viewpoint of the victims – wounded, plundered, humiliated, ravished, en-slaved – the behaviour of heroes and demigods cannot be admirable. If the domestication of the human animal is progress, *ressentiment* must be recognized as its most important cultural implement.[170] But Nietzsche's point is that we have regressed. The blond beast is frightening, but does less damage than the atrophied mediocrity of the modern world. When he says that contemporary Europe stinks with sickly men,[171] we are reminded of Zarathustra's sensitivity to the odours exuded by his visitors, and Nietzsche goes on to equate nihilism with the disappearance of human love, reverence and hopes for humanity. 'We are tired *of Man*.'[172] When people were not ashamed of their cruelty, life on earth had been gayer than it was now.[173]

The second essay, titled 'Guilt, Bad Conscience and the Like', leads up to an explanation of bad conscience as 'the grave illness humanity had to contract when it underwent the most fundamental of all its transformations – when it finally found itself constricted by society and peace.'[174] Nietzsche's concept of *Verinnerlichung* (internalization) anticipates Jung's 'introversion', reviving a seventeenth-century word to suggest the process by which libido is turned inwards. As Nietzsche puts it, 'All instincts that cannot be released outwards will turn inwards',[175] and he equates this with the development of 'soul'. 'The whole inner world, originally as thin as if stretched between two membranes, expanded outwards and upwards, acquiring depth, breadth and height as outward discharge was blocked.'[176] Destructiveness and aggressive cruelty were therefore turned inwards against the self. Here Nietzsche could draw analogically on the results of self-observation during his life-long experience of 'self-conquest'. He contended that the change in humanity had not been gradual or voluntary or a mere matter of organic adaptation to new circumstances, that it had not only been inaugurated by violence but maintained by violence.[177] The violence done (or threatened) by the state while imposing discipline on the individual was parallel to the violence done by the individual to himself. No one could have been a better witness than Nietzsche was of

this secret self-ravishment, this artistic cruelty, this lust to impose form on oneself as on a tough, resistant, suffering material, cauterizing into oneself a will, a criticism, a contradiction, a contempt, a negation; this uncanny, weirdly enjoyable labour of a voluntarily divided soul making itself suffer out of pleasure in causing suffering, finally this whole, *active* 'bad conscience' – you can guess already – as the true womb of all ideal and imaginative experience.[178]

Bad conscience is a physical disorder comparable with pregnancy.

In the third essay, 'The Significance of Ascetic Ideals,' Nietzsche will admit that at one time the philosophic spirit could not have existed without an aura of holiness: the caterpillar priest would turn into the butterfly philosopher.[179] And in the second essay Nietzsche uses his experience of siding severely against himself as a base for thinking his way into the Christian cruelties. In the tribe based on a nexus of blood relationships, the communal sense of indebtedness to the forefathers grew insepar-able from worship. The idea of bad conscience became integral to the idea of God.[180] Whereas the Greeks had used their gods as an antidote to guilt feelings, blaming bad behaviour on divinely induced delusions, the Christians would always have a good reason for thinking themselves unworthy when animal instincts were interpreted as disobedience to God's will.[181] Guilt feelings spread like a polyp until the irredeemable indebtedness gives rise to the ideas of eternal punishment and original sin. The debt has become so great that God has to pay it by sacrificing himself.[182] But the idea of crucifixion derives from man's cruelty to himself: he is declaring himself bankrupt by increasing his indebtedness to an amount that he will never be able to repay.

Analysing the relationship between the sense of guilt and the idea of debt, Nietzsche could point to the German word *Schuld*, which means both guilt and debt, but his findings are relevant to all religious, moral and legal systems. Taking the opposite view from Kant's, he maintained that autonomy and morality were mutually exclusive: the 'sovereign individual' would have to break free from 'the morality of *mores*'.[183] But disciplinary systems function on the assumption that the wrongdoer becomes a debtor to the community.[184] The creditor – Church or state – must be allowed to demonstrate its power by inflicting pain and humiliation on the culprit: in this way accounts can be balanced.[185] In a discussion of punishment which substantially anticipates the book by Michel Foucault,[186] Nietzsche gives horrendous examples of judicial savagery,[187] but his contention is that there was nothing unhealthy about the 'disinterested malice' of spectators at public torture and executions.[188] Suffering was never pointless either for the Christian, who had built such an elaborate superstructure of salvation on it, or for ancient man, who always connected it with either the spectator or the aggressor.[189] The modern mistake was to confuse the origin of punishment with its purpose. The attitude behind it was parallel to that taken towards the captive enemy: 'Woe to the loser!'[190] The idea of justice could not have been evolved before a legal code was instituted, because nature operates through aggression and exploitation.[191] Legality is an artificial state based on the restriction of the will to life and the will to power,[192] while punishment is hardly ever 'useful' in the way it is expected to be. The worm of conscience can seldom bite into the hardened skin of the convict.[193]

The essay on the meaning of ascetic ideals is the least intrinsically interesting of the three, and the least relevant to the main subject, but it contains some indirect self-portraiture. Philosophers, he tells us, always feel 'irritable and rancorous' towards sensuality.[194] 'We admire silence, coldness, nobility, distance, in general everything that does not put the soul on the defensive.'[195] Schopenhauer had treated sexuality as a personal enemy,[196] and 'Every artist knows how damaging intercourse is in states of great spiritual tension or preparation; those with the greatest power and the best instincts do not need to learn this from experience, from unfortunate experience. For the benefit of the evolving work their "maternal" instinct disposes ruthlessly of all other stored or accumulated energy, all animal vigour.'[197]

The argument in this essay becomes more confused than anywhere else in the book, partly, perhaps, because Nietzsche is trying (though not explicitly) to validate the authority of the sick philosopher. Since the healthy cannot be expected to take care of the sick, we need doctors and nurses who are themselves sick.[198] The healthy man can digest his misdeeds as he does his meals, even if there are tough morsels to be chewed,[199] but sickliness is normal. Man is the sick animal, insecure, inconstant, indeterminate.[200] The feeling 'if only I could be someone else' is all too common,[201] and self-disgust is the strongest factor in the formation of a herd.[202] The ascetic ideal is prompted by a self-protective instinct in a degenerating life trying to keep itself alive: the wounds man inflicts on himself compel him to live.[203] Nietzsche, unable to resolve the conflict between his criticisms of the life-denying impulses in asceticism and his defence of reclusiveness in the philosopher, promises a full-scale history of European nihilism under the title *Der Wille zur Macht: Versuch einer Umwertung aller Werte* (*The Will to Power: Attempt at a Revaluation of All Values*). He describes this as a 'work in progress', but it seems he had no intention of publishing it, or anything else, for some time. *Genealogie* was to be the last of his 'efforts to make my previous writing comprehensible, and nothing will be printed for several years now – I must withdraw absolutely into myself and wait until I may shake the last fruit from my tree.'[204] He knew he was setting himself an almost impossible task, but before he had started on

Zarathustra, the prospect of writing it had been hardly less daunting.

The book was written very quickly. The manuscript of *Genealogie*, begun, so far as Nietzsche could remember, about 10 July, using notes that dated from January, was sent off to the printer on 30 July.[205] 'I worked very hard all through July', he told his mother. 'It seems that both my health and my spiritual strength have returned. I have also made several improvements in my daily routine, with decidedly favourable results.'[206] He was getting up at five to drink a glass of bitter cocoa, going back to sleep, getting up again at six, dressing, and then drinking a large cup of tea before starting work. Instead of eating the *table d'hôte* meal in the hotel, as he had last year, he paid the same price for a solitary meal half an hour earlier, eating the same food each day – a beef-steak with spinach and a large omelette with apple jelly. In the evening he had a few slices of ham, two egg-yolks and two rolls. Nor was he drinking any wine or spirits. 'In July I had only three big attacks of my headache with vomiting all day, which, compared with the previous month, is real progress.'[207]

It was an unusually hot summer. Both the hotels in Sils were full, and almost every family in the village was renting a room or two to visitors. About 18 July Meta von Salis came to spend seven weeks there with a friend, Hedwig Kym. Meta now had a doctorate in history, having written a thesis on Agnès de Poitou, mother of Henri IV.[208]

Almost every morning and sometimes in the afternoon Nietzsche came to see us. When the weather was fine and the heat moderate, he would take us for walks; otherwise we would have intimate conversations in our room. . . . Nietzsche loved to 'recover' in my company from his loneliness, his work and sometimes from tiresome visitors. In my room, which was full of flowers, we would sit for hours, I with work in my hand, he talking about what he had been thinking, reading, or experiencing. . . . After the expenditure of spiritual strength, tracing morality to its deepest roots without ever fighting shy of the results, after grim inner tension and uncomfortable discoveries, Nietzsche needed relaxation for a while in friendly surroundings. He himself was kind, easily wounded, conciliatory, anxious not to give offence, but his task demanded uncompromising harshness, bringing pain and bitterness both to him and other people.[209]

When he went boating with them on Lake Silvaplana they taught him how to use the rudder. On their last evening in Sils they went for a walk on the sandy shore. There was a light breeze, and the waves, he said, looked 'as though they wanted to reach out their hands in farewell'. As they walked for the last time, over the barren strip of field between the lake and the village, he said: 'Now I'm a widower and orphan again.'[210]

By the end of August the Sils hotels were emptying, but Nietzsche stayed on for nearly three weeks of September. At the beginning of the month Paul Deussen, who had just been appointed to a professorship of philosophy in Berlin, and who was on his way to Greece, made a detour to visit Nietzsche, bringing a copy of his translation, *Sutras of the Vedanta*, newly published at the expense of the Berlin Academy of Sciences. He was currently working on the *Upanishads*. Nietzsche felt quite proud to have introduced him to Schopenhauer's work, which had been the springboard to his interest in oriental culture.

Nietzsche was planning to leave Sils on about 20 September to spend a couple of months in Venice, having asked Gast to find accommodation for him, preferably near St Mark's Square. 'I need a chaise-longue (to stretch myself out on): I am so often ill.' A thunderstorm over Lake Como gave him an uneasy journey but, once settled, he found 'conditions more tolerable than at other times. The air, too, now *limpida elastica*.'[211] But he planned to stay only for four weeks. 'The light is extremely trying for my eyes; because of the humidity it is quite different from the light in Sils.'[212] But he had fine weather, 'clear, fresh, clean, cloudless, almost like Nice.'[213] Gast was in good spirits, and Nietzsche still stubbornly maintained that he was producing 'the most beautiful music now being written'.[214]

Once again his birthday, his forty-third, reminded him uncomfortably of his isolation: the only greetings to arrive were from his mother.[215] Unfavourable newspaper reviews of *Jenseits* – 'higher nonsense', 'diabolically calculating', 'psychiatric and pathological' – had more of a provoking than a depressing effect on him. 'My intention is to move to Nice on 21 October for a long, hard-working winter,'[216] though his career as a writer had so far cost him three thousand francs in printers' bills, and earned him nothing by way of royalties.[217] He could not even expect to publish future books except at his own expense.[218] But he was sure that his most important work was still to be done.[219] In the same way that he defended Taine, whose 'life takes on the quality of a mission: his attitudes to problems are determined by a necessity',[220] Nietzsche believed that 'the destiny which lies upon me'[221] was to provide an alternative to nihilism: 'I have still not despaired of finding the way out, the hole that will lead us to "something".'[222] When he was speaking of himself, the words 'task' and 'destiny' were interchangeable. 'This task has made me ill. It will make me healthy again, and not only healthy but more philanthropic.'[223]

He left Venice on 21 October. The journey was unpleasant: 'Between Genoa and Milan a dangerous incident (in the tunnel, at night); two hours delay. Arrival in Nice with violent headache. My trunk open, lock broken.'[224] But by evening he was in good spirits.[225] Nice had recovered from the earthquake: 'It has never been cleaner; the houses are better painted; the cooking in the hotels has improved.'[226] In his north-facing room at the Pension de Genève it was cold, 'like January',[227] and on his fifth evening a fishbone stuck in his throat. The following morning it was still there. Depressed as he was, his fingers blue with cold, he felt the accident to be 'full of symbolism and meaning'.[228] He tried to cheer himself up by reading Montaigne. Rather than pay the fifty francs it would have cost to hire a stove for the season, he had asked his mother to send him one from Naumburg, but it did not arrive until late in the rainy November that had followed the cold October.[229] 'Until today I was shivering and blue-fingered, which was no benefit to my philosophy. It is almost intolerable when you feel death's icy breath in your own room – when going home is not like returning to a *castle* but like being *dragged back to prison*.'[230]

The Swiss owners of the *pension*, who had known him since 1883, were giving him his room and two meals a day for only 5½ francs, while the other guests were paying a daily rate of 8–10 francs. But Nietzsche's whole pension, which should have stopped in 1886, was only three thousand francs. The room was newly decorated, with a *chaise-longue* and a dark reddish brown carpet he had chosen for himself. He got up each morning at six, lit his stove, made himself tea, ate a few biscuits. He went for two brisk walks every day, an hour in the morning, three hours in the afternoon, following the same route, day after day. He would have breakfast at midday and his main meal at six in the evening, drinking only water with it. Afterwards he would sit until nine by a shaded light in the lounge, 'almost entirely surrounded by Englishmen and English ladies'.[231]

When *Genealogie* was published on 10 November he sent a copy to Burckhardt, saying that he regarded him and Taine as his only two readers. 'If only you were *here*!!'[232] He posted a copy to Erwin Rohde, who did not even acknowledge it, and one to Carl von Gersdorff, who responded enthusiastically. 'You are living in a beautiful, free world, and I bless you for being able to live as a philosopher.'[233] Nietzsche answered: 'Seldom in my life has a letter caused me so much joy.'[234]

The most gratifying reaction of all was from a stranger, the eminent Danish critic Georg Brandes, who had written a book on Kierkegaard (1877). He had not replied when Nietzsche sent him *Jenseits*, but, on receiving *Genealogie*, he wrote: 'You are one of the few men with whom I should like to speak,' and he used the phrase 'aristocratic radicalism'.[235] This delighted Nietzsche, who called it 'the shrewdest comment on me I have so far read'.[236] In his next letter Brandes said, 'You are without doubt the most exciting of all German writers.'[237]

In December he was feeling the need to 'depersonalize' his life even further, to 'draw a line' under everything he had so far done. The phrases occur in letters both to Carl Fuchs and to Gast.[238] A week before Christmas, when he reread *Genealogie*, he was surprised to find how passionate it was – proof, he thought, that his previous achievements were a mere 'promise' of what was yet to come.[239] 'We are still in the "overture" to my philosophy.'[240] He could have no notion of how soon the final curtain was to fall.

He was working on *Der Wille zur Macht* (*The Will to Power*), which he completed only in a sketch that failed to satisfy him, numbering 372 paragraphs from his notes and arranging them into four books. In the draft of a letter to Overbeck written on 3 February 1888 he said that he had completed the first draft of his *Umwertung aller Werte* (*Revaluation of All Values*). 'The whole sketch for it was the longest torture I have ever suffered, a real sickness.'[241] In the letter this sentence is suppressed, but he wrote of 'grim hours, entire days and nights when I no longer knew how to go on living, and when a black despair, unlike any I have known, took hold of me. . . . No more beautiful things should be expected of me now, any more than a suffering, starving animal can be expected to devour its prey elegantly.'[242] Writing to Gast ten days later, and again using the word 'torture', Nietzsche gives the projected title as *Versuch einer Umwertung* (*Attempt at a Revaluation*). The draft does not correspond to the book with 1,067 numbered sections which was posthumously published as *Der Wille zur Macht*.

In Germany there was still no Brandes to support Nietzsche, which provoked him into making critical statements about his own importance, rather in the way that the schizophrenic, isolated from all meaningful relationships, tries, in R. D. Laing's words, 'to be in an unreal, impossible way, all persons and things to himself. The imagined advantages are safety for the true self, isolation and hence freedom from others, self-sufficiency and control.'[243] Writing in 1874 about Wagner's 'spurious omnipotence', Nietzsche had said: 'No one is more honestly against himself than the man who believes only in himself.' After thirteen years, manically unbalanced, Nietzsche had turned against himself in this sense. The fanfare of self-praise he published in *Ecce Homo* is privately prefigured in a February letter to von Seydlitz and his wife: 'Between ourselves – the three of us – it is not inconceivable that I am the foremost philosopher of the era, perhaps even somewhat more, a bridge between two millennia, decisive and doom-laden.'[244] A letter to Brandes, written a week later, contains a brief, self-justifying commentary on Nietzsche's earlier works.[245] Taken together the two letters almost form a synopsis for *Ecce Homo*, which seems madder because the self-praise and self-justification are addressed to the unconverted.

At the beginning of March the weather was still cold, but the sunlight was already becoming painful.[246] He was ill for three days in the middle of the month, and on the 20th he had a sleepless night trying to decide where to spend the spring.[247] At the end of the month he was still in Nice, but he had decided to leave for Turin on 2 April. 'I have heard favourable reports of the *dry* air there, the quiet streets, the extraordinary extensiveness of the town, so that I can go for long walks without exposing myself to the sunlight.'[248]

He had good reasons for hating journeys, and this was one of his worst. 'Really I am no longer fit to travel on my own. I get so worked up that I behave stupidly.'[249] Changing at Savona, he boarded the wrong train, which made him feel so ill that he found a hotel in San Pier d'Arena, outside Genoa, where he stayed for two days, while his luggage went on to Turin. Arriving in Genoa the next day, he found it so beautiful that he wandered around the streets, lost in admiration. After another night in a hotel he finally reached Turin, where he rented a room in a newsvendor's third-floor flat near the Palazzo Carignano. The city delighted him. He had expected a modern metropolis but found a princely residence, where the 'aristocratic calm' of the seventeenth century had been preserved.[250] 'There are no tiresome suburbs; there is unity of taste even in the colours (the whole city is yellow or reddish-brown). And for the feet, as for the eyes, it is a classical place . . . and everything much more dignified than I had expected! The most beautiful cafés I have seen.'[251] He ate regularly; in a trattoria – minestra or risotto, meat, vegetables and bread.[252]

When he collected his *poste restante* mail he found a letter from Brandes, who had been 'seized with a kind of anger that no one in Scandinavia knows of you, and had quickly decided to make you well known at one blow'.[253] He was going to deliver a series of open lectures at the University of Copenhagen on Nietzsche's work. In answering his request for biographical details, Nietzsche felt either free to depart from the facts or unable to distinguish between fact and fantasy: he had been born 'on the battlefield of Lützen'; the first name he had heard spoken was Gustavus Adolphus; his ancestors were Polish aristocrats called Niezky; outside Germany he was usually taken for a Pole; he had been an officer in the artillery, and had been 'indescribably intimate' with the Wagners.[254]

Wagner was the subject of the 'little pamphlet about music' he was writing.[255] *Der Fall Wagner* (*The Case of Wagner*) is more of a polemic than *Genealogie*, more unbalanced than any of Nietzsche's previous works, and more indicative of mental illness. 'I have given the Germans the most profound books they have.'[256] In the preface, Wagner is described as 'merely one of my diseases',[257] and at the beginning of the book Nietzsche enthuses about *Carmen*: 'How such a work brings one to perfection. One becomes a "masterpiece" oneself.'[258] He has now heard it twenty times, 'and each time it seemed to me I became more of a philosopher, a better philosopher. ... I become a better man when this Bizet speaks to me.'[259] Don José's trite line 'Yes, *I* have killed her, *I* – my adored Carmen' is praised for 'translating the tragic essence of love into a formula'. 'Such a conception of love, the only one worthy of the philosopher, is rare.'[260] Wagner, on the other hand, had fallen prey to the danger that threatened all Romantics: 'chewing the cud of moral and religious absurdities until they choke'.[261]

Wagner is presented as the epitome of modernism, the epitome of decadence. 'His art is the most seductive blend of everything the world today most wants – the three great stimulants of the effete – the *brutal*, the *artificial* and the innocent (idiotic).'[262] Dostoevsky had made these two words synonymous for him.[263] Some of Nietzsche's bombardment is well aimed: he calls the *Lohengrin* Prelude 'only too enticing, only too well gauged, an example of how music can be a means of hypnotizing';[264] he emphasizes the theatrical rhetoric in Wagner's style, calling him 'the Victor Hugo of music as language'.[265] But when it becomes apparent that Nietzsche has arrived at his understanding of Wagner by means of self-observation, some of his criticism gets blown back in his own face. 'If anything about Wagner is interesting, it is the logic by which a physiological defect moves progressively, step by step, as method and procedure, as innovatory principles, as a crisis of taste.'[266] Twenty years of intermittent obsession with Wagner had taught Nietzsche more than he knew he had learned. He sent the manuscript of *Der Fall Wagner* straight to the printer Naumann, who found it illegible. Nietzsche had to rewrite it at the end of July.[267]

In Copenhagen, Brandes was enjoying a great success with his Nietzsche lectures, which were attracting audiences of about three hundred and were being reviewed in the newspapers.[268] 'I am so relieved, so invigorated, in such a good mood. ... Am I not indebted for all this to the genial *north winds*, which do not always come from the Alps? Sometimes they come from *Copenhagen*!'[269] At the end of the final lecture there was a big ovation. 'Your name is now very *popular* in all Copenhagen's intellectual circles, and at least *known* throughout Scandinavia.'[270] Nietzsche could at last believe he had a public, and he could write to Brandes, as he once had to Rohde, feeling he had a powerful ally, a respectable academic actively engaged in campaigning for him. He volunteered an explanation of his phrase 'revaluation of all values': only the alchemist who made gold was genuinely enriching humanity; everyone else was merely engaged in exchanging and bartering. 'This time my task is quite curious: I have asked myself what humanity has most hated, feared and despised – from just that have I made my "gold".'[271]

'Wonder upon wonders,' Nietzsche wrote on 13 May, 'I have had
a remarkably *cheerful* spring so far. The first for ten, fifteen years –
perhaps even longer!'[1] To his mother he had written that Turin
'would really be the place where I would one day dearly love to have
my old mother'.[2] Before he left for Sils on 5 June, he received a letter
from an American journalist, Karl Knortz, who wanted to write
an article on him,[3] so there were at last grounds for thinking his
reputation outside Germany was growing.

But on the journey to Switzerland he had to spend a night,
already feeling ill, at Chiavenna, and, arriving in Sils, he had a
whole day of vomiting.[4] It took him six days to recover.[5] The
weather was freakish, too. After a week as hot as any he could
remember in Sils, it began to snow persistently.

In June Kaiser Friedrich died, to be succeeded by Wilhelm 11,
who was barely thirty. Bismarck (who was seventy-three) continued in office, but Nietzsche was apprehensive that power would
go to Adolf Stöcker, an ex-preacher who had tried to form a
Christian-Social Workers' party. 'I know that Germany will be
the first country in which my *Wille zur Macht* is suppressed.'[6]

Writing to Knortz, Nietzsche presented a rosy picture of
developments. He claimed never to have lifted a finger in self-
advertisement, though in fact both feet had often left the ground,
and he had been angry when Fritzsch refused to publicize the
success of Brandes's lectures.[7] He called *Zarathustra* 'the profoundest work in the German language', and his books 'in the
front rank by virtue of the richness of the psychological experience,
the courage in face of the greatest dangers, and their sublime frank-
ness'.[8] Later in the month, writing to Malwida, he self-indulgently
distorted the nature of Knortz's interest: describing the 'brilliant
success' of Brandes's lectures, Nietzsche added: 'I have just been
offered the prospect of something similar in New York.'[9] At the

same time he tried to entice Carl Fuchs into writing an essay on him:

> I have never yet been characterized as a *psychologist* or as a *writer* ('poet' too) or as the inventor of a new kind of pessimism (Dionysian, born out of *strength* and taking pleasure in seizing the problem of existence by its horns) or as an *immoralist* (until now the highest form of 'intellectual rectitude', which is entitled to treat morality as illusion when it has itself become *instinctive* and *unavoidable*). It is not at all necessary or even desirable to side with me; on the contrary, a dose of curiosity, as if confronted with some unfamiliar plant, and an ironic resistance would be an incomparably *more intelligent* position to adopt.[10]

But the euphoria and the strenuous self-promotion were drawing extravagantly on his energy. 'My *stamina* is so feeble, I shall never be able to make up the losses sustained in more than ten years of living on my "capital" while earning nothing, nothing, nothing. With great art and caution I keep myself more or less on my feet, but so much time is lost when I feel weak, which ought not to happen at my age. . . . I have been in an indescribably bad state almost the whole time. A deeply ensconced headache ensuing on a fit of retching; no desire or strength for walking; revulsion against my –' (the rest of the sheet is torn off).[11] The oscillation between the extremes is symptomatic of the tension that led up to the breakdown at the end of the year. In the autumn he sometimes felt confident that during 1889 he would be able to complete his *Umwertung*, 'the most independent book in existence'.[12] Only madness could save him from the realization that he would never bring it into existence.

In July the weather in Sils was still abnormally wintry, and his landlady put extra blankets on his bed. On the 20th he wrote: 'Nothing has improved, neither the weather nor my health – both are still absurd.'[13] He complained of symptoms 'cloaking a profound nervous exhaustion in which the whole machine is worth nothing.'[14] He had never suggested, even to Overbeck, that his father might be the source of his ailments, but he could no longer ignore the possibility: 'I am not suffering at all from headaches or stomach-ache, but pressure brings on the manifestations of a nervous exhaustion (which is partly acquired, partly inherited) from my father, who also died after apparently losing all his stamina.'[15] But he may still have been ignoring the possibility of congenital syphilis, though he was by now convinced that he was descended from the nobility. He may have thought there was more racial 'purity' in the Polish nobility than in the German nobility, which he had characterized as syphilitic.

But even now, instead of sinking into desperation or apathy, he made his self-diagnosis into a base for philosophical generalization. *Götzendämmerung oder Wie man mit dem Hammer philosophiert* (*Twilight of the False Gods or How to Philosophize with a Hammer*) was started at the end of June and completed at the end of September. His original title for it was *Müssigang eines Psychologen* (*A Psychologist at Leisure*), but he responded to Gast's agitation for something more dignified. In the book he built up an analogy between a degenerate young man – effete, prematurely aged – and a degenerate people. It is not viciousness and luxury that causes decadence: the increasing need for strong stimulants is the result of physiological deterioration in the race, just as the young man's sickness is not the cause but the consequence of hereditary exhaustion.[16] From the book it would be impossible to guess what Nietzsche had been writing in his letters: his association of ugliness with physical deterioration is remarkably impersonal and lucid: ugliness 'reminds one of decay, danger, impotence: it actually causes a loss of energy, while beauty has the opposite effect.'[17] 'Ugliness is interpreted as a sign and symptom of degeneration. . . . Each indication of exhaustion, heaviness, age, weariness, each kind of restriction, constriction or paralysis, above all the smell, colour, form of dissolution, decay . . . all this provokes the same reaction – the value judgement "ugly".'[18] With remarkable immunity to self-pity, Nietzsche even condemns the invalid who wants to go on living at any cost: 'Society should have only a profound contempt for the man who survives like a vegetable in cowardly dependence on doctors and medicine after he has lost the meaning of his life, the right to live.'[19] It is ironic that he was to win the admiration of German society only when he was surviving like a vegetable.

The subject of the sick philosopher is broached earlier in the book. Socrates said on his deathbed that he owed a cock to Asclepius – the debt conventionally incurred on recovering from an illness – his implication being that life had been a disease.[20]

Perhaps we should look more closely, Nietzsche suggests, at the wisest men of each period. Are they all moribund? Does wisdom appear on earth like a raven attracted by the smell of carrion?[21] As in *Geburt der Tragödie*, he accuses Socrates and Plato of being symptoms of decay, agents of dissolution, anti-Greek, negative in their relation to life.[22] Socrates, who was as ugly and decadent as a typical criminal,[23] admitted to all the evil appetites, but claimed to have mastered them.[24] Did 'this shrewdest of self-deceivers'[25] ever understand that 'having to combat one's own instincts is the formula for decadence'?[26] So long as life is progressive, happiness is indistinguishable from instinct.[27]

Rejecting the evidence of the senses in favour of an ideal world, Plato determined the course philosophy was to follow: 'For thousands of years philosophers have handled nothing but mummified concepts; nothing has come out of their hands alive.'[28] If nothing is real except essences, anything that changes or dies is unreal, so the philosopher feels entitled to disregard both history and the experience of living.[29] But really it is not our senses that mislead us, it is reason, which forces us to falsify the evidence they give us,[30] prejudicing us with commitment to belief in unity, identity, duration, substance, cause, materiality and being.[31] Built on the subject–predicate relationship, our language conditions us into thinking in terms of an ego-substance which produces an effect.[32] Believing that we originate the act of willing, we have always assumed that we can catch causality red-handed.[33] Nor have we doubted that the antecedents of each action can be discovered in the consciousness as motives.[34] But 'will', 'motive', and 'ego' were no longer plausible, while the concept of the 'thing' was no more than a reflection of the belief in the ego as cause.

In the section titled 'What the Germans Lack', Nietzsche seems to be drawing on memories of undergraduate life and of Franconia, especially in the complaint, 'How much tiresome heaviness, lameness, dampness, dressing-gown dilatoriness – how much *beer* there is in the German intellect!'[35] In one of the aphorisms at the beginning of the book he had suggested that 'German spirit' had been a contradiction in terms since the beginning of the *Reich*, eighteen years ago,[36] and in this section he makes the point by saying that 'Deutschland, Deutschland über Alles' was the end of German philosophy.[37] Too much seriousness and willpower is squandered on politics,[38] while the expansion of higher education necessitated by military privileges had led to a lowering of standards.[39] Everything in the schools was adjusted 'to the most dubious mediocrity'; culture had been democratized,[40] and modern man had become 'too indolent for the vices which depend on strong will'.[41] Privately disinclined to blame anyone — even his father — for his sufferings, Nietzsche wrote that complaining was always useless, always a sign of weakness. He castigated the socialists for blaming their sufferings on other people, and the Christians for blaming themselves.[42] The Christian condemns 'the world', while the socialist condemns 'society'. Altruistic morality was always a sign of decadence: ' "Not pursuing one's own interest" — that is only the moral fig-leaf for a quite different actuality, physiological in fact: "I no longer know how to find my own interest." '[43] The root of all modern stupidity was the degeneration of instinct. Over the labour question, for instance. the workers were already far too well placed not to go on asking for more; if one wants slaves, why educate them to be masters?[44] Nietzsche hated the 'Rousseauesque morality' of the French Revolution, which was 'still an active force, enlisting everything shallow and mediocre'.[45] Nothing was more poisonous than the idea of equality. That such bloody events had followed in its wake 'has given this modern idea *par excellence* a kind of glory and a gleaming fieriness, so that the theatricality of the revolution has seduced even the noblest spirits'.[46]

While writing the book he received two thousand marks from Deussen, who told him it came from anonymous admirers in Berlin to subsidize his printing costs.[47] 'I hope', Deussen wrote, 'you will be glad to give sympathetic understanding to it if individuals try to make up to you *for the transgressions of humanity*.'[48] Nietzsche suspected Deussen was handing over his own money. Meta von Salis, who arrived in Sils 'a little thinner and still paler than before',[49] also contributed a thousand marks to his printing expenses. He was too proud to pocket either sum willingly, but in four years he had spent over four thousand francs on printing, and it was essential that he should have some money in reserve for the great work to come.

He enjoyed spending time with Meta and a Hamburg pianist, Karl von Holten, who rehearsed and memorized one of Gast's compositions. When he played it for Nietzsche, he wanted to hear it six times.[50] But the Turin euphoria had receded, and despite these distractions he was finding his time in Sils 'an endurance test of the most extreme kind: anything more horrible is unimaginable. Very often I did not know how I was going to lift myself out of an incredible melancholy and weakness.'[51] But he was not too dispirited or too solipsistic to go on campaigning for Gast. Hans von Bülow was now director of the opera house at Hamburg, and Nietzsche took the risk of recommending his friend's opera *Der Löwe von Venedig*.[52]

He was intending to stay on for another month, until mid-September, before returning to Turin. Another August visitor to Sils was Julius Kaftan, a theologian who had been at Basel University from 1873 until he took up a post ten years later in Berlin. On his first morning in Sils, Nietzsche paid him a surprise visit, and they had a great many philosophical conversations. 'For three weeks in Sils-Maria we saw each other every day,' Kaftan testified. 'We went for long walks together discussing everything fully and without reserve, as if we were old friends. Which we were not.'[53] Nietzsche could lead a much more sociable life than he had in Turin: 'The company in the hotel is not bad, and what distinguished people there are all want to meet me.'[54]

On 3 September he wrote what he intended as the preface to his *Umwertung* – 'perhaps the proudest preface ever written', he called it.[55] 'This book belongs to the very few. Perhaps none of them are alive yet. . . . Only the day after tomorrow belongs to me. Some men are born posthumously.' Among the prerequisites for understanding him were habituation to mountain altitudes, to seeing 'the pitiful gossip about politics and national interest *from above* . . . the brave man's predilection for questions that intimidate his contemporaries, courage for the forbidden. . . . A new conscience for truths which have kept silent. . . . Reverence for oneself, love for oneself, unlimited freedom with oneself.' It was only readers with these qualities that he wanted. 'The rest are merely humanity.'[56]

But it was not so easy to embark on the task he had set himself. He was aware 'that my life in the last weeks fell into some disorder. Several times I got up at two o'clock in the morning, "troubled in my spirit", and wrote down what had been going through my head.'[57] *Der Fall Wagner* and *Götzendämmerung* were 'really only convalescences in the middle of an unmeasurably taxing and decisive task'.[58] It was harder to come to grips with it than to relish the results it would have when successfully fulfilled. '*When it is understood*, it will split the history of mankind into two halves. ... Much that has been free will be *free no longer*: the realm of *tolerance* is reduced by value judgements of the first importance to mere cowardice and feebleness of character. To be a Christian – I am mentioning just one consequence – will from then on be *indecent*. A great deal of this, the most radical subversion humanity has known, is already under way inside me.'[59] He had, in fact, been working since the beginning of September on *Der Antichrist*, which he later announced as the first volume of his *Umwertung*. According to one of the plans in his notebooks, the first book was to be subtitled 'Attempt at a Critique of Christianity', the second was to be 'The Free Spirit: Critique of Philosophy as a Nihilistic Movement', the third 'The Immoralist: Critique of the Most Fatal Kind of Ignorance, Morality', and the fourth, 'Dionysus: Philosophy of Eternal Recurrence'.

In the spring of 1888 Nietzsche had been reading the work of the radical theologian Julius Wellhausen, who had published his history of Israel in a new version (1883), following it, in 1885, with a book of biblical criticism presenting Jesus as a historical figure. It is possible, as Curt Janz suggests,[60] that Nietzsche had been discussing Wellhausen with Kaftan, and that the discussions influenced *Der Antichrist*, which was begun just after Kaftan left Sils. But instead of starting on a revaluation of all values, the book reiterates many of the points Nietzsche has made already about power, weakness, decadence, pity, Christianity. Again the Judaeo-Christian morality is characterized as deriving from *ressentiment*;[61] again the priest is characterized as a man with a vested interest in making people sick.[62] Discussing whether Jesus can be viewed historically or psychologically, Nietzsche ridicules Ernest Renan's attempt in *La Vie de Jésus* (1863) to portray him as a genius and a hero. Physiologically, his morbid susceptibility to the sense of touch must indicate an instinctive hatred of all external reality,[63] while his compulsion to ostracize all feelings of hostility indicates an extreme capacity for suffering. 'The fear of all pain, even of the infinitely small, cannot do otherwise than end in a religion of love.'[64] The 'glad tidings' of the Gospels are that there are no more opposites; the faith proclaimed is not one that has been won by struggling. 'It is like a return to childishness on a spiritual level. ... That nothing he says shall be taken literally is precisely the precondition for this anti-realist to be able to speak at all.'[65] Sin, guilt, punishment and reward are abolished: blessedness is the only reality.[66] History, time, space, external reality are reduced to signs, occasions for metaphor.[67] The profoundest saying in the Gospels was 'Resist not evil.'[68] It is indecently hypocritical to call oneself a Christian while defending oneself or pursuing one's advantage or preserving one's honour.[69] 'There has been only one Christian, and he died on the cross.'[70] St Paul had shifted the balance of Christian doctrine by focusing on crucifixion, salvation, the other world, the immortal soul.[71] 'Paul was the greatest of all apostles of revenge.'[72] The God whom Paul invented for himself, who 'confounds the wisdom of the world', is really only Paul's determination to do so, to call his own will God.[73]

Writing without access to his own books – when he wanted to quote from *Menschliches, Allzumenschliches* he had to ask Overbeck to copy out a passage for him[74] – he had no means of checking whether he was making points he had previously made only in his notebooks, or whether he was publicly repeating himself. As a book, *Der Antichrist* is on roughly the same level as *Der Fall Wagner* – a much lower level than *Jenseits* or *Genealogie*. But he had become incapable of self-criticism: when the book was half finished he wrote: 'It has an energy and a transparency which have perhaps never been achieved by a philosopher. It seems to me as though all at once I have learned to *write*. ... The work cuts clean through the centuries. I swear that everything that has been said or thought in criticism of Christianity is pure childishness in comparison.'[75]

He was in the middle of writing *Der Antichrist* when his copies of *Der Fall Wagner* reached him. Sending one to Brandes and announcing his *Umwertung*, he said: 'Europe will need to discover a new Siberia where it can exile the originator of these experiments in valuation.'[76] He sent copies of *Der Fall Wagner* to Burckhardt, who did not reply, in spite of being told 'A single word from you would make me happy,' and to Malwida, claiming 'to have disposed of Wagner while engaged on my immeasurably difficult life-task'.[77]

He had intended to leave for Turin in the middle of September, but there were abnormal downpours of rain and snow, together with flooding. When he was able, finally, to travel on the 20th, he arrived in Milan at midnight and had to cross the narrow wooden bridges over the flooded Lake Como by torchlight.[78] But once he was in Turin he felt relaxed. He stayed at the same lodgings as before, but found a fifty per cent improvement in tidiness, cleanliness and attentiveness, while in the *trattorie* he had the impression of a hundred per cent improvement in quality and quantity.[79] He could even tolerate bad weather here better than elsewhere, and he was able to work every day.[80]

He had enthused, previously, about Venice, Nice and Sils, but never as euphorically as about Turin – a 'superb and strangely beneficent city'.[81] His room was 'a hermit's retreat among extraordinarily beautiful broad streets'.[82] If only he had discovered the city ten years earlier! If only he had spent his summers here 'instead of in the unspeakably dreadful Engadin!'[83] He thought other people were reacting to him preferentially and lovingly. 'Everywhere I am given the most distinguished treatment. If only you could see how pleased everyone here is when I arrive, and how in all quarters they involuntarily bring the best, the most tactful parts of their nature to the fore, putting on their best, their most considerate manners.'[84] This illusion persisted until his breakdown. 'What is most remarkable', he wrote later, 'is that here in Turin I exercise a perfect fascination. Everybody glances at me as if I were a prince – there is a special distinction in the way doors are held open for me, meals set out.'[85]

He went for regular afternoon walks outside the city. 'The clearest October light everywhere, the superb tree-lined road which led me for about an hour close alongside the Po, scarcely yet touched by autumn. I am now the most grateful man in the world, *autumnally* minded in every good sense of the word: it is my great *harvest time*.' 'Everything comes easily to me, everything succeeds, although it is not likely that anyone has ever had such great things on his hands.'[86] When he saw himself in the mirror, he thought he looked different. 'In admirably good humour, well nourished and ten years younger than I should be. What is more, since choosing Turin as my home, I am greatly changed in the honours I do myself – I am glad to have an excellent tailor . . . in my trattoria I am undoubtedly given the best food there is. . . . Here day after day dawns with the same boundless sun-filled perfection: the superb foliage in glowing yellow, the sky and the great river delicately blue, the purest possible air.'[87] In fact Turin has an average of 107 rainy days each year, and the Via Carlo Alberto is neither broad nor bright. The houses are tall and identical. Twenty-five years later his landlord, Davide Fino, could still remember how lonely his tenant had been, and how he would sit for hours in the evening, improvising at the piano. According to Fino's daughter, what he played was mostly Wagnerian music.[88]

The delusions of grandeur made Nietzsche peremptory with friends and acquaintances. After Hans von Bülow had kept Gast's opera for eight weeks without replying, Nietzsche wrote: 'You shall never hear from me again, I promise you that. I think you do not realize that the foremost mind of the period has expressed a wish to you.'[89] To Malwida's tactfully worded arguments against *Der Fall Wagner* he replied: 'These are not things on which I tolerate contradiction. On questions of decadence I am the highest court of appeal there is on earth. Present-day humanity, with its miserably vitiated instincts, should think itself lucky to have someone who, in the obscurer cases, can pour out clean wine.'[90] He informed Elisabeth that his life had reached its zenith, that he had suddenly recovered his strength and his self-confidence in time to 'fulfil tasks such as, perhaps, no man has ever yet set himself.'[91] (The ineffectual word 'perhaps' is recurrent in his most extravagant claims.) This letter is signed 'Your brother, now *quite a great person*'.

On 15 October, his forty-fourth birthday, he heard from none of his friends except Gast, but indifference to him and his work could be interpreted as a sign of the times:

No moment in history has been more important; but *who would know anything about it?* . . . While humanity's highest problem is being annexed with an undreamed-of loftiness and freedom of intellectual passion, which is calling for a *decision* on human destiny, the all-pervading pettiness and obtuseness *must* dissociate itself all the more vigorously. There is still no 'hostility' whatever towards me: people are simply deaf to anything I say. *So* there is neither a *for* nor an *against*.[92]

Adopting, as he was, more and more insane strategies to achieve self-sufficiency, he celebrated his birthday single-handed by starting *Ecce Homo*. 'Seeing that before long', he wrote in the preface, 'I must confront humanity with the gravest demand ever made of it, it seems essential to say *who I am*. . . . The disproportion between the greatness of my task and the *smallness* of my contemporaries has found expression in their having neither heard nor seen me.' He goes on to claim that *Zarathustra* is the highest and deepest book in existence, 'an inexhaustible spring, into which no bucket descends without coming back laden with gold and goodness . . . it is an incomparable privilege to be a listener here. . . . It was not in vain that today I buried my forty-fourth year. I was entitled to bury it – whatever life there was in it is saved, is immortal.'[93] Such chapter-headings as 'Why I Am So Wise' and 'Why I Write Such Good Books' could hardly fail to irritate, but his rationalization was that the book must win exemption from current ideas about what was permissible.[94] The exorbitant self-praise, which he had previously confined to his letters, is now made public; he had forgotten what he had written in *Die fröhliche Wissenschaft* about the noisiness of self-applause.

Summarizing his physical ailments, he claims that they have made him uniquely qualified as a commentator on decadence: 'From the perspective of illness to *healthier* concepts and values, and, conversely, from the fullness and self-confidence of a *rich* life to the covert working of the instinct for decadence – this was my most continuous training, my most personal experience, which gave me mastery of this, if of anything.'[95] He goes on to claim that he is both a decadent and the opposite. The typical decadent chooses what is disadvantageous for him, but Nietzsche had refused to let himself be cared for, had chosen solitude. Though this could, by his own definition, be adduced as evidence of decadence, he presented it as proof that he had known how to make himself healthy again.[96] Fortified with delusions, he was at last strong enough to entertain the possibility that his disease was hereditary: 'I regard it as a great privilege to have had such a father: it even seems to me that this explains all my other privileges, except for life, the great Yes to life.' To enter into the world of higher experiences, all he had to do was wait, and, once there, he felt at home. 'Almost paying with my life for this privilege was not buying it at too high a price.'[97]

In 'Why I am So clever' he recommends his private habits as worthy of emulation: no alcohol, but a hearty meal is easier to digest than a small one; no coffee, strong tea in the morning, but start the day with thick, oil-less cocoa; sit as little as possible and never believe the ideas that occur to you indoors.[98] Live somewhere with dry air and clear skies, so that your metabolism will be accelerated.[99] Keep the surface of consciousness clear from all great imperatives, and do not try to know yourself. 'The precondition for becoming what one is is not to have the least notion of what one is.'[100]

Citing facts from his past, Nietzsche was misleadingly selective. Von Bülow, for instance, is quoted as saying that he had never seen anything like the *Manfred* music on paper, and that it was a rape of Euterpe. The 'days of Tribschen' are characterized as 'days of trust, gaiety, sublime coincidences, *profound* moments . . . *our* heaven never became clouded'.[101]

As a writer he ranked himself with Heine as one of the two greatest artists using the German language.[102] That the contention is valid does not prove that the observations on which he based it were any more objective than those which led him to write that wherever he went in Turin, people's faces lit up, and that market women gave him the sweetest grapes from their stalls.[103] As in his letters and autobiographical summaries, he was tending, more and more, to romanticize the past. He claimed that it was while he was on duty as a medical orderly outside the walls of Metz that he thought his way through the problems of *Geburt der Tragödie*, and that it was only after the book was published that Wagner's name began to arouse high hopes.[104] Nietzsche's understanding of the Dionysian made him the first tragic philosopher. 'Before me this transposition of the Dionysian into philosophical pathos did not exist: tragic wisdom was lacking.'[105] This claim is not untenable, but sometimes the writing sinks to the level of a brochure advertising Nietzsche's work: 'One should listen to the world-historical accent with which the concept "tragic attitude" is introduced: this text is full of world-historical accents.'[106]

It would be pointless to calculate how many attempts Nietzsche had made at autobiography between his schoolboy efforts and *Ecce Homo*. As he says of the *Unzeitgemässe Betracht-ungen*, 'I do not wish to deny that at bottom they speak only of me.'[107] And he is right to insist that his concept of the philosopher is 'miles distant from any concept that includes even a Kant, not to mention the academic cud-chewers and other professors of philosophy.'[108] But now the publicist is pulling at the elbow of the spiritual autobiographer. Nietzsche is concerned about his image. His life must not seem to have been devoid of sexual relationships. When he fled from Bayreuth, 'a charming Parisienne tried to console me'.[109] A few paragraphs later there is a casual reference to 'my companion'.[110] But he could still read his earlier books like old diaries. When he looks at *Morgenröte* 'almost each sentence turns into a net in which I fish up something incomparable from the depths: its whole skin trembles with delicate thrills of memory'.[111]

Most of *Ecce Homo* is inferior writing, failing to communicate those thrills from the past, but the final section, 'Why I am Destiny', looks impressively at the future. Nietzsche was no nihilist, but in this chapter he comes close to facing the consequences of his wish to annihilate mediocrity when the vast bulk of humanity is irredeemably mediocre. What will happen now that he has cut the lifeline of lies that Judaism and Christianity held out? 'One day my name will be associated with something catastrophic – a crisis such as there has never been on earth, the most profound collision of conscience. . . . I am not a man, I am dynamite.' Here he is echoing Widmann's review, but he expands on the idea. 'When truth starts battling with the lies of millennia, we shall have convulsions, a spasm of earthquakes, a displacement of mountain and valley such as no one has dreamed of.'[112] Having condemned Aquinas and the Book of Revelations for vengefully predicting a holocaust, he is doing so himself, and with an accuracy that suggests the wars of the twentieth century. 'The concept of politics will be assimilated wholly into ideological warfare, all the power structures of the old society will be blown up – they are all founded on lies. There will be wars such as there have never been on earth.'[113]

In claiming to be the first immoralist, he also claims the right to indulge his powers of destruction and his pleasure in them. 'I obey my Dionysian nature which does not know how to separate negation from affirmation.'[114] What sets him apart from the rest of humanity, he declares, is that he was the first to expose Christian morality.[115] 'Everything previously called "truth" is recognized as the most damaging, insidious, underground form of lie; the sacred pretext of "improving" humanity as a stratagem for *sucking* the blood out of life itself. Morality as *vampirism*.'[116] This is lucid enough, but the discussion of *Zarathustra* is confusing in merging Zoroaster with Nietzsche's character and with Nietzsche himself. The first man to treat the conflict between good and evil 'as the very wheel in the machinery of things', he must also be the first to recognize his error. And he is 'more truthful than any other thinker'.[117] Who is?

Nietzsche was also tending to confuse mental events with external events. Writing to Meta von Salis ten days after finishing the chapter that predicts a spasm of earthquakes, he said: 'Considering what I have written between 3 September and 4 November, I fear there may soon be a small earthquake . . . two years ago, when I was in Nice, it happened, appropriately, there. Indeed, yesterday's report from the observatory mentioned a slight tremor.'[118] Six days later, writing to Brandes about *Ecce Homo*, he said: 'It ends by pitching such thunder and lightning against everything Christian or contaminated by Christianity. . . .'[119] He was becoming more solipsistic: cosmic and meteorological imagery reflect the tendency to think of himself as a world.

About the end of September, Brandes had given a copy of *Der Fall Wagner* to August Strindberg, 'whom I have completely won over for you'.[120] Reading his 1887 play *Comrades* in a French translation, Nietzsche felt 'the most wholehearted admiration, my only reservation being the feeling that this is also self-admiration on my part'.[121] And after reading *The Father* twice, he wrote to Strindberg, congratulating him on a 'masterpiece of hard psychology' and introducing himself as 'the most independent and perhaps the most powerful spirit of our day'. He said that he wanted Strindberg's advice on how to get himself read in France.[122] Receiving no reply, he wrote again on 7 December, asking whether Strindberg would be willing to translate *Ecce Homo* into French. This letter crossed in the post with one from Strindberg saying: 'Without doubt you have given humanity the profoundest book it possesses, and what is not least you have had the courage – and perhaps you can afford – to spit these words. I am ending all my letters "Read Nietzsche". This is my *Carthago est delenda*.'[123] He would have been willing, as he said in his next letter, to translate *Ecce Homo* if Nietzsche did not object to the high fee he would have to charge. Otherwise he would be glad to track down a reliable translator.[124]

There was no abatement in Nietzsche's euphoria. In October he had been suffering from the cold, but November began mildly, and he was still delighted with Turin, not least because of the food and the feeling that everywhere he ate meals or bought fruit, he was given preferential treatment. 'I had never known what it was to have a good appetite: really, I eat four times as much as I did in Nice, pay *less*, and have not yet had the least trouble with my stomach.'[125] 'With the best will in the world, my old friend Overbeck, I cannot think of anything bad to tell you about myself. Both in my work and in my good spirits, things go on and on at a *tempo fortissimo*.'[126]

By the end of November he was finding it hard to control his features. 'I play so many stupid tricks with myself and privately do such inspired clowning that sometimes I go about the streets *grinning* – there is no other word for it – half an hour on end. . . . For the last four days I have been unable to compose my features into seriousness.'[127] And six days later at a concert: 'My face continually made grimaces in order to get over my extreme pleasure – including, for ten minutes, the grimace of tears.'[128]

Rereading his own books he felt full of pleased amazement at how good they were, and, in a letter signed 'the Phoenix', he seems confident that Gast will be delighted to read in *Ecce Homo* that 'psychologically' there is nothing about Wagner or Schopenhauer in the third and fourth *Unzeitgemässe Betrachtungen*: 'Both speak only of me.'[129] He wanted to recover all the copies of *Zarathustra* Part IV which had been given to friends: he was thinking of leaving it unpublished until 'after a few decades of world crises – wars!'[130] And in December he was manically convinced that nothing was beyond his powers: 'The most unheard-of tasks are easy as a game; my health like the weather, coming up daily with boundless brilliance and assurance. The world will be inverted for the next few years: since the old god has abdicated, I shall be ruling the world.'[131] On Christmas Day he predicted: 'In two months I shall be the foremost name on earth.'[132]

He believed he had godlike powers, that his thoughts could control events: 'There are no coincidences any more, either. If I think of someone, a letter from him comes politely through the door.'[133] And in the draft of a letter breaking off relations with his sister: 'You have no conception of what it means to be closely related to the man and the destiny in whom the question of millennia has been resolved – quite literally, I hold the future of humanity in the palm of my hand.'[134] With his pamphlet *Nietzsche contra Wagner*, a selection of what he had already written, he believed he had disposed finally of 'the Wagner question',[135] and his anti-German feelings came to a head in his belief that he could intervene politically: 'I am myself now working on a memorandum for the European courts, with a view to forming an anti-German league. I want to sew up the "*Reich*" in an iron shirt and to provoke a war of desperation. My hands will not be free until the young Kaiser and all his attachments are in my power.'[136] There is no clear point at which he had come to believe insanely in his omnipotence; the progression had been gradual. But in a note to Gast dated 31 December, he wrote: 'When your card came, *what* was I doing? . . . It was the famous Rubicon. . . . I no longer know my address: let us assume that it will shortly be the Palazzo del Quirinale.'[137] No change in his handwriting is noticeable until October, and the main change does not come until the end of the year. As Overbeck wrote, 'His madness – and no one had closer experience of his outbreak than I did – had been as abruptly catastrophic as I originally believed. It occurred between Christmas Eve 1888 and Epiphany 1889.' To Strindberg Nietzsche later wrote: 'I have ordered a convocation of princes in Rome. I want to have the young Kaiser shot.' He signed the note 'Nietzsche Caesar'.[138] This is the last letter to include his own name in the signature. Strindberg's reply, written entirely in Greek and Latin, started with a quotation from an Anacreontic poem, 'I want, I want to be mad,' and ended 'Meanwhile it is a joy to be mad.' It was signed 'Strindberg (Deus, optimus maximus)'.[139]

On the morning of 3 January Nietzsche had just left his lodgings when he saw a cab-driver beating his horse in the Piazza Carlo Alberto. Tearfully, the philosopher flung his arms around the animal's neck, and then collapsed. The small crowd that gathered around him attracted Davide Fino, who had his lodger carried back to his room. After lying unconscious or at least motionless for a while on a sofa, Nietzsche became boisterous, singing, shouting, thumping at the piano. He probably thought he was clowning deliberately. Both Socrates and Shakespeare, he maintained, had been obliged to play the buffoon, and in his Christmas letter to Overbeck he had complained of never being able to speak confidentially to anyone.[140] But the 'inspired clowning' which had already been hard to control by the end of November was now in unchallengeable possession of his mind. He wrote notes to the King of Italy ('My beloved Umberto'), the royal house of Baden ('My children'), and the Vatican Secretary of State. He would go to Rome on Tuesday, he said, to meet the pope and the princes of Europe, except for the Hohenzollerns. He advised the other German princes to ostracize them, for the *Reich* was still the enemy of German culture. Writing to Gast, Brandes and Meta von Salis, Nietzsche signed himself 'The Crucified',[141] and writing to Burckhardt, Overbeck and Cosima Wagner, signed himself 'Dionysus'. The note to Meta runs: 'The world is transfigured, for God is on the earth. Do you not see how all the heavens are rejoicing? I have just seized possession of my kingdom, am throwing the pope into prison, and having Wilhelm, Bismarck and Stöcker shot.' The note to Burckhardt starts: 'That was the little joke for which I condone my boredom at having created a world.'[142]

To Cosima he wrote, 'Ariadne, I love you.'[143] In a dramatic fragment about Naxos written in 1885 and in an 1888 reworking of Ariadne's lament in *Zarathustra* Part IV, Nietzsche had associated Theseus with Wagner and himself with the god finally to be reunited with Ariadne. But it was only now, in his madness, that he could make an overt declaration of love. He wrote again to Burckhardt, a day or two later:

Actually I would much rather be a Basel professor than God, but I have not ventured to carry my private egoism so far as to desist from creating the world on his account. You see, one must make sacrifices, however one may be living, and wherever. ... Since I am condemned to while away the next eternity with bad jokes, I have a writing business here which really leaves nothing to be desired – very pleasant and not at all exhausting. The unpleasant thing, which offends my modesty, is that fundamentally I am every name in history. As for the children I have brought into the world, I have to consider with some suspicion, whether all those who enter the 'Kingdom of God' do not also come out of God.[144]

Burckhardt showed this letter to Overbeck who immediately wrote to Nietzsche asking him to come to Basel, but the following day Overbeck received a letter from Turin saying that Nietzsche had just had all the anti-Semites shot.[145] On consulting Professor Wille, director of Basel's psychiatric clinic, Overbeck was advised to go immediately to Turin. He left the same evening, to arrive the following afternoon in the Via Carlo Alberto. He found Nietzsche sitting in the corner of a sofa revising *Nietzsche contra Wagner*. They threw themselves into each other's arms and burst into tears; Nietzsche especially 'broke into a convulsive trembling and groaning'.[146] After the Finos had given him a bromide he was able to talk more calmly, but, between playing fragments, very softly, at the piano, he spoke of himself as successor to the dead god, and, as the effects of the calmative wore off, he clowned excitedly, leaping about, dancing, shouting, gesturing obscenely. 'So far Nietzsche is quite harmless – in many ways like a child – for other people, at least those who are close to him, terrible, but not at all dangerous.'[147] Fino had not yet called the police, but if Overbeck had arrived any later in Turin, Nietzsche's condition might not have been the only obstacle in the way of taking him back to Basel.[148]

When the time came Nietzsche refused to get out of bed, but Overbeck had enlisted the help of Miescher, a German dentist experienced in handling the insane, and he told Nietzsche that receptions were going to be laid on for him in Basel, together with pageants and musical festivals. At the station, where they had to wait for half an hour, and at Novara, changing trains and waiting for three hours, Nietzsche wanted to address the crowds and to embrace everybody, but Miescher convinced him that he was too eminent not to travel incognito. On the train he slept most of the time, drugged with chloral, but when he woke he sang, sometimes quite loudly. They arrived at Basel on the morning of 10 January at 7.45 and went straight to Dr Wille's clinic in a taxi. Nietzsche failed to recognize Wille, and Overbeck was nervous of mentioning his name. When the doctor introduced himself, Nietzsche responded quietly: 'Wille? Ah, you are an alienist. Some years ago I had a talk with you about religious mania *à propos* a madman called Adolf Vischer, who was living here.' After Nietzsche let himself be taken away by another doctor, Overbeck produced the two most recent letters Nietzsche had written to Burckhardt and to him. Wille decided Nietzsche could not be released, and he made contact with Baumann, a doctor who had seen him once in Turin. He sent a signed statement diagnosing 'mental degeneration': 'Claims he is a famous man and asks for women all the time.'

According to the records of the clinic, Nietzsche apologized for the bad weather. 'For you, good people, I shall prepare the loveliest weather tomorrow.' He devoured his breakfast ravenously and enjoyed his bath. To questions he gave only fragmentary answers, but said that during his 'attacks' he would have liked to embrace everyone in the street and to climb up walls. Kept in bed, he ate well. During the afternoon he sometimes broke into singing and screaming. He talked desultorily, saying he had infected himself on two occasions. During the night he went on talking and got up several times to wash and to clean his teeth. He stayed in bed all morning, and, taken for a walk in the afternoon, he threw his hat down and sometimes lay on the ground. He reproached himself with ruining the lives of several people. The next day, 12 January, he got four or five hours of interrupted sleep after being given sulfonal, and another dose was administered to him at two o'clock. He slept better that night, and the following day he had an enormous appetite. In the afternoon, taken for another walk in the garden, he sang, whimpered and shouted, again lying on the ground several times after taking off his jacket and waistcoat.

Overbeck had written to Nietzsche's mother, who arrived in Basel on the evening of the 13th. After spending the night at the Overbecks' house, she went to the nursing home, where she told the doctors that her husband's brain disease had been caused by falling downstairs. According to their notes, one of her brothers died in a nerve sanatorium and her husband's sisters had been hysterical and eccentric. When she was taken in to see her son, he embraced her delightedly: 'My dear good mama, I am so glad to see you.' After talking quite soberly about family affairs he shouted: 'Behold in me the tyrant of Turin.' What he said afterwards was so confused that she was asked to leave.

Though Wille and Overbeck both tried to dissuade her, she made up her mind to take her son back to Germany with her. She would have liked to look after him at home. Wille said this was out of the question, but eventually he agreed to let Overbeck write to Otto Binswanger, head of the clinic at Jena University, asking for Nietzsche to be accepted as a patient there so that his mother could visit him regularly. On 10 January the muscle on the left side of his face had been described as 'almost normal', but on his last day in the clinic the partial paralysis there was 'much more noticeable than during the last few days'. Wille's diagnosis was 'progressive paralysis'.

On the evening of 17 January 1889, Nietzsche was taken to the station at Basel in a cab with his mother, a young doctor, Ernst Mähly, and an attendant. Overbeck was at the station in time to watch his friend walk stiffly, with hurried, lurching steps, towards the reserved compartment. Before the train left, Overbeck went into the compartment to say goodbye. Getting up to embrace him, Nietzsche groaned and told Overbeck he was the man he had loved most of all.

The journey began well. The mother fed her son with ham sandwiches and cherries. He ate them appreciatively, saying he had been in a lunatic asylum but would be all right again as he was quite young, only twenty-two. But before long he flew into a rage with her and threw one of his gloves out of the window. She moved into another compartment, leaving him with the doctor and the attendant. When they changed trains at Frankfurt, she 'held his dear head, supporting his chin, once again and kissed his forehead all over'.[149] Alone in Basel, Overbeck felt that he had betrayed his friend: 'It would have been a far more genuine act of friendship to take his life. . . . It is all over with Nietzsche.'[150]

In Jena on Friday 18 January he was admitted to the psychiatric clinic, and a three-day medical examination was begun on the Saturday. According to the notes taken, his face was very flushed, his tongue slightly furred. The pupil of his right eye was wider than the left. While walking he spasmodically screwed up his left shoulder, and he was in a state of hyperaesthesia. When he was led into the psychiatric department, he kept bowing politely, and

he strode majestically into his room, thanking the attendants for
the 'magnificent reception'. He kept wanting to shake hands with
the doctor and to sing his poems. He talked disconnectedly and
almost incessantly, grimacing all the while. The doctors diagnosed
'a paralytic psychic disturbance'. He became a second-class patient
when his mother decided that she could not afford to pay for first-
class treatment. He was noisy and slept little, despite the tran-
quillizers he was given. He complained of headaches. After three
weeks of confinement he was enraged, frequently screaming word-
lessly. On 9 February his mother came to see him, bringing
cherries and a new pair of gloves. She was unable to persuade
Binswanger to take any interest in Nietzsche's recent notebooks.
'It would be impossible to read them,' he said, though the one she
was offering contained such highly readable epigrams as

> Loneliness
> does not torture; it matures –
> So you must have the sun as a girl-friend.

and

> You run too fast!
> only now when you tire
> does your luck catch up with you.

Nor did Binswanger want to read any more of *Ecce Homo* than the
preface.

Though Nietzsche always knew who the doctors were, he
thought Cosima had brought him to the asylum,[151] and he was
confused about his own identity, sometimes calling himself the
Duke of Cumberland or the Kaiser,[152] and once saying 'I was
Friedrich Wilhelm IV the last time.'[153] His appetite continued to
be large, and he gained fourteen pounds in weight between 1
March and 1 April. White hairs were growing on the right side of
his moustache,[154] and he often complained of neuralgia on the
right side. From 20 March till 17 August he was treated with
Ung. ciner, which was used for aggressive paralysis. In April he
was less prone to delusions of grandeur and more conscious of being
ill, complaining of headaches and pains around the eyes. He spoke
little to the other patients, and often spoke in French. Accustomed
to spending his summers in the Engadin he found it an ordeal to

stay in Jena, and Binswanger noticed how the heat unsettled him. In June he smashed a window,[155] and in July a tumbler, wanting 'to protect his approaches with glass splinters'.[156] The presence of other people irritated him, and he wanted to spend most of the day in bed.[157] He was complaining of headaches on the right side of his head. He thought the chief warder was Bismarck. Believing that he was being tortured every night, he begged for help.[158]

When his mother came to see him on 29 June, they were taken to the consulting room. 'A magnificent room isn't it? This is where I give my lectures to a select public, and I've had the best offers from Leipzig.' When he found a pencil, he wrote delightedly on an old envelope his mother had, and on the way back he took a pencil and some of the paper that was in the 'lecture theatre'. 'Now I shall have something to do when I creep into my cave.'

In the middle of August he smashed more window-panes, saying he had seen the barrel of a rifle behind them. In the autumn he was less prone to violence, and from October onwards his mother was allowed to see him more often. He looked 'just the same as in his healthiest days, and he has a healthy look in his eyes too'.[159] She tried to make him write to Elisabeth. He was quite willing to, but his handwriting was indistinct, and the letter rapidly deteriorated into nonsense.

In December a self-professed disciple, Julius Langbehn, who believed he could cure Nietzsche, managed to win both his mother's and Binswanger's confidence. He started taking him out for walks – two hours in the morning, two in the afternoon. He wanted to bring Nietzsche to Dresden, and to obtain funds for setting up a household in which Nietzsche would be treated like a royal child, rather like Pirandello's Enrico IV. Langbehn would play the role of a major-domo, with attendants to make up the retinue. Gast believed in him but Overbeck was sceptical, and Nietzsche's mother finally baulked when Langbehn wanted to become her son's legal guardian.

On 21 January 1890 Gast came to visit his friend. 'He did not look very ill. I almost had the impression that his mental disturbance consists of no more than a heightening of the humorous antics he used to put on for an intimate circle of friends. He recognized me immediately, embraced and kissed me, was highly delighted to see me, and gave me his hand repeatedly as if unable to believe

I was really there.'[160] Going for long walks with Nietzsche every day, Gast could see that he did not want to be cured: 'it seemed – horrible though this is – as if Nietzsche were merely feigning madness, as if he were glad for it to have ended in this way'. This tallies with Overbeck's feelings when he came to Jena in February: 'I cannot escape the ghastly suspicion ... that his madness is simulated. This impression can be explained only by the experiences I have had of Nietzsche's self-concealments, of his spiritual masks. But here too I have bowed to facts which overrule all personal thoughts and speculations.' Apparently neither of them remembered what he had written in *Morgenröte* about ancient Greeks who feigned madness or prayed for delirium.

Every day Gast took him six doughnuts, and on 1 February, Nietzsche said: 'No, my friend, I do not want to get sticky fingers now because I want to play a little first.' Then he sat down to improvise. 'Not one wrong note! Interweaving tones of Tristan-like sensitivity ... Beethoven-like profundity and jubilant songs rising above it. Then again reveries and dreams.' Gast left the asylum feeling 'enormously strengthened in my belief we shall have our Nietzsche back again'.

In the middle of February his mother moved into a small flat in Jena, where he would soon be able to live with her. Every morning at nine o'clock she called to collect him from the clinic, and he stayed with her and Gast until six-thirty in the evening. Most of the time he was childishly docile now, and easily reduced to tears. Overbeck, who arrived on 24 February to spend a few days in Jena, soon formed the opinion that his mind had deteriorated since last year.[161] In the street Nietzsche would sometimes try to hit dogs or passers-by. He could talk lucidly about events before his breakdown, but Overbeck failed to draw him into discussing the more recent past. 'Your chocolate is in N's hands,' Overbeck wrote to his wife. 'He rushed at it, I mean at the packet, to make it disappear into his pocket.'[162]

Binswanger was no less patronizing towards his patients than most contemporary directors of asylums. Explaining Nietzsche's symptoms to some visitors, Binswanger told him to walk up and down the room, and when he responded lethargically, he was told: 'Now, Professor, an old soldier like you must still be able to march nicely!' 'His eyes lit up, his body tensed, and he started striding firmly through the room!'[163] Immune to humiliation, Nietzsche was not at first eager to move out of the clinic into the flat with his mother but was happy to spend time with her, especially when she read to him. When he did not want to do what she told him, she had only to threaten to go away and he would immediately try to appease her with a hug, even in the street, or by holding her arm more tightly. When he talked incoherently or gesticulated wildly, she would imitate him, saying: 'Suppose I did that to you and made such queer movements with my hands, would you under-stand me?' This would make him laugh. Sometimes he would want to shake hands with strangers in the street, but usually the couple would cross the road or change direction when anyone approached.[164]

On 24 March 1890 he was released from the asylum, and he stayed in the flat with her until 13 May when they left for Naum-burg. Mostly his behaviour was inoffensive, but one morning before the end of the month he left the house without her and started to undress on the pavement, wanting to bathe in a puddle, until a policeman stopped him. Her overriding fear was that she would lose him once again to the clinic, but she managed to keep him with her for the rest of her life. Sometimes she would take him to visit friends, the Gelzer-Thurneysens. She would coax him into playing their piano by sitting down herself to strike a few chords. At first he would play standing up, but she would push him onto the stool, and once absorbed he would go on for hours, leaving her free to talk in another room. Looking after him with no one to help her but the elderly maid, Alwine, she was con-stantly tired, and so long as she could hear piano music in the background she could relax.[165]

In December 1890 she was to see her daughter again. Bernhard Förster, who had been defrauding his colonists, had committed suicide in June 1889, and after keeping control of Nueva Germania for more than a year since his death, Elisabeth came back. With his mother, Nietzsche waited for her at the railway station, holding a bunch of roses. At home he seemed not to follow her stories about Paraguay, but listened with pleasure when she read to him from *Zarathustra*. According to Gast, who visited them in February 1891, she spent little time with Nietzsche, busying her-self with correspondence and trips to Berlin. She seemed disappointed that he appeared so indifferent to her, but he was no longer able to carry on a conversation, just smiling or shaking his head or making inconsequential remarks. Since Gast's visit to the asylum his memory had deteriorated, and though he still tried to play the piano, he had lost his sense of rhythm.[166] His mother tried to stimulate his memory by asking about old friends or posing such questions as 'Who was Zola?' or 'Who was Aristophanes?' Usually he could supply the basic facts, but like a schoolboy who had been forced to learn them. When Deussen, who came to see him in the autumn, tried to turn the conversation to Schopenhauer, he said, 'Arthur Schopenhauer was born in Danzig.'[167]

Elisabeth had been planning to write a book that would redeem her husband's reputation, but when articles began to appear in newspapers and periodicals about the sick philosopher, she realized they might arouse interest in Nietzsche's work. In the 1889 edition of Meyer's *Konversationlexikon* there is no mention of the name Nietzsche, but she was astute enough to guess that with help from a commercially-minded publisher a market could soon be created for his work. She also knew that Gast was the only man accustomed to deciphering Nietzsche's handwriting, so she assured him that no decision would be taken without his consent. Eventually she agreed terms with Naumann. Instead of going back to Paraguay at the end of 1891 as she had intended, she stayed on until July 1892, making arrangements for a cheap edition of her brother's works.

His mother was devoting virtually all her time to looking after him, taking him out for three or four hours of walking every day, and at least three times a week to the river-water baths. She read to him a good deal; when left with a book he would read out loud, bending close to the page and straining till the veins stood out on his forehead.[168] She would also let him sit alone on the veranda or play the piano, not so much singing as speaking texts to his own accompaniment.[169] He would often remain silent for most of the day, leafing through books and taking only two or three words from a page, or staring for a long time at his hands as if they did not belong to him, stuffing them finally into his trouser pockets. But he looked quite healthy, and there was no sign of paralysis.

Visiting him again in February 1892, Gast found him more passive. Only when he read would he become excited, making loud barking or rumbling noises until the book was taken away from him. Mostly he would read only the number on the page, the first line, and a line from the middle of the page, obviously without understanding.[170] When he went out for walks with his mother, there would often be 'a laughing expression on his face, which does not suit him, but I let him keep it, because it must draw pleasant pictures through his soul, and only when we meet someone do I remind him to "make his nice serious professorial face", which mostly he does, but he often seems not quite to understand what is wanted'.[171]

His mother's presence was certainly a comfort to him. When she put her hand on his brow, he would sometimes say: 'You have a *good* hand,' and when she read to him from the table he would often lie next to her on the sofa, holding her right hand pressed against his chest for hours at a stretch.[172] He would sit for hours in the armchair facing the window, childishly examining the favourite objects he had accumulated in five purses. Certain sentences he would say again and again: 'I am dead because I am stupid' or 'I am stupid because I am dead,' 'I have a fine feeling for things', and 'I do not like horses', though he persisted, despite correction, in saying '*ich bebe*' instead of '*ich liebe*'.[173]

Alongside the childlike goodwill towards his mother was a hostility which could seldom have found any outlet, but in the archive at Weimar there are four pages of crayon scrawl in red and blue, probably written before Elisabeth sailed for Paraguay in July 1892. One of the many strange features about the cryptic, discontinuous sentences is that when he used the first person he was not referring to himself, but performing a harshly critical ventriloquism, with either his mother or his sister as object. 'Only where did the illness in the family come from? For little Marie was indeed a very strong girl and the Herr Pastor even more so I got to know him at the wedding They used to say it always fell on the fourth child.'[174] 'Marie' must refer to his mother, and he seems to have been harbouring a morbid suspicion that she had once had an incestuous affair with her brother Edmund, pastor at Gorenzen:

Edmund *heartily* loved both your good children and loved the Bl wife so much he was now another guardian of our Fritz and more Indeed he was declared incurable at the court of Prof. Binzwanger [sic] and from that moment on I had no peace in being able at least to look after him myself Indeed I had my fun finding out whether he was engaged for all the ones that came to me were either engaged or got engaged so he said I've had my fingers burnt so I prefer not to move in Do they have children? Do you remember when I said uninvited guests have to stand in the corner It was too much grief for a mother's heart was it not she still has 3 children? of her own Does either of us resemble him? He is so similar to him in character too so gently dignified They could both control themselves so well.[175]

At the same time he was capable of a much more sympathetic identification with the old lady, even if he was partially aware that she was glad to repossess him, to become as indispensable to him as in infancy. 'Otherwise he feels abandoned But the love for me has also remained Already he has become too accustomed to me again It makes it so difficult for me to say goodbye.'[176] 'It is better here but when one can still do something to help and here I can.'

When Elisabeth is the subject, the insane ventriloquism is unambivalently hostile. '*As mother of the colony* I still have so much to do for all the colonists! That is the main pleasure for Fritz I am monstrously good. I do not know whether I am [leaving] my husband's work in the lurch.' And he is probably mimicking her when he writes: 'For me everything was over a long time ago, what I have lost I have lost. Only if my private property increases in value will I be able to recover the greater part of my capital. Money is nothing to me! God has always helped me! And I am very *glad* to give.'[177]

On these four pages all the references to himself are in the second person or the third. 'Always great things expected from you.' 'Loyal, loyal, loyal.' 'He is very pleased to have visits He is often livelier, it varies Today is a quiet day. . . . He recognizes voices from old times. Always kindly and pleasant.'[178] 'He has always been so *noble*.'

There is only one reference to Wagner: 'That is a *famous* glass. Present from Wagner.' And there is one reference to the daily walks with his mother: 'We go walking in the beechwood for three or four hours every day and indeed winter and summer In the morning until quarter to two and in the evening before supper.'[179]

Towards the end of 1892 he had several months of almost sleepless nights, rubbing at his left side with his right hand, working himself up, groaning and sweating profusely. His mother consulted Binswanger, who alarmed her by saying it might be necessary to take him back into the clinic. Gast, who visited him again in January 1893, was worried by the vehement way he would seize uncomprehendingly on two or three words out of what was said to him, and it looked as though he was liable to become violent with his mother.[180] But within a few weeks the over-excitement subsided, and by the spring he was again sleeping peacefully.[181] His appetite was good, though he never asked for food or drink. He would often say: 'Is your name perhaps Franziska?' or 'More light', or 'Summary death', or 'I lived in a place with excellent people. The place was called Basel, I believe.' Some days he would go on talking, inconsequentially, until he had exhausted himself and his eyelids closed.[182] When they were out walking, she would silence him whenever anyone approached, so that his nonsense would not be overheard.[183] When it became impossible to silence him, she gave up taking him out for walks. Several times, on coming home, she broke down in tears. She was terrified, above all, of losing him to Binswanger again.

When Elisabeth came back from Paraguay in September 1893 she found him much more abstracted than when she had left fifteen months earlier, but the demand for his books had increased so steeply that Naumann had decided to bring out the collected works, edited by Gast, who was also planning to write a biography. This idea she quickly scotched, wanting to be the biographer herself. With her mother's reluctant consent she had a wall removed to create space for a Nietzsche Archive on the ground floor of the house, and she retrieved all the manuscripts in Gast's possession. She then ousted him from his editorial position in favour of Fritz Koegel, a young man who had been on the point of entering the consular service. Leaving her mother and Alwine to look after Nietzsche, she devoted her formidable energy to writing a two-volume biography, drawing freely on *Ecce Homo*, which was still unpublished, to supervising preparations for the collected edition, and to building up the archive. Overbeck refused to trust her with her brother's letters to him, but virtually all his other correspondents either donated or sold their material to her. To link herself more obviously to him she began to sign herself

Elisabeth Förster-Nietzsche, obtaining a court order to validate the change.

At Easter 1894, Erwin Rohde accepted her invitation to visit Nietzsche: 'he is completely apathetic, recognizes no one but his mother and sister, speaks scarcely a single sentence for a month at a stretch. His body is shrivelled and weak, though his complexion is healthy. . . . But obviously he no longer feels anything – neither happiness nor unhappiness.'[184] On his fiftieth birthday Paul Deussen came to the house with a bouquet: 'Only the flowers seemed to engage his attention for a moment, but then they too lay unnoticed.'[185] It may have been as a result of lying in bed so much that the right-hand side of his body became immobilized. As Professor Wille wrote to Peter Gast in 1906, he had no doubt that Nietzsche had progressive paralysis, and Binswanger was of the same opinion. Doctor Ziehen, who attended him both at the Jena clinic and at home in Naumburg, called it atypical *dementia paralytica*, and the old family doctor, Gutjahr, confirmed the diagnosis. The mistake was typical of the period.

Uncomfortable at having her daughter and Koegel working together downstairs while the invalid was lying upstairs, his mother objected strongly enough to provoke her daughter into renting a large flat. In September 1894 Elisabeth moved into it, together with the archive. The first volume of her biography was completed early in 1895. After the young Rudolf Steiner published his book on Nietzsche, she invited him to work for her. When he realized that she had no understanding of her brother's philosophy, he offered to give her lessons, which she accepted from him.

The royalty earnings were extremely high: at the end of 1894 Naumann paid fourteen thousand marks into Nietzsche's account, and the Machiavellian Elisabeth secured six thousand for herself – more than twice as much as her brother's pension had been. Her next objective was to obtain sole control of her brother's work. With help from her friends she raised enough money to offer her mother a regular income for the rest of her life on condition that she surrendered her rights. The old lady was reluctant, but her daughter made out that the archive needed funds and that donations were available subject to the proviso that she was in sole charge. Her mother finally submitted, and signed the document on 18 December 1895.

In September 1895, Overbeck paid his last visit to his friend:

> I saw him only in his room, half-crouching like a wild animal mortally
> wounded and wanting only to be left in peace. He made literally not one
> sound while I was there. He did not appear to be suffering or in pain,
> except perhaps for the expression of profound distaste visible in his
> lifeless eyes. . . . He had been living for weeks in a state of alternation
> between days of dreadful excitability, rising to a pitch of roaring and
> shouting, and days of complete prostration.[186]

The longest of Nietzsche's friendships, it had resembled his boyhood relationships with Lutheran pastors and theologians such as
Buddensieg.

In August 1896 Elisabeth moved into a flat near the centre of
Weimar, taking the archive with her. When Koegel became
engaged to Emily Gelzer, Elisabeth made up her mind to get rid
of him, at first hoping Steiner would take over from him as chief
editor and later thinking of editing the books herself, together with
Meta von Salis, who had become a friend and investor. In April
1897 Elisabeth was called back to Naumburg; her mother was ill
with influenza and needed help in looking after her son. Then, on 20
April, the seventy-one-year-old woman died. Elisabeth did not
want to live in Naumburg again and there was not enough room
in the flat to accommodate her brother, so she persuaded Meta to
buy a villa on the outskirts of Weimar, the Villa Silberblick, which
could accommodate the archive, the philosopher, and his sister.
Meta would have been a frequent visitor had she not been outraged
by the ostentatious alterations Elisabeth made to the house without even consulting her. Her opinion of Elisabeth sank even lower
when she read a newspaper article by a journalist who had been
allowed to observe Nietzsche during his sleep and then awake,
watching him crouching on a chair as pieces of cake were fed to
him.[187] According to Elisabeth, his condition improved after the
move to Weimar: he began to make comments on what was read
to him, and, as it became easier for him to move, even tried to write.

Another investor, Count Harry Kessler, came to stay at the
Villa Silberblick in August 1897, and before breakfast on his
second day there he was taken into the invalid's room:

> He was asleep on a sofa. His mighty head had sunk half-way down to
> the right as if it were too heavy for his neck. His forehead was truly

colossal; his manelike hair is still dark brown, like his shaggy, protruding moustache. . . . In the lifeless, flabby face one can still see deep wrinkles dug by thought and willpower, but softened, as it were, and getting smoothed out. There is infinite weariness in his expression. His hands are waxen, with green and violet veins, and slightly swollen, as on a dead body. A table and a high-backed chair had been positioned at the edge of the sofa to prevent the heavy body from slipping down. . . . He looked less like a sick man or a lunatic than like a corpse.[188]

Two months later Kessler again went to stay at the villa. About fifteen minutes after switching off his light for the night, he was startled by a loud roar from the sick-room. 'I half got up and again heard once or twice the long, coarse, moaning sounds he was uttering with full force.'

He was unaware that his books, now prodigiously lucrative, were supporting Elisabeth's social life. The name Nietzsche was constantly appearing in the papers, and while he did not benefit from his fame, she was delightedly receiving the artists and aristocrats who came to the villa. She could afford to employ a cook, a maid, a private secretary, a liveried coachman, gardeners and an editorial staff – sometimes four people. At the same time she was consciously cultivating a Nietzsche myth. In the summer of 1898 she cut off a lock of his hair and put it in an envelope for the archive. She dressed him in a white pleated robe that made him look like a Brahmin. Whoever saw him, wrote Rudolf Steiner, 'had the impression that this man could not die, but that his eye would rest for all eternity upon mankind and the whole world of appearance.'[189]

But in the summer of 1898, when he had a minor stroke, his condition deteriorated, and after a more serious one in May 1899 he was weaker, and able to talk only with so much difficulty that he did not want other people to hear his voice. 'I do not speak nicely.' But when he was given a new book, he said: 'Didn't I write good books too?'[190]

In 1899–1900 he was treated by Doctor Vulpius for inflammation in the iris of the left eye. The pigment spots on the front of the lens capsule and the failure of the pupil to react to light made him conclude that the disease was syphilitic.[191] On Monday 20 August 1900 Nietzsche caught a cold. His temperature went up, and it was hard for him to breathe. 'At about midday on Friday the

24th, as I was sitting opposite him, his whole expression suddenly changed, and as the stroke came, he sank back unconscious.'[192] He was dead. It was seven weeks before his fifty-sixth birthday. Elisabeth had the body laid out on white linen and damask in a heavy oak coffin between potted plants and flowers in the archive room. She invited an eminent art-historian, Kurt Breysig, to deliver the funeral oration. He was given her sewing box to use as a lectern, and, reading from a manuscript, he spoke at inordinate length. A critic remarked: 'The same sterile scholasticism Nietzsche had always fought followed him to his grave. If he could have arisen, he would have thrown the lecturer out of the window and chased the rest of us out of his temple.'[193]

He was buried the next day at Röcken next to his father. Elisabeth had arranged for a traditional Lutheran funeral, so the author of *Der Antichrist* was buried to the sound of church bells and the village choir singing hymns. The coffin was decorated with a silver cross. Gast, who had made his peace with Elisabeth, gave the benediction, ending with the words: 'Hallowed be thy name to all future generations.'

Nietzsche maintained that for men capable of greatness, considerations of pleasure and pain should always be secondary. Schopenhauerian man, as characterized in the 1874 essay *Schopenhauer als Erzieher*, despises all thoughts of comfort or discomfort: his strength lies in his capacity for forgetting himself. In the 1880s Nietzsche wrote derogatory notes about metaphysicians who brought the problem of pleasure and pain into the foreground: 'For the courageous and the creative, pleasure and pain are *never* ultimate values – they are epiphenomena: if one is to achieve anything one must desire both.'[1] It is possible to desire both without making them into ultimate values, but to a man who prides himself, as Nietzsche did, on not letting a day go by without 'lopping off some comforting belief', they are not secondary considerations. For those condemned to life-long malaise, with life-long poverty to exacerbate the suffering, physical comfort is in any case unavailable, but it is not everyone who defies the winter, as Zarathustra does, by taking cold baths. It was not for nothing that the boys at Pforta called Nietzsche a *Quälgeist*, a thorn in the flesh. Even then his intolerance towards easy-going mediocrity must have seemed neurotic, and the inclination to prove a point about Mucius Scaevola by holding lighted matches in the palm of his hand belongs to the same pattern as the inclination to impose penances on himself, as he did after first reading Schopenhauer, rationing himself for two weeks to four hours' sleep a night. Otto Rank has pointed out that as with the obsessional neurotic, Nietzsche's combination of politeness, mildness and delicacy with glorification of cruelty derived from a suppression of the sado-masochistic impulse.[2]

The habit of self-punishment was formed long before the theories about self-conquest. The will to power may have functioned in him through the belief that self-mastery was the necessary preliminary for winning power over others, but it is obvious that the satisfaction he gained from self-frustration motivated some of his most crucial decisions, as when he blanketed his strong inclination to become an artist. The commitment to classical philology was an act of submission to a discipline he expected to be stringent, and in his undergraduate research on Theognis, *Suidas*, Diogenes and Democritus, he made self-denial into a method of proceeding. Habituating himself to a rigorous scepticism, a dutiful intolerance towards all but the minority of scholarly assumptions that could withstand close critical scrutiny, he was already on the track that would lead to the rejection of Schopenhauer and Wagner. It would have been intolerably comfortable to go on believing in them. 'Isolated though I was,' he wrote, looking back on the situation after the *volte-face*, 'I now took sides *against* myself and *for* everything that would hurt *me* – me especially – and come hard to me.'[3]

When he was working on the Schopenhauer essay, he obviously believed in his own capacity for forgetting himself. 'If he considers himself at all,' he wrote of Schopenhauerian man, 'it is to gauge the remoteness of his exalted goal, and he seems to see a paltry mound of slag behind himself, and underneath.'[4] Within seven years he had to acknowledge that it was impossible to keep the slag out of the writings. 'There is something about them that constantly offends my sense of shame: they are mirror-images of an incomplete, suffering creature with scarcely any control over his vital organs.'[5] But he had not recognized that this was inevitable, nor would he admit it publicly. In *Jenseits* he wrote: 'Mistrusting the possibility of self-knowledge, I have never thought about myself much or with any enthusiasm.' This is doubly misleading. Freud was right to praise the unique depth of his self-knowledge, and no one – not even Artaud – has left a more detailed documentation of his physical suffering, but it was only when he was on the brink of madness that Nietzsche could see he had always been thinking and writing about himself, even when concerning himself with Jesus or Socrates or Wagner: 'I am all the names in history.' Yet the statement in *Jenseits* is an accurate index of his intentions: he had not wanted to think about himself, and though the ideas were like the physical discomforts in seeming to arrive, uninvited, from somewhere outside his body, they were unlike physical discomforts in seeming to have meaning in relation to what was outside. The vigorous attempt at self-denial had led not to self-absorption but to a vigorously extroverted solipsism.

In relation to the human condition, as to the conditions of his own life, Nietzsche had no choice but to move painfully and fruitfully between passive acceptance and violent rebellion, between *amor fati* and outrage. Without needing to oscillate so much, we are all caught in the same trap. To agree wholeheartedly to the living conditions we are given is to accept the prospect of death cheerfully: is this masochism or realism? For Kafka, who was about fifteen when he started reading Nietzsche, and who emulated him in taking sides against himself ('Everything I possess is directed against me'), it seemed that the best things he had written had their basis in 'this capacity of mine to die contentedly. ... I positively enjoy my own death in the dying character's.' Kierkegaard wrote: 'As a sick man longs to cast off his bandages, so does my mind long to cast off ... that sweaty, sodden poultice which is the body and its weakness.' Like Kafka, he had the feeling that he was always outside himself. Nietzsche sometimes had the impression that he could sidestep the unsatisfactory present by mortgaging his life to writing which would give him a posthumous hold on the future. The living might cross him off their list, but the day after tomorrow would belong to him. He was no less solitary than Kafka or Kierkegaard, no less inept and half-hearted in making plans for marrying, but, unlike them, he launched himself into paeans of exuberant praise for life. The euphoria he finally experienced in Turin is prefigured in passage after passage of jubilantly affirmative prose in *Morgenröte*, in *Die fröhliche Wissenschaft*, in *Zarathustra*. But sooner or later negativity would always gain the upper hand. 'I do not wish for life again. How have I borne it? Creatively. What gives me strength to bear the sight of it? The prospect of the superior man, the affirmer of life. I have tried myself to affirm it – ah!'[6] Like Artaud, who was badgered by pain into making insane proposals for the improvement of the human body, Nietzsche took refuge in biological futurology. 'Perhaps the whole evolution of the spirit rests on the body; it is the history of the development of a superior body that surfaces in our sensibility. ... In the long run it is not a question of humanity: it is to be overcome.'[7] The difficulty of reconciling the doctrine of eternal recurrence with the idea of the superior man derives from this inescapable ambivalence of Nietzsche's towards everything he meant by the word *life*. 'Wholeheartedly I love only life', says Zarathustra, 'and verily never more than when I hate it.' Self-defeat is, for Nietzsche, as inextricably intertwined with self-conquest as self-denial is with self-transcendence.

Discussing Rimbaud, Leo Bersani has suggested that the repudiation of the self in *'Je est un autre'*, the disjunction between subject and thought, may be connected with his ambition to make poetry mean as little as possible.[8] He rejected his family, his country, religion, society, and almost the entire history of litera-ture. There was no equivalent to Rimbaud's violence in Nietzsche's equable behaviour, but he, too, effectively rejected his family and his country, exiling himself from society while repudiating the whole tradition of idealist philosophy. He was trying to deny the whole of contemporary reality in favour of the vision he expressed with his image of the superior man. He would have been mortified to think that he was paralleling Wagner's ambition for Siegfried, but the anterior impulse of rejection is the same: 'Wotan represents the totality of the intelligence of the present, whereas Siegfried is the man of the future. We want him and wish for his arrival, but we cannot create him – he must create himself by means of our annihilation.'[9] But is there any connection between Nietzsche's self-denial, his denial of self as an entity, and his wholesale repudiation of contemporary reality?

In advocating self-control, the overcoming of the lower instincts in favour of the higher, Nietzsche's *oeuvre* is not alone in nine-teenth-century German literature and philosophy. Goethe, in *Wilhelm Meisters Lehrjahre*, puts a highly educable young man into a series of situations that bring him closer to the self-realization which has always been his conscious objective. In Adalbert Stifter's *Nachsommer*, Heinrich may fail to learn from his mistakes, but the intention is that the reader should. Schopen-hauer's assumption is that it is only through suffering that we can discover the truth about life, and he recommends withdrawal into cultured leisure as an escape from the degrading enslavement to will. He also represents the ideal existence as being independent of other people. Nietzsche may have abandoned the plans for educational reform that required him to surround himself with friends in Basel, but he never ceased to regard himself as a teacher, and, through Zarathustra, he preaches a gospel which is more liberal and more psychologically enlightened than Christianity. We should not repay evil with good or want to have too many virtues. We should not bear false witness or commit adultery, for we will sleep badly if we do, but we should not feel obliged to love our neighbours or despise our bodies. 'There is more reason in your body than in your best wisdom.'[10] But if this corresponds to what Nietzsche believed, why is sexuality almost always either repressed or sublimated in his work? Eroticism is seldom admitted to his verse, and hardly ever to his prose, except in the second part of *Zarathustra*, when the recent humiliation at the hands of Lou Salomé was making it a painful pleasure to work blunted declarations of love into the narrative. The occasional discussions of sexuality, such as the one that occurs in the fourth part, may seem uninhibited, but they are disingenuous. Zarathustra tells us that he always suspects the motives of men who embrace chastity, but Nietzsche usually tries to convey the impression either that he was not sexually inexperienced or that he had sublimated sexual desire for the sake of his work. There is no genuine attempt to translate the body's wisdom into philosophy, or to preach a self-realization in which physical and intellectual desires can be reconciled with intellectual aspirations. In fact he seems to have been profoundly frightened of sexual desire as a destructive force. His prophecies of a future holocaust may have little in common with the fantasies of mass destruction in *Justine* and *Juliette*, but when he was near to madness he showed an unmistakable relish in associating himself with the disasters that would come after his death, and this is reminiscent of Lady Clairwil's dreams of committing such large-scale crimes that the resultant chaos outlasts her. As Gilles Deleuze argues, the apathy of the Sadean libertine depends on the masochistic pleasure of 'denying nature within the self and outside of the self, and denying the self itself'.[11] This is what Nietzsche did.

At the same time, it must be recognized that his inversion of Platonism and his attacks on Christianity precipitated an affirmation of the self which was revolutionary. Though he called himself an immoralist, he was really a moralist who exposed the self-deceptions inherent in previous moralizing. After self-observation had sharpened his awareness of the pleasure to be had from inflicting pain and curbing self-indulgence, he was able to apply the rigour he had cultivated as a philologist to his critical scrutiny of the priesthood, while his analysis of *ressentiment* highlighted the flaws and absurdities in the facade of meekness and self-righteousness that can all too easily be erected by the Christian. Nietzsche's praise for the morality he admires – 'master' morality or 'noble' morality – is based on the claim that it 'grows out of a triumphant affirmation of the self', whereas 'slave' morality is based on denial, rejection, 'and this No is its creative act'.[12] One of Nietzsche's major achievements as a philosopher was that he reasoned his way towards a new humanism, a way of apprehending good and evil without divine sanctions. As Heidegger wrote, 'This metaphysics, which includes the doctrine of the *Übermensch*, is unlike any previous metaphysics in casting man in the role of the sole and unconditioned measure of all things.'[13]

The problem of whether Nietzsche should be categorized as a metaphysician may be taken together with the problem of how his private self-denial is compatible with his revolutionary affirmation of the self. The imagery that came most naturally to him was the imagery of disease. He saw Christianity as a debilitating malady with a firm grip on European civilization, and he compared the impossibility of refuting Christianity with the impossibility of refuting a disease of the eye.[14] How can logic or intelligence be pitted against either? Logic is a clumsy weapon anyway, when it can 'handle only formulas for what remains the same',[15] while reality is in a constant state of flux. But the current state of civilization was such that all the 'higher sentiments' were 'intermingled with illusion and extravagance': they were urgently in need of 'purification', which could take effect on them only gradually.[16] Language may be incapable of encapsulating the objective truth about reality, but for Nietzsche there could be no question of abandoning the mental activity that was impossible without it: 'we cease to think when we refuse to do so under the constraint of language. . . . Rational thought is interpretation according to a scheme we cannot jettison.'[17] In face of disease, usefulness may be a more important criterion than truth.

Nietzsche is still often reprimanded for inconsistency and for flouting the law of non-contradiction, but, like Kierkegaard, he had little respect for it, and it was one of his major achievements to show that its value was limited. His attacks on language and logic were launched most cogently in work he left unpublished – the essay on truth and falsehood and the notebooks. His formulations of 1886–7 do not substantially diverge from his formulations of 1873, except in dropping the contrast he had drawn between concepts and intuitive awareness. Though he often referred, as an empiricist would, to the evidence of the senses, for him 'the antithesis of this phenomenal world is not "the real world" but the formless unformulable world of the chaos of sensations – *another kind* of phenomenal world, "unknowable" to us'.[18] He consistently believed that 'the fictitious world of subject, substance, "reason" etc. is indispensable. . . . "Truth" is the will to be master over the multiplicity of sensations. . . . In this . . . we take phenomena as *real*.'[19] But, being indescribable, the character of a world in a state of becoming may seem false or self-contradictory.[20] If language and logic can cope only with a fictional world in which everything remains static, the law of non-contradiction can be no more binding on us than, say, the rule of the three unities. 'The conceptual ban on contradiction proceeds from the assumption . . . that the concept not only designates the essence of a thing but *comprehends* it. . . . Logic is an attempt to comprehend actuality by means of a scheme of being we have ourselves proposed.'[21]

The two unsteady supports which Nietzsche had for his cerebration and his attempts at communication were his uncomfortable sense of his own physical existence and his sense of his own enormous potential. In so far as he believed that the individual's life could be shaped into a work of art, he had himself as excitingly malleable material with tantalizing limitations, but, despite his lack of faith in logic, he could try to argue himself into a position of superiority by fighting his own disease at the same time as fighting Europe's, refuting neither but trying to overcome both, if only by visualizing a future without them. This is one of the ways in which the relentless struggle against himself was linked to the rejection of contemporary reality, while his awareness of disunity inside himself led (or at least contributed) to his disbelief in the self generally as a coherent entity. It also made it easier for him to envisage a moral perspective in which the upward and downward pulls were not oriented in relation to a transcendent ideal of goodness. Goethe's Faust may have been aware of having two souls within his breast, but the differentiation had been realized in terms of a God–devil polarity.

Nietzsche was too impressed by the pre-Socratic philosophers, who set great store by cosmology, to be uninterested in the possibilities of looking at humanity from a hypothetical viewpoint outside it and trying to imagine the world as a whole. It can be said that this is to adopt a transcendental perspective, but if we are dealing in fictions anyway, the cosmological hypothesis must be admissible, so long as it is presented tentatively. Nietzsche was aware that what he had to offer was not facts but interpretations or simplifications. 'He is a thinker: that is to say he knows how to take things as being simpler than they are.'[22] Many of Nietzsche's ideas are metaphysical in the sense of taking an overall view of humanity – his scepticism about free will, God and the soul all fall into this category, as does his doctrine of eternal recurrence – but he does not insist on these ideas as Kant does on his categories and his *a priori* judgements, claiming that they apply necessarily and universally because without them experience could not be apprehended or comprehended. Nietzsche, the frustrated artist, had already argued in *Die Geburt der Tragödie* that experience could be justified only as an aesthetic phenomenon, and his achievement, before withdrawing into the fictional world of madness, was to draw truth and fiction closer together than they had ever been before, damaging, if not quite destroying, the barrier between them. But the danger of looking at the individual life as a potential work of art and at the world as an aesthetic phenomenon is that one has no good reason for fighting shy of a tragic ending. On the contrary, isn't the work of art likely to be greater if the ending is catastrophic? In the 1874 essay on history Nietzsche had already written: 'I know of no purpose in life better than being destroyed by what is great and impossible,' and in a note of 1884 he wrote: 'One must learn from war (1) to associate death with the interests for which one fights – that makes *us* venerable; (2) one must learn to sacrifice many and to take one's cause seriously enough not to spare human lives; (3) rigid discipline, and to allow oneself force and cunning in war.'[23] In other notes (which he left unpublished but which were selected, arranged in non-chronological order and published by his Fascistic sister) he discusses the possibilities of selective breeding and of educating a ruling caste, 'the masters of the earth', tyrants who can 'work as artists on "man" himself'.[24] He speaks of the need to *create conditions* that *require stronger men*, who for their part need ... a physical-cum-spiritual discipline to *strengthen them*'.[25] Though the improvement he wanted in the quality of living had nothing to do with the changes that the Nazis effected, it is undeniable that formulations such as these were useful for Hitlerian propaganda, but there is no reason to believe that twentieth-century European history would have been any different if these notebooks had remained unpublished. It is misleading to say, as J. P. Stern does in his discussion of German, Italian and French Fascism, 'It cannot be denied that the intellectual super-structure of these political movements is as inconceivable without Nietzsche's ideas as these movements are without their super-structure.'[26] This is tantamount to blaming Nietzsche for the whole phenomenon.

He is open to the charge of being excessively non-political, arguing as he did that in a well-ordered state it should not be necessary for anyone but politicians to take an interest in political affairs. Certainly he was antidemocratic: his intolerance towards the lower orders was in line with his intolerance towards the lower instincts. But he would have hated the Third *Reich* even more, if possible, than he hated the Second.

While it is easy to exaggerate Nietzsche's political influence on our century, it is hard to exaggerate his intellectual and cultural influence. He was (to take just one aspect of it) the great pioneer of discontinuity. It may have been mainly his headaches, his habit of thinking while walking and making hasty notes, that habituated him to organizing his books in brief units, but his intuitive insight into the value of fragmentation worked hand in hand with his assumption that philosophy should concern itself not with building abstract systems but with the minutiae of human behaviour. It can be said that Nietzsche placed too little trust in the possibility of coherence and system-building, but extremism is often the concomitant of originality, and there was no shortage of systematic thinkers or system-builders among Nietzsche's contemporaries. He may have been influenced by Baudelaire, who made the point, *à propos* Corot's paintings, that 'there is a world of difference between a "completed" subject and a "finished" subject, and that in general what is "completed" is not "finished" ', but influence is less important than affinity: both writers were forerunners of modernism, and in both the interest in the sketchy, the discontinuous, was connected with an antipathy to representationalism or a disbelief that representation was feasible. Nietzsche, much more than Kant, was the philosophical prophet of the painters who saw art not so much as a matter of imitating nature as of arranging pigments on a canvas.

Nietzsche's *penchant* for discontinuity had helped to form a mental habit which enabled him, when he was writing his impressionistic historical commentaries, to isolate contradictions and moments of disjunction, instead of focusing, as most contemporary historians did, on personalities, trends, and periods circumscribed by dates. As a historian Nietzsche was brilliant, if erratic. Partly because of his eyesight, he could not read enough to equip himself for panoptic generalizations about Western civilization, and there may even have been a defensive motivation behind the impressionistic style which camouflaged the lack of substantiation for them. Similarly his scientific and theological pronouncements were based more on inspired guesswork and self-observation than on reading or research. When we compare him – as we cannot help comparing him – with Wittgenstein, his language seems coarsegrained, approximate, outmoded. He uses words like 'truth', 'life', 'man', and 'spirit' without definition or precision, though he was well in advance of his period in his awareness of the extent to which language forced him to deal in fictions. It was impossible to redefine the words 'good' and 'evil' – their meaning could not but be contingent on previous usage – but his genealogical approach to morality undeniably tends towards clarification. What seems odd is that his unrivalled understanding of the way morality had evolved did not prevent him from believing in the feasibility of moral revolution. He convinced himself not only that he would be able to revalue all values, but that his revaluation would be generally accepted, that he had somehow won the right to make a demand which humanity would find irresistible. It was insane to believe this when all his earlier books had made so little impact on the reading public, but we shall never be able to isolate a point at which disease began to unbalance his thinking. It is obvious that he would never have written in the way he did had he been healthy; and even if Freud and Adler were wrong in their long-distance diagnosis of his malaise, they usefully summed up how much Nietzsche had in common with paretics. Alfred Adler noticed that in paretics unconscious instincts often rise freely to consciousness, not being held back by their cultural ideals. This accounts for their violent changes of mood. As Freud said, paretics could go on achieving extraordinary artistic results as Maupassant did, until shortly before collapsing. The loosening process that results from paresis 'gave Nietzsche the tenacity for a quite extraordinary achievement of seeing through all layers and recognizing them at the very base [of everything]. In that way he placed his paretic disposition at the service of science.'[27]

After a life so full of suffering, it was fortunate, at least, that the final euphoria should make him immune to guilt feelings at failing to accomplish his self-imposed task. It was unjust that his sister should be the chief beneficiary of his fame, and that in 1892 he should have been aware only that great things had been expected of him, not that great things had been achieved. It may be that there was an element of *ressentiment* in his final predictions of holocaustic warfare and in his demands for the sacrifice of other people's lives. Perhaps he was, in spite of himself, seeking revenge for an inner pollution, dancing like a will-o'-the-wisp around the swamp in which humanity was to sink. But his main influence was towards unmasking, demystification. He was one of the great liberators.

Notes

Details of books are given in these notes only when they are not listed in the Bibliography. The abbreviation 's.' indicates a section.

Introduction

1 Minutes of the Vienna Psychoanalytic Society, vol. 2, 1908–10 (New York 1967).
2 Albert Camus, *L'Homme révolté* (Paris 1951).
3 'Fragment from the History of Posterity', notes 1872–5.
4 Jacques Derrida, *L'Ecriture et la différence* (Paris 1967). Translated by Alan Bass as *Writing and Difference* (Chicago and London 1978).
5 Ibid.
6 Hegel, letter to Windischmann, 27 May 1810.
7 Karl Rosenkranz, *Hegels Leben* (Berlin 1844).
8 Hegel, 'Erstes Systemprogramm des Deutschen Idealismus', in Johannes Hofmeister (ed.), *Dokumente zu Hegels Entwicklung* (Stuttgart 1936).
9 Rosenkranz, *Hegels Leben*.
10 Hegel, *Philosophie des Rechts*.
11 Letter from Goethe to Schiller, 25 November 1797.
12 *Götzendämmerung*.
13 Letter from Goethe to Schiller, 22 January 1802.
14 *Also sprach Zarathustra*, Part II, 'On Self-Conquest'.
15 Ludwig Feuerbach, *Briefe*, vol. 2.
16 *Der Wille zur Macht*, s. 1051.
17 Ibid., s. 1050.
18 Dostoevsky, *The Brothers Karamazov*, Book 5, Chap. 4.
19 *Der Wille zur Macht*, s. 1052.
20 Letter to Jacob Burckhardt, 6 January 1889.

Chapter 1

1 Letter from Pastor Gustav Adolf Osswald, 14 October 1849.
2 Quoted by Elisabeth Förster-Nietzsche.
3 Letter from Karl Marx to Arnold Ruge, 25 January 1843.
4 Otto von Bismarck, *Memoirs*, in *Gesammelte Werke* (Berlin 1924ff).
5 'Aus meinem Leben'.
6 *Ecce Homo*.
7 Cited by Blunck.
8 Friederike Dächsel, letter of August 1849.

9 'Aus meinem Leben'.
10. Ibid.
11 Paul Deussen.
12 Professor Pitzker writing in the *Tägliche Rundschau* during the summer of 1893. Cited by Elisabeth Förster-Nietzsche.
13 'Aus meinem Leben'.

Chapter 2

1 Postscript to autobiography sent to Wilhelm Pinder in the middle of February 1859.
2 Letter to his mother, 9 October 1859.
3 In an essay written in commemoration of the school's tercentenary.
4 Ibid.
5 Letter to Wilhelm Pinder, 11 December 1859.
6 Letter to his mother, mid-November 1859.
7 Letter to Wilhelm Pinder, beginning of November 1859.
8 Letter to Wilhelm Pinder, 3 December 1859.
9 Letter to Wilhelm Pinder, 11 December 1859.
10 Postscript to autobiography.
11 Diary, 11 August 1859.
12 Letter to his mother, 9 October 1859.
13 Letter to Wilhelm Pinder, late April or early May 1860.
14 Diary, 16 August 1859.
15 Letter to his mother and sister, 21 August 1859.
16 Diary, 10 August 1859.
17 Diary, 22 August 1859.
18 Paul Deussen.
19 Letter to Wilhelm Pinder, 17 March 1860.
20 Letter to Wilhelm Pinder and Gustav Krug, 14 January 1861.
21 Letter to his mother, mid-January 1861.
22 Letter to his mother, 2 February 1861.
23 Letter to his mother, 16 February 1861.
24 Ibid.
25 Letter to his mother, end of February 1861.
26 Paul Deussen.
27 Ibid.
28 Letter to Edmund Oehler, beginning of April 1861.
29 Letter to his mother and sister, April 1861.
30 Letter to his mother and sister, 10 November 1863.
31 Letter to his mother and sister, 20 August 1861.
32 Letter to Wilhelm Pinder, mid-May 1860.
33 Letter to his mother and sister, 25 August 1861.
34 Elisabeth Förster-Nietzsche.
35 Diary, 24 August 1859.

36 Letter to Rosalie Nietzsche, 11 January 1862.
37 Letter to his mother, end of February 1862.
38 Letter to his sister, end of April 1862.
39 Letter from Goethe to Eckermann, 5 July 1829.
40 Letter to his mother, 10 November 1862.
41 Letter to his mother, 19 November 1862.
42 Letter to Rosalie Nietzsche, 12 January 1863.
43 'Vor dem Kruzifix'.
44 Letter to his mother, 16 April 1863.
45 Ibid.
46 Letter to his mother, 27 April 1863.
47 Letter to his mother, 11 May 1863.
48 Letter to his mother, end of May or beginning of June 1863.
49 Ibid.
50 Letter to his mother and sister, beginning of December 1863.
51 Letter to his mother and sister, 13 March 1864.
52 Kant, *Idee zu einer allgemeinen Geschichte in weltbürgerlicher Absicht* (1864).
53 Letter to Wilhelm Pinder and Gustav Krug, 12 February 1864.
54 Letter to Wilhelm Pinder, 4 July 1864.
55 Letter to Paul Deussen, 8 July 1864.
56 Ibid.

Chapter 3

1   Elisabeth Förster-Nietzsche.
2   Letter to his mother and sister, 27 September 1864.
3   Ibid.
4   Ibid.
5   Paul Deussen.
6   Ibid.
7   Letter to his mother and sister, 8 October 1864.
8   Ibid.
9   Paul Deussen.
10 Letter to his mother and sister, 17–18 October 1864.
11 Letter to his mother and sister, 24–5 October 1864.
12 Letter to his mother and sister, 7–9 December 1864.
13 Letter to his mother and sister, 24–5 October 1864.
14 Letter to his mother and sister, 7–9 December 1864.
15 Letter to his mother and sister, 11–12 December 1864.
16 Paul Deussen.
17 Ibid.
18 *Über die Zukunft unserer Bildungsanstalten.*
19 Paul Deussen.
20 Letter to his mother and sister, Christmas 1864.

21 Letter to his mother and sister, end of December 1864.
22 Ibid.
23 Paul Deussen.
24 Thomas Mann, 'Nietzsches Philosophie', in *Neue Studien*.
25 Cited by Blunck.
26 Letter to his mother and sister, 18 February 1865.
27 Paul Deussen.
28 Letter to his mother and sister, 2 February 1865.
29 Ibid.
30 Letter to his mother and sister, end of February 1865.
31 Ibid.
32 Letter to his mother, end of February 1865.
33 Letter to his mother, 29 May 1865.
34 Letter to his sister, 11 June 1865.
35 Letter to his mother, 10 May 1865.
36 Letter to Hermann Mushacke, 30 August 1865.
37 Letter to his mother, 10 May 1865.
38 Letter to Carl von Gersdorff, 25 May 1865.
39 Letter to Carl von Gersdorff, 4 August 1865.
40 Letter to Carl von Gersdorff, 25 April 1865.
41 Ibid.
42 Letter to his mother, second half of June 1865.
43 Letter to Hermann Mushacke, 30 August 1865.
44 Letter to his mother, second half of June 1865.
45 Ibid.
46 Letter to his sister, 11 June 1865.
47 Letter to his mother and sister, 5 August 1865.
48 Letter to Hermann Mushacke, 30 August 1865.
49 *Werke und Briefe: Historisch-Kritische Gesamtausgabe* (Munich 1933–42). III 292.
50 'Rückblick auf meine zwei Leipziger Jahre', 17 October 1865–10 August 1867, written autumn 1867.
51 Letter to Eduard Mushacke, 19 October 1865.
52 Letter to his mother, 22 October 1865.
53 'Rückblick auf meine zwei Leipziger Jahre'.
54 Ibid.
55 Letter to his mother and sister, 5 November 1865.
56 Letter to his mother and sister, after 12 November 1865.
57 'Rückblick auf meine zwei Leipziger Jahre'.
58 Letter to his mother, 31 January 1866.
59 Letter to his mother and sister, 22 April 1866.
60 Elisabeth Förster-Nietzsche.
61 Letter to his mother and sister, 3 March 1866.
62 Ibid.
63 'Rückblick auf meine zwei Leipziger Jahre'.
64 Letter to Carl von Gersdorff, 7 April 1866.
65 Ibid.

66 Ibid.
67 A fragment, probably written in Leipzig late in 1865 or early in 1866.
68 Letter to his mother and sister, 22 April 1866.
69 Letter to Hermann Mushacke, 27 April 1866.
70 Letter to his mother and sister, 22 April 1866.
71 Letter to Hermann Mushacke, 27 April 1866.
72 Ibid.
73 Letter to his mother and sister, 28 April 1866.
74 Letter to his mother and sister, beginning of July 1866.
75 Ibid.
76 Ibid.
77 Postscript to the same letter.
78 Letter to Wilhelm Pinder, 7 July 1866.
79 Ibid.
80 Letter to Hermann Mushacke, 11 July 1866.
81 Letter to Carl von Gersdorff, 12 July 1866.
82 Letter to Carl von Gersdorff, 15 August 1866.
83 Letter to Carl von Gersdorff, end of August 1866.
84 Letter to Wilhelm Pinder, 5 July 1866.
85 Letter to Carl von Gersdorff, end of August 1866.
86 Ibid.
87 Postscript to a letter to Hermann Mushacke, November 1866.
88 Letter to Hermann Mushacke, 15 August 1866.
89 Letter to his mother and sister, 18 August 1866.
90 Elisabeth Förster-Nietzsche.
91 Letter to Carl von Gersdorff, 11 October 1866.
92 Letter to Hermann Mushacke, November 1866.
93 Letter to his mother and sister, 18 December 1866.
94 Letter to Hermann Mushacke, 4 January 1867.
95 Ibid.
96 Letter to Carl von Gersdorff, 20 February 1867.
97 Letter to Carl von Gersdorff, 6 April 1867.
98 Ibid.
99 Ibid.
100 Ibid.
101 Ibid.
102 *Menschliches, Allzumenschliches*, Part II, s. 20.
103 Letter to Carl von Gersdorff, 6 April 1867.
104 Elisabeth Förster-Nietzsche dates these 'before the middle of 1867'.
105 Letter to Paul Deussen, 4 April 1867.
106 Letter from Carl von Gersdorff, 31 March 1866.
107 Letter to Carl von Gersdorff, end of August 1866.
108 Letter from Erwin Rohde to Wilhelm Wisser, 29 November 1867.
109 'Rückblick auf meine zwei Leipziger Jahre'.
110 Letter to his mother and sister, end of June 1867.
111 Letter to Hermann Mushacke a few days before 15 July 1867.
112 Elisabeth Förster-Nietzsche.

Chapter 4

1 Letter to Erwin Rohde, 3 November 1867.
2 Letter to Hermann Mushacke, 4 October 1867.
3 Letter to Erwin Rohde, 3 November 1867.
4 Fragment of a letter to Paul Deussen, 10 November 1867.
5 Letter to Friedrich Ritschl, 25 October 1867.
6 Letter to Carl von Gersdorff, 24 November and 1 December 1867.
7 Letter to Erwin Rohde, 3 November 1867.
8 Ibid.
9 Letter to Carl von Gersdorff, 24 November and 1 December 1867.
10 'Über Demokrit' (fragment).
11 Ibid.
12 Letter to Carl von Gersdorff, 16 February 1868.
13 'Über Demokrit'.
14 Letter to Carl von Gersdorff, 16 February 1868.
15 Letter to Erwin Rohde, 1–3 February 1868.
16 Ibid.
17 Letter to Carl von Gersdorff, 16 February 1868.
18 Ibid.
19 Letter to Erwin Rohde, 3 April 1868 (started earlier).
20 Letter to Friedrich Ritschl, 26 May 1868.
21 Kant, *Kritik der Urteilskraft*.
22 *Bildung und Umbildung organischer Naturen*.
23 Letter to Erwin Rohde, 16 June 1868.
24 Letter to Erwin Rohde, 8 October 1868.
25 Letter to Paul Deussen, second half of October 1868.
26 Letter to Erwin Rohde, 9 November 1868.
27 Letter to Paul Deussen, second half of October 1868.
28 Letter to Erwin Rohde, 27 October 1868.
29 Letter to Paul Deussen, second half of October 1868.
30 Letter to Erwin Rohde, 27 October 1868.
31 'Wirkung eines Musikstücks', fragment reprinted in Elisabeth Förster-Nietzsche.
32 Letter to Erwin Rohde, 9 November 1868.
33 Ibid.
34 Ibid.
35 Feuerbach, *Briefe*, vol. 1, p. 407.
36 Wagner, *Mein Leben*.
37 Letter from Richard Wagner to August Röckel, 23 August 1856.
38 Ibid.
39 Richard Wagner, *Die Walküre*, Act II, Scene 2.
40 Letter to Erwin Rohde, 20 November 1868.
41 Letter to Erwin Rohde, 9 December 1868.
42 Ibid.

43 Letter to his mother and sister, end of November/beginning of December 1868.
44 Letter to Erwin Rohde, 10 January 1869.
45 Ibid.
46 Letter from Friedrich Ritschl to Wilhelm Fischer-Bilfinger, 10 January 1869.
47 Letter to his mother and sister, second half of February 1869.
48 Letter to Erwin Rohde, 22 and 28 February 1869.
49 Letter to Carl von Gersdorff, 11 April 1869.
50 Ibid.
51 'Aus den Jahren 1868–9'.
52 Ibid.
53 Letter to his mother and sister, 21 April 1869.

Chapter 5

1 Letter to Friedrich Ritschl, 10 May 1869.
2 Elisabeth Förster-Nietzsche.
3 Letter to Friedrich Ritschl, 10 May 1869.
4 Letter to his mother, May 1869.
5 Letter to Erwin Rohde, 29 May 1869.
6 Letter to Richard Wagner, 22 May 1869.
7 Letter to his sister, 29 May 1869.
8 Draft of letter to Sophie Ritschl, 26 July 1869.
9 Cf. Hugh Lloyd-Jones, 'Nietzsche and the Study of the Ancient World', in O'Flaherty, Sellner and Helm.
10 Letter to his mother, mid-June 1869.
11 Letter from Richard Wagner, 3 June 1869.
12 Cosima's diary. Entry for 5 June 1869 in her handwriting.
13 Cosima's diary. Entry for 5 June 1869 in Richard Wagner's handwriting.
14 Letter to Erwin Rohde, 16 June 1869.
15 Letter to his mother, first half of July 1869.
16 Letter to Erwin Rohde, 16 June 1869.
17 Ibid.
18 Letter to Paul Deussen, July 1869.
19 Letter to Erwin Rohde, mid-July 1869.
20 Letter to his mother, first half of July 1869.
21 Letter to Erwin Rohde, mid-July 1869.
22 Cosima's diary, 31 July 1869.
23 Letter from Cosima von Bülow, 5 August 1869.
24 Cosima's diary, 28 August 1869.
25 Letter to Carl von Gersdorff, 4 August 1869.
26 Cosima's diary, 28 August 1869.
27 Letter to Gustav Krug, 4 August 1869.

28 Letter from Cosima von Bülow, 26 August 1869.
29 Cosima's diary, 17 May 1869.
30 Gottfried Semper, *Stil im deutschen technischen und tektonischen Künsten* (1860–3).
31 Letter to his mother, beginning of September 1869.
32 Letter from Carl von Gersdorff, 8 September 1869.
33 Letter to his mother and sister, end of September 1869.
34 Letter to Carl von Gersdorff, 28 September 1869.
35 Letter to his sister, end of September 1869.
36 Letter to Carl von Gersdorff, 28 September 1869.
37 Letter to Erwin Rohde, mid-July 1869.
38 Letter to Erwin Rohde, 7 October 1869.
39 *Nachgelassene Fragmente*, autumn 1869.
40 Letter to Paul Deussen, 25 August 1869.
41 Letter to Erwin Rohde, 3 September 1869.
42 *Nachgelassene Fragmente*.
43 Ibid.
44 Ibid.
45 Letter to Sophie Ritschl, Christmas Day 1869.
46 Letter to Erwin Rohde, end of January and 15 February 1870.
47 Letter from Richard Wagner, 14 January 1870.
48 Letter from Erwin Rohde, 5 November 1869.
49 Letter to Erwin Rohde, end of January and 15 February 1870.
50 Letter to Paul Deussen, February 1870.
51 'Das griechische Musikdrama'.
52 Letter to Paul Deussen, February 1870.
53 *Nachgelassene Fragmente*, winter 1869/70–spring 1871.
54 Ibid.
55 Ibid.
56 Ibid.
57 Ibid.
58 This is a misquotation from Goethe's poem 'Epilog zu Schillers Glocke'.
59 Letter to Carl von Gersdorff, 11 March 1870.
60 Ibid.
61 Letter to Carl von Gersdorff, 2 July 1870.
62 Letter from Erwin Rohde to his mother, 9 June 1870.
63 Letter to Cosima von Bülow, 19 June 1870.
64 Letter to Erwin Rohde, 19 July 1870.
65 Ibid.
66 Letter to his mother, 19 July 1870.
67 Letter to Sophie Ritschl, 20 July 1870.
68 Letter to Carl von Gersdorff, 7 November 1870 and slightly earlier.
69 Letter from Cosima von Bülow, 9 August 1870.
70 *Nachgelassene Fragmente*, August–September 1870.
71 Letter to his mother, 29 August 1870.
72 Letter to Richard Wagner, 11 September 1870.

73 Letter to Carl von Gersdorff, 10 October 1870.
74 Letter to Richard Wagner, 11 September 1870.
75 Ibid.
76 Letter to Wilhelm Vischer-Bilfinger, 19 October 1870.
77 Letter to his mother and sister, 23–4 October 1870.
78 Letter to Erwin Rohde, 23 October 1870.
79 See Paul Maas, *Greek Metre*, trans. Hugh Lloyd-Jones (O.U.P.1962).
80 Letter to Erwin Rohde, 23 October 1870.
81 Ibid.
82 Ibid.
83 Letter to Erwin Rohde, 23 November 1870.
84 *Nachgelassene Fragmente*, September 1870–January 1871.
85 Letter to Richard Wagner, 10 November 1870.
86 Ibid.
87 Letter to Carl von Gersdorff, 12 December 1870.
88 Letter to Erwin Rohde, 15 December 1870.
89 Ibid.
90 Ibid.
91 *Nachgelassene Fragmente*, September 1870–January 1871.
92 Ibid.
93 *Nachgelassene Fragmente*, end of 1870–April 1871.
94 Hegel, *Vorlesungen über die Aesthetik*. Delivered 1820–6, published 1835.
95 *Nachgelassene Fragmente*, September 1870–January 1871.
96 *Nachgelassene Fragmente*, end of 1870–April 1871.
97 Ibid.
98 Ibid.
99 Ibid.
100 *Nachgelassene Fragmente*, September 1870–January 1871.
101 Ibid.
102 Ibid.
103 *Nachgelassene Fragmente*, end of 1870–April 1871.
104 *Nachgelassene Fragmente*, September 1870–January 1871.
105 Ibid.
106 *Nachgelassene Fragmente*, end of 1870–April 1871.
107 Ibid.
108 Ibid.
109 Letter to Wilhelm Vischer-Bilfinger, probably January 1871.
110 Letter to Erwin Rohde, 8 February 1871.
111 Letter to his mother and sister, probably 21 January 1871.
112 Letter to his mother and sister, 6 February 1871.
113 Letter to his mother, 1 March 1871.
114 Elisabeth Förster-Nietzsche.
115 Letter to Erwin Rohde, 29 March 1871.
116 Draft of letter to Wilhelm Engelmann, 20 April 1871.
117 Letter to Erwin Rohde, 29 March 1871.
118 Elisabeth Förster-Nietzsche.

119 *Die Geburt der Tragödie*, s. 4.
120 Draft of letter to Wilhelm Engelmann, 20 April 1871.
121 Letter to Wilhelm Vischer-Bilfinger, 27 May 1871.
122 Ibid.
123 Pamphlet later titled *The Civil War in France*.
124 Letter to Carl von Gersdorff, 18 November 1871.
125 Letter to Carl von Gersdorff, 21 June 1871.
126 Letter to Erwin Rohde, 19 July 1871.
127 Letter to Erwin Rohde, 17 June 1871.
128 Letter to Paul Deussen, 2 July 1871.
129 Elisabeth Förster-Nietzsche (ed.), *The Wagner–Nietzsche Correspondence*.
130 Letter to Carl von Gersdoff, 18 September 1871.
131 Letter to Carl von Gersdorff, 18 November 1871.
132 Letter to Erwin Rohde, 4 August 1871.
133 Letter from Cosima Wagner, 3 September 1871.
134 Letter to his sister, 15 September 1871.
135 Letter from Cosima Wagner, 17 September 1871.
136 Letter from Richard Wagner, 16 October 1871.
137 Letter to his mother and sister, 26 October 1871.
138 Letter to his mother, 2 September 1871.
139 Letter to Erwin Rohde, 23 November 1871.
140 Letter to Erwin Rohde, after 21 December 1871.
141 Letter to his mother, 2 September 1871.
142 Draft of letter to Richard Wagner, presumably written 2 January 1872.
143 Letter to Richard Wagner, 2 January 1872.
144 Letter to Gustav Krug, 31 December 1871.
145 Ritschl's diary, 31 December 1871.
146 Letter to Friedrich Ritschl, 30 January 1872.
147 Ritschl's diary, 2 February 1872.
148 Letter from Friedrich Ritschl, 14 February 1872.
149 Letter to Erwin Rohde, mid-February 1872.
150 Letter from Richard Wagner, beginning of January 1872.
151 Letter from Richard Wagner, 10 January 1872.
152 Letter from Cosima Wagner, 18 January 1872.

Chapter 6

1 Letter to Ernst Wilhelm Fritzsch, 22 March 1872.
2 Letter from Jacob Burckhardt to Arnold von Salis, 12 April 1872.
3 Letter to his mother and sister, 24 January 1872.
4 Letter to Richard Wagner, 24 January 1872.
5 Letter to Erwin Rohde, 28 January 1872.
6 Ibid.
7 Letter to Erwin Rohde, 12 May 1872.

8 Letter to Carl von Gersdorff, 1 May 1872.

9 Letter to Erwin Rohde, 30 April 1872.

10 Ibid.

11 Letter to Carl von Gersdorff, 4 February 1872.

12 Ibid.

13 Letter to Erwin Rohde, 4 February 1872.

14 Letter to Erwin Rohde, 15 March 1872.

15 Letter to Friedrich Ritschl, 6 April 1872.

16 Letter from Cosima Wagner, 24 April 1872.

17 See the essays by Hugh Lloyd-Jones and Walter Kaufmann in O'Flaherty, Sellner and Helm.

18 Letter to Erwin Rohde, 12 May 1872.

19 Letter to Erwin Rohde, 4 May 1872.

20 'Richard Wagner in Bayreuth'.

21 'Nachklang einer Sylvesternacht'.

22 *Ecce Homo*.

23 Letter to Hans von Bülow, 20 July 1872.

24 Letter from Hans von Bülow, 24 July 1872.

25 Letter to Gustav Krug, 24 July 1872.

26 Letter to Hans von Bülow, October 1872.

27 Letter to his mother, 1 October 1872.

28 Ibid.

29 Letter to Erwin Rohde, 5 October 1872.

30 Letter to Richard Wagner, October 1872.

31 Letter to Erwin Rohde, 25 October 1872.

32 Letter from Cosima Wagner, 12 February 1873.

33 Letter to his mother and sister, 31 January 1873.

34 Letter to Carl von Gersdorff, 24 February 1873.

35 Ludwig Wilhelm Kelterborn, Memoir written in the form of a letter from Boston to Elisabeth Förster-Nietzsche (August 1901).

36 Postcard to Franz Overbeck, 30 July 1881.

37 Cosima Wagner's diary, 7 February 1881.

38 Letter to Richard Wagner, April 1873.

39 Ibid.

40 *Nachgelassene Fragmente*, summer 1872–beginning of 1873.

41 *Unzeitgemässe Betrachtungen* 1, *David Strauss der Bekenner und der Schriftsteller*.

42 Cited by Karl Heinrich Hoefele.

43 *Die Grenzboten* XXXII no. 4, 1873.

44 Letter to Carl von Gersdorff, 11 February 1874.

45 A.J.Ayer, interview with Bryan Magee. Reprinted in Bryan Magee (ed.), *Men of Ideas* (London, 1978).

46 Nietzsche is here using the word *Verhalten* (attitude) as cognate with *Verhältnis* (relationship).

47 Wittgenstein, *Philosophical Investigations*, 119. I am indebted here to Erich Heller, who has shown in his essay on 'Wittgenstein and

Nietzsche' how easy it is to mistake a pronouncement by one for a pronouncement by the other.

48 Letter from Carl von Gersdorff to Elisabeth Nietzsche, 18 July 1873.
49 Letter to Erwin Rohde, 18 October 1873.
50 Ibid.
51 Goethe, *Gespräche*, Weimar ed., vol. IV, 22.
52 *Vom Nützen und Nachteil der Historie im Leben*, s. 6.
53 Ibid.
54 S. 7.
55 S. 7.
56 S. 9.
57 S. 8.
58 S. 9.
59 S. 2.
60 S. 5.
61 S. 8.
62 S. 10.
63 S. 4.
64 S. 10.
65 Ss. 2 and 6.
66 S. 3.
67 S. 9.
68 Ritschl's diary, 30 December 1873.
69 Letter from Jacob Burckhardt, 25 February 1874.
70 Letter to his mother and sister, 14 January 1874.
71 Letter to his mother, 1 February 1874.
72 Letter to his mother and sister, 18 February 1874.
73 Letter to his mother and sister, 26 March 1874.
74 Letter to his mother and sister, 14 January 1874.
75 Letter to Carl von Gersdorff, 1 April 1874.
76 Cosima Wagner's diary, 4 April 1874.
77 Letter from Richard Wagner, 27 February 1874.
78 Letter from Cosima Wagner, February 1874.
79 Letter from Richard Wagner, June 1874.
80 Letter to Carl von Gersdorff, 4 July 1874.
81 Ibid.
82 Letter to Carl von Gersdorff, 26 July 1874.
83 Letter to his sister, 22 July 1874.
84 Letter to his mother towards the end of July 1874.
85 Letter to Marchesa Guerrieri-Gonzaga, 10 May 1874.
86 Letter to Erwin Rohde, 14 May 1874.
87 Ibid.
88 *Schopenhauer als Erzieher*, chap. 1.
89 Chap. 3.
90 Chap. 1.
91 Goethe, *Wilhelm Meisters Lehrjahre*, Book 8, chap. 5.
92 *Schopenhauer als Erzieher* chap. 4.

93 Ibid.
94 Ibid.
95 Ibid.
96 Ibid.
97 Chap. 8.
98 Chap. 7.
99 Chap. 5.
100 Ibid.
101 Letter to Erwin Rohde, 14 June 1874.
102 *Nachgelassene Fragmente*, beginning of 1874–spring 1874.
103 Richard Wagner, 'Das Judentum in der Musik', in *Die Neue Zeit-schrift für Musik* (1850). See Albert Goldmann and Evert Sprinchorn (eds.), *Wagner on Music and Drama* (London 1970).
104 Elisabeth Förster-Nietzsche.
105 Letter to Carl von Gersdorff, 24 September 1874.
106 Letter to Franz Overbeck and Heinrich Romundt, 2 October 1874.
107 Letter to Erwin Rohde, 7 October 1875.
108 Ibid.
109 Letter from Richard Wagner, second day of Christmas 1874.
110 Letter to Malwida von Meysenbug, 2 January 1875.
111 Ibid.
112 Ibid.
113 Letter to Hans von Bülow, 2 January 1875.
114 Letter to Erwin Rohde, 5 February 1875.
115 Letter to Marie Baumgartner, 9 February 1875.
116 The word *Saalentleerer* first occurred in Rohde's letter of 23 October 1873. *Lehrer* means teacher.
117 Letter to Erwin Rohde, 28 February 1875.
118 Letter to Carl von Gersdorff, 17 April 1875.
119 Ibid.
120 Letter to Carl von Gersdorff, 1 August 1875.
121 Letter to his sister, 26 March 1875.
122 Letter to his sister, 5 May 1875.
123 Letter to his sister, 9 May 1875.
124 Letter to Carl von Gersdorff, 21 May 1875.
125 Letter to Richard Wagner, 24 May 1875.
126 Letter to Carl von Gersdorff, June 1875.
127 Letter to Carl von Gersdorff, 7 June 1875.
128 Ibid.
129 Letter to his mother and sister, 17 July 1875.
130 Letter to Carl von Gersdorff, 21 July 1875.
131 Letter to Erwin Rohde, 1 August 1875.
132 Ibid.
133 Letter to his mother, 10 August 1875.
134 Letter to Malwida von Meysenbug, 11 August 1875.
135 Ibid.
136 Ibid.

137 Letter to Erwin Rohde, 29 August 1875.
138 Letter to Carl von Gersdorff, 26 September 1875.
139 Ibid.
140 Ibid.
141 Ibid.
142 Letter to Erwin Rohde, 7 October 1875.
143 Letter to Carl von Gersdorff, 26 September 1875.
144 Letter to Erwin Rohde, 26 September 1875.
145 Letter to Erwin Rohde, 7 October 1875.
146 Ibid.
147 Letter to Erwin Rohde, 8 December 1875.
148 Letter to Carl von Gersdorff, 13 December 1875.
149 Ibid.
150 Letter to Carl von Gersdorff, 18 January 1876.
151 Ibid.
152 Letter to his mother and sister, 8 March 1876.
153 Letter to Franz Overbeck, 5 April 1876.
154 Letter to Mathilde Trampedach, 11 April 1876.
155 *Richard Wagner in Bayreuth*, chap. 9.
156 Chap. 5.
157 Chap. 7.
158 Chap. 3.
159 Ibid.
160 Chap. 4.
161 Chap. 8.
162 Ibid.
163 Ibid.
164 Ibid.
165 Chap. 9.
166 Ibid.
167 Ibid.
168 Letter to Erwin Rohde, 7 July 1876.
169 Draft of letter to Richard Wagner, July 1876. The letter he actually sent has not been found.
170 Letter from Richard Wagner, 11 July 1876.
171 Letter to Carl von Gersdorff, 21 July 1876.
172 Letter to his sister, 25 July 1876. (She dates the letter 1 August. For a detailed exposure of her deception, see Ernest Newman, vol. 4.)
173 Letter to his sister, 28 July 1876 (dated by her 4 August 1876).
174 Cosima Wagner's diary, 28 July 1876.
175 Letter to his sister, 6 August 1876.
176 Ibid.
177 *Ecce Homo*.
178 Ibid.
179 Letter to Louise Ott, 30 July 1876.
180 Letter to Richard Wagner, 27 September 1876.
181 *Morgenröte*, s. 287.

Chapter 7

1 *Ecce Homo*, chapter on *Menschliches, Allzumenschliches*.
2 Ibid.
3 Ibid.
4 Letter from Malwida von Meysenbug, 30 April 1876.
5 Letter to Reinhardt von Seydlitz, 24 September 1876.
6 Paul Rée writing a year later.
7 Albert Brenner, letter to his relations in Basel, 1 October 1876. Reprinted in Bernoulli.
8 Malwida von Meysenbug, *Lebensabend einer Idealistin*.
9 Elisabeth Förster-Nietzsche (ed.), *The Nietzsche–Wagner Correspondence*.
10 Richard Wagner in *Bayreuther Blätter*.
11 Letter to Reinhardt von Seydlitz, 4 January 1876.
12 Paul Rée, letter to Franziska Nietzsche, 8 November 1876.
13 *Lebensabend einer Idealistin*.
14 Ibid.
15 Malwida von Meysenbug, letter to her daughter, 20 November 1876.
16 Postcard to his mother and sister, 8 January 1877.
17 Postcard to his sister, 20 January 1877.
18 Ibid.
19 Paul Rée, letter to Elisabeth Nietzsche, 20 February 1877.
20 Letter to his sister, 31 March and 25 April 1877.
21 Letter to Paul Rée, 17 April 1877.
22 Letter to Malwida von Meysenbug, 13 May 1877.
23 Ibid.
24 Ibid.
25 Letter to his sister, 2 June 1877.
26 Letter to his mother and sister, 12 June 1877.
27 Letter to Malwida von Meysenbug, 1 July 1877.
28 Letter to his mother and sister, 25 June 1877.
29 Letter from Erwin Rohde, 29 June 1877.
30 Letter to Erwin Rohde, 28 August 1877.
31 Letter to Siegfried Lipiner, 28 August 1877.
32 Letter to Reinhardt von Seydlitz, 4 January 1878.
33 Letter to Erwin Rohde, 28 August 1877.
34 Letter to Franz Overbeck, end of August 1877.
35 Letter to Carl Fuchs, 27 July 1877.
36 Letter to Paul Deussen, beginning of August 1877.
37 *Menschliches, Allzumenschliches* Part I, s. 1.
38 S. 57.
39 S. 102.
40 S. 107.
41 Ibid.

42 Ibid.
43 St Luke XVIII, 14.
44 *Menschliches, Allzumenschliches*, Part I, s. 87.
45 S. 137.
46 S. 141.
47 S. 142.
48 *Der Wanderer und sein Schatten*, s. 16.
49 *Menschliches, Allzumenschliches*, Part I, s. 1.
50 *Ecce Homo*, chapter on *Menschliches, Allzumenschliches*.
51 S. 10.
52 *Vom Nützen und Nachteil der Historie im Leben*, s. 2.
53 S. 7.
54 *Menschliches, Allzumenschliches* Part I, s. 43.
55 S. 70.
56 S. 81.
57 S. 92.
58 S. 98.
59 S. 68.
60 S. 114.
61 S. 12–14.
62 S. 169.
63 S. 213.
64 S. 209.
65 S. 210.
66 S. 291.
67 S. 283.
68 S. 292.
69 S. 235.
70 Ibid.
71 S. 438.
72 S. 450.
73 S. 452.
74 S. 385.
75 S. 379.
76 S. 406.
77 S. 638.
78 Letter from Ernst Schmeitzner, 25 January 1878.
79 S. 147.
80 S. 149.
81 S. 164.
82 S. 109.
83 Letter to Ernst Schmeitzner, 3 December 1877.
84 Dr Otto Eiser's report, 6 October 1877.
85 Ibid.
86 Letter from Richard Wagner to Dr Eiser, 27 October 1877. Cited by Westernhagen.

87 Letter from Cosima Wagner to Malwida von Meysenbug, mid-June 1878.

88 Letter from Dr Eiser to Franz Overbeck, 9 February 1878.

89 Erwin Rohde, letter of 16 June 1878.

90 Letter from Cosima Wagner to Marie von Schleinitz, May 1878.

91 Letter from Malwida von Meysenbug, June 1878.

92 Letter from Reinhardt von Seydlitz, 19 June 1878.

93 Letter from Marie Baumgartner, 28 April 1878.

94 Letter from Heinrich Romundt, 3 May 1878.

95 32-page letter from Siegfried Lipiner, no longer extant.

96 Letter to Paul Rée, 10 August 1878.

97 *Nachgelassene Fragmente*, 11, 7, 142.

98 Letter to Reinhardt von Seydlitz, 4 January 1878.

99 *Menschliches, Allzumenschliches*, s. 235.

100 Letter to Mathilde Maier, 15 July 1878.

101 *Bayreuther Blätter*, August–September 1878.

102 Letter to Ernst Schmeitzner, 3 September 1878.

103 Letter to Franz Overbeck, 3 September 1878.

104 Letter to Franz Overbeck, 17 September 1878.

105 Letter from Ernst Schmeitzner to Heinrich Köselitz, 29 September 1878.

106 Letter to Gustav Krug, 14 November 1878.

107 Unpublished notebook in Weimar archive.

108 Letter to Marie Baumgartner, 28 October 1878.

109 Letter to Reinhardt von Seydlitz, 18 November 1878.

110 Letter to Heinrich Köselitz, 5 December 1879.

111 *Menschliches, Allzumenschliches* Part II, *Vermischte Meinungen und Sprüche*, s. 343.

112 S. 407.

113 S. 152.

114 S. 401.

115 S. 20.

116 S. 83.

117 S. 309.

118 S. 240.

119 S. 357.

120 S. 405.

121 S. 372.

122 S. 90.

123 S. 5.

124 S. 33.

125 S. 171.

126 Ibid.

127 S. 99.

128 S. 173.

129 Ibid.

130 S. 200.

131 S. 107.
132 Postcard to Ernst Schmeitzner accompanying text of *Menschliches,
      Allzumenschliches*, Part II, 31 December 1878.
133 Letter to his mother and sister, 17 December 1878.
134 Letter to his mother and sister, 27 December 1878.
135 Letter to his mother and sister, 18 January 1879.
136 Letter from Louis Kelterborn to Elisabeth Förster-Nietzsche,
      August 1901.
137 Letter to Peter Gast, 22 January 1879.
138 Letter to his mother and sister, 9 February 1879.
139 Letter to his mother and sister, 17 February 1879.
140 Letter to Peter Gast, 1 March 1879.
141 Letter from Peter Gast, 7 March 1879.
142 Letter to his mother and sister, 9 March 1879.
143 Ibid.
144 Letter to his mother and sister, 30 March 1879.
145 Letter from Jacob Burckhardt, 3 April 1879.
146 Letter from Reinhardt von Seydlitz, 7 April 1879.
147 Letter from Cosima Wagner to Elisabeth Förster-Nietzsche, 9 March
      1879.
148 Letter to Franz Overbeck, 11 April 1879.
149 Letter to his mother and sister, 12 April 1879.
150 Letter to Paul Rée, 23 April 1879.
151 Elisabeth Förster-Nietzsche.
152 Letter to his sister, 31 May 1879.
153 Letter to Franz Overbeck, 8 June 1879.
154 Letter to his sister, 24 June 1879.
155 Letter to his sister, 6 July 1879.
156 Ibid.
157 Letter to his mother, 21 July 1879.
158 Letter to his sister, 14 August 1879.
159 Letter from Franz Overbeck, 27 August 1879.
160 Letter to Paul Rée, end of July 1879.
161 Letter to Peter Gast, 11 September 1879.
162 Letter from Peter Gast to Cäcilie Gusselbauer, 12 September 1879.
163 Letter to Peter Gast, 5 October 1879.
164 Ibid.
165 Letter to Peter Gast, 5 November 1879.
166 *Der Wanderer und sein Schatten*, s. 16.
167 S. 5.
168 S. 216.
169 Ibid.
170 S. 217.
171 S. 230.
172 S. 320.
173 S. 84.
174 *Menschliches, Allzumenschliches* Part II, s. 94.

175 *Der Wanderer und sein Schatten*, s. 86.
176 S. 38.
177 S. 52.
178 S. 44.
179 S. 22.
180 Ibid.
181 Ibid.
182 S. 60.
183 S. 181.
184 S. 285.
185 Ibid.
186 Ibid.
187 Elisabeth Förster-Nietzsche.
188 Letter to his sister, 10 October 1879.
189 Letter to Franz Overbeck, 24 October 1879.
190 Postcard to Peter Gast, 4 October 1879.
191 Letter to Peter Gast, 30 September 1879.
192 The phrase occurs in letters to his sister and to Ida Overbeck, both 5 November 1879.
193 Letter to Franz Overbeck, 14 November 1879.
194 Letter to Franz Overbeck, 11 December 1879.
195 Letter to Ernst Schmeitzner, 18 December 1879.
196 Letter to his sister, 29 December 1879.
197 Letter from Erwin Rohde, 22 December 1879.
198 Letter to Franz Overbeck, 28 December 1879.
199 Letter to Dr Eiser, early January 1880.
200 Letter to Franz Overbeck, 28 December 1879.
201 Letter to Dr Eiser early January 1880.
202 *Morgenröte*, s. 118.

Chapter 8

1 Letter from Peter Gast to Cäcilie Gusselbauer, 24 February 1880. Cited by Podach.
2 Letter from Peter Gast to Cäcilie Gusselbauer, 28 February 1880.
3 Letter from Peter Gast to Cäcilie Gusselbauer, 4 March 1880.
4 Letter from Peter Gast to Cäcilie Gusselbauer, 13 March 1880.
5 Ibid.
6 Letter from Peter Gast to Franz Overbeck, 26 March 1880.
7 Postcard to his mother and sister, 2 April 1880.
8 Postcard to his mother, 15 March 1880.
9 Letter from Peter Gast to Cäcilie Gusselbauer, 15 March 1880.
10 Ibid.
11 Letter from Peter Gast to Cäcilie Gusselbauer, 8 April 1880.
12 Letter from Peter Gast to Cäcilie Gusselbauer, 14 June 1880.

13 Letter from Peter Gast to Cäcilie Gusselbauer, 24 September 1880.
14 *Morgenröte*, s. 76.
15 Ibid.
16 S. 89.
17 S. 72.
18 S. 13.
19 Ibid.
20 S. 68.
21 S. 14.
22 Ibid.
23 Ibid.
24 Elisabeth Förster-Nietzsche.
25 Letter to his mother and sister, 24 November 1880.
26 Letter to Franz Overbeck, 22 June 1880.
27 Letter to his mother and sister, 5 July 1880.
28 Letters to Franz Overbeck and to his mother and sister, 14 October 1880.
29 Letter to Peter Gast, 5 July 1880.
30 Letter to Peter Gast, 18 July 1880.
31 Preface to *Morgenröte*, autumn 1886.
32 *Morgenröte*, s. 129.
33 S. 133.
34 Ibid.
35 S. 128.
36 S. 120.
37 S. 119.
38 Ibid.
39 Letter to Peter Gast, 20 August 1880.
40 Letter to Peter Gast, 18 July 1880.
41 Letter to Peter Gast, 20 October 1880.
42 Letter to his mother and sister, 14 October 1880.
43 Letter to Franz Overbeck, 31 October 1880.
44 *Morgenröte*, s. 356.
45 S. 369.
46 S. 262.
47 S. 334.
48 S. 215.
49 Letter to Paul Rée, 31 October 1880.
50 Postcard to Peter Gast, 17 November 1880.
51 Letter to his sister, 5 December 1880.
52 Letter to his mother and sister, 8 January 1881.
53 Letter to Franz Overbeck, November 1880.
54 *Morgenröte*, s. 381.
55 *Morgenröte*, s. 437.
56 *Menschliches, Allzumenschliches, Der Wanderer und sein Schatten*, s. 131.
57 *Morgenröte*, s. 463.

58 S. 463.
59 S. 477.
60 Letter to Franz Overbeck, November 1880.
61 *Morgenröte*, s. 481.
62 S. 497.
63 S. 500.
64 S. 516.
65 Ibid.
66 S. 548.
67 Ibid.
68 S. 553.
69 Letter to Peter Gast, 10 April 1881.
70 Letter from Peter Gast to Cäcilie Gusselbauer, 8 May 1881.
71 Letter to his mother and sister, 18 May 1881.
72 Letter to Franz Overbeck, 31 May 1881.
73 Letter to his sister, 19 June 1881.
74 Letter to Peter Gast, 8 July 1881.
75 Ibid.
76 Letter to his sister, 7 July 1881.
77 Ibid.
78 Letter to Peter Gast, 21 July 1881.
79 Letter to Franz Overbeck, 30 July 1881.
80 Ibid.
81 Letter to Peter Gast, 14 August 1881.
82 Ibid.
83 Ibid.
84 Letter to his sister, 18 August 1881.
85 Letter to Paul Rée, August 1881.
86 *Ecce Homo*, chapter on *Also sprach Zarathustra*.
87 *Die fröhliche Wissenschaft*, s. 341.
88 Ibid.
89 Heinrich Heine, Elster ed., vol. 3. The book Nietzsche had was Adolf Strodtman (ed.), *Letzte Gedichte und Gedanken* (Hamburg 1869).
90 *Der Wille zur Macht*, s. 99.
91 S. 1063.
92 S. 1061.
93 S. 99.
94 See Janz, vol. 11, chap. 2.
95 Postcard to Peter Gast, 22 September 1881.
96 Letter to Franz Overbeck, 18 September 1881.
97 Ibid.
98 Letter to Peter Gast, 21 August 1881.
99 Letter to Peter Gast, end of August 1881.
100 Ibid.
101 Ibid.
102 Postcard to Peter Gast, 22 September 1881.

103 Postcard to Peter Gast, 4 October 1881.
104 Postcard to Peter Gast, 6 November 1881.
105 Postcard to Peter Gast, 28 November 1881.
106 Postcard to Peter Gast, 8 December 1881.
107 *Der Fall Wagner*.
108 Letter to his sister, 29 November 1881.
109 Letter from T. S. Eliot to Stephen Spender, 1931.
110 Letter to Franz Overbeck, 14 November 1881.
111 *Die fröhliche Wissenschaft*, s. 1.
112 S. 4.
113 Ibid.
114 S. 130.
115 S. 55.
116 S. 49.
117 S. 55.
118 S. 27.
119 S. 76.
120 Ibid.
121 S. 54.
122 S. 58.
123 S. 111.
124 S. 125.
125 Ibid.
126 S. 117.
127 Ibid.
128 S. 182.
129 S. 266.
130 Letter to Peter Gast, 25 January 1882.
131 Ibid.
132 Letter to Peter Gast, 5 February 1882.
133 S. 276.
134 S. 341.
135 S. 332.
136 S. 144.
137 S. 283.
138 Ibid.
139 S. 285.
140 Ibid.
141 S. 288.
142 S. 305.
143 S. 309.
144 Letter to Peter Gast, 25 January 1882.
145 Letter to his mother and sister, 10 February 1882.
146 Ibid.
147 Letter to Peter Gast, 21 January 1887.

Chapter 9

1 Letter from Paul Rée, 20 April 1882.
2 Lou Andreas-Salomé, *Lebensrückblick*, ed. Ernst Pfeiffer (Zürich and Weisbaden 1951).
3 Draft of letter to Georg Rée, early August 1883.
4 Letter from Paul Rée, 20 April 1882.
5 Letter to Paul Rée, 8 May 1882.
6 Lou Andreas-Salomé, *Lebensrückblick*.
7 Ibid.
8 Lou Andreas-Salomé, *Nietzsche in seinen Werken*.
9 Ibid.
10 Carl Albrecht Bernoulli, *Franz Overbeck und Friedrich Nietzsche: eine Freundschaft*.
11 Ida Overbeck, quoted by Bernoulli.
12 Ibid.
13 Lou Salomé's diary, 18 August 1882.
14 Ida Overbeck, quoted by Bernoulli.
15 Lou Salomé's diary, 14 August 1882.
16 Letter from Franz Overbeck to Peter Gast, 25–6 June 1882.
17 Ida Overbeck, quoted by Bernoulli.
18 Ibid.
19 Letter to Peter Gast, 13 July 1882, and letter from Peter Gast, 17 July 1882.
20 Letter to Franz Overbeck, 24 June 1882.
21 Letter from Paul Rée to Lou Salomé, about 18 May 1882.
22 Letter to Lou Salomé, 28 May 1882.
23 Ibid.
24 Letter to Lou Salomé, 7 June 1882.
25 Letter from Lou Salomé, 4 June 1882.
26 Letter to Lou Salomé, 18 June 1882.
27 Ibid.
28 Ibid.
29 Letter from Paul Rée to Lou Salomé, August 1882.
30 Letter to Lou Salomé, 18 June 1882.
31 Letter from Lou Salomé, 2 August 1882.
32 Letter to Lou Salomé, 2 August 1882.
33 Letters from Elisabeth Nietzsche to Clara Gelzer, 24 September and 2 October 1882.
34 Lou Salomé's diary, 14 August 1882.
35 Lou Salomé's diary, 21 August 1882.
36 Lou Salomé's diary, 14 August 1882.
37 Letter to Franz Overbeck, mid-September 1882.
38 Letter to Peter Gast, 20 August 1882.

39 Franz Overbeck, quoted by Bernoulli.
40 Letter from Lou Salomé to Paul Rée, 18 August 1882.
41 Ibid.
42 Letter to Franz Overbeck, mid-September 1882.
43 Letters from Elisabeth Nietzsche to Clara Gelzer, 24 September and 2 October 1882.
44 Binion, chapter 2.
45 Lou Salomé's diary, August 1882.
46 Letters from Elisabeth Nietzsche to Clara Gelzer, 24 September and 2 October 1882.
47 Letters from Elisabeth Nietzsche to Clara Gelzer, 24 September and 2 October 1882.
48 Letter to Lou Salomé, beginning of September 1882.
49 Quoted in letter to Franz Overbeck, mid-September 1882.
50 Quoted in letter to his sister, early September 1882 and to Franz Overbeck, mid-September 1882.
51 Letter to Lou Salomé, early September 1882.
52 Letter from Paul Rée to Lou Salomé, inaccurately dated by her 12 August 1882.
53 The letter was later stuck into her diary for 1900–3.
54 Quoted in letter to Lou Salomé, mid-September 1882.
55 Letter to Lou Salomé, mid-September 1882.
56 See Binion.
57 Postscript to letter to Peter Gast, 16 September 1882.
58 Letter to Franz Overbeck, October 1882.
59 Letter to Franz Overbeck, beginning of November 1882.
60 Letter from Peter Gast to Franz Overbeck, 14 November 1882.
61 Lou Salomé's diary, October 1882.
62 Draft of letter to Paul Rée, December 1882.
63 Letter to Lou Salomé, 8 November 1882.
64 Ida Overbeck, quoted by Bernoulli.
65 Letter to Paul Rée, December 1882.
66 Letter to Peter Gast, 23 November 1882.
67 Letter to Paul Rée, end of November 1882.
68 Letter to Lou Salomé, end of November 1882.
69 Letter to Heinrich von Schleinitz, beginning of December 1882.
70 Note in *Nachgelassene Fragmente*.
71 Letter to Lou Salomé and Paul Rée, December 1882. The other letters have not survived except in drafts which probably differ substantially from the letters he sent.
72 Letter to his sister, end of November 1882.
73 Letter to Franz Overbeck, March 1883, not published in Bernoulli's collected edition but quoted in his unpublished essay 'Nietzsche and Lou' (summer 1931) now in the Basel archive.
74 Letter to Franz Overbeck, 25 December 1883.
75 Letter to his sister, 27 April 1883.
76 Letter to Franz Overbeck, 25 December 1882.

Chapter 10

1 Letter to Malwida von Meysenbug, 1 January 1883.
2 Ibid.
3 *Also sprach Zarathustra*, Part I, s. titled 'On Reading and Writing'.
4 'Zarathustra's Prologues'.
5 'On Reading and Writing'.
6 'On Believers in a Beyond'.
7 Letter to Franz Overbeck, *c.* 9 February 1883.
8 'On the Adder's Bite'.
9 'On the Despisers of the Body'.
10 'Zarathustra's Prologues'.
11 'On the Despisers of the Body'.
12 'On Believers in a Beyond'.
13 'On the Despisers of the Body'.
14 Ibid.
15 Letter to Peter Gast, 4 August 1882.
16 *Also sprach Zarathustra*, Part I, 'On Chastity'.
17 Ibid.
18 'On Little Old Women and Young Ones'.
19 Ibid.
20 Ibid.
21 'On the Flies in the Market Place'.
22 'On the Way of the Creator'.
23 'Neighbourly Love'.
24 'On War and Warriors'.
25 'On the New Idol'.
26 Ibid.
27 Letter to Franz Overbeck, *c.* 9 February 1883.
28 Ibid.
29 'On Reading and Writing'.
30 'Zarathustra's Prologues'.
31 Ibid.
32 *Also sprach Zarathustra*, Part III, 'On the Old and the New Commandments'.
33 Letter to Franz Overbeck, *c.* 9 February 1883.
34 Letter to Peter Gast, 19 February 1883.
35 Letter to Peter Gast, 7 March 1883.
36 Letter to Peter Gast, 17 March 1883.
37 Ibid.
38 Letter to Peter Gast, 20 March 1883.
39 Letter to Peter Gast, 22 March 1883.
40 Ibid.
41 Letter to Franz Overbeck, *c.* 22 February 1883.
42 Ibid.

43 Letter to Peter Gast, 2 and 6 April 1883.
44 Letter to Peter Gast, 6 April 1883.
45 Letter to Peter Gast, 6 April 1883.
46 Ibid.
47 Letter to Peter Gast, 10 May 1883.
48 Letter to Peter Gast, 20 May 1883.
49 Elisabeth Förster-Nietzsche.
50 Letter to Marie Baumgartner, 28 May 1883.
51 *Ecce Homo*.
52 Letter to his mother and sister, 21 June 1883.
53 *Also sprach Zarathustra* Part II, 'On the Tarantulas'.
54 'On the Virtuous'.
55 'On Redemption'.
56 Ibid.
57 Ibid.
58 'On Self-Conquest'.
59 Ibid.
60 Ibid.
61 Ibid.
62 Part I, 'On the Thousand and One Goals'.
63 Part II, 'On Priests'.
64 'On the Exalted'.
65 William Blake, *The Marriage of Heaven and Hell*, 'The Voice of the Devil'
66 'On the Exalted'.
67 William Blake, 'For the Sexes: the Gates of Paradise'.
68 *Also sprach Zarathustra*, Part II, 'On the Compassionate'.
69 William Blake, *The Marriage of Heaven and Hell*, 'Proverbs of Hell'.
70 *Also sprach Zarathustra*, Part II, 'Night Song'.
71 Ibid.
72 'The Dance Song'.
73 Ibid.
74 Letter to Peter Gast, end of August 1883.
75 Ibid.
76 'The Hour of Deepest Silence'.
77 Letter to Franz Overbeck, summer 1883.
78 Ibid.
79 Letter to Peter Gast, 26 August 1883, from a section suppressed in Gast's edition of the letters.
80 Letter to Ida Overbeck, mid-July 1883.
81 Letter to Malwida von Meysenbug, end of November 1882.
82 Letter to Ida Overbeck, mid-July 1883.
83 Letter to Franz Overbeck, beginning of September 1883.
84 Ibid.
85 Letter to Peter Gast, 3 September 1883.
86 Letter to his mother and sister, December 1883.
87 Letter to his mother and sister, 25 December 1883.

88 Ibid.
89 Conversation reported by Dr Josef Paneth in a letter to Sophie Schwab. Quoted by Elisabeth Förster-Nietzsche.
90 Letter to Franz Overbeck, c. 24 January 1884.
91 *Also sprach Zarathustra*, Part III, 'On Involuntary Bliss'.
92 'On the Old and the New Commandments'.
93 'The Wanderer'.
94 Ibid.
95 'On Involuntary Bliss'.
96 'On the Virtues that Make for Smallness'.
97 'Upon the Mount of Olives'.
98 Ibid.
99 'On Passing On'.
100 Ibid.
101 'On the Vision and Riddle'.
102 'On the Spirit of Gravity'.
103 'On the Old and the New Commandments'.
104 Ibid.
105 Ibid.
106 'The Convalescent'.
107 'The Seven Seals or the Song of Yes and Amen'.
108 Letter to Franz Overbeck, 8 February 1884.
109 Letter to Erwin Rohde, 22 February 1884.
110 Letter to Malwida von Meysenbug, 12 February 1884.
111 Letter to Heinrich von Stein, 21 May 1884.
112 Letter to Franz Overbeck, 7 April 1884.
113 Letter to Franz Overbeck, beginning of April 1884.
114 Letter to Malwida von Meysenbug, early May 1884.
115 Letter to Franz Overbeck, beginning of June 1884.
116 Letter to Franz Overbeck, 7 April 1884.
117 Letter to Peter Gast, 25 July 1884.
118 Letter from Peter Gast to Cäcilie Gusselbauer, 5 June 1884.
119 Letter to Franz Overbeck, 21 May 1884.
120 Letter from Franz Overbeck to Erwin Rohde, 27 July 1884.
121 Ibid.
122 Letter to Peter Gast, 25 July 1884.
123 Meta von Salis.
124 Letter to Franz Overbeck, 1 August 1884.
125 Letter to Peter Gast, 2 September 1884.
126 Ibid.
127 Letter to his mother, 10 August 1884.
128 Resa von Schirnhofer. Cited by Janz.
129 Ibid.
130 Letter from Heinrich von Stein to Daniela von Bülow, 31 August 1884.
131 Ibid.
132 Letter to Franz Overbeck, 14 September 1884.

133 Ibid.
134 Letter to his mother, 4 October 1884.
135 Letter to Franz Overbeck, 4 October 1884.
136 Letter to Franz Overbeck, end of October 1884.
137 Letter to Franz Overbeck, 4 October 1884.
138 Letter to Gottfried Keller postmarked 16 September 1884.
139 Letter from Gottfried Keller, 28 September 1884.
140 Elisabeth Förster-Nietzsche. Commentary in her edition of the letters.
141 Letter to Peter Gast, 14 October 1884.
142 Letter from Franz Overbeck, 21 December 1884.
143 Letter to his mother and sister, 7 November 1884.
144 Letter to his mother and sister, *c.* 19 November 1884.
145 Letter to his mother and sister, 28 November 1884.
146 Letter to his mother and sister, beginning of January 1885.
147 Letter to Malwida von Meysenbug, 13 February 1885.
148 Letter to his mother and sister, beginning of January 1885.
149 Letter to Franz Overbeck, 22 December 1885.
150 Letter to Franz Overbeck, 31 March 1885.
151 *Also sprach Zarathustra*, Part IV, 'The Sign'.
152 'On the Higher Men'.
153 'The Honey Sacrifice'.
154 'The Voluntary Beggar'.
155 'The Greeting'.
156 'On the Higher Men'.
157 'The Cry of Distress'.
158 Ibid.
159 'Retired from Service'.
160 Ibid.
161 Ibid.
162 Ibid.
163 'The Shadow'.
164 Ibid.
165 Letter to his mother and sister, 21 March 1885.
166 'The Magician'.
167 Ibid.
168 See Janz, vol. II, p. 376.
169 Letter to Franz Overbeck, 31 March 1885.
170 Letter to Franz Overbeck, end of May 1885.
171 Letter to Franz Overbeck, 31 March 1885.
172 'The Donkey Festival'.
173 'The Song of Dejection'.
174 Notebooks.
175 Letter to Peter Gast, 21 March 1885.
176 Letter to Carl von Gersdorff, 12 February 1885.
177 Letter to Carl von Gersdorff, 9 May 1885.
178 Letter to Franz Overbeck, end of May 1885.

179 Letter to his mother, 4 October 1884.
180 Letter to Carl Fuchs, December 1884.
181 Ibid.
182 Letter to Malwida von Meysenbug, 13 March 1885.
183 Ibid.
184 'Einsiedlers Sehnsucht'.
185 Letter to Peter Gast, 30 March 1885.
186 Letter to Franz Overbeck, 4 July 1885.
187 Letter to his mother, April 1885.
188 Ibid.
189 *Nachlass*, April–June 1885.
190 Letter to his sister, April 1885.
191 Letter to his sister, 20 May 1885.
192 Letter to his mother, end of May 1885.
193 Ibid.

Chapter 11

1 Letter to Peter Gast, 23 July 1885.
2 Letter to Franz Overbeck, 2 July 1885.
3 Ibid.
4 Letter to Peter Gast, 23 July 1885.
5 Adolf Ruthardt, writing in 1921.
6 Letter to his mother and sister, 6 September 1885.
7 Ibid.
8 Letter to Peter Gast, 22 September 1885.
9 Letter to Franz Overbeck, October 1885.
10 Letter to Heinrich von Stein, 15 October 1885.
11 Letter to Franz Overbeck, 17 October 1885.
12 Ibid.
13 Letter to Peter Gast, 21 August 1885.
14 Letter to his mother, 23 October 1885.
15 Letter to Franz Overbeck, 9 January 1886.
16 Letter to Peter Gast, 6 December 1885.
17 Letter to his mother and sister, beginning of January 1886.
18 Letter to his mother and sister, 7 November 1885.
19 Ibid.
20 Letter to his mother, 7 November 1885.
21 Letter to his sister, November 1885.
22 Letter to Peter Gast, 24 November 1885.
23 Ibid.
24 Letter to Peter Gast, 6 December 1885.
25 Letter to his mother, December 1885.
26 Letter to his sister, November 1885.
27 *Jenseits von Gut und Böse*, s. 1.

28 S. 59.
29 S. 295.
30 Ibid.
31 S. 2.
32 S. 3.
33 Ibid.
34 S. 4.
35 S. 16.
36 S. 17.
37 Siegmund Freud, *Das Ich und das Es*.
38 See Georg Groddeck, *The Meaning of Illness*, ed. Lore Schacht (London 1977).
39 Georg Groddeck, 'Von der Sprache', in *Hin zu Gottnatur*, 3rd ed. (Leipzig 1913). Trans. in *The Meaning of Illness*.
40 Rimbaud, letter to Georges Izambard, 13 May 1871.
41 *Jenseits*, s. 19.
42 Ibid.
43 S. 36.
44 S. 289.
45 Ibid.
46 S. 290.
47 S. 42.
48 S. 211.
49 S. 244.
50 S. 241.
51 Ibid.
52 S. 242.
53 S. 203.
54 S. 62.
55 Ibid.
56 S. 240.
57 S. 195.
58 S. 197.
59 S. 201.
60 S. 202,
61 For a detailed examination of the affinity between Sade and Nietzsche, see the chapter 'Juliette or Enlightenment and Morality' in Max Horkheimer and Theodor Adorno.
62 *Jenseits*, s. 259.
63 S. 257.
64 S. 258.
65 S. 260.
66 S. 262.
67 S. 260.
68 S. 61.
69 S. 269.
70 S. 296.

71 Letter to his mother, end of January 1886.
72 Ibid.
73 Letter to his sister, 12 March 1886.
74 Letter to Franz Overbeck, 10 March 1886.
75 Letter to Peter Gast, 27 March 1886.
76 Letter to his mother, 25 February 1886.
77 Letter to his sister, February 1886.
78 Letter to Erwin Rohde, 23 February 1886.
79 Letter to Franz Overbeck, late March or early April 1886.
80 Letter to Bernhard and Elisabeth Förster, April 1886.
81 Letter to Franz Overbeck, late March or early April 1886.
82 Letter to Franz Overbeck, 1 May 1886.
83 Letter to Irene von Seydlitz, 7 May 1886.
84 Letter to Peter Gast, 7 May 1886.
85 Letter to his mother, 9 May 1886.
86 Letter to Franz Overbeck, 14 July 1886.
87 Ibid.
88 Letter to Franz Overbeck, 20 June 1886.
89 Letter to his sister, 2 September 1886.
90 Letter from Erwin Rohde to Franz Overbeck, 24 January 1889.
91 Letter from Erwin Rohde to Franz Overbeck, 1 September 1886.
92 Letter to Franz Overbeck, 5 August 1886.
93 Ibid.
94 Letter to Franz Overbeck, 20 June 1886.
95 Letter to his mother, end of July 1886.
96 Letter to his mother, 17 August 1886.
97 Quoted in letter to Franz Overbeck, 5 August 1886.
98 Letter to Franz Overbeck, 24 July 1886.
99 Letter to Peter Gast, 31 October 1886.
100 *Menschliches, Allzumenschliches*, Part II, preface.
101 Ibid.
102 Preface to 1886 edition of *Die Geburt der Tragödie*.
103 Ibid.
104 Letter to Peter Gast, 2 September 1886.
105 Letter from Jacob Burckhardt, 26 September 1886.
106 *Der Bund*, 16–17 September 1886.
107 Letter to Malwida von Meysenbug, 24 September 1886.
108 Letter to Peter Gast, 10 October 1886.
109 Letter to Reinhardt von Seydlitz, 26 October 1886.
110 *Die fröhliche Wissenschaft*, s. 367.
111 S. 347.
112 Siegmund Freud, *Civilisation and Its Discontents*, standard edition, vol. 21.
113 Robert Musil, *Der Mann ohne Eigenschaften*, vol. 1.
114 *Die fröhliche Wissenschaft*, s. 357.
115 Ibid.
116 S. 370.

117 Ibid.
118 Ibid.
119 S. 371.
120 S. 349.
121 S. 373.
122 Ibid.
123 Ibid.
124 Letter to Hippolyte Taine, 4 July 1887.
125 Letter to Franz Overbeck, 29 October 1886.
126 Letter to his sister, 3 November 1886.
127 Letter to his mother, November 1886.
128 Letter to Franz Overbeck, 25 December 1886.
129 Ibid.
130 Postcard to Franz Overbeck, 4 January 1887.
131 Letter to Peter Gast, 9 December 1886.
132 Postcard to Franz Overbeck, 9 January 1887, and letter to him, 12 February 1887.
133 Letter to Franz Overbeck, 12 February 1887.
134 Letter to Peter Gast, 21 January 1887.
135 Letter to Franz Overbeck, 23 February 1887.
136 Ibid.
137 Letter to Peter Gast, 7 March 1887.
138 Letter to Reinhardt von Seydlitz, 24 February 1887.
139 Ibid.
140 Letter to Franz Overbeck, 24 March 1887.
141 Postcard to Peter Gast, 4 April 1887.
142 Postcard to Peter Gast, 12 April 1887.
143 Letter to his sister, 20 April 1887.
144 Ibid.
145 Ibid.
146 Letter to Franz Overbeck, 17 June 1887.
147 Letter to his sister, 5 June 1887.
148 Letter to Franz Overbeck, 14 April 1887.
149 Ibid.
150 Letter to Peter Gast, 19 April 1887.
151 Postcard to Peter Gast, 26 April 1887.
152 Letter to his mother, 10 May 1887.
153 Letter to Franz Overbeck, 13 May 1887.
154 Letter to Franz Overbeck, 17 June 1887.
155 Ibid.
156 Ibid.
157 Ibid.
158 Letter to Peter Gast, 22 June 1887.
159 Letter to Peter Gast, 18 July 1887.
160 Ibid.
161 Letter to Peter Gast, 27 June 1887.

162 *Zur Genealogie der Moral*, first essay, 'Gut und Böse, Gut und Schlecht, s. 2.
163 S. 5.
164 S. 6.
165 S. 10.
166 S. 14.
167 S. 15.
168 S. 16.
169 S. 11.
170 Ibid.
171 Ibid.
172 S. 12.
173 Second essay, '"Schuld" "Schlechtes Gewissen" und Verwandtes', s. 6.
174 S. 2.
175 S. 16.
176 Ibid.
177 S. 17.
178 S. 19.
179 Third essay, 'Was bedeuten Asketische Ideale?', s. 16.
180 Second essay, s. 21.
181 S. 22.
182 S. 21.
183 S. 2.
184 S. 4.
185 S. 5.
186 Michel Foucault, *Surveiller et punir: Naissance de la prison* (Paris 1975).
187 Second essay, s. 3.
188 S. 6.
189 S. 7.
190 S. 9.
191 S. 11.
192 Ibid.
193 S. 14.
194 Third essay, s. 7.
195 S. 8.
196 S. 7.
197 S. 8.
198 S. 15.
199 S. 13.
200 S. 15.
201 S. 14.
202 S. 18.
203 S. 13.
204 Letter to Franz Overbeck, 30 August 1887.
205 Letter to Peter Gast, 8 August 1887.

206 Letter to his mother, 3 August 1887.
207 Ibid.
208 Letter to Franz Overbeck, 30 August 1887.
209 Meta von Salis.
210 Ibid.
211 Postcard to Franz Overbeck, 24 September 1887.
212 Ibid.
213 Postcard to his mother, 3 October 1887.
214 Postcard to his mother, 1 October 1887.
215 Letter to his mother, 18 October 1887.
216 Postcard to his mother, 3 October 1887.
217 Letter to his sister, 15 October 1887.
218 Ibid.
219 Ibid.
220 Letter to Erwin Rohde 21 May 1887.
221 Letter to Erwin Rohde, 11 November 1887.
222 Letter to Erwin Rohde, 23 May 1887.
223 Letter to Franz Overbeck, 12 November 1887.
224 Postcard to Peter Gast, 23 October 1887.
225 Postcard to his mother, 23 October 1887.
226 Letter to Peter Gast, 27 October 1887.
227 Ibid.
228 Ibid.
229 Postcard to Franz Overbeck, 23 November 1887.
230 Letter to Peter Gast, 24 November 1887.
231 Letter to his mother, 20 March 1888, and letter to Franz Overbeck, 23 December 1887.
232 Letter to Jacob Burckhardt, 14 November 1887.
233 Letter from Carl von Gersdorff, 30 November 1887.
234 Letter to Carl von Gersdorff, 20 December 1887.
235 Letter from Georg Brandes, 26 November 1887.
236 Letter to Georg Brandes, 2 December 1887.
237 Letter from Georg Brandes, 11 January 1888.
238 Letter to Carl Fuchs, 14 December 1887, and letter to Peter Gast, 20 December 1887.
239 Letter to Peter Gast, 20 December 1887.
240 Postcard to Franz Overbeck, 4 January 1888.
241 Draft of letter to Franz Overbeck, 3 February 1888.
242 Letter to Franz Overbeck, 3 February 1888.
243 R.D.Laing, The Divided Self (London 1960).
244 Letter to Reinhardt von Seydlitz, 12 February 1888.
245 Letter to Georg Brandes, 19 February 1888.
246 Letter to Franz Overbeck, 3 March 1888.
247 Letter to Peter Gast, 21 March 1888.
248 Letter to Peter Gast, 31 March 1888.
249 Letter to Peter Gast, 7 April 1888.
250 Ibid.

251 Ibid.
252 Letter to Franz Overbeck, 10 April 1888.
253 Letter from Georg Brandes, 3 April 1888.
254 Letter to Georg Brandes, 10 April 1888.
255 Letter to Peter Gast, 20 April 1888.
256 *Der Fall Wagner*, second postscript.
257 Preface.
258 S. 1.
259 Ibid.
260 S. 2.
261 S. 3.
262 S. 5.
263 Walter Kaufman, in his edition of *The Birth of Tragedy* and *The Case of Wagner*, makes the point that Nietzsche's fondness for the word 'idiotic' dates from his reading of Dostoevsky.
264 *Die fröhliche Wissenschaft*, s. 7.
265 S. 8.
266 S. 7.
267 Letter to his mother, 2 August 1888.
268 Letter to Franz Overbeck, 3 May 1888.
269 Letter to Georg Brandes, 4 May 1888.
270 Letter from Georg Brandes, 23 May 1888.
271 Letter to Georg Brandes, 23 May 1888.

Chapter 12

1 Letter to Reinhardt von Seydlitz, 13 May 1888.
2 Letter to his mother, 25 April 1888.
3 Mentioned in letter to Franz Overbeck, 27 May 1888.
4 Letter to his mother, 10 June 1888.
5 Letter to his mother, 14 June 1888.
6 Letter to Peter Gast, 20 June 1888.
7 Letter to Peter Gast, 14 June 1888.
8 Letter to Karl Knortz, 21 June 1888.
9 Letter to Malwida von Meysenbug, end of July 1888.
10 Letter to Carl Fuchs, 29 July 1888.
11 Letter to his mother, 25 June 1888.
12 Letter to Meta von Salis, 7 September 1888.
13 Letter to Franz Overbeck, 20 July 1888.
14 Letter to Franz Overbeck, 4 July 1888.
15 Ibid.
16 *Götzendämmerung*, 'The Four Prime Fallacies', s. 2.
17 'Contentions of a Man at Odds with his Times', s. 20.
18 Ibid.
19 S. 36.

20 'The Problem of Socrates', s. 1.
21 Ibid.
22 S. 2.
23 S. 3.
24 S. 9.
25 S. 12.
26 S. 11.
27 Ibid.
28 'Reason in Philosophy', s. 1.
29 Ibid.
30 S. 2.
31 S. 5.
32 Ibid.
33 'The Four Prime Fallacies', s. 3.
34 Ibid.
35 'What the Germans Lack', s. 2.
36 'Sayings and Arrows', no. 23.
37 'What the Germans Lack', s. 1.
38 S. 4.
39 S. 5.
40 Ibid.
41 'Contentions of a Man at Odds with his Times', s. 18.
42 S. 34.
43 S. 35.
44 S. 40.
45 S. 48.
46 Ibid.
47 Letter to his mother, 23 July 1888.
48 Quoted in letter to his mother, 23 July 1888.
49 Letter to his mother, 2 August 1888.
50 Letter to Carl Fuchs, 26 August 1888.
51 Letter to his mother, 13 August 1888.
52 Letter to Hans von Bülow, 10 August 1888.
53 Julius Kaftan, 'Aus der Werkstatt des Übermenschen'. Article published 10 November 1905.
54 Letter to his mother, 2 August 1888.
55 Letter to Meta von Salis, 7 September 1888.
56 Preface to *Der Antichrist*.
57 Ibid.
58 Letter to Paul Deussen, 14 September 1888.
59 Ibid.
60 Janz, vol. 2.
61 *Der Antichrist*, s. 24.
62 Ibid.
63 S. 28.
64 S. 30.
65 S. 32.

66 S. 33.
67 S. 34.
68 S. 29.
69 S. 39.
70 S. 38.
71 S. 42.
72 S. 45.
73 S. 47.
74 Postcard to Franz Overbeck, 8 October 1888.
75 Letter to Franz Overbeck, September 1888.
76 Letter to Georg Brandes, 13 September 1888.
77 Letter to Malwida von Meysenbug, September 1888.
78 Letter to Peter Gast, 27 September 1888.
79 Ibid.
80 Ibid.
81 Letter to Peter Gast, 14 October 1888.
82 Ibid.
83 Letter to his sister, end of October 1888.
84 Ibid.
85 Letter to Meta von Salis, 29 December 1888.
86 Letter to Franz Overbeck, 18 October 1888.
87 Letter to Peter Gast, 30 October 1888.
88 Karl Strecker, *Nietzsche und Strindberg* (Munich 1921).
89 Letter to Hans von Bülow, 9 October 1888.
90 Letter to Malwida von Meysenbug, 18 October 1888.
91 Letter to his sister, end of October 1888.
92 Letter to Franz Overbeck, 18 October 1888.
93 *Ecce Homo*, preface and epigraph.
94 Letter to Peter Gast, 30 October 1888.
95 *Ecce Homo*, 'Why I Am So Wise', s. 1.
96 S. 2.
97 S. 3.
98 'Why I Am So Clever', s. 1.
99 S. 2.
100 S. 9.
101 S. 5.
102 S. 4.
103 'Why I Write Such Good Books', s. 2.
104 *Die Geburt der Tragödie*, s. 1.
105 S. 3.
106 S. 4.
107 'The Unseasonable Ones', s. 3.
108 Ibid.
109 *Menschliches, Allzumenschliches*, s. 2.
110 S. 3.
111 *Morgenröte*, s. 1.
112 'Why I Am Destiny', s. 1.

113 Ibid.
114 S. 2.
115 S. 7.
116 S. 8.
117 S. 3.
118 Letter to Meta von Salis, 14 November 1888.
119 Letter to Georg Brandes, 20 November 1888.
120 Letter from Georg Brandes, 6 October 1888.
121 Letter to Georg Brandes, 20 November 1888.
122 Letter to August Strindberg, end of November 1888.
123 Letter from August Strindberg, received 7 December 1888.
124 Letter from August Strindberg, December 1888.
125 Letter to his mother, 17 November (inaccurately dated 3 November) 1888.
126 Letter to Franz Overbeck, 13 November 1888.
127 Letter to Peter Gast, 26 November 1888.
128 Letter to Peter Gast, 2 December 1888.
129 Letter to Peter Gast, 9 December 1888.
130 Ibid.
131 Letter to Carl Fuchs, 11 December 1888.
132 Ibid.
133 Ibid.
134 Draft of letter to his sister, December 1888.
135 Letter to Carl Fuchs, 27 December 1888.
136 Letter to Franz Overbeck, received 28 December 1888.
137 Letter to Peter Gast, 31 December 1888.
138 Letter to August Strindberg, undated.
139 Letter from August Strindberg, January 1889.
140 Letter to Franz Overbeck, 25 December 1888.
141 Letters to Peter Gast, Georg Brandes and Meta von Salis, postmarked 4 January 1889.
142 Letter to Jacob Burckhardt, postmarked 4 January 1889.
143 Letter to Cosima Wagner, begining of January 1889.
144 Letter to Jacob Burckhardt, dated 6 January but posted 5 January 1889.
145 Letter to Franz Overbeck, received 7 January 1889.
146 Letter from Franz Overbeck to his wife, 8 January 1889.
147 Ibid.
148 Letter from Franz Overbeck to Peter Gast, 15 January 1889.
149 Letter from his mother to Franz Overbeck, January 1889.
150 Letter from Franz Overbeck to Peter Gast, 20 January 1889.
151 Remark of 27 March quoted in the records of the clinic.
152 10 March 1889.
153 23 February 1889.
154 24 March 1889.
155 10 June 1889.
156 4 July 1889.

157 14 June 1889.

158 16 June 1889.

159 Letter from his mother to Franz Overbeck, October 1889.

160 Letter from Peter Gast to Carl Fuchs, January 1890.

161 Letter from Franz Overbeck to his wife, 24 February 1890.

162 Ibid.

163 Dr S. Simchowitz, article in *Frankfurter Zeitung*, 7 September 1900. Cited by Podach.

164 Letter from his mother to Franz Overbeck, 22 March 1890.

165 Evidence of a relation of the Gelzers. Cited by Podach.

166 Letter from Peter Gast to Franz Overbeck, 26 February 1890.

167 Paul Deussen, op. cit. Deussen confuses the date of the visit with that of one to Naumburg and Jena in Easter 1889.

168 Letter from his mother to Franz Overbeck, summer 1891.

169 Letter from his mother to Franz Overbeck, 5 October 1891.

170 Letter from Peter Gast to Franz Overbeck, 26 February 1892.

171 Letter from his mother to Franz Overbeck, 31 March and 1 April 1892.

172 Letter from his mother to Franz Overbeck, 3 July 1892.

173 Letter from his mother to Franz Overbeck, 26 September 1892.

174 Unpublished manuscript in the Nietzsche collection in the Goethe–Schiller Archiv at Weimar.

175 Ibid.

176 Ibid.

177 Ibid.

178 Ibid.

179 Ibid.

180 Letter from Peter Gast to Franz Overbeck, 5 January 1893.

181 Letter from his mother to Franz Overbeck, 31 March 1893.

182 Ibid.

183 Letter from his mother to Franz Overbeck, 29 June 1893.

184 Letter from Erwin Rohde to Franz Overbeck, 27 December 1894.

185 Paul Deussen, op. cit.

186 Letter from Franz Overbeck to Erwin Rohde, 31 December 1895.

187 See Karl Böttcher, 'In geistiger Umnachtung', in *Auf Studienpfaden* (Zürich 1900).

188 Count Harry Kessler's diary, 8 August 1897.

189 Rudolf Steiner, quoted in Bernoulli, vol. 2.

190 Kurt Hildebrandt.

191 Ibid.

192 Elisabeth Förster-Nietzsche.

193 Fritz Schumacher, *Erinnerungen eines Baumeisters* (Stuttgart 1949).

Chapter 13

1 *Der Wille zur Macht*, s. 579 (notes of 1883–8).
2 Minutes of the Vienna Psychoanalytic Society, vol. 1, 1906–8 (New York 1962).
3 1886 preface to *Menschliches, Allzumenschliches*, Part II.
4 Bruford suggests that the slag image may derive from a 1782 letter from Goethe to Fritz Jacobi about the slag hammered out of his nature by the difficulties of his life in Weimar.
5 Letter to Peter Gast, end of August 1881.
6 *Werke: Kritische Gesamtausgabe*, Abteilung VII, vol. 1.
7 *Der Wille zur Macht*, s. 676 (note of 1883–8).
8 Leo Bersani, *A Future for Astyanax: Character and Desire in Literature* (New York 1976, London 1978).
9 Letter from Richard Wagner to August Röckel, 25 January 1854.
10 *Zarathustra* Part I, 'On the Despisers of the Body'.
11 Gilles Deleuze, *Présentation de Sacher-Masoch* (Paris 1967).
12 *Genealogie der Moral*, s. 10.
13 Heidegger, vol. 2.
14 *Der Fall Wagner*, Epilogue.
15 *Der Wille zur Macht*, s. 517 (note of 1887).
16 *Morgenröte*, s. 33.
17 *Der Wille zur Macht*, s. 522 (note of 1886–7).
18 *Der Wille zur Macht*, s. 569 (note of 1887).
19 *Der Wille zur Macht*, s. 517 (note of 1887).
20 Ibid.
21 S. 516 (note of 1887, revised 1888).
22 *Die fröhliche Wissenschaft*, s. 189.
23 *Der Wille zur Macht*, s. 982 (note of 1884).
24 *Der Wille zur Macht*, ss. 958 (note of 1884) and 960 (note of 1885–6).
25 S. 981 (note of 1887).
26 J. P. Stern.
27 Minutes of the Vienna Psychoanalytic Society, vols. 1 and 2.

Bibliography

Nietzsche's Works

1872 *Die Geburt der Tragödie aus dem Geiste der Musik* (*The Birth of Tragedy from the Spirit of Music*)

1873 *Unzeitgemässe Betrachtungen* (*Untimely Reflections*),
1. *David Strauss, der Bekenner und der Schriftsteller* (*David Strauss, the Confessor and the Writer*)

1874 2. *Vom Nützen und Nachteil der Historie für das Leben* (*On the Uses and Disadvantages of History for Life*)
3. *Schopenhauer als Erzieher* (*Schopenhauer as Educator*)

1876 4. *Richard Wagner in Bayreuth*

1878 *Menschliches, Allzumenschliches: ein Buch für freie Geister* (*Human, All Too Human, a Book for Free Spirits*)

1879 Anhang: *Vermischte Meinungen und Sprüche* (Appendix: *Assorted Opinions and Sayings*)

1880 *Der Wanderer und sein Schatten* (*The Wanderer and His Shadow*)

1881 *Die Morgenröte: Gedanken über die moralischen Vorurteile* (*Sunrise: Thoughts on Moral Prejudices*)

1882 *Die fröhliche Wissenschaft* (*The Joyful Wisdom*) Books I–IV

1883 *Also sprach Zarathustra: ein Buch für Alle und Keinen* (*Thus Spoke Zarathustra: a Book for Everyone and No One*) Parts I and II

1884 Part III

1885 Part IV (limited edition)

1886 *Jenseits von Gut und Böse: Vorspiel einer Philosophie der Zukunft* (*Beyond Good and Evil: Prelude to a Philosophy of the Future*)
Menschliches, Allzumenschliches (new version consisting of the original, the appendix and *Der Wanderer und sein Schatten*)

1887 *Zur Genealogie der Moral* (*On the Genealogy of Morals*)
Die fröhliche Wissenschaft Book V

1888 *Der Fall Wagner: ein Musikanten-Problem* (*The Case of Wagner:
      a Musician's Problem*)

1889 *Die Götzendämmerung oder Wie man mit dem Hammer philosophiert*
      (*Twilight of the False Gods or How to Philosophize with a Hammer*)

1891 *Dionysus Dithyramben* (*Dionysus Dithyrambs*)

1892 *Also sprach Zarathustra* Part IV (public edition)

1895 *Der Antichrist*
      Nietzsche contra Wagner. Aktenstücke eines Psychologen (*Documents
      of a Psychologist*)

1908 *Ecce Homo. Wie man wird, was man ist* (*How One Becomes What
      One Is*)

Collected Edition

Werke: Kritische Gesamtausgabe, ed. Giorgio Colli and Mazzino
    Montinari (Berlin, De Gruyter 1967 onwards).

Abteilung I
      Vol. 1 Letters from Nietzsche, 1850–64 and to him, 1849–64
      Vol. 2 Letters from Nietzsche, September 1864–June 1869
      Vol. 3 Letters to Nietzsche, October 1864–March 1869

Abteilung II
      Vol. 1 Letters from Nietzsche, 1864–71
      Vol. 2 Letters to him, 1864–71
      Vol. 3 Letters from Nietzsche, 1872–4
      Vol. 4 Letters to him, 1872–4

Abteilung III
      Vol. 1 *Geburt der Tragödie: Unzeitgemässe Betrachtungen*, nos.
              1–3
      Vol. 2 *Nachgelassene Schriften* 1870–3
      Vol. 3 *Nachgelassene Fragmente* autumn 1869–autumn 1872
      Vol. 4 *Nachgelassene Fragmente* summer 1872–end of 1874

Abteilung IV
      Vol. 1 *Unzeitgemässe Betrachtungen* No. 4; *Nachgelassene Frag-
              mente* beginning of 1875–spring of 1876

Vol. 2 *Menschliches, Allzumenschliches* Part 1; *Nachgelassene Fragmente* 1876–winter 1877–8

Vol. 3 *Menschliches, Allzumenschliches* Part 11; *Nachgelassene Fragmente* spring 1877–November 1879

Vol. 4 *Nachbericht* to *Abteilung* IV

Abteilung V

Vol. 1 *Morgenröte; Nachgelassene Fragmente* beginning of 1880 to spring 1881

Vol. 2 *Idyllen aus Messina; Die fröhliche Wissenschaft; Nachgelassene Fragmente* spring 1881–summer 1882

Abteilung VI

Vol. 1 *Also sprach Zarathustra*

Vol. 2. *Jenseits von Gut und Böse*
and *Zur Genealogie der Moral*

Vol. 3 *Der Fall Wagner* and *Götzendämmerung; Nachgelassene Schriften* August 1888–January 1889; *Der Antichrist; Ecce Homo; Dionysus Dithyramben; Nietzsche contra Wagner*

Of the earlier, less reliable collected editions, the most accessible is *Werke in drei Bänden*, ed. K. Schlechta (Munich 1954–6), and the most useful the Musarionausgabe, 23 vols. (Munich 1920–9).

Select Bibliography of Translations

The Complete Works of Friedrich Nietzsche, 18 vols., ed. Oscar Levy (New York 1909–11, reissued 1964).

Selected Letters of Friedrich Nietzsche, trans. and ed. Christopher Middleton (Chicago 1969).

The Portable Nietzsche, ed. Walter Kaufmann (New York 1954). Contains *Thus Spoke Zarathustra, Twilight of the Idols, The Antichrist* and *Nietzsche contra Wagner* plus selections.

Basic Writings of Nietzsche (New York 1968). Contains *Beyond Good and Evil, The Birth of Tragedy, The Case of Wagner, On the Genealogy of Morals* and *Ecce Homo*. Trans. with commentary by Walter Kaufmann. (R. J. Hollingdale collaborated on the translation of *On the Genealogy of Morals*.) These translations are also available in paperback (New York 1966–8), 3 vols.

The Will to Power, trans. Walter Kaufmann and R. J. Hollingdale, with commentary (New York 1967).

The Gay Science, trans. Walter Kaufmann (New York 1974).

The Use and Abuse of History, trans. Adrian Collins (Indianapolis 1949).

A Nietzsche Reader, selected and trans. R. J. Hollingdale (Harmondsworth 1977).

Human, All Too Human, trans. Helen Zimmern, 2 vols (New York 1974).

Thoughts Out of Season, trans. J. M. Kennedy, 2 vols (New York 1974).

The Dawn of Day, trans. Anthony M. Ludovici (New York 1974).

Historical

Craig, Gordon A., *Germany 1866-1945* (Oxford 1978).

Hamerow, Theodore S., *Restoration, Revolution, Reaction: Economics and Politics in Germany 1815-1871* (Princeton, New Jersey 1958).

Hoffele Karl Heinrich, *Geist und Gesellschaft der Bismarckzeit 1870-1890* (Göttingen 1967).

Mander, John, *Berlin: the Eagle and the Bear* (London 1959).
  Our German Cousins: Anglo-German Relations in the 19th and 20th Centuries (London 1974).

Passant, E. J., *A Short History of Germany 1815-1845* (Cambridge 1959).

Taylor, A. J. P., *The Course of German History* (London 1945).
  The Struggle for Mastery in Europe 1848-1918 (Oxford 1954).

Thomson, David, *Europe since Napoleon* (London 1957).

Vansittart, Peter, *Worlds and Underworlds: Anglo-European History through the Centuries* (London 1974).

Literary, Philosophical and Psychological

Barrett, William, *Irrational Man: a Study in Existential Philosophy* (New York 1958).

Dodds, E. R., *The Greeks and the Irrational* (Berkeley, Los Angeles and London 1954).

Kohn, Hans, *The Mind of Germany: the Education of a Nation* (London 1961).

Löwith, Karl, *Von Hegel zu Nietzsche. Der revolutionäre Bruch im Denken des 19. Jahrhunderts* (Stuttgart 1964), trans. D. E. Green as *From Hegel to Nietzsche: the Revolution in 19th Century Thought* (New York 1964, London 1965).

Lukacs, Georg, *Deutsche Literatur im Zeitalter des Imperialismus* (Berlin 1946).

Ricoeur, Paul, *Freud and Philosophy: an Essay in Interpretation*, trans. Denis Savage (New Haven and London 1970).

Stern, J. P. *Idylls and Realities: Studies in 19th Century German Literature* (London 1971).
Reinterpretations: Seven Studies in 19th Century German Literature (London 1964).

Biographical, Critical and Interpretative

Alderman, Harold, *Nietzsche's Gift* (Athens, Ohio 1977).

Allison, David B. (ed.), *The New Nietzsche: Contemporary Styles of Interpretation* (New York 1977).

Andler, Charles, *Nietzsche: sa vie et pensée*, 6 vols. (Paris 1920–31).

Andreas-Salomé, Lou, *Friedrich Nietzsche in seinen Werken* (Vienna 1894).

Bernoulli, Carl A., *Franz Overbeck und Friedrich Nietzsche: eine Freundschaft*, 2 vols. (Jena 1908).

Binion, Rudolph, *Frau Lou: Nietzsche's Wayward Disciple* (Princeton, New Jersey 1968).

Blunck, Richard, *Friedrich Nietzsche: Kindheit und Jugend* (Munich and Basel, 1953).

Brandes, Georg, *Friedrich Nietzsche*, trans. A. G. Chater (London 1914).

Brann, Helmut Walther, *Nietzsche und die Frauen* (Leipzig 1931).

Camus, Albert, 'Nietzsche et le nihilisme' in *L'Homme révolté* (Paris 1951).

Dannhauser, Werner, J., *Nietzsche's View of Socrates* (Ithaca 1974).

Deleuze, Gilles, *Nietzsche* (Paris 1965).
　　　　　　Nietzsche et sa philosophie (Paris 1970).

Deussen, Paul, *Erinnerungen an Friedrich Nietzsche* (Leipzig 1901).

Fink, Eugen, *Nietzsches Philosophie* (Stuttgart 1960).

Förster-Nietzsche, Elisabeth, *Das Leben Friedrich Nietzsches*, 3 vols (Leipzig 1895–1904), trans. as *The Young Nietzsche* (by A. M. Ludovici) and *The Lonely Nietzsche* (by P. V. Cohn) (London 1912–15).

Granier, Jean, *Le Problème de la verité dans la philosophie de Nietzsche* (Paris 1966).

Haar, Michael, 'Nietzsche and Metaphysical Language', in *Man and World*, vol. 4, November 1971.

Heidegger, Martin, *Nietzsche*, 2 vols. (Pfüllingen 1961).

Heller, Erich, 'Burckhardt and Nietzsche', 'Nietzsche and Goethe' and 'Nietzsche and Rilke', in *The Disinherited Mind* (Cambridge and Philadelphia, 1952).
　　　　　　'The Importance of Nietzsche' and 'Wittgenstein and Nietzsche', in *The Artist's Journey into the Interior* (New York 1965).
　　　　　　'Nietzsche in the Waste Land', in *The Poet's Self and the Poem* (London 1976).

Heller, Peter, *Dialectrics and Nihilism: Essays on Lessing, Nietzsche, Mann and Kafka* (Amherst, Mass. 1966).

Hildebrandt, Kurt, *Gesundheit und Krankheit in Nietzsches Leben und Werk* (Berlin 1926).

Hollingdale, R. J., *Nietzsche: The Man and his Philosophy* (Baton Rouge and London 1965).
　　　　　　Nietzsche (London 1973).

Horkheimer, Max and Theodor Adorno, *Dialektik der Aufklärung* (Frankfurt 1944), trans. John Cumming as *Dialectic of Enlightenment* (New York 1972).

Howey, Richard Lowell, *Heidegger and Jaspers on Nietzsche: a Critical Examination of Heidegger's and Jaspers's Interpretations of Nietzsche* (The Hague 1973).

Janz, Curt Paul, *Die Briefe Friedrich Nietzsches: Textprobleme und ihre Bedeutung für Biographie und Doxographie* (Zürich 1972).
   Friedrich Nietzsche: Biographie, 3 vols. (Munich and Vienna, vol. 1 1977, vol. 2 1978).

Kaufmann, Walter, *Nietzsche: Philosopher, Psychologist, Antichrist* (Princeton 1950, 4th ed. 1974).
   'How Nietzsche Revolutionized Ethics', 'Nietzsche and Rilke', and 'Jasper's Relation to Nietzsche', in *From Shakespeare to Existentialism* (Boston 1959).

Klossowski, Pierre, *Nietzsche et le cercle vicieux* (Paris 1969).

Laruelle, François, *Nietzsche contre Heidegger* (Paris 1977).

Lauret, Bernard, *Schulderfahrung und Gottesfrage bei Nietzsche und Freud* (Munich 1977).

Lea, F.A., *The Tragic Philosopher: a Study of Friedrich Nietzsche* (New York 1957).

Love, Frederick R., *Young Nietzsche and the Wagnerian Experience* (Chapel Hill 1963).

Magnus, Bernard, *Nietzsche's Existential Imperative* (Bloomington and London 1978).

Mann, Thomas, 'Nietzsches Philosophie', in *Neue Studien* (Stockholm 1948).

Manthey-Zorn, Otto, *Dionysus: The Tragedy of Nietzsche* (Westport, Connecticut 1975).

Möbius, Paul J., *Über das Pathologische bei Nietzsche* (Wiesbaden 1902).

Montinari, Mazzino, 'Ein neuer Abschmitt in Nietzsches *Ecce Homo*', in *Nietzsche Studien*, vol. 1 (Berlin and New York 1972).

Morgan, George A., *What Nietzsche Means* (Cambridge, Mass. 1941).

Newman, Ernest, *The Life of Richard Wagner*, vol. 4 (London and New York, 1972).

O'Flaherty, James, Timothy F. Sellner and Robert M. Helm, *Studies in Nietzsche and the Ancient World* (Chapel Hill 1976).

Pasley, Malcolm (ed.), *Nietzsche: Imagery and Thought* (London 1978).

Podach, Erich F., *Nietzsches Zusammenbruch: Beitrag zu einer Biographie auf Grund unveröffentlichter Dokumente* (Heidelberg 1930), trans. F.A.Voigt as *The Madness of Nietzsche* (New York 1931).
　　　Gestalten um Nietzsche mit unveröffentlichten Dokumenten zur Geschichte seines Lebens und seines Werkes (Weimar 1932).
　　　Der Kranke Nietzsche: Briefe seiner Mutter an Franz Overbeck (Vienna 1937).

Salis, Meta von, *Philosoph und Edelmann* (n.d.).

Seigel, Jerrold, *Marx's Fate: the Shape of a Life* (Princeton, New Jersey 1978).

Solomon, Robert C. (ed.), *Nietzsche: a Collection of Critical Essays* (New York 1973).

Stambaugh, Joan, *Nietzsche's Thought of Eternal Return* (Baltimore and London, 1972).

Stern, J.P., *Nietzsche* (London 1978).
　　　A Study of Nietzsche (Cambridge 1979).

Strong, Tracy B., *Nietzsche and the Politics of Transfiguration* (Berkeley 1975).

Symposium, Syracuse University Press, spring 1974. Special issue devoted to Nietzsche.

Vaihinger, Hans, 'Nietzsche and His Doctrine of Conscious Illusion', in *Die Philosophie des Als-Ob* (Leipzig 1911), trans. C.K.Ogden as *The Philosophy of As-If* (New York 1924).

Wagner, Cosima, *Diaries*, vol. I, 1869–77, ed. Martin Gregor Dellin and Dietrich Mack, trans. Geoffrey Skelton (London and New York 1978).

Westernhagen, Curt von, *Wagner: a biography*, trans. Mary Whittall, 2 vols. (Cambridge 1979).

Wilcox, John T., *Truth and Value in Nietzsche: a Study in His Metaphysics and Epistemology* (Ann Arbor 1974).

Wolff, Hans M., *Friedrich Nietzsche: der Weg zum Nichts* (Bern 1956).

Index

Note: N refers to Friedrich Nietzsche; Elisabeth to Elisabeth Nietzsche;
RW to Richard Wagner; and letters to letters from Nietzsche.

abstinence, 197, 225, 283–4,
  306–10, 355
Adler, Alfred, 5, 361
Aeschylus, 67, 106, 115, 117, 120,
  134, 136, 153; W. Dindorf's
  lexicon, 81, 84
aesthetics, *see* art
Agoult, Comtesse Marie d', 107,
  108, 140
Altenburg, court of, 15, 19
Anacreon, 38
Apocalypse of St John, 307, 331
Apollo, 134–6; *see also* Dionysus
Aquinas, St Thomas, 307, 331
aristocracy, 296; nobility, 306;
  master morality, 293–4, 306–7,
  356
army: Bismark reorganizes, 52, 55;
  Junkers, 55, 69; N accepted for,
  53, 88, 89; N considers enlisting,
  65, 76, 79, 88; N in artillery,
  1867–8, 89–91; N wounded,
  93–6; N medical orderly, 1870,
  127–9
art: definition of, 117, 147;
  Dionysian, 7–8, 131–2, 134–6,
  302, 330; function of, 136–7; and
  genius of the people (Wagner),
  114; life as, 358; painting, 360;
  and philosophy, 117–18; romantic, 7, 209, 215–16, 302, 317;
  and self-oblivion, 123
Artaud, Antonin, 352, 353

ascetic ideals, 308–10; *see also*
  abstinence
Augustine, St, 281
Austria: 1848, 16; 1859 war, 32;
  1860s, Schleswig-Holstein, 52–3;
  1863, and Prussia, 69; 1866, 76,
  78–9; defeated, 79, 80, 131;
  1871, 133
Ayer, A. J., 163

Bach, St Matthew Passion, 123
Bakunin, Mikhail, 99
Basel, Switzerland, 106; N takes
  university chair of philology,
  101–5; timetable, 106, 205;
  lodgings, 106, 111, 205; lives
  with Elisabeth, 181, 203, 205;
  inaugural lecture, 109–10; as
  professor, 106–7, 108–10, 111–
  12, 114–21, 125, 129–31, 133,
  137–8 143–5, 148–52, 156–8,
  160, 162, 165, 171, 176, 177–80,
  183–4, 189; applies for chair of
  philosophy, 137–8, 139; leave of
  absence, 190–1; returns to, 202,
  205–6, 210–12; resigns, 212;
  leaves, 212–13; considers returning, 262; visits, 269, 274; patient
  at psychiatric clinic, 336–8
Baudelaire, Charles, 359–60
Baumgartner, Adolf, 169, 175
Baumgartner, Marie, 204, 206, 207
Bayreuth: festival planned, 142,

145, 150; opera house foundation stone laid, 153–4; N appeals for funds, 165–6, 184; *RW in Bayreuth* essay, 170, 181, 184–6; Wagners' home at, 157, 159, 160, 170–1, 174–5; 1876 festival, 186–9, 190; 1883 festival, 248

Bayreuther Blätter, 202, 206

Beethoven, Ludwig van, 133, 154, 236; N's comment on, 186; RW's essay on, 131, 133

Berlin: 1848 revolution, 16; N visits, 1865, 70; plans to go to, 88; in army at, 89; anti-Semitism, 268; Lou Salomé in, 1882, 247; capital of Reich, 293

Bernhardt, Sarah, 242

Betz, Franz, 188

Bible: translated by Luther, 15; Apocalypse, 307, 331; *see also* Christianity

Biedermann, Professor, 96

Binswanger, Otto, 338, 339, 340, 341–2, 344, 346, 347

Bismarck, Otto von: 1848, 16; 1862, 52–3; *Junkers*, 55; 1865, 69; 1866, 76, 78–80; 1870, 126, 127, 130; 1871, 141; 1872, 152; and religious tolerance, 268–9; 1885, 292–3; 1888, 319

Bizet, Georges, *Carmen*, 236, 261, 316–17

Blake, William, 265, 266

'blond beast', 306–7

body, the, 258, 355; *see also* sickness, sexuality

Bonn University, N student at, 55, 58, 59–68, 69–70; lodgings, 59–60; Ritschl leaves, 67, 71, 87

Borgia, Cesare, 294

Brahms, Johannes, 174, 305; *Triumphlied*, 174, 175

Brandes, Georg: reacts to *Genealogie*, 314; lectures re N, 316, 317–18, 319; letters to, 315, 326, 332

Brenner, Albert, 191, 192, 193

Breysig, Kurt, 350

Brockhaus, Hermann, 97, 112, 143

Brockhaus, Ottilie (née Wagner), 97, 100, 112

Buchbinder, Professor, 29, 57

Buddensieg, Professor, 32, 41, 42, 348

Bülow, Cosima von, *see* Wagner, Cosima

Bülow, Hans von, 151, 324, 328; and Cosima, 107, 112; and N's music, 155, 330

Burckhardt, Jacob: lecturer at Basel, 108–9, 130, 148, 158, 247; friend to N, 125, 143; reacts to N's books, 146, 168, 211–12, 252, 274, 300; letters to, 314, 326, 335–6, 337

Byron, Lord George Gordon, 43, 46

Camus, Albert, 2

Catholic Church: mass, 117; Romundt joins, 178; campaign against, 268

Chekhov, Anton, 196

cholera epidemic, 1866, 83

Christianity: music of, 117, 123; N confirmed, 38–9; rejects, 44–5, 50, 62–3, 66–7, 77; 'Thoughts about –', 77; RW and, 192; and sin, 223–4; morality of attacked, 197, 230, 262–3, 280, 294–5, 299–300, 301–2, 306–9, 323, 325–6, 331–2, 355–6; compared with Greek religion, 199, 309

Chur, 218, 305

Cologne, 105; brothel at, 64; King Wilhelm appears in, 69

Comte, Auguste, 91–2

conflict and contests: Greek, 87, 109, 159; and hatred, 237; lessons of war, 358

Copenhagen University, lectures on N, 316, 317

Corssen (teacher), 43, 56, 57

Counter-Reformation, 205

Credner, Hermann, 288, 295 ,297
Crentzel, Friedrich, 113
Curtius, Professor, 78

Dächsel (lawyer), 18
Darwinism, 167, 199, 302
death: N considers, 214–15;
    suicide, 284; will to die, 301;
    of God, see God
Delbrück, Rudolf von, 268, 292
democracy, 201, 293–4, 359
Democritus, essay on, 88, 91, 92–3
Derrida, Jacques, 3
Descartes, René, 290, 291
Deussen, Marie, 59
Deussen, Paul: at school, 20, 35,
    38–9, 172; 1864 holiday, 58–9;
    at Bonn University, 59–60, 62–3,
    64–5; studies theology, 83;
    letters to, 55–6, 96, 119, 142,
    196; Die Elemente der Meta-
    physik, 195–6; meetings with
    Nietzsche, 1871, 143; 1887, 312;
    1888, gift of money, 323; 1891,
    343; 1894, 347
Deutsche Allgemeine, 96
Dindorf, Wilhelm, 81, 84
Dionysus, 6–9, 120, 131, 299; in
    Jenseits, 289–90, 291; Dionysian
    attitude, 131–2, 133, 134–6, 302,
    330; music, 145
discontinuity and dispersal, 8–9,
    359–60
disease, see sickness
Dostoevsky, Feodor, 8, 304, 317;
    The Idiot, 8; The Possessed, 280
drama: origin of, 57, 115; and
    self-oblivion, 123; music and,
    57, 117–18, 120–1, 134; see also
    music-drama, tragedy
dreams, 200, 140; N's, 18–19, 32,
    63–4, 227; Zarathustra's, 271
Dresden, Saxony; Elisabeth at, 46;
    opera house, 99, 102; 1849 revolt
    at, 99; RW at school at, 113
drunkenness, 50–1, 61–2, 68

education: N's ideal, 132, 167–8;
    Greek, 132, 159; lectures on
    German system, 148–50; essay
    on Schopenhauer, 171, 172–4,
    175–6, 351; see also teaching
Eiser, Dr Otto, 203–4, 219
Elberfeld, Rhineland, 58
Eliot, George, 62–3
Eliot, T. S., 134, 236
Empedocles, 41, 42, 131
Engelmann (publisher), 141, 144
epilepsy, 8, 10, 17
Erlangen, army training course at,
    128, 129
Ermanarich, saga of, 39–41
ethics, 196–7; see also morality
Euripides, 120–1, 134, 136, 153

faith, 66–7
Falk, Adalbert, 268
Fascism, 359
Fate, essays on, 44–5
Favre, Jules, 129
Feuerbach, Ludwig, 7, 99
Fino, Davide, 328, 335, 336
Flims, Switzerland, 1873 visit, 165
Förster, Bernhard: and anti-
    Semitism, 267–8, 269, 287;
    colonies, 276–7, 287, 296;
    marriage, 283, 284–5; N meets,
    287–8; death, 342
Förster-Nietzsche, Elisabeth, see
    Nietzsche, Elisabeth
Foucault, Michel, 3, 309
France: war with Austria, 32; with
    Prussia, 126–9, 130, 133; Revo-
    lution in '82, 323; 'Commune',
    141; see also Paris
Franconia fraternity, Basel, 61–2,
    63, 64, 65–6, 68, 70, 78, 322
Frankfurt: 1863 conference, 69;
    1866 Diet, 79
fraternities, student, 61, 68; in
    Basel, see Franconia; in Berlin,
    70; Teutonia, 32, 61
Freud, Sigmund, 244, 361; N as
    precursor of, 2, 103, 140, 197,

200, 202, 290–1, 301; on the unconscious, 73; *Das Ich und das Es*, 290; on N, 1, 10, 11, 352

Freytag, Gustav, 161–2

Friedrich III, Kaiser, 33, 319

Friedrich Wilhelm III, King of Prussia, 15

Friedrich Wilhelm IV, King of Prussia, 14, 15–16, 33

Fritzsch, Ernst Wilhelm (publisher), 144, 162, 166, 168, 170, 171; N returns to, 1886, 297, 298, 319

Fuchs, Carl, letters to, 195, 282, 314, 320

Gast, Peter (Heinrich Köselitz): in Basel, 184; works on N's MSS, 184, 198, 202–4, 210, 218–19, 222, 231, 246–7, 282, 298, 299–300; leaves for Venice, 204; with N in Italy, 221–3, 231; relationship with N, 211, 215, 221, 235, 283; reviews *Menschliches*, 213; music by, 231, 235, 252, 274, 276, 323–4, 325; opera, *Der Löwe von Venedig*, 277, 283, 297, 324; 1882, 242, 246, 252; 1884, 274; 1885, 283, 289; 1886, 296, 298; 1886, 303; 1887, 312; 1888, 328; letters to, 210, 211, 214–15, 226, 227, 228, 233, 240, 251, 253, 258–9, 261, 314, 315, 333, 334; after N's madness 340–1, 342–3, 346; and N's MSS, 346; at N's funeral, 350

Gelzer, Emily, 348

Gelzer, Professor Heinrich and Frau, 249, 250

Geneva, 183–4, 211, 212

Genoa, 225, 228, 229, 235, 242, 253, 260, 261, 269, 316

German People's Party, 269

Germania, 36–7, 40, 41, 43, 44, 45, 68, 137–8, 148–9

Germany: unification of, 69, 79, 126; North German Confeder-

ation, 80; 1871, 133–4; nationalism, 80, 113, 124–5, 126; Parliament proposed, 78; Reich, 126, 292–3, 322–3, 334, 359; Nazis, 142, 359; N's attitude to, 127–8, 282–3, 292–3; lectures on education in, 148–50

Gersdorff, Baron Carl von: at school, 40, 49; at University, 67–8, 76, 87; in army, 80, 85, 90; diet, 115–16; and Wagners, 159; letters to, 67–8, 80, 82–3, 86, 124–5, 130, 132, 141–2, 159–60; 1871, 143, 144; 1873, 162, 165; 1874, 171, 176; 1875, 177–8, 181, 182; 1876, 183; 1885, 282; on *Genealogie*, 314

God: identified with N's father, 26; prayers to, 29; existence of, 94; of Christianity, 199; of Greeks, 7, 136; of Jews, 7, 136; and guilt, 309; death of, 34, 136, 216, 225, 238–9, 264, 280; *see also* Christianity, Dionysus, religion

Goethe, Johann Wolfgang von: at Leipzig, 71, 75; beliefs, 5, 6, 110, 172; on Byron, 46; on history, 166; N reads in youth, 23; quotes, 94; N's view of, 1, 167, 230, 272–3; *Faust*, 6, 46–7, 358; *Iphigenie in Tauris*, 6; *Wilhelm Meister*, 172, 354

good and evil, 196–7, 355, 356; notions of, 199; redefinition of, 236–7; in *Zarathustra*, 264; evolution of concepts of, 306–7; *Beyond Good and Evil, see Jenseits under* Nietzsche; virtue, 262; *see also* morality

Granier, Raimund, 47–8

Greek: N studies as child, 21, 22, 27, 34; RW studies, 113–14; conflict, 87, 109, 159; culture, unity of, 7, 167; education, 132, 159; gods, 136, *see also* Dionysus; philosophy, essay on, 160; slavery, 158; tragedy, 57, 113–14,

115, 120–1, 134–6, see also *Die Geburt der Tragödie*, under Nietzsche; music in tragedy, 140; verse, metre, 129–30; see also under individual names of writers

Grenzboten, 168

Groddeck, Georg, 290–1

Grossmann, Friederike, 65–6

guilt, 307–9

Gusselbauer, Cäcilie, 221, 222

Gustavus Adolphus Society, Bonn, 70

Gutjahr, Dr, 17, 347

Halle, 95; University, 15, 54; philological congress at, 89

Hase, *Leben Jesu*, 39

health, see madness, sickness

Hegar, Friedrich, 276, 277

Hegel, Georg Wilhelm, 4–6, 72, 122, 123, 124, 130, 134, 173, 239, 302; and history, 167; at thirty, 177

Heidegger, Martin, 1, 3, 356

Heidelberg University, 55

Heine, Heinrich, 330; *Letzte Gedichte und Gedanken*, 233–4; *Zur Geschichte der Philosophie*, 239

Heinse, Dr, 41, 43, 50

herd morality, 293–4; see also slaves

heroes, 50, 271–2; Homeric, 306; Wagnerian, 113; see also Superior Man

Hersing, Professor, 64

Herzen, Natalie, 193

Herzen, Olga, 154, 156

Hesiod, and Homer, 87, 155–6

history: N's insights into, 102; aphorisms on, 86; and fate, 44–5; philosophy of, 109; essay, 'Uses and Disadvantages of', 166–70, 173, 199

Hölderlin, Friedrich, 5; poems of, 41–2, 109, 284

Holten, Karl von, 323–4

Homer: as poet, 110; N reads in youth, 22; and Hesiod, 87, 155–6; characters of, 306; re conflict, 159; RW on, 114

horse-riding, 87, 90, 93, 100

idealism, 32, 82, 322; rejected, 215, 230, 302

Immermann, Professor, 180, 183

indexes prepared by N, 84, 90, 95

Jahn, Otto, 60, 67

Janz, Curt Paul, 281, 325

Jena, Saxony: N visits in youth, 31–2, 61; medical consultation in, 48; Elisabeth in, 249; psychiatric clinic, 338–42

Jesus Christ, 201, 216–17, 325; parodied, 279; see also Christianity

Jews: God of, 136; concept of sin, 223–4; restrictive measures against, 268; anti-Semitism, 268–9, 277, 287; N's attitude, to 78, 108, 125, 142, 146, 151, 195, 269; Wagner's attitude to, 108, 125, 151, 175, 204

Jung, Carl, 11, 308

Junkers, 55, 69

justice, 199, 262, 309

Kafka, Franz, 9, 353

Kaftan, Julius, 324, 325

Kant, Immanuel, 54, 72, 82, 164, 174, 358; idealism, 32; N writes on, 94, 215–16

Karlsruhe, Germany, 105; wartime journey to, 129

Keller, Gottfried, 276, 277

Kelterborn, Ludwig Wilhelm, 160, 210

Kessler, Count Harry, 348–9

Kierkegaard, Soren, 353, 357

Kiessling, Adolf, 101, 111

Kleist, 6

Koberstein (teacher), 39–40, 42–3, 290

Koegel, Fritz, 346, 347, 348

Kohl, Otto, 87
Königswinter, 59
Köselitz, Heinrich, see Gast, Peter
Krug, Gustav: childhood friend, 20, 22, 49, 52; in Germania Society, 36–7, 40, 43; letters to, 113, 146, 155, 206; later, 143, 176
Kruger, Dr Otto, 203
Kym, Hedwig, 311

Laertius, Diogenes, essay on, 83–4, 88, 91
Langbehn, Julius, 340
Lange, F. A., 86, 88, 94; Geschichte des Materialismus, 82
language: N's childhood experience of, 14–15, 197; compared with music, devalued, 122–3; development of linguistic philosophy, 163; evolution of, 306; and morality, 196–7; and truth, 162–5, 356–7; N's use of, 360; see also philology
Lanzky, Paul, 278, 280, 288, 300
laughter, 200
Lautréamont, Comte de (Isidore Ducasse), Les Chants de Maldoror, 47
Lawrence, D. H., 2, 132
Leibniz, Gottfried von, 301
Leipzig, Germany, 70; N studies at University, 67, 71–88, 96–102; awarded doctorate, 102; lodgings, 70–1, 76, 78, 96; philology club, 74, 75, 81, 83, 96; King Wilhelm visits, 76; Wagner visits, 97; Elisabeth studies at, 118; later visits to, 143, 168, 287, 288, 297, 298; with Lou Salomé, 1882, 251–3
Leopardi, Giacomo, 267, 284; translated by von Bülow, 151, 155
Lessing, Gotthold, 85, 117
Levi, Hermann, 297
Lichtenberg, Georg Christoph, 85, 86, 290

Lipiner, Siegfried, 195, 204; Der entfesselten Prometheus, 204
Liszt, Franz, 88, 281; on Die Geburt der Tragödie, 147; 'Consolations', 53; Sainte Elisabeth, 112; daughters, 107; see also Wagner, Cosima
Literarisches Zentralblatt, 96
Löen (theatre director), 113
logic, 120, 356–7
loneliness, 2
love, 259, 294
Lucerne, Switzerland, 133, 177, 246
Ludwig II, King of Bavaria, 133; and Wagner, 107, 112–13, 118, 154, 186, 188
Lugano, Switzerland, 138–40
Luther, Martin, 15, 27, 224, 272–3

Machiavelli, Niccolo, Il Principe, 44
Macmahon (French commander), 128, 129
madness, 3–5, 7–11; Dionysian, 299, 302, see also Dionysus; epilepsy, 8, 10, 17; schizophrenia, 315; Strindberg re, 334; and morality, 224, 237–9; N foresees his own, 103, 225, 275–6; N's feigned?, 10, 340–1; overtakes N, 315–18, 319–50, diagnosis of, 347, 361
Mähly, Dr Ernst, 338
Mann, Thomas, Doktor Faustus, 6, 64
Mannheim, RW concerts at, 143, 145
Marienbad, 225, 226, 227
marriage: N contemplates, 184, 193, 194, 283, 353; proposes, 184, 245, 246; writes on, 201, 202
Marx, Karl, 134, 149, 201, 293; editor Rheinische Zeitung, 16; and 1871 Commune, 141
Marxism, 218
Massini, Rudolf, 203–4, 212

'master morality', 293–5, 306–7, 356

mathematics, 57

Mayer, Julius Norbert, *Mechanik der Wärme*, 234

Mazzini, Giuseppe, 138

Meiningen, music festival, 88

Mendelssohn, Felix, 23, 151

Mendelssohn, Karl Bartholdy, 151

Menippus, lecture on, 96

Messina, Sicily, 242–3

metaphysics, 3, 356, 358

Meyerbeer, Giacomo, 114, 151

Meysenbug, Malwida von, 135, 273; N meets, 154; 1872, 156; 1875, 182; 1876, 187, 191, 192–3; 1877, 203; 1878, on *Menschliches*, 204; 1882, 'Roman club', 244; and Lou Salomé, 244, 248, 267; 1883, 269; letters to, 300, 319, 326–7, 328

Michelet, Jules, *La Bible de l'Humanité* 135

morality: Christian, *see* Christianity; genealogy of, 199–200, 306–7, 360; herd, 293–4; and language, 196–7; prejudices of attacked, 223–5, 226, 227; 'slave' and 'master', 293–5, 306–7, 356; *see also* good and evil, *Genealogie* and *Die Morgenröte under* Nietzsche

Mosengel, Adolf, 127, 128, 129

motherhood, 196, 202, 262

motives, 196, 226–8, 262

Munich, 288, 297; *Das Rheingold* production at, 113, 118

Mushacke, Hermann, 70–1, 76, 83, 84–5, 88

music, 117–18, 122–3; compared to words, 122–3; RW's philosophy of, 131–2; Christian, 117, 123; and drama, 115, 117–18, 120–1, 134; N as infant, 17; N's education, 23, 49, 67, 104; school choir, 33; composed by N, 37, 40, 49, 56, 63, 65, 144,

Hymnus an die Einsamkeit, 176–7, '*Manfred* Meditation', 154–5; performed by N, 58; after madness, 341, 342, 343; *see also under individual names of composers, opera*

music-drama, 115, 117–18; Greek, 120, 121; renaissance of, 134; *see also* opera, Wagner, Richard

Musil, Robert, 301

names, 3, 124; *see also* language

Napoleon III, 44, 76, 78, 126, 129

nationalism, German, 80, 113, 124–5, 126

natural forces, 77

nature: and culture, 173–4; in fable on truth, 158, 162

Naumann, C. G. (printer), 297, 317, 343, 346, 347

Naumburg, Germany; N family move to, 19; schools, 20, 27, Dom Gymnasium, 22–5, 27, 28; 1856 homes in, 25; N returns to, 36–7, 38, 39, 88, 129, 143, 144, 157, 183, 206, 246, 267, 287, 288; cholera in, 83; N in army in, 89–96; rents tower and garden, 1879, 214, 218; after madness, 342–8; N Archive, 346, 347

Nazis, 142, 359

negation, 92–3

negativism, 10, 123–4, 353

Nice, 269–70, 273–4, 275, 288–9, 296, 313, 315; earthquake, 304; Pension de Genève, 278, 283, 288, 300, 303, 304, 313–14; rue des Ponchettes, 303–4; St François de Paule, 288–9

Nietzsche, Augusta (aunt of N), 14, 25

Nietzsche, Elisabeth Förster-(sister of N): birth, 17; childhood, 19, 21, 22–3, 25; N at Pforta, 28, 32, 52; at Dresden, 46; relations with N, 52, 63, 180; N at university, 66, 75; religion,

66, 75; helps N index, 95; 1866,
83; 1868, slackening ties, 101;
1869, 116, 118; 1870, 127; and
Wagners, 127, 142, 177; travels
with N, 1871, 138–9, 142–3, 145–
6; 1872 travels, 156; 1873 travels, 165; 1874, 174, 175; 1875,
179, 180; lives with N in Basel,
181, 203; 1878 breach, 205, 210;
1879 N leaves Basel, 212–13,
214, 218; 1880, 225; 1882, 247,
248, 250; and Lou Salomé, 248–
9, 251, 267, 273, 284; breach,
254; reconciled, 262; strained
relations, 267; and Förster,
267–8, 269; 1884 breach with N,
273; together, 276–7; anti-
Semitism, 268; marriage, 276–7,
283–5; and N after marriage,
287; to Paraguay, 296; asks for
money, 303; letters to, 39, 43–4,
61–2, 66–7, 108–9, 115, 328, 334;
death of husband, 342; after N's
madness, 340, 342–3, 344;
writes re N, 345; takes control of
N's works, 343, 346–7, 359, 351;
new flat, 347; at Weimar, 348–
50; biography of N, 15, 43, 58,
83, 88, 103, 192, 346, 347

Nietzsche, Erdmuthe (grandmother of N), 14, 18, 19, 20, 25

Nietzsche, Franziska (mother of
N); early life, 14; marriage, 13–
14, 17, 18; widow with young
children, 19, 20, 23, 24, 25, 27;
while N at Pforta, 28, 32, 39, 41,
48, 49; and N's religion, 60, 66;
poems to, 63; letters to N, 74,
115; in N's holidays, 70; letters
to, 36, 38, 39, 41, 46, 48, 50,
51–2, 61, 65, 71, 73–4, 102, 112,
115; 1868, slackening bond, 101;
1869, 116; 1870, 127; 1871, 138,
144, 145; 1872 travels, 156;
1874, 168; resents Elisabeth living elsewhere, 177, 180; 1876,
183; 1878, 205; 1882, 251,

breach, 254; 1883, 269; 1884,
273, 276; 1885, 282, 285; 1886,
303; 1887, 311, 312; 1888, 319;
after N's madness, Basel clinic,
337–8; Jena, 339–42, Naumburg,
342–8; death, 348

Nietzsche, Friedrich Wilhelm,
LIFE: childhood, 13–27; relations
with father, 17, 18; childhood
language, 14–15, 17; dreams,
18–19, 32, 63–4, 227; schools, 19,
20–1, 22–5, Pforta, 27–57; confirmed, 38–9; student at Bonn,
58–70, at Leipzig, 71–88, 96–
102; in army, 53, 89–96, 127–9;
awarded doctorate, 102; takes
Swiss nationality, 104–5; professor at Basel, 106–213; year of
absence, 190–202; years of
travel, 213–315; madness 313–15;
death, 349–50; character and
outlook, 351–61; appearance,
229, 245, 274, 275, 283, 348–9;
sexuality, 11, 64–5, 283;
marriage contemplated, 184, 193,
194, 245, 246, 283; as lecturer,
96, 120–1, 148–50; as teacher,
132, 142, 355; reviewer, 96;
finances, 65–6, 115, 206–7, 303,
313, 323; royalties, 347; works in
demand, 343, 346, 349, 361;
ill health 3, 20, 24, 30, 35, 37–8,
45–6, 48, 51, 69–70, 76, 138, 154,
159, 168–9, 179–81, 182–3, 186,
190, 193, 200, 203, 207, 210–11,
219, 221, 222–3, 225, 229, 231,
242, 261, 269–70, 273, 275–6,
298, 305, 315, 319, 320; effect of
health on writings, 360–1; eyes,
24, 29–30, 53, 88, 162, 165, 179,
190, 195, 203, 210–11, 212, 232,
236, 296–7, 349; diet, 168, 180,
181, 225, 311, 330, 333; diagnosis and treatment, 203–4, 254;
abstinence, 225, 283–4; writing,
1–4, 23–5, 85, 121–2, 200; biography and philosophy, 1–11

WORKS: *Die Geburt der Tragödie*, 56–7, 113, 120, 121, 127, 139–41; published, 144, 145, 146–7; 168; reception, 148, 152–3; reviews, 152, 153; 2nd edition, 168, 176; 1886 preface, 298, 299. *Unzeitgemässe Betrachtungen*, 162, 169, 197, 240. *David Strauss*, 160–2, 168, 176, 292. *Vom Nützen*, 166–8, 169–70, 173, 199. *Schopenhauer*, 171, 172–4, 175–6, 351. 'RW in Bayreuth', 170, 181, 184–6, 315. *Menschliches*, 4, 197–204, 229; reactions, 204–5; Part II, 207, 209, 210–12; sales, 213; revised 1885, 286, 288; preface to new edition, 298–9. *Der Wanderer*, 214–18, 219; *Die Morgenröte*, 4, 223–5, 226, 227–8, 229–31. *Die fröhliche Wissenschaft*, 233, 236–40, 247, 255, 273; reactions, 252; Book V, 300–1. *Also sprach Zarathustra*, 233, 245–6, 255–61, 354; reactions, 261, 276, 304; N writes re book, 272–3; Part II, 262–6, 270–2, 355; Part III, 267, 283; Part IV, 278–82, 283–4. *Jenseits*, 280, 289–96, 352; publication, 297; reactions, 297–8, 305, 312. *Genealogie*, 199, 306–11; reactions, 314. *Der Fall Wagner*, 316–17. *Die*, 326–7, 328. *Götzendämmerung*, 321–3. *Der Antichrist*, 325–6. *Ecce Homo*, 10, 315, 329–33. *Nachgelassene Fragmente*, 134–7. *Idyllen aus Messina*, 242. *Aus meinem Leben*, 26. *Euphorion*, 47, 50. *Gods on Olympus* (play), 22. *Prometheus*, 30. 'Fate and History', 44–5. 'Free Will and Fate', 45. school essays, 49–50. 'Über Stimmungen', 53–4, 73. 'A New Year's Dream', 63–4. 'Aphorismen', 86, 94. 'Gedanken über das Christentum', 77. 'Über Demokrit', 88,

91, 92–3. 'Die Teleologie seit Kant', 94–5. 'Selbstbeobachtung', 103–4. *Über Wahrheit*, 162. *Empedokles*, 131. 'Fragment from the history of posterity', 3. five prefaces, 1872 157–9. *Wir Philologen*, 178. *Der Wille zur Macht*, 314–15. *Umwertung*, 314–15, 320, 324. poems, 24–5, 30–1, 35, 37, 41, 43, 47–8, 57, 63; letters, 34, 67–8, 84–5; *see also under individual correspondents' names*, music

Nietzsche, Joseph (brother of N), 17, 18–19

Nietzsche, Karl Ludwig (father of N): early career and education, 15; marriage and household, 13–14; politics, 16–17; epilepsy, 10, 17; health, 10, 24, 320–1, 337; death of, 17–18; N dreams of, 18–19; N recalls, 13, 26, 60; resembles RW, 98; tombstone, 288

Nietzsche, Rosalie (aunt of N), 14, 17, 20, 43, 66; letters to, 44, 50; death of, 84

Norddeutsche Allgemeine Zeitung, 153, 157

Novalis, 32, 197

Oehler, Pastor David Friedrich (grandfather of N), 14, 26, 32

Oehler, Edmund (uncle of N), 36, 344

opera: RW's theory of, 113–14; N visits, 1881, 235–6; *Carmen*, 236, 261, 316–17; Gast's, 277, 283, 297, 324; *see also* Bayreuth, music-drama, Wagner, Richard

Orta, Sacro Monte, 245, 246

Osswald, Pastor Gustav Adolf, letter from, 13, 15, 36

Ott, Louise, 189

Overbeck, Franz: at Basel, 144, 178; leaves, 179; holiday 1875, 182; 1877, 194, 203; 1878, 204,

206; 1879, 212, 214; 1882, 245, 246; and Lou Salomé, 247; letters to, 227, 254, 281, 286, 296, 298, 333, 335; 1883, 261–2, 267; 1884, 274, 277; 1885, 285; 1886, 303, 305; 1888, 314, 326, notes madness, 334, 336; collects N from Turin, 336–8; after N's madness, 3, 340, 341; last meeting, 348; and Elisabeth, 346

Overbeck, Ida, 203, 206, 245–6, 253

Paraguay, Aryan colony, 269, 296, 303, 342

Paris: 1848 rising, 16; N plans a year in, 102, 106; 1870 revolt, 129; seige, 130, 133; 1871 commune, 141

Paul, St, 4, 224, 326

Paul, Jean, 119

pessimism, 159, 302, 320; classical, 87

Pforta school, 27–57, 58, 60, 61, 65, 67

philology: N chooses as career, 56; studies, 60, 67; inaugural lecture on, 109–10; Leipzig societies, 74–5, 81, 83, 96; N professor of, 106–213; essay on philologists, 178; and philosophy, 76–7, 82, 96, 137; see also language

philosophy: and completion, 359–60; and personality, 1, 251; and philology, 76–7, 82, 96, 137; and sickness, 1, 302–3, 310, 321–2; N applies for chair of, 137–8, 139

Pinder, Herr (judge), 20, 22, 23

Pinder, Wilhelm: childhood friend, 20, 22–3, 24, 33, 34; writes on N, 20–1; holiday together, 36; Germania society, 36–7, 40, 41; at University, 55; letters to, 29, 30, 34, 35–6, 41, 55, 79; 1871, 143; 1874, 176

Plato, 109, 120, 218, 230; idealism, 302, 322; on madness, 4, 224;

dialogue method, 148–9; *Phaedo*, 106

pleasure and pain, 351–3, 355–6; see also sickness, suffering

Pobles village, Saxony, 14, 26, 30, 32

Polish ancestry, N. claims, 273–4, 316, 321

power, 230–1, 264; will to, 9, 227–8, 263, 351–2; 'master morality', 293–5, 306–7, 356; see also Superior Man

Prometheus, 30, 34, 256–7

Prussia: in 1840s, 15–16; 1860s, Schleswig-Holstein, 52–3; 1865, 69; 1866 war, 76, 78–9; in North German Confederation, 80; 1870 war with France, 126–9, 130–1, 133, 136; campaign against Catholics and Jews, 268–9; N's attitude to, 131, 133, 161

psychology, 2; see also Freud, Sigmund

punishment, 309; self-, 6, 351–2

racism: RW and, 108, 124–5; see also Jews, nationalism

Redtel, Anna, 52, 59

Rée, Georg, 248, 267

Rée, Paul: N meets, 182; *Psychologische Beobachtungen*, 182, 198; 1876, 189, 191, 192, 193, 197; 1878, 195, 204–5, 206; N's friends' attitude to, 204–5; 1880, 221; 1881, 233; 1882, 242; and Lou Salomé, 244–54, 255, 265; 1884, 273

religion: N's, 38–9, 197; faith, 66–7; Romundt turns to, 178; RW and, 192; see also Christianity, God

Renaissance, the, 27, 205; to come, 134

Renan, Ernest, *La vie de Jésus*, 325–6

Rheinische Museum für Philologie,

81, 100, 101, 102, 156; N indexes, 90, 95

Rheinische Zeitung, 16

Richter, Hans, 113, 133, 145

riding, *see* horse-riding

Rimbaud, Arthur, 291, 354

Ritschl, Albrecht: lecturer at Bonn, 60–1, 67, 71; moves to Leipzig, 67, 71, 87; at Leipzig, 74–6, 77, 78, 83, 86–7, 88; on N's essay on Theognis, 75, 81; promotes N's work and career, 81, 84, 90, 91, 101–2; friendship with N, 86–7; illness, 86, 89; editor, *Rheinische Museum*, 81, 90, 100, 101, 156; 1871, 143; on *Die Geburt*, 146; N attacks, 150, 1872, 155, 156; 1873, 168

Ritschl, Sophie, 75, 97, 100, 109

Riva, Italy, 221–2

Rochefoucauld, François La, 197–8

Röcken village, Saxony: parsonage, 13–14, 15, 18–19; graveyard, 18–19, 350

Roder-Widerhold, Louise, 286

Rohde, Erwin: student at Leipzig, 87–8; holiday with N, 1867, 88; relationship with N, 90, 91, 111, 119–20, 318; N recommends for Chair, 137, 139, 142; letters to, 98, 100, 101, 102–3, 111, 112, 119, 131, 139, 140, 144–5, 150–1, 152, 162, 165, 296; 1870 visits, 125–6; 1871, 143, 144; reviews *Die Geburt*, 152, 153; Professor at Kiel, 153; *Afterphilologie*, 157; 1874, 176; 1875, 178, 181, 182; 1877, 195; 1878, 204; 1879, 219; 1882, 252; 1884, 272–3; at Leipzig, last meeting, 297; on *Jenseits*, 297–8; on *Genealogie*, 314; visits N when mad, 347

Rohn, Herr, 70–1; family, 76; second-hand bookshop, 72, 74

Romanticism, 7, 209, 215–16, 302, 317

Rome: 'Roman club', 244; N with Lou Salomé, 244–5; 1883, with Elisabeth, 262

Romundt, Heinrich: at Leipzig, 96, 100, 142; 1871, 142, 143; 1873, 165; 1874, 175; wants to become priest, 178; on *Menschliches*, 204

Roscher, Wilhelm, 74, 97

Rousseau, Jean-Jacques, 172; *Emile*, 48

Ruthardt, Adolf, 287

Sade, Marquis de, 220; *Juliette*, 279, 294, 355

sado-masochism, 28, 351, 355

St Moritz, 213–14, 219, 231–2

Salis, Meta von: N meets, 274–5; 1886 in Sils, 300; 1887 meetings, 305, 311–12; 1888, gives money, 323; letter to, 323; and Elisabeth, 348

Salomé, Lou: 1882, friendship with N and Rée, 244–54; photographed together, 246; at Bayreuth, 248; in Tautenburg, 249–51; and Elisabeth, 248–9, 251, 267, 273, 284; looked back on, 4, 255, 258, 265–7, 355; cited on RW, 273

Saussure, Ferdinand de, 164

Saxony, invaded, 1866, 79

Schaarschmidt (at Bonn), 60

Schenk, Dr Emil (uncle of N), 31–2

Schiller, Friedrich, 6, 7, 125; *Die Räuber*, 43; *Wallensteins Lager*, 50

Schirnhofer, Resa von, 273–4, 275–6, 304

Schleswig-Holstein, 52–3; 1866, 79–80

Schmeitzner, Ernst (publisher), 171, 175, 186, 203, 209, 210, 213, 219, 235; 1878 visit, 206; anti-Semitism, 277; bankrupt, 277, 282, 288; blocks other publishers for N, 297

Schopenhauer, Arthur, 52, 82, 109,

132, 167, 291, 354; *Die Welt als Wille*, 72–3, 74, 121, 133–4; N first reads, 72–4, 351; influence on N, 72–4, 76, 77, 80, 86, 87, 90, 102, 103, 117, 127, 138, 215; on words/music, 122–3; artistic vision, 137; and RW, 98–100; method of writing, 121–2; N writes on, 133–5, 136, 137, 159; essay, S. as educator, 171, 172–4, 175–6, 351, 352; N reacts against, 190, 195, 208–9, 263

Schumann, Robert, 52, 63, 77; *Faust*, 97

science, 196, 291

self: and body, 258; concept of, 11, 290–1; -denial and -affirmation, 351–61; -oblivion, and art 123; -observation, 1–2, 4–5, aphorisms on, 103; -punishment, 6, 351–2; -transcendence, 9–10, 207, 241–2; consciousness, 301–2

Semper, Gottfried, 115

Senger, Hugo von, 183–4

sexuality, 197, 310, 355; N's, 11, 64–5, 283; *see also* abstinence, marriage, women

Seydlitz, Irene von, 193, 288

Seydlitz, Reinhardt von, 193–4, 195, 288; on *Menschliches*, 204, 212; letters to, 207, 315

Shakespeare, William, 43–4, 239

sickness: N's attitude to, 1, 179, 190, 200, 207–8, 230, 236, 240–1, 299, 302–3, 321; and electricity, 232, 235; imagery of, 356; and philosophy, 1, 302–3, 310, 321–2; N's ill-health, *see under* Nietzsche, Friedrich; *see also* madness, suffering, syphilis

Sils-Maria, Switzerland, N in: 1881, 232–5; 1883, 262; 1884, 275–6; 1885, 286–7; 1886, 298, 300; 1887, 305, 311–12; 1888, 319–20, 323–4

slaves: necessity for, 158, 201;

modern, 7, 200; morality, 293–5, 306–7, 356

Social Democratic Party, 293

Social Democratic Workers' Party, 166

socialism, 201, 218

Socrates, 134, 148–9, 160, 216–17, 322; and Euripides, 153; N lectures re, 120–1; death, 320

Sophocles, 120, 135, 136; N's commentaries on, 57, 67

Sorrento, 1876, 191–4

Spinoza, Baruch, 1, 160, 230, 302; N discovers works of, 232

Spitteler, Carl, *Prometheus und Epimetheus* 256–7

state, the, 173–4, 259, 359

Stein, Baron Heinrich von, 276, 283, 305–6

Steiner, Rudolf, 347, 348, 349

Steinhardt, Professor (at Pforta), 32, 39, 43, 56, 67

Stendhal, 192

Stifter, Adalbert, *Nachsommer*, 354

Stöcker, Adolf, 319

Strasbourg, 157; University, 152

Strauss, David, 162; *Der alte und der neue Glaube*, 160–1; *Das Leben Jesu*, 62–3, 82; N's essay on, 160–2, 168, 176, 292

Strindberg, August, 332–3, 334

suffering, 351–6; punishment, 309; self-inflicted, 6, 351–2; sado-masochism, 28, 351, 355

Suidas, tenth-century lexicon, 81

Superior Man (Übermensch), 9–10, 230, 241, 258, 264–5, 353–4; 'blond beast', 306–7; intellect, 230; *see also* heroes, 'master morality', power

syphilis: whether N suffered from, 10–11, 24, 95, 129, 273, 349; attitude to, 284, 321

systematization, 104

Swiss: nationality, N takes, 104–5, 126, 127–8; neutrality, 126, 127–8

Taine, Hippolyte, 300, 302–3, 313, 314
Tautenburg, Thuringia, 1882, 248, 249–51
teaching, 132, 142, 355; N as lecturer, 96, 120–1, 148–50; *see also* education
Teutonia fraternity, 32, 36, 61
Theognis of Megara, 306; N's dissertation on, 54–5, 67, 70, 75; edition of, 76, 77, 78, 81, 85
tragedy: German, 6, 57, 115; Greek, 57, 113–15, 120–1, 134–6; renaissance of, 134; RW's theory, 113–15, 134
see also Die Geburt der Tragödie under Nietzsche, Friedrich; drama
Trampedach, Mathilde, 183–4
Tribschen, Wagner's Swiss villa; N visits, 107–8, 110–11, 112, 116, 118–19, 125–6, 131, 132–3, 140, 142, 143, 148, 151; Rohde at, 125–6; Elisabeth at, 127; 'T. Idyll', 132–3; Wagner's departure from, 151; 1882 visit, 246; 1888, 330
truth: 'The Pathos of', 158, 162; and fiction, 358; and history, 166; and language, 163–5, 356–7; will to, 289, 301, 357
Turin, Italy, 1888, 315, 316, 319, 324, 327–8, 329, 333–6, 353

Upanishads, 73, 312
Usener, Professor, 157

vanity, 217–18
vegetarianism, 115–16
Venice, 22–3, 225, 274, 283, 286, 296–7, 312–13
virtue, 262; altruism, 196, 226, 323; *see also* good and evil
Vischer-Bilfinger, Professor Wilhelm, 101–2, 127–8, 137
Volkmann, Dr (teacher), 54

Volkmann, Richard von (doctor), 95

Wagner, Adolph, portrait of, 118
Wagner, Cosima (von Bülow): at Tribschen, 107, 108, 112, 113; birth of Siegfried, 110–11; divorce, 112; letters from, 114, 118, 125–6, 128, 147; sends N on errands, 118; N's relations with, 122, 131, 145, 151; 1870 birthday, 132–3; 1870, 140; 1871, 142, 143–4, 144, 145; on *Geburt*, 147; 1872, 151, 153; prefaces dedicated to, 157–9; 1873, 159; on essay on history, 169–70; 1875, 177; 1876, 187, 189, 191; on *Menschliches*, 204, 212; and Bernhardt, 242; death of RW, 261; letter to, 1889, 335
Wagner, Eva, 108
Wagner, Isolde, 108
Wagner, Minna, 107
Wagner, Richard: appearance, 108; education, 113; political career, 98–9; marriages, 107; N meets, 97–100; relations with N, 100–1, 102, 108, 122, 125, 151; 1869 letter to, 108; and Schopenhauer, 98–100, 108; at Tribschen, *see* Tribschen; birth of Siegfried, 110–11; recommends books to N, 113; racism, 108, 124–5; N champions, 40, 114–15, 120–2, 124–5, 134–5, 140–1, 150–1, 160–1, 162, 165–6; 1871 'Foreword to', 135; publisher becomes N's, 144; at Bayreuth, 145, 154, 187, 188, 248; on *Geburt*, 146–7; 1872, 148, 157; 1873, 159–61; and D. Strauss, 160–2; on essay on history, 169–70; Wahnfried, home, 170–1, 174–5, 177; dispute re Brahms, 174–5; 1874 Christmas, 176; essay, *RW in Bayreuth*, 170, 181, 184–6, 315; 1875 letter to,

179: N reacts against, 188–9, 195, 202, 204, 205–6, 302; end of friendship, 189, 190; last meetings, 191–2; in *Menschliches*, 202, 209; and N's doctor, 203; and N, attitude to each other after breach, 206, 214, 222, 227, 239, 242–3, 281, 282–3, 345; in *Zarathustra*, 281; *Der Fall W*, 316–17, 326–7, 328; *N contra W*, 334; essays, 113–15, 131; pamphlet on conducting, 118; newspaper attack on N, 206; death, 260–1; *see also* Bayreuth, Tribschen, Ludwig II

Music: theory of, 113–14, 134; N's attitude to, 37, 49, 97, 117, 282–3, 293; *Lohengrin*, 99, 317; *Tristan*, 97, 132, 282–3; *Die Meistersinger*, 97, 98, 105; *Der Ring*, 99–100, 113, 187–8, *Das Rheingold*, 112–13, 118, 188; *Siegfried*, 107, 108, 354; *Götterdämerung*, 112, 187; *Parsifal*, 118, 191–2, 195, 205, 243; *Siegfried Idyll*, 132–3; *Kaisermarsch*, 140

war: lessons of, 358; 1866, 79–80; 1870–1, 126–9, 130–1, 133
Weber (headmaster), 21
Weimar, Germany, 348–50
Wellhausen, Julius, 325
Wenkel, Friedrich August, 77

Widemann, Paul, 203, 204, 298
Widmann, J. V., 300, 305, 331
Wiel, Dr, 180–1
Wilamowitz-Möllendorf, Ulrich von, *Zukunftsphilologie*, 153, 157
Wilhelm I of Prussia, 33, 52; at Cologne, 69; at Leipzig, 76; Emperor, 133; at Bayreuth, 188
Wilhelm II, Kaiser, 319
Wilke, Superintendent, 18
will: free, 45, 226–7; to power 227–8, 263, 301; Schopenhauer, 72–3, 82, 137, 208–9, 228, 263; to truth, 289, 301, 357; to death 301
Wille, Professor (Basel clinic), 336–7, 338, 347
Windisch, Ernst, 97, 98
Wittgenstein, Ludwig, 163, 164–5, 208, 360
Wolzogen, Hans von, 202
women: need for, 283–4; Zarathustra on, 259; *see also* marriage, motherhood
Wullner, Franz, 118

Zarncke, Friedrich, 78, 96, 152
Zeitschrift für Musik, 37
Zimmermann, Dr, 37, 38, 48
Zola, Emile, 196
Zoroaster, 245–6
Zürich: RW in, 99; L. Salomé at University, 244; N at, 274, 276, 282, 283, 286, 305